PRECIOUS SEED

PRECIOUS SEED

DISCOURSES

BY

SCOTTISH WORTHIES

SOLID GROUND CHRISTIAN BOOKS
BIRMINGHAM, ALABAMA USA

Solid Ground Christian Books
715 Oak Grove Rd
Birmingham, AL 35209
205-443-0311
sgcb@charter.net
http://solid-ground-books.com

PRECIOUS SEED: DISCOURSES OF SCOTTISH WORTHIES

Taken from 1877 edition by John Grieg & Son, Edinburgh

Solid Ground Classic Reprints

First printing of new edition February 2007

Cover work by Borgo Design, Tuscaloosa, AL
Contact them at borgogirl@bellsouth.net

Cover image from Ric Ergenbright
View his work at ricergenbright.com

SPECIAL THANKS: We are grateful to Gary M. Carnie of San Antonio, Texas for informing us of this volume, and for allowing us to use his precious copy for this edition.

ISBN: 1-59925-097-7

PREFATORY NOTE.

―――o―――

The following "Discourses by Scottish Worthies" have been gathered together mainly for the purpose of affording to a new generation an intelligent idea of the character of the pulpit ministrations of men who did great things in their day for the truth of God. It seemed desirable that those who never heard them unfold the "oracles of God" should become familiar with their mode of expounding and applying the Divine Word, and their distinguished ability as preachers of the everlasting gospel. It is to be hoped that this effort to perpetuate the influence of their life-work will tend in some measure to aid in moulding the personal and national life of the Scottish people, and thus though dead, these Worthies will continue to speak to future generations.

The Editor begs gratefully to acknowledge the readiness with which relatives furnished Manuscript Discourses for this Volume, and he has specially to thank Messrs Blackwood & Sons for liberty to reprint No. IV.; Messrs Nisbet & Co., London, for No. XVI.; Messrs Oliphant & Co. for Nos. XIII. and XVIII.; Messrs T. & T. Clark for No. XV.; and Messrs Edmonston & Douglas for No. XXIV.

CONTENTS.

I. GLORYING IN THE CROSS OF CHRIST.
PAGE

"But God forbid that I should glory, save in the cross of our Lord Jesus Christ, by whom the world is crucified unto me, and I unto the world."—GAL. vi. 14.   .   1

By the REV. JOHN M'LAURIN, Glasgow.

II. THE PROSPECTS OF THE CHURCH OF CHRIST.

"Lift up thine eyes round about, and behold: all these gather themselves together, and come to thee. As I live, saith the Lord, thou shalt surely clothe thee with them all, as with an ornament, and bind them on thee, as a bride doeth."—ISAIAH xlix. 18.   38

By the REV. JOHN LOVE, D.D., Glasgow.

III. CHRIST'S DEATH AND RESURRECTION.

"For I delivered unto you first of all that which I also received, how that Christ died for our sins according to the Scriptures; and that he was buried, and that he rose again the third day according to the Scriptures," &c.—1 COR. xv. 3-8.   .   50

By the REV. SIR H. MONCREIFF WELLWOOD, BART., D.D., Edinburgh.

IV. THE LOVE OF THE SPIRIT.

"Now I beseech you, brethren, for the love of the Spirit."—ROM. xv. 30   .   64

By the REV. THOMAS M'CRIE, D.D., Edinburgh.

V. LOVERS OF PLEASURE MORE THAN LOVERS OF GOD.

"Lovers of pleasures more than lovers of God."—2 Tim. iii. 4. . . . 85

By the Rev. Andrew Thomson, D.D., Edinburgh.

VI. THE TERRORS OF THE LORD.

"Knowing therefore the terrors of the Lord, we persuade men."—2 Cor. v. 11. . 100

By the Rev. James Martin, M.A., Edinburgh.

VII. ALL THINGS ARE YOURS.

"All things are yours; whether Paul, or Apollos, or Cephas, or the world, or life, or death, or things present, or things to come; all are yours; and ye are Christ's; and Christ is God's."—1 Cor. iii. 21-23. . , . . . 114

By the Rev. David Welsh, D.D., Edinburgh.

VIII. PEACE IN BELIEVING.

"Peace in Believing."—Romans xv. 13. 129

By the Rev. Thomas Chalmers, D.D., LL.D., Edinburgh.

IX. THE RIGHTEOUSNESS OF GOD MANIFESTED FOR THE JUSTIFICATION OF SINNERS.

"But now the righteousness of God without the law is manifested."—Rom. iii. 21. 139

By the Rev. John Macdonald, D.D., Ferintosh.

X. MAN'S REDEMPTION THE JOY OF ANGELS.

"Which things the angels desire to look into."—1 Pet. i. 12. . . . 156

By the Rev. Alexander Stewart, Cromarty.

XI. THE GLORY OF GOD THE INSTRUMENT OF OUR SANCTIFICATION.

"But we all, with open face beholding as in a glass the glory of the Lord, are changed into the same image, from glory to glory, even as by the Spirit of the Lord." —2 Cor. iii. 18. 179

By the Rev. Patrick M'Farlan, D.D., Greenock.

CONTENTS.

XII. DEATH SWALLOWED UP IN VICTORY.

PAGE

"He shall swallow up death in victory."—ISA. xxv. 8. . . . 196

By the REV. ANDREW SYMINGTON, D.D., Paisley.

XIII. CONVICTION OF SIN.

"And when he [the Comforter] is come, he will reprove the world of sin, and of righteousness, and of judgment."—JOHN xvi. 8. 221

By the REV. ROBERT MURRAY M'CHEYNE, Dundee.

XIV. THE INVITATION OF CHRIST TO SINNERS.

"Come unto me, all ye that labour and are heavy laden, and I will give you rest." —MATT. xi. 28. 233

By the REV. ROBERT GORDON, D.D., Edinburgh.

XV. GODLINESS.

"He that cometh to God must believe that he is, and that he is a rewarder of them that diligently seek him."—HEB. xi. 6. 248

By the REV. WILLIAM CUNNINGHAM, D.D., Edinburgh.

XVI. THE LAMB OF GOD.

"The next day John seeth Jesus coming unto him, and saith, Behold the Lamb of God, which taketh away the sin of the world!"—JOHN i. 29. . . . 264

By the REV. JAMES HAMILTON, D.D., London.

XVII. THE PURE IN HEART.

"Blessed are the pure in heart, for they shall see God."—MATT. v. 8. . . 278

By the REV. ALEXANDER DYCE DAVIDSON, D.D., Aberdeen.

XVIII. THE EQUITY AND BENIGNITY OF THE DIVINE LAW.

"Wherefore the law is holy, and the commandment holy, and just, and good."— ROM. vii. 12. 299

By the REV. JOHN BROWN, D.D., Edinburgh.

XIX. GOD'S TRUTH AND MAN'S FREEDOM.

                                                                                                   PAGE

"The truth shall make you free."—JOHN viii. 32.   .   .   .   318

By the REV. THOMAS GUTHRIE, D.D., Edinburgh.

XX. THE SIMPLICITY THAT IS IN CHRIST.

"But I fear, lest by any means, as the serpent beguiled Eve through his subtilty, so your minds should be corrupted from the simplicity that is in Christ."—2 COR. xi. 3.   336

By the REV. ROBERT SMITH CANDLISH, D.D., Edinburgh.

XXI. SALVATION BY WATER AND BLOOD.

"This is he that came by water and blood, even Jesus Christ; not by water only, but by water and blood. And it is the Spirit that beareth witness, because the Spirit is truth."—1 JOHN v. 6.   360

By the REV. PATRICK FAIRBAIRN, D.D., Glasgow.

XXII. SIN, DEATH, AND VICTORY OVER THEM.

"So when this corruptible shall have put on incorruption, and this mortal shall have put on immortality, then shall be brought to pass the saying that is written, Death is swallowed up in victory."—1 COR. xv. 54.   374

By the REV. ROBERT BUCHANAN, D.D., Glasgow.

XXIII. APOSTASY AND RECOVERY.

"All we, like sheep, have gone astray; we have turned every one to his own way; and the Lord hath laid on him the iniquity of us all."—ISA. liii. 6.   .   .   389

By the REV. CHARLES C. MACKINTOSH, D.D., Dunoon.

XXIV. THE DRAWING POWER OF THE CROSS.

"Now is the judgment of this world: now shall the prince of this world be cast out. And I, if I be lifted up from the earth, will draw all men unto me. This he said, signifying what death he should die."—JOHN xii. 31-33.   .   .   .   400

By the REV. JOHN DUNCAN, LL.D., Edinburgh.

XXV. WALKING WITH GOD.

"Enoch walked with God."—GENESIS v. 24.   417

By the REV. JOHN MACDONALD, A.M., Calcutta.

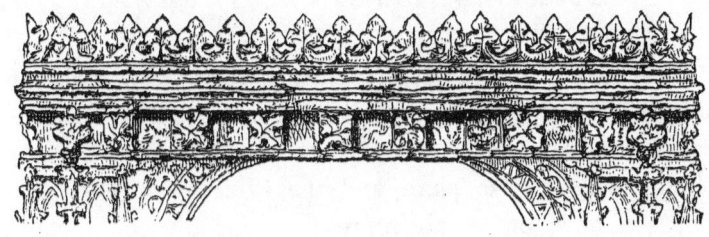

I.

Glorying in the Cross of Christ.

BY THE REV. JOHN M'LAURIN.

"BUT GOD FORBID THAT I SHOULD GLORY, SAVE IN THE CROSS OF OUR LORD JESUS CHRIST, BY WHOM THE WORLD IS CRUCIFIED UNTO ME, AND I UNTO THE WORLD."—GAL. VI. 14.

IT is an old and useful observation, that many of the most excellent objects in the world are objects whose excellency does not appear at first view; as, on the other hand, many things of little value appear more excellent at first than a narrower view discovers them to be. There are some things we admire because we do not know them, and the more we know them, the less we admire them. There are other things we despise through ignorance, because it requires pains and application to discover their beauty and excellency.

This holds true in nothing more than in that glorious despised object mentioned in the text. There is nothing the world is more divided about in its opinion than this. To the one part it is altogether contemptible; to the other it is altogether glorious. The one part of the world wonders what attractives others find in it; and the other part wonders how the rest of the world are so stupid as not to see them, and are amazed at the blindness of others, and their own former blindness.

It is said of the famous reformer, Melancthon, when he first saw the glory of this object at his conversion, he imagined he could easily, by plain persuasion, convince others of it; that the matter being so plain, and the evidence so strong, he did not see how, on a fair representation, any could stand out against it. But upon trial he was forced to express himself with regret, that old Adam was too strong for young Melancthon, and that human corruption was too strong for human persuasion without divine grace.

The true use we should make of this is certainly to apply for that enlightening grace to ourselves which the apostle Paul prays for in the behalf of the Ephesians (Eph. i. 17), "That the God of our Lord Jesus Christ . . . may give us the spirit of wisdom and revelation in the knowledge of Him." But as here, and in other cases, prayers and means should be joined together, so one of the principal means of right knowledge of the principal object of our faith and ground of our hope, is to meditate on the glory of that object, asserted so strongly in this text, and that by one who formerly had as diminishing thoughts of it as any of its enemies can have.

In the verses preceding the text, the apostle tells the Galatians what some false teachers among them gloried in; here he tells what he gloried in himself. They gloried in the old ceremonies of the Jewish law, which were but shadows; he gloried *in the cross of Christ*, the substance. He knew it was an affront to the substance to continue these shadows in their former force after the substance itself appeared, therefore he regrets that practice with zeal, and at the same time confines his own glorying to that blessed object which the shadows were designed to signify. "God forbid that I should glory, save in the cross of Christ," &c.

Here the apostle sheweth us both his high esteem of the cross of Christ and the powerful influence of it upon his mind. The cross of Christ signifies in Scripture sometimes our sufferings for Christ, sometimes his suffering for us. As the latter is the chief, and most natural sense of the words, so there is reason to think it is the sense of the apostle here. This is the sense of the same expression in the twelfth verse of this chapter, which speaks of persecution (that is our suffering) for the cross of Christ, *i.e.* the doctrine of Christ's cross. Besides, it is certain that it is not our sufferings, but Christ's sufferings, which we are chiefly to glory in, to the exclusion of other things; and it is not the former chiefly, but the latter, that mortifies our corruptions, and crucifies the world to us.

The cross of Christ may signify here not only his death, but the whole of his humiliation, or all the sufferings of his life and death; of which sufferings the cross was the consummation. The apostle, both here and elsewhere, mentions the cross, to remind us of the manner of his death, and to strengthen in our minds those impressions which the condescension of that death had made, or ought to have made, in them. That the Author of liberty should suffer the death of a slave; the fountain of honour, the height of disgrace; that the punishments which were wont to be inflicted upon the meanest persons for the highest offences should be inflicted on the greatest person that could suffer. This is the object that the apostle gloried in.

There are not two things more opposite than glory and shame; here the apostle joins them together. The cross in itself is an object full of shame; in this case it appeareth to the apostle full of glory. It had been less remarkable had he only said, he gloried in his Redeemer's exaltation after he left the world, or in the glory he had with the Father before he came to it, yea, before the world was. But the object of the apostle's glorying is the Redeemer, not only considered in the highest state of honour and dignity, but even viewed in the lowest circumstances of disgrace and ignominy, not only as a powerful and exalted, but as a condemned and crucified Saviour.

Glorying signifies the highest degree of esteem; the cross of Christ was an object of which the apostle had the most exalted sentiments, and the most profound veneration; this veneration he took pleasure to avow before the world, and was ready to publish on all occasions. This object so occupied his heart and engrossed his affections, that it left no room for anything else; he gloried in nothing else; and, as he telleth us in other places, he counted everything else but loss and dung, and would know nothing else, and was determined about it (1 Cor. ii. 2).

The manner of expressing his esteem of this object has a remarkable force and vehemence in it, *God forbid*, or let it by no means happen; as if he had said, "God forbid, whatever others do, that ever it should be said that Paul, the old persecutor, should glory in anything else but in the crucified Redeemer; who plucked him as a brand out of the fire, when he was running farther and farther into it; and who pursued him with mercy and kindness, when he was pursuing Him in his members with fierceness and cruelty. I did it through ignorance (and it is only through ignorance that any despise him); he has now revealed himself to me, and God forbid that the light that met me near Damascus should ever go out of my mind; it was a light full of glory, the object it discovered was all glorious, my all in all, and God forbid that I should glory in anything else."

His esteem of that blessed object was great, and its influence on him proportionable. By it the world was crucified to him, and he was crucified to the world; here is a mutual crucifixion. His esteem of Christ was the cause why the world despised him, and was despised by him; not that the cross made him hate the men of the world, or refuse the lawful enjoyments of it. It allowed him the use of the latter, and obliged him to love the former; but it crucified these corruptions, which are contrary both to the love of our neighbour and the true enjoyment of the creatures. This is called fighting, warring, wrestling, and killing. The reason is, because we should look upon sin as our greatest enemy, the greatest enemy of our souls, and of the Saviour of our souls; this was the view the apostle had of sin, and of the corruption that is in the world through lust (2 Peter i. 4), he looked upon it as the murderer of his Redeemer, and this inspired him with a just resentment against it; it filled him with these blessed passions against it mentioned by himself (2 Cor. vii. 11), as the native fruits of faith, and repentance, zeal, indignation, revenge; that is, such a detestation of sin as was joined with the most careful watchfulness against it.

This is that crucifying of the world meant by the apostle; the reason of the expression is, because the inordinate love of worldly things is one of the chief sources of sin; the cross of Christ gave such a happy turn to the apostle's affections, that the world was no more the same thing to him that it was to others, and that it had been formerly to himself. His soul was sick of its pomp, and the things he was most fond of before had now lost their relish with him; its honours appeared now contemptible, its riches poor, its pleasures nauseous; its examples and favours did not allure, nor its hatred terrify him; he considered the love or hatred of men, not chiefly as it affected him, but themselves, by furthering or hindering the success of his doctrine among them; all these things may be included in that *crucifying of the world*, mentioned in the last clause of the verse. But the intended ground of the discourse being the first clause, the doctrine to be insisted on is this:—
"That the cross of Christ affords sinners matter of glorying above all other things; yea, that it is in a manner the only thing they should glory in. The whole humiliation of Christ, and particularly his death for the sake of sinners, is an object that has such incomparable glory in it, that it becomes us to

have the most honourable and exalted thoughts of it." As this is evidently contained in the text, so it is frequently inculcated on us in other scriptures (2 Cor. iv. 6 ; 2 Cor. iii. 18 ; 1 Cor. i. 19 and 24), it is plain that when the scriptures speak of the glory of God, in the face of Jesus Christ, it is meant chiefly of his glory in the face of Christ crucified; that is, in the work of redemption finished on the cross.

In discoursing on this subject, it will be proper, first, to consider briefly, *What it is to glory in any object;* and then, *What ground of glorying we have in this blessed object proposed in the text.*

To *glory* in any object includes these two things—first, a high esteem of it, and then some concern in it. We do not glory in the things we are interested in unless we esteem them ; nor in the things we admire and esteem, unless we are some way interested in them. But although all professing Christians are some way concerned to glory in the cross of Christ, because of their outward relation to Him by their baptismal covenant, and because the blessed fruits of His cross are both plainly revealed and freely offered to them, yet it is those only who have sincerely embraced those offers that can truly glory in that object. Yet what is their privilege is the duty of all ; all should be exhorted to glory in this object, and to have a high esteem of it, because of its excellency in itself; to fix their hearts in it by faith, because it is offered to them ; to shew their esteem of it, by seeking an interest in it ; and having a due esteem of it, and obtained an interest in it, to study a frame of habitual triumph in it. But the nature of this happy frame of mind is best understood by considering the glory of the object of it.

The ancient prophets, who foretell Christ's coming, appear transported with the view of his glory. Not only the New Testament, but also the Old, represents the Messias as the most remarkable and most honourable person that ever appeared on the stage of the world. It speaks of him as a glorious Governor, a Prince, a King, a Conqueror, besides other magnificent titles of the greatest dignity, shewing that his government should be extensive and everlasting, and that his glory should fill the whole earth. But, while the prophets foretell his greatness, they foretell also his meanness; they shew, indeed, he was to be a glorious king, but a king who would be rejected and despised of men. And that after all the great expectation the world would have of him, he was to pass over the stage of the world disregarded and unobserved, excepting as to the malicious treatment he was to meet with on it.

About the time of his coming, the Jews were big with hopes of him as the great Deliverer and chief ornament of their nation. And if history may be credited, even the heathens had a notion about that time, which possibly was derived from the Jewish prophecies, that there was a Prince of unparalleled glory to rise in the east, and even in Judea in particular, who was to found a kind of universal monarchy. But their vain hearts, like that of most men in all ages, were so intoxicated with the admiration of worldly pomp, that that was the only greatness they had any notion or relish of; this made them form a picture of Him, who was the desire of all nations, very unlike the original.

A king which the world admires, is one of extensive power, with numerous armies, a golden crown and sceptre, a throne of state, magnificent palaces, sumptuous feasts, many attendants of high rank; immense treasures to enrich them with, and various posts of honour to prefer them to.

Here was the reverse of all this; for a crown of gold, a crown of thorns; for a sceptre, a reed put in his hand, in derision; for a throne, a cross; instead of palaces, not a place to lay his head in; instead of sumptuous feasts to others, ofttimes hungry and thirsty himself; instead of great attendants, a company of poor fishermen; instead of treasures to give them, not money enough to pay tribute, without working a miracle; and the preferment offered them, was to give each of them his cross to bear. In all things the reverse of worldly greatness from first to last; a manger for a cradle at his birth, not a place to lay his head sometimes in his life, nor a grave of his own at his death.

Here unbelief frets and murmurs, and asks, Where is all the glory, that is so much extolled? For discovering this, faith needs only look through that thin vail of flesh; and under that low disguise appears the Lord of glory, the King of kings, the Lord of hosts, strong and mighty (Ps. xxiv. 8). The Lord mighty in battle; the heavens his throne, the earth his footstool, the light his garments, the clouds his chariots, the thunder his voice, his strength omnipotence, his riches all-sufficiency, his glory infinite, his retinue the hosts of heaven, and the excellent ones of the earth, on whom he bestows riches unsearchable, an inheritance incorruptible, banquets of everlasting joys, and preferments of immortal honour, making them kings and priests unto God, conquerors, yea and more than conquerors, children of God, and mystically one with himself.

Here appears something incomparably above all worldly glory, though under a mean disguise. But the objection is still against that disguise; yet even that disguise, upon due consideration, will appear to be so glorious, that its very meanness is honourable. It was a glorious disguise, because the designs and effects of it are so; if he suffered shame, poverty, pain, sorrows, and death, for a time, it was that we might not suffer these things for ever. That meanness therefore was glorious, because it was subservient unto an infinitely glorious design of love and mercy.

It was subservient more ways than one; it satisfied the penalty of the law, it put unspeakable honour on the commandments of it. It was a part of Christ's design to make holiness (that is, obedience to the law) so honourable, that everything else should be contemptible in comparison of it; love of worldly greatness is one of the principal hindrances of it. We did not need the example of Christ to commend earthly grandeur to us, but very much to reconcile us to the contrary, and to make us esteem holiness, though accompanied with meanness. Christ's low state was an excellent mean for this end. There was therefore greatness, even in his meanness. Other men are honourable by their station, but Christ's station was made honourable by him; he has made poverty and meanness, joined with holiness, to be a state of dignity.

Thus Christ's outward meanness, that disguised his real greatness, was in itself glorious, because of the design of it. Yet that meanness did not wholly becloud it; many beams of glory shone through it.

His birth was mean on earth below. But it was celebrated with hallelujahs by the heavenly host in the air above; he had a poor lodging, but a star lighted visitants to it from distant countries. Never prince had such visitants so conducted. He had not the magnificent equipage that other kings have, but he was attended with multitudes of patients, seeking and obtaining healing of soul and body; that was more true greatness than if he had been attended with crowds of princes. He made the dumb that attended him sing his praises, and the lame to leap for joy, the deaf to hear his wonders, and the blind to see his glory. He had no guard of soldiers, nor magnificent retinue of servants; but, as the centurion, that had both, acknowledged, health and sickness, life and death, took orders from him. Even the winds and storms, which no earthly power can control, obeyed him; and death and the grave durst not refuse to deliver up their prey when he demanded it. He did not walk upon tapestry, but when he walked on the sea, the waters supported him. All parts of the creation, excepting sinful men, honoured him as their Creator. He kept no treasure, but when he had occasion for money, the sea sent it to him in the mouth of a fish. He had no barns, nor corn-fields, but when he inclined to make a feast, a few loaves covered a sufficient table for many thousands. None of all the monarchs of the world ever gave such entertainments. By these and many such things, the Redeemer's glory shone through his meanness, in the several parts of his life. Nor was it wholly clouded at his death; he had not, indeed, that fantastic equipage of sorrow that other great persons have on such occasions. But the frame of nature solemnised the death of its Author; heaven and earth were mourners. The sun was clad in black; and if the inhabitants of the earth were unmoved, the earth itself trembled under the awful load; there were few to pay the Jewish compliment of rending their garments, but the rocks were not so insensible; they rent their bowels. He had not a grave of his own, but other men's graves opened to him. Death and the grave might be proud of such a tenant in their territories, but he came not there as a subject, but as an invader, a conqueror; it was then the king of terrors lost his sting, and on the third day the Prince of life triumphed over him, spoiling death and the grave. But this last particular belongs to Christ's exaltation; the other instances shew a part of the glory of his humiliation, but it is a small part of it.

The glory of the cross of Christ, which we are chiefly to esteem, is the glory of God's infinite perfections displayed in the work of redemption, as the apostle expresses it, *the glory of God in the face of Christ Jesus* (2 Cor. iv. 6). *Even of Christ crucified* (1 Cor. ii. 2). It is this which makes any other object glorious, according as it manifests more or less of the perfections of God. This is what makes the works of creation so glorious; the heavens declare God's glory, and the firmament his handiwork. And we are inexcusable for not making more pains to contemplate God's perfections in them, his almighty power and incomprehensible wisdom, and particularly his infinite goodness. But the effects of the Divine goodness, in the works of creation, are only temporal favours; the favours purchased to us by the cross of Christ are eternal. Besides, although the works of creation plainly shew that God is in himself good, yet they also shew that God is just, and that he is displeased with us for our sins; nor do they point out to us the way how we may be reconciled to him. They publish the Creator's glory, they publish at the same time his laws and our obligations to obey them. Our consciences tell us we have neglected these obligations, violated these laws, and consequently incurred the Lawgiver's displeasure. His works declaring his glory, shew that in his favour is life, and consequently that in his displeasure is death and ruin; yea, they lay us in some measure under his displeasure already. Why else do natural causes give so much trouble in life, and pain in death? From all quarters the works of God revenge the quarrel of his broken law. They give these frail bodies subsistence for a time, but it is a subsistence embittered with many vexations, and at last they crush them, and dissolve them in dust.

The face of nature, then, is glorious in itself, but it is overcast with a gloom of terror to us; it shews the glory of the Judge to the criminal, the glory of the offended Sovereign to the guilty rebel. This is not the way to give comfort and relief to a criminal; it is not the way to make him glory and triumph. Accordingly the enemies of the cross of Christ, who refuse to know God otherwise than by the works of nature, are so far from glorying in the hopes of enjoying God in heaven, that they renounce all those great expectations, and generally deny that there is any such blessedness to be had. Conscience tells us we are rebels against God, and nature does not shew how such rebels may recover His favour; how in such a well-ordered government as the divine government must be, the righteous Judge and Lawgiver may be glorified, and the criminal escape, much less how the Judge may be glorified, and the criminal obtain glory likewise.

The language of nature, though it be plain and loud in proclaiming the glory of the Creator, yet it is dark and intricate as to his inclination towards guilty creatures. It neither assures peremptorily that we are in a state of despair, nor gives sure footing for our hopes. If we are favourites, whence so many troubles? If we are hopeless criminals, whence so many favours? Nature shews God's glory and our shame; his law our duty, and consequently our danger. But about the way of escape it is silent and dumb. It affords many motives for exciting desires after God, but it shews not the way to get these desires satisfied. Here in the text is an object which gives us better intelligence. It directs us not merely to seek by feeling in the dark (Acts xvii. 27), if haply we may find, but to seek him so as certainly to find Him. Unlikely doctrine to a carnal mind: that there should be more of God's glory manifested to us in the face of Christ crucified than in the face of heaven and earth—the face of Christ, in which sense discovers nothing but marks of pain and disgrace—that bloated, mangled visage, red with gore, covered with marks of scorn, swelled with strokes, and pale with death—that would be the last object in which the carnal mind would seek to see the glory of the God of life; a visage clouded with the horror of death, it would with more pleasure and admiration view the same face when transfigured, and shining like the sun in its strength. Divine glory shone indeed then in a bright manner in that face on the mount, but not so brightly as on mount Calvary. This was the more glorious transfiguration of the two. Though all the light in the world, in the sun and stars, were collected together into one stupendous mass of light, it would be but darkness to the glory of this seemingly dark and melancholy object. For it is here, as the apostle expresses it (2 Cor. iii. 18), "We all, as with open face, may behold the glory of God."

Here shines spotless justice, incomprehensible wisdom, and infinite love all at once. None of them darkens or eclipses the other; every one of them gives a lustre to the rest. They mingle their beams, and shine with united eternal splendour. The just Judge, the merciful Father, and the wise Governor. No other object gives such a display of all these perfections; yea, all the objects we know give not such a display of any one of them. Nowhere does justice appear so awful, mercy so amiable, or wisdom so profound.

By the infinite dignity of Christ's person, his cross gives more honour and glory to the law and justice of God than all the other sufferings that ever were or will be endured in the world. When the apostle is speaking to the Romans of the gospel, he does not tell them only of God's mercy, but also of his justice revealed by it (Rom. i. 18). God's wrath against the unrighteousness of men is chiefly revealed by the righteousness and sufferings of Christ. The Lord was pleased for his righteousness sake (Isa. xlii. 21). Both by requiring and appointing that righteousness, he magnified the law and made it honourable. And though that righteousness consists in obedience and sufferings which continue for a time, yet since the remembrance of them will continue for ever, the cross of Christ may be said to give eternal majesty and honour to that law which it satisfied, that awful law, by which the universe (which is God's kingdom) is governed, to which the principalities and powers of heaven are subject; that law, which in condemning sin banished the devil and his angels from heaven, our first parents from paradise, and peace from the earth. Considering, therefore, that God is the Judge and Lawgiver of the world, it is plain that his glory shines with unspeakable brightness in the cross of Christ as the punishment of sin. But this is the very thing that hinders the lovers of sin from acknowledging the glory of the cross, because it shews so much of God's hatred of what they love. It would be useful for removing such prejudices, to consider, that though Christ's sacrifice shews the punishment of sin, yet if we embrace that sacrifice, it only *shews* it to us—it takes it off our hands, it leaves us no more to do with it. And surely the beholding our danger, when we behold it as prevented, serves rather to increase than lessen our joy; by seeing the greatness of our danger, we see the greatness of our deliverance. The cross of Christ displays the glory of infinite justice, but not of justice only.

Here shines chiefly the glory of infinite mercy. Nothing in the world more lovely or glorious than love and goodness itself, and this is the greatest instance of it that can be conceived. God's goodness appears in all his works; this is a principal part of the glory of the creation. We are taught to consider this lower world as a convenient habitation, built for man to dwell in; but, to allude to the apostle's expression, Heb. iii. 3. This gift we are speaking of should be accounted more worthy of honour than the world, inasmuch as he who hath built the house hath more honour than the house.

When God gave us his Son, he gave us an infinitely greater gift than the world; the Creator is infinitely more glorious than the creature, and the Son of God is the Creator of all things. God can make innumerable worlds by the word of his mouth; he has but one only Son, and he spared not his only Son, but gave him to the death of the cross for us all.

God's love to his people is from everlasting to everlasting. But from everlasting to everlasting there is no manifestation of it known or conceivable by us that can be compared to this. The light of the sun is always the same, but it shines brightest to us at noon. The cross of Christ was the noontide of everlasting love, the meridian splendour of eternal mercy; there were many bright manifestations of the same love before, but they were like the light of the morning, that shines more and more unto the perfect day; and that perfect day was when Christ was on the cross, when darkness covered all the land.

Comparisons can give but a very imperfect view of this love which passeth knowledge. Though we should suppose all the love of all the men that ever were, or shall be, on the earth, and all the love of the angels in heaven, united in one heart, it would be but a cold heart to that which was pierced with the soldier's spear. The Jews saw but blood and water, but faith can discern a bright ocean of eternal love flowing out of these wounds. We may have some impression of the glory of it by considering its effects; we should consider all the spiritual and eternal blessings received by God's people for four thousand years before Christ was crucified, or that have been received since, or that will be received till the consummation of all things; all the deliverances from eternal misery; all the oceans of joy in heaven, the rivers of water of life, to be enjoyed to all eternity, by multitudes as the sand of the sea-shore. We should consider all these blessings as flowing from that love that was displayed in the cross of Christ.

Here shines also the glory of the incomprehensible wisdom of God, which consists in promoting the best ends by the fittest means. The ends of the cross are best in themselves, and the best for us that can be conceived; the glory of God, and the good of man. And the means by which it advances these ends are so fit and suitable, that the infinite depth of contrivance in them will be the admiration of the universe to eternity.

It is an easy thing to conceive the glory of the Creator manifested in the good of an innocent creature; but the glory of the righteous Judge manifested in the good of the guilty criminal, is the peculiar mysterious wisdom of the cross. It is easy to conceive God's righteousness declared in the punishment of sins; the cross alone *declares his righteousness in the remission of sins* (Rom. iii. 25). It magnifies justice in the way of pardoning sin, and mercy in the way of punishing it. It shews justice more awful than if mercy had been excluded, and mercy more amiable than if justice had been dispensed with. *It magnifies the law, and makes it honourable* (Isa. xlii. 21). It magnifies the criminal who broke the law; and the respect put upon the law makes him honourable likewise (1 Cor. ii. 7). Yea, this is so contrived, that every honour done to the criminal is an honour done to the law, and all the respect put upon the law puts respect also on the criminal; for every blessing the sinner receives is for the sake of obedience and satisfaction made to the law, not by himself, but by another, who could put infinitely greater dignity on the law. And the satisfaction of that other for the sinner puts the greatest dignity on him that he is capable of. Both the law and the sinner may *glory in the cross of Christ.* Both of them receive eternal honour and glory by it.

The glories that are found separately in the other works of God are found united here. The joys of heaven glorify God's goodness, the pains of hell glorify his justice; the cross of Christ glorifies both of them in a more remarkable manner than heaven or hell glorifies any of them. There is more remarkable honour done to the justice of God by the sufferings of Christ, than by the torments of devils; and there is a more remarkable display of the goodness of God, in the redemption of sinners, than in the joy of angels. So that we can conceive no object in which we can discover such manifold wisdom, or so deep contrivance for advancing the glory of God.

The like may be said of its contrivance for the good of man. *It heals all his diseases, it pardons all his sins* (Ps. ciii.). It is the sacrifice that removes the guilt of sin; it is the motive that removes the love of sin; it mortifies sin and expiates it. It atones for disobedience, it excites to obedience; it purchases strength for obedience, it makes obedience practicable, it makes it delightful, it makes it acceptable, it makes it in a manner unavoidable, it constrains to it (2 Cor. v. 14). It is not only the motive to obedience, but the pattern of it. It satisfies the curse of the law, and fulfils the commands of it. Love is the fulfilling of the law, the sum of which is the love of God and of our neighbour. The cross of Christ is the highest instance of both. Christ's sufferings are to be considered as actions. Never action gave such glory to God, never action did such good to man. And it is the way to shew our love to God and man, by promoting the glory of the one, and the good of the other.

Thus the sufferings of Christ teach us our duty, by that love whence they flowed, and that good for which they were designed. But they teach us not only by the design of them, but also by the manner of his undergoing them. Submission to God and forgiveness of our enemies are two of the most difficult duties; the former is one of the chief expressions of love to God, and the latter of love to man; but the highest submission is, when a person submits to suffering though free of guilt; and the highest forgiveness is, to forgive our murderers, especially if the murderers were persons who were obliged to us, as if a person not only should forgive them who took away his life, even though they owed him their own life, but also desire others to forgive them, pray for them, and as much as possible excuse them. This was the manner of Christ's bearing his sufferings—*Father, thy will be done;* and, *Father, forgive them, for they know not what they do.*

Thus we see how fit a mean the cross is for promoting the best ends, for justification and sanctification. It would be too long to insist here in shewing its manifold fitness for promoting also joy and peace here, and everlasting happiness hereafter. For no doubt it will be a great part of the future happiness to remember the way it was purchased, and to see the Lamb that was slain at the right hand of Him that gave him for that end. The things already adduced shew that the incomprehensible wisdom of God is gloriously displayed in the cross of Christ, because it hath such amazing contrivance in it for advancing the good of man as well as the glory of God. For that is the design of it, to shew the glory of God and goodwill towards man.

But it is not only the glory of divine wisdom that shines in this blessed object, but also the glory of divine power. This to them who know not Christ is no small paradox. But to them who believe, *Christ crucified is the wisdom of God and the power of God* (1 Cor. i. 24). The Jews thought Christ's crucifixion a demonstration of his want of power; hence they upbraided him, that he who wrought so many miracles suffered himself to hang on the cross. But this itself was the greatest miracle of all. They asked, Why He who saved others saved not himself? They named the reason without taking heed to it; that was the very reason why at that time he saved not himself, because he saved others—because he was willing and able to save others. The motive of his enduring the cross was powerful, divine love, stronger than death; the fruits of it powerful, divine grace, the power of God to salvation (Rom. i. 16), making new creatures, raising souls from the dead—these are acts of Omnipotence. We are ready to admire chiefly the power of God in the visible world, but the soul of man is a far nobler creature than it. We justly admire the power of the Creator in the motion of the heavenly bodies; but the motion of souls towards God as their centre is far more glorious—the effects of the same power far more eminent and far more lasting.

The wounds of Christ seemed effects of weakness; but it is easy to observe incomparable strength appearing in them. We should consider what it was that bruised Him—*He was bruised for our iniquities.* The Scripture represents them (Isa. liii.) as a great burden, and describes us all lying helpless under it, as a people laden with iniquity. Christ bore our sins in his own body on the tree; he bore our griefs, and carried our sorrows, not these we feel here only, but those we deserved to feel hereafter. We should consider who laid this burden on Him, *The Lord laid on Him the iniquities of us all* (Isa. liii. 6). We might well say with Cain, our punishment was more than we were able to bear; this might be said to every one of us apart, but it was not the sins of one that he bore, he bore the sins of many, of multitudes as the sand on the seashore, and the sins of every one of them, as numerous. This was the heaviest and most terrible weight in the world.

The curse of the law was a weight sufficient to crush a world. They who first brought it on themselves found it so. It sunk legions of angels who excel in strength, when they had abused that strength against the law, from the heaven of heavens to the bottomless pit. The same weight that had crushed rebel angels threatened man for joining with them. Before man could bear it, before any person could have his own proportion of it, it behoved, as it were, to be divided into numberless parcels. Man, after numberless ages, would have borne but a small part of it. *The wrath to come* would have been always wrath to come to all eternity; there would have been still infinitely more to bear. Christ only had strength to bear it all; to bear it all in a manner at once, to bear it all alone. None of the people were with Him; our burden and our help was laid on One who was mighty. And his bearing it was a glorious manifestation of his might, of the noblest kind of might, that he was *mighty to save.*

It is true, that load bruised Him; but we would not be surprised at that if we considered the dreadfulness of the shock. Could we conceive the weight of eternal justice, ready to fall down, like lightning, with violence upon a world of malefactors, and view that sacred body interposed betwixt the load of wrath from above and the heirs of wrath below, we would not wonder at these bruises, we would not despise them. We should consider the event had that wrath fallen lower; had it met with no obstacle it would have made havoc of another kind—this world would have been worse than a chaos, and been covered with the dismal effects of vindictive justice and divine righteous vengeance.

Although his sacred flesh was both mangled and marred with that dismal load, yet we should consider that it sustained it. Here was incomparable strength, that it sustained that shock which would have grinded mankind into powder, and He sustained it (as was said before) alone. He let no part of it fall lower. They who take sanctuary under this blessed covert are so safe that they have no more to do with that load of wrath but to look to it (John iii. 14). To allude to the psalmist's expressions (Ps. xci. 7, 8), "It shall not come nigh them, only with their eyes they shall behold, and see the reward of their wickedness;" but they shall see it given to that righteous One. And all that in effect is left to them in this matter, is by faith to look and behold what a load of vengeance was hovering over their guilty heads, and how that guiltless and spotless body interposed, they will see it crushed at a sad rate. But it is the end of the conflict that shews on what side the victory is; in that dreadful struggle Christ's body was brought as low as the grave. But though the righteous fall, he rises again. Death was undermost in the struggle (1 Cor. xv. 27); it was Christ that conquered in falling, and completed the conquest in rising. The cause, design, and effects of these wounds shew incomparable power and strength appearing in them; the same strength appeared in his behaviour under them, and the manner in which he bore them, we see in the history of his death. He bore them with patience, and with pity and compassion towards others. A small part of his sorrow would have crushed the strongest spirit on earth to death. The constitution of man is not able to bear too great violence of joy or grief. Either the one or the other is sufficient to unhinge our frame. Christ's griefs were absolutely incomparable, but his strength was a match for them.

These considerations serve to shew that it is the greatest stupidity to have diminishing thoughts of the wounds of the Redeemer. Yet, because this has been the stumbling-block to the Jews, and foolishness to the Gentiles, and many professing Christians have not suitable impressions of it, it is proper to consider this subject a little more particularly. It is useful to observe how the Scripture represents the whole of Christ's humiliation as one great action, by which He defeated the enemies of God and man, and founded a glorious everlasting monarchy. The prophets, and particularly the psalmist, speak so much of Christ as a powerful conqueror, whose enemies were to be made his footstool, that the Jews do still contend that their Messiah is to be a powerful temporal prince, and a great fighter of battles, one who is to subdue their enemies by fire and sword, and by whom they themselves are to be raised above all the nations of the world. If pride and the love of earthly things did not blind them, it were easy to see that the descriptions of the prophets are vastly too high to be capable of so low a meaning. This will be evident by taking a short view of them, which at the same time will shew the glory of that great action just now spoken of, by shewing the greatness of the design and the effects of it.

The prophets ofttimes speak more expressly of the Messias as a great King, which is a name of the greatest earthly dignity. The hand of Pilate was overruled to cause write that title of honour even on his cross. The glory of the kingdom that He was to found is represented in very magnificent expressions by the prophet Daniel (chap. ii. 35, 45 ; vii. 9, 10, 13, 14). Here are lively representations of unparalleled greatness : an everlasting kingdom to be founded, strong obstacles to be removed, powerful enemies to be defeated.

It is useful to observe the universal importance of this design. No part of the universe was unconcerned in it.

The glory of the Creator was eminently to be displayed, all the divine persons were to be gloriously manifested, the divine attributes to be magnified, the divine works and ways to be honoured ; the earth was to be redeemed, hell conquered, heaven purchased, the law to be magnified and established (Isa. xlii. 21). Its commandments to be fulfilled, its curse to be suffered, the law was to be satisfied, and the criminal that broke it be saved, and his tempter and accuser to be defeated ; the head of the old serpent was to be bruised, his works to be destroyed, and the principalities and powers of darkness to be spoiled and triumphed over openly (Col. ii. 15). The principalities and powers of heaven were to receive new matter of everlasting hallelujahs, and new companions to join in them ; the fallen angels were to lose their old subjects, and the blessed angels to receive new fellow-citizens. No wonder this is called the making a new heaven and a new earth, and even the face of hell was to be altered. Surely a more glorious design cannot be contrived ; and the more we consider it, the more we may see the greatness of the action that accomplished it.

As the design was great, the preparations were solemn. The stage of it was to be this earth ; it was chiefly concerned in it. It was solemnly prepared for it. This is the view given us of the providences that preceded it ; they fitted the stage of the world for the great event in the fulness of time. If we saw clearly the whole chain of them, we would see how they pointed towards this as their centre, and how they contributed to honour it, or rather it reflected the greatest honour upon them. The fore-cited prophecies in Daniel, besides several others, are instances of this. They shew how the great revolutions in the heathen world were subservient to this design, particularly the succession of the four monarchies represented in Nebuchadnezzar's dream. Their rise and overthrow were subservient to the rise of this monarchy, never to be overthrown.

We see but a small part of the chain of providence, and even that very darkly. But this perhaps is worth the observing briefly, that universal empire came gradually from the eastern to the western parts of the world, from the Assyrians and Persians to the Greeks and Romans. By this means greater communication and correspondence than formerly was opened up between distant nations of the earth, from the rising to the setting of the sun. The kingdom represented by the stone cut out of the mountain was to extend to both (Dan. ii. 34, 35). However we think of this, it is certain that if we saw the plot of providence unfolded, we would see these and other revolutions contributing to the fulness of times, and adjusting the world to that state and form of things that was fittest for the Redeemer's appearance.

These were a part of the preparations for the work in view; but they were but a part of them. For all the sacrifices offered every morning and evening for so many ages, were preparations for it and shadows of it. The same may be said of other figures and types. The church of God for four thousand years waited with longing looks for this salvation of the Lord. They were refreshed with the sacrifices that prefigured it. The heathens themselves had their sacrifices. They had sinfully lost the tradition of the true religion and the Messiah handed down from Noah; yet Providence ordered it so, that they did not wholly lose the rite of sacrificing. There is reason to acknowledge a particular providence preserving tradition in this point; for how otherwise could it enter into men's heads to serve their gods by sacrificing their beasts? It was useful that the world should not be entirely unacquainted with the notion of a sacrifice; the substitution of the innocent in the room of the guilty all pointed towards this great oblation which was to make all others to cease. The predictions of the prophets in different ages, from Moses to Malachi, were also preparations for this great event. John the Baptist appeared as the morning-star, the harbinger of the Day-spring from on high. It was his particular office to prepare the way of the Lord before him. The evidence of the prophecies was bright; the Jews saw the time approaching, their expectations were big. Counterfeit Messiah took advantage of it; and not only the Jews, but even the heathens, probably by report from them, had a notion of an incomparably great person who was to appear about that time. These, besides many other great things, serve to shew what glorious preparations and pomp went before the great work we are speaking of.

Here it may perhaps occur to some, that it is strange an action that had such great preparations before it happened, was so little observed when it did happen. Strictly speaking, this was not true. It was not much noticed indeed among blind and ignorant men—this was foretold; but it had a noble theatre, the whole universe were in effect spectators of it. The Scripture teacheth us to reflect on this: particularly to consider the principalities and powers in heavenly places, as attentive onlookers on this glorious performance. We may infer this (besides other scriptures) from Eph. iii. 10.

These morning-stars shouted for joy, and sang together at the old creation (Job xxxviii. 7). This was a new creation to sing at, a more amazing spectacle than the old. In that, the Son of God acted in the form of God; now, he was to act in the low form of a servant. Nor was that the lowest part of it: he was to suffer in the form of a criminal. The Judge in the form of a malefactor, the Lawgiver in the room of the rebel. The creation was a mean theatre for so great an event, and the noblest creatures unworthy judges of such an incomprehensible performance; its true glory was the approbation of its infinite contriver, and that He, at whose command it was done, was fully well pleased with it.

Yet to us, on whose natures example has so much influence, it may be useful to consider that honourable crowd of admirers and spectators that this performance had, and to reflect how heaven beheld with veneration what was treated on earth with contempt; it was a large theatre, multitudes as sand on the seashore, a glorious company. In Scripture, angels, in comparison of men, are called gods. We are not sensible of their glory, which struck prophets almost dead with fear, and tempted an apostle to idolatry; but these, when the first-begotten is brought into the world (Heb. i. 6 compared with Ps. xcvii. 7), all these gods are commanded to worship him; the place of Scripture where angels are called gods, is the place where they are commanded to worship Christ. And according to the same apostle (Heb. i. 6), it was a special time of his receiving this glory from the hosts of heaven, when his glory was to be vailed among the inhabitants of the earth. It is evident that they were spectators of all that he did in that state, and no doubt they were attentive spectators; they desired to look, as it were, with outstretched necks into these things (1 Peter i. 12), nor could they be unconcerned spectators. They were on divers accounts interested in it. They did not need a redemption themselves; but they delighted in ours. They loved Christ, and they loved his people. Their love interested them in the glory of the one and the other. All we know of their work and office, as Luther expresses it, is to sing in heaven and minister on earth; our *redemption* gave occasion for both; they sang for joy when it began at Christ's birth (Luke ii. 13), they went with gladness on messages of it beforehand to the prophets, and to the virgin Mary. They fed Christ in the desert, they attended him in his agony and at his resurrection, and accompanied him at his ascension. They were concerned to look into these things in time, that were to be remembered to all eternity; and into that performance on earth that was to be the matter of eternal hallelujahs in heaven.

It should not therefore hinder our esteem of this great work that the great men on earth took no notice of it. They were but mean, blind, ignorant, vulgar, compared to these powers and thrones just now mentioned who beheld it with veneration. It is no disparagement to an excellent performance that it is not admired by ignorant persons who do not understand it.

The principalities in heaven understood, and therefore admired; nor were the principalities and powers of darkness wholly ignorant of it. Their example should not be a pattern to us; but what they beheld with anguish, we should behold with transport. Their plot was to make the earth, if possible, a province of hell; they had heard of that glorious counterplot; they were alarmed at the harbingers of it; they looked on, and saw their plot step by step defeated, and the projects of eternal mercy going on. All the universe therefore were interested onlookers at this blessed undertaking. Heaven looked on with joy, and hell with terror, to observe the event of an enterprise that was contrived from everlasting, expected since the fall of man, and that was to be celebrated to all eternity.

Thus we have before us several things that shew the glory of the performance in view :—The Design, of universal importance; the Preparation, incomparably solemn; a company of the most honourable attentive Spectators. As to the performance itself, it is plain it is not a subject for the tongues of men ; the tongues of men are not for a subject above the thoughts of angels ; they are but desiring to look into it, they have not seen fully through it : that is the work of Eternity. Men may speak and write of it, but it is not so proper to describe it as to tell that it cannot be described. We may write about it, but if all its glory were described, the world would not contain its books (John xxi. 25) ; we may speak of it, but the most we can say about it is to say that it is unspeakable. And the most that we know is that it passes knowledge. It is He that performed this work that can truly declare it. It is He who contrived that can describe it. It is He who knows it. None knows the Father but the Son, or he to whom he shall reveal him. It is from Him we should seek this knowledge (Eph. i. 17) ; what of it is to be had here is but in part (2 Cor. xiii. 9) ; but it leads us to the place where it will be perfect. Here we think as children, we speak as children. Yet we are not therefore to neglect thinking or speaking of it ; our thoughts are useless without contemplating it, our speech useless without praising it. The rest of the history of the world, except as it relates to this, is but a history of trifles or confusions, dreams and vapours of sick-brained men. What we can know of it here is but little ; but that little incomparably transcends all other knowledge. And all other earthly things are but loss and dung to it (Phil. iii. 3, 11). The least we can do is with the angels, to desire to look into these things, and we should put up these desires to Him, who can satisfy them, that He may shine in our hearts by the light of the knowledge of the glory of God (2 Cor. iv. 6). The true object of this knowledge is the glory of God ; the means of obtaining it, is *light shining* from God ; and as to the place into which it shines, it is into our hearts. We are therefore to desire that light from Him who is light itself ; but our prayers should be joined with other means, particularly that meditation which Paul recommends to Timothy (1 Tim. iv. 15), we ought to meditate on these things, so as to give ourselves wholly to them. Our meditation should be as lively and as like to seeing the object before us as possible. But it is not by strength of imagination that the soul is profited in this case, but by having the eyes of the understanding enlightened (Eph. i. 18).

The makers and worshippers of images pretend to help us in this matter, by pictures presented to the eye of the body. But it is not the eye of sense or force of imagination, but the eye of faith, that can give us true notions and right conceptions of this object (2 Cor. v. 16). Men may paint Christ's outward suffering, but not that inward excellency from whence their virtue flowed, viz., his glory in himself, and his goodness to us. Men may paint one crucified; but how can that distinguish the Saviour from the criminals? On each side of him we may paint his hands and his feet fixed to the cross; but who can paint how these hands used always to be stretched forth for relieving the afflicted and curing the diseased; or how these feet went always about doing good, and how they cure more diseases and do more good now than ever? We may paint the outward appearance of his sufferings, but not the inward bitterness or invisible causes of them. Men can paint the cursed tree, but not the curse of the law that made it so. Men can paint Christ bearing the cross to Calvary, but not Christ bearing the sins of many. We may describe the nails piercing his sacred flesh; but who can describe eternal justice piercing both flesh and spirit? We may describe the soldier's spear, but not the arrows of the Almighty; the cup of vinegar which he but tasted, but not the cup of wrath which he drank out to the lowest dregs; the derision of the Jews, but not the desertion of the Almighty forsaking his Son, that he might never forsake us who were his enemies.

These sorrows he suffered and the benefits he purchased are equally beyond description. Though we describe his hands and his feet mangled and pierced, who can describe how in one hand, as it were, he grasped multitudes of souls ready to sink into ruin, and in the other hand an everlasting inheritance to give them; or how these bruised feet crushed the old serpent's head, and trampled on death and hell, and sin the author of both? We may describe the blood issuing from his body, but not the waters of life streaming from the same source, oceans of spiritual and eternal blessings. We may paint how that blood covered his own body, but not how it sprinkles the souls of others, yea, sprinkles many nations. We may paint the crown of thorns he wore, but not the crown of glory he purchased. Happy were it for us if our faith had as lively views of this object as our imaginations ofttimes have of incomparably less important objects, then would the pale face of our Saviour shew more powerful attractives than all the brightest objects in nature besides. Notwithstanding of the gloomy aspect of death, it would discover such transcendent majesty as would make all the glory in the world lose its relish with us; we would see then indeed the awful frowns of justice, but these frowns are not at us, but at our enemies, our murderers, that is, our sins. The cross shews Christ's pitying his own murderders, but shews no pity to our murderers; therefore we may see the majesty of eternal justice tempered with the mildness of infinite compassion. Infinite pity is an object worth looking to, especially by creatures in distress and danger; there death doth appear in state, as the executioner of the law, but there he appears also deprived of his sting with regard to us. There we may hear also the sweetest melody in the world to the awakened sinner; that peace-speaking blood, that speaks better things than that of Abel; the sweetest and loudest voice in the world, louder than the thunder on Sinai. Its voice reacheth heaven and earth, pleading with God in behalf of men, and beseeching men to be reconciled to God; speaking the most comfortable and the most seasonable things in the world, to objects in distress and danger, that is, *salvation and deliverance.*

Of the various views we can take of this blessed work, this is the most suitable, to consider it as the most glorious deliverance that ever was or will be. Other remarkable deliverances of God's people are considered as shadows and figures of this. Moses, Joshua, David, and Zerubbabel were types of this great Joshua; according to his name, so is he JESUS a Deliverer. The number of the persons delivered shew the glory of this deliverance to be unparalleled; it was but one single nation that Moses delivered, though indeed it was a glorious deliverance, relieving sixty thousand at once, and a great deal more; but this was incomparably more extensive. The apostle John calls the multitude of the redeemed a multitude that no man could number (Rev. vii. 9), of all nations, kindreds, people, and tongues. The unparalleled glory of this deliverance appears not only in the number of the delivered, but also in the nature of the deliverance. It was not men's bodies only that it delivered, but immortal souls, more valuable than the world (Matt. xvi. 26). It was not from such a bondage as that of Egypt, but one as far beyond it, as eternal misery is worse than temporal bodily toil. So that nothing can equal the wretchedness of the state from which they are delivered, but the blessedness of that to which they are brought.

But here we should not forget the opposition made against this deliverance. It was the greatest that can withstand any good design. The apostle (Eph. vi. 12) teaches to consider the opposition of flesh and blood as far inferior to that of principalities and powers, and spiritual wickedness in high places. The devil is called the god of this world (2 Cor. iv. 4), and himself and his angels the rulers of the darkness of this world

(Eph. vi. 12). They had obtained a dominion over the world (excepting that small corner, Judea) for many ages by the consent of the inhabitants. They found them not only pliable, but fond of their chains, and in love with their bondage. But they had heard of this intended enterprise of supreme power and mercy, this invasion and descent upon their dominions. They had heard of the design of bruising their head, overturning their government, making their slaves to revolt. Long experience had made them expert in the black art of perdition; long success made them confident, and their malice still pushed them on to opposition, whatever be the success. As they were no doubt apprised of this designed deliverance, and alarmed at the signs of its approach, they made all preparations to oppose it, mustered all their forces, employed all their skill, and, as all was at stake, made their last efforts for a kind of decisive engagement; they armed every proper instrument, and set every engine of spiritual destruction a-working; temptations, persecutions, violence, slander, treachery, counterfeit Messiahs, and the like.

Their Adversary appeared in a form that did not seem terrible, not only as a man, but as one despised of the people (Ps. xxii. 6), accounted as a worm, and no man. But this made the event more glorious. It was a spectacle worth the admiration of the universe to see the despised Galilean turn all the artillery of hell back upon itself. To see one in the likeness of the Son of man, wresting the keys of hell and death out of the hands of the devil; to see him entangling the rulers of darkness in their own nets, and making them ruin their designs with their own stratagems. They made one disciple betray him, and another deny him; they made the Jews accuse him, and the Romans crucify him. But the wonderful Counsellor was more than match for the old serpent, and the lion of the tribe of Judah too hard for the roaring lion. The devices of these powers of darkness were in the event made means of spoiling and triumphing over themselves (Col. ii. 15). The greatest cruelty of devils and their instruments was made subservient to the designs of the infinite mercy of God; and that hideous sin of the sons of men, overruled in a perfectly holy manner, for making an end of sin, and bringing in everlasting righteousness (Dan. ix. 24). The opposition made to this deliverance did but advance its glory, particularly the opposition it met with from those for whose good it was intended, that is, sinners themselves. This served to enhance the glory of mysterious long-suffering and mercy.

It would take a long time to insist on all the opposition He met with, both from the enemies of sinners, and from sinners themselves; but at last He weathered the storm, surmounted difficulties, led captivity captive, obtained a perfect conquest, purchased an everlasting inheritance, founded an everlasting kingdom, triumphed on the cross, died with the publishing his victory in his mouth, That it was finished.

The world is represented as silent before the Lord when he rose up to work this great deliverance. And, as was shewn before, no part of the world was unconcerned in it. The expectation was great, but the performance could not but surpass it. Every part of it was perfect, and every circumstance graceful; nothing deficient, nothing superfluous, nothing but what became the dignity of the person, and the eternal wisdom of the contrivance. Everything was suited to the glorious design, and all the means proportioned to the end. The foundation of the everlasting kingdom was laid before it was observed by the men that opposed it, and so laid that it was impossible for the gates of hell to prevail against it; all things adjusted for completing the deliverance, and for securing it against all endeavours and attempts to overturn it. The great Deliverer in that low disguise wrought through his design, so as none could oppose it without advancing it, to the full satisfaction of that infinite wisdom that devised it, and the eternal admiration of the creatures that beheld it.

The Father was well pleased; heaven and earth rejoiced, and was astonished; the powers of hell fell down like lightning. In heaven loud acclamations and applauses, and new songs of praises began that are not ended yet, and never will; they will still increase; still new redeemed criminals from earth, saved from the gates of hell, and entering the gates of heaven, with a new song of praise in their mouths, add to the ever-growing melody, of which they shall never weary; for that is their rest, their labour of love, never to rest, day nor night, giving praise and glory to Him that sits on the throne, and to the Lamb at his right hand, who redeemed them from all nations and tongues, washing them in his own blood, and making them kings and priests unto God.

But still an objection may be made concerning the little honour and respect this work met with on earth where it was performed. This, duly considered, instead of being an objection, is a commendation of it. Sin had so corrupted the taste of mankind, that it had been a kind of reflection on this work if it had suited it. Herein the beauty of it appears, that it was above that depraved, wretched taste which it was designed to cure; and that it did actually work that change on innumerable multitudes of nations.

If the cross of Christ met with such contempt on earth, it met also with incomparable honour. It made the greatest revolution in the world that ever happened since the creation, or that ever will happen till Shiloh come again. A more glorious, a more lasting change than ever was produced by all the princes and conquerors in the world. It conquered multitudes of souls, and established a sovereignty over men's thoughts, wills, and affections. This was a conquest to which human power hath no proportion. Persecutors turned apostles; and vast numbers of Pagans, after knowing the cross of Christ, suffered death and torments cheerfully to honour it. The growing light shone from east to west; and opposition was not only useless, but subservient to it. The changes it produced are sometimes described by the prophets in the most magnificent expressions; thus for instance Isa. vii. : *It turned the parched grounds into pools of waters, made the habitations of dragons to become places of grass and reeds and rushes; made wildernesses to bud and blossom as the rose.* It wrought this change among us in the utmost isles of the Gentiles. We ought to compare our present privileges with the state of our forefathers before they knew this blessed object; and we will find it owing to the glory of the cross of Christ, that we who are met here to-day to worship the living God in order to the eternal enjoyment of him, are not worshipping sun, moon, and stars, or sacrificing to idols.

But the chief effects of the cross of Christ, and which shew most of its glory, are its inward effects on the souls of men. There (as was before hinted) it makes a new creation; Christ is formed in them, the source and the hope of glory. This is a glorious workmanship: the image of God on the soul of man. But since these effects of the cross of Christ are secret, and the shame put upon it ofttimes too public, and since human nature is so much influenced by example, it will be useful to take such a view of the honour done to this object as may arm us against the bad example of stupid unbelievers.

The cross of Christ is an object of such incomparable brightness, that it spread a glory round it to all the nations of the earth, all the corners of the universe, all the generations of time, and all the ages of eternity. The greatest actions or events that ever happened on earth filled, with their splendour and influence, but a moment of time and a point of space.

The splendour of this great object fills immensity and eternity. If we take a right view of its glory, we will see it contemplated with attention, spreading influence, and attracting looks from times past, present, and to come; heaven, earth, and hell, angels, saints, devils. We will see it to be both the object of the deepest admiration of the creatures, and the perfect approbation of the infinite Creator; we will see the best part of mankind, the church of God for four thousand years looking forward to it before it happened; new generations yet unborn rising up to admire and honour it, in continual successions, till time shall be no more; innumerable multitudes of angels and saints looking back to it with holy transport, to the remotest ages of eternity. Other glories decay by length of time; if the splendour of this object change, it will be only by increasing. The visible sun would spend his beams in process of time, and as it were grow dim with age; this object hath a rich stock of beams which eternity cannot exhaust. If saints and angels grow in knowledge, the splendour of this object will be still increasing; it is unbelief that intercepts its beams: unbelief takes place only on earth, there is no such thing in heaven or in hell. It will be a great part of future blessedness, to remember the object that purchased it; and of future punishment, to remember the object that offered deliverance from it. It will add life to the beams of love in heaven, and make the flames of hell burn fiercer; its beams will not only adorn the regions of light, but pierce the regions of darkness. It will be the desire of the saints in light, and the great eye-sore of the prince of darkness and his subjects.

Its glory produces powerful effects wherever it shines. They who behold this glory are transformed into the same image (2 Cor. iii. 18). An Ethiopian may look long enough to the visible sun before it change his black colour; but this does it. It melts cold and frozen hearts, it breaks stony hearts, it pierces adamants, it penetrates through thick darkness. How justly is it called marvellous light (1 Peter ii. 9)! It gives eyes to the blind to look to itself, and not only to the blind, but to the dead. It is the light of life, a powerful light: its energy is beyond the force of thunder, and it is more mild than the dew on the tender grass.

But it is impossible fully to describe all its effects, unless we could fully reckon up all the spiritual and eternal evils it prevents, all the riches of grace and glory it purchases, and all the divine perfections it displays. It has this peculiar to it, that as it is full of glory itself, it communicates glory to all that behold it aright. It gives them a glorious robe of righteousness; their God is their glory; it calls them to glory and virtue; it gives them the spirit of God and of glory; it gives them joy unspeakable and full of glory here, and an exceeding great and eternal weight of glory hereafter.

It communicates a glory to all other objects, according as they have any relation to it: it adorns the universe; it gives a lustre to nature and to providence. It is the greatest glory of this lower world, that its Creator was for a while its inhabitant. A poor landlord thinks it a lasting honour to his cottage that he has once lodged a prince or emperor; with how much more reason may our poor cottage, this earth, be proud of it that the Lord of glory was its tenant from his birth to his death, yea, that he rejoiced in the habitable parts of it, before it had a beginning, even from everlasting (Prov. viii. 31).

It is the glory of the world that he who formed it, dwelt on it; of the air, that he breathed in it; of the sun, that it shone on him; of the ground, that it bore him; of the sea, that he walked on it; of the elements, that they nourished him; of the waters, that they refreshed him; of us men, that he lived and died among us, yea, that he lived and died for us; that he assumed our flesh and blood, and carried it to the highest heavens, where it shines as the eternal ornament and wonder of the creation of God. It gives also a lustre to providence. It is the chief event that adorns the records of time, and enlivens the history of the universe. It is the glory of the various great lines of providence, that they point at this as their centre; that they prepared the way for its coming; that after its coming they are subservient to the ends of it, though in a way indeed to us at present mysterious and unsearchable. Thus we know that they either fulfil the promises of the crucified Jesus or his threatenings; and shew either the happiness of receiving him, or the misery of rejecting him.

II.

The Prospects of the Church of Christ.

BY THE REV. JOHN LOVE, D.D.

"Lift up thine eyes round about, and behold: all these gather themselves together, and come to thee. As I live, saith the Lord, thou shalt surely clothe thee with them all, as with an ornament, and bind them on thee, as a bride doeth."—Isaiah xlix. 18.

"GREAT and marvellous," saith the assembly of redeemed spirits in heaven, "Great and marvellous are thy works, Lord God Almighty, just and true are thy ways, thou King of saints." It is, however, through thickets of apparent contrariety and contradiction that the eternal wisdom makes its way to fulfil the designs and purposes which, when accomplished, shall occupy the search and the wonder of everlasting ages.

The complaint recorded (ver. 14 of this chapter) hath a very glorious sound. It hath been frequently in the mouths of individual believers, and hath staid them when their feet were stumbling on the dark mountains. And if we consider the prospects of the Christian Church, the foundation on which she rests, the words of divine promise put in her mouth, and the spiritual weapons of warfare she holds in her hands, and compare with these the present state of religion through the habitable parts of this whole earth, it may perhaps be considered as a complaint to be justly assumed by the whole multitude of Christian believers now in the world, as a collective body. The Zion now existing on the earth may say, "The Lord hath forsaken me, and my Lord hath forgotten me." Such expostulations, however, cease to appear strange when we consider such words as we see recorded (ver. 4) as coming from the lips of the beloved of the Eternal Father, in whom his soul delighteth. "Then I said," I, whom Jehovah hath called from the womb, whose name he hath mentioned with delight from the bowels of my mother, I, whom he hath made a polished shaft and hid in his quiver; I, to whom He said, thou art my servant, O Israel, in whom I will be glorfied; I said, pierced with anguish, and worn down with disappointment, "I have laboured in vain, I have spent my strength for nought, and in vain." But the reply to such complaints from the Church and from her Redeemer, complaints that, as it were, touch the heart-strings of Deity, is emphatical indeed.

To the majestic though humbled Redeemer the answer is in these terms: "It is a light thing that thou shouldest be my servant, to raise up the tribes of Jacob; I will also give thee for a light to the Gentiles, that thou mayest be my salvation to the ends of the earth. In an acceptable time have I heard thee, and I will give thee for a covenant of the people, to establish the earth, that thou mayest say to the prisoners, Go forth; to them that are in darkness, Show yourselves."

And to the spouse of the Redeemer the answer issues forth from on high in accents of still more tender condolence: "Can a woman forget her sucking child, that she should not have compassion on the son of her womb? yea, they may forget, yet will I not forget thee. Behold, I have graven thee on the palms of my hands; thy walls are continually before me."

From the same bowels of compassion and love, but in a tone which rises with each sentence in grandeur, significance, and triumph, proceed the words of the text: "Lift up thine eyes round about, and behold : all these gather themselves together, and come to thee. As I live, saith the Lord, thou shalt surely clothe thee with them all, as with an ornament, and bind them on thee, as a bride doeth."

Where is the faith which is prepared to meet such words as these, and to follow them out to their vast extent ? It shall be created, it shall be expanded, it shall be inspired with conquering vigour, while we inquire into the meaning and certainty, while we drink in the sweetness, while we bow to the authority and grace of those words of the living God.

I. The Church's attention is summoned to a *vast multitude of converts* pouring in upon her from every side, " Lift up thine eyes round about, and behold : all these gather themselves together, and come to thee." " Lift up thine eyes," thy dejected eyes, suffused with tears, those eyes which conviction of sin hath sharpened, and which have looked far into eternity, those eyes which have seen scenes of desolation, defilement, and mourning, those dove-like eyes, which nothing can delight but the view of thy Redeemer coming in the glory of his kingdom. Behold the object which will soothe every drooping spirit, which will satiate and replenish every sorrowful soul. See what a throng ! How numerous ! How beautiful ! Multitudes ! Multitudes ! not in the valley of decisive judgment, but in the fields of blessing. Myriads ! Nations ! A world travailing in birth ! A world newly created !

The early promises of grace opened wide the door of hope. They spread out an ample bosom prepared to embrace immense numbers of perishing sinners. But through a long series of ages, the Church was taught the preciousness of salvation by its rareness. Hope was sustained by a succession of converts, small in number, and forming to the eyes of sense an inconsiderable minority in the midst of crowds who passed on into eternity, under the curse and power of iniquity.

But the enlarged promises of the everlasting covenant assume a largeness of grace worthy of the love of Him, before whom all nations are as the drop of a bucket, in whose eyes systems of worlds appear little objects.

The spirit of promise draws the picture of a whole earth, thick set with living converts, like the sky bespangled with stars, or like the surface of the earth, whose shrubs and trees twinkle with the dew of the morning. He displays a multitude which no man can number, which no imagination can completely apprehend, a multitude surpassing far, it is to be believed, the number of those hosts which fell from heaven, yea, probably far surpassing the hosts of blessed angels which remain there; a multitude sufficient to occupy the whole habitable places of this great earth, successively through a long train of blessed ages.

What an object is this to the truly illuminated Church which understands the value of salvation, and perceives how many salvations are wrapped up in that of a single soul. For it is not a mere crowd, important by mere numbers, which stands held forth in the promise as the ultimate result of infinite love, and of the travail of the Mediator's soul. It is a crowd, every individual of which appears rich with divine glory. For we must notice—

II. That this great multitude *is a selected throng of human beings*, on each individual of which the distinguishing electing love of God hath particularly and personally rested from eternity, and in connection with this, a particular influence of the power of Jehovah is to be recognised as universally impressed on this whole multitude, wherein the Church is permitted to triumph. Causes and effects must be proportioned to one another. But sometimes great effects are produced with such ease, and seem so congenial to these subjects, that the cause is almost overlooked. This is the case in the ordinary works of the Almighty. When we stand on the bank of a great river, and observe its waters moving forward in silent majesty, we are apt to forget, while the movement seems so easy and natural, that there is implied in it an operation of immense power, and that, in a manner which no philosopher has yet been able to explain, the power of the Creator, in what is called gravitation, is impressed on every particular drop in the great body of flowing waters. So while the benevolent Christian forms ideas, corresponding to the promises of God, of countless multitudes flowing together to the goodness and salvation revealed in his Church, the movement seems so desirable and so reasonable, that he needs to be reminded of the greatness of that power by which an effect so great is produced. It is proper, therefore, to think of the strong native opposition in each individual who comes truly to the Saviour. It is necessary to think of the accumulating force of that combined opposition which hath formed, through so many ages, that fatal course or current of the world which hath appeared irresistible. Then it will be necessary to apprehend a greatness of power, not merely resembling that which secretly bears on the waters of the river in their natural course, but rather like that which turned back the overflowing streams of Jordan towards their source, or which divided the waters of the roaring ocean.

We contemplate the revealed arm of Jehovah as the immediate cause of this confluence of true converts. Still, however, a further cause must be sought. Why is that arm of power which lay hid through so many ages, while millions on millions were perishing, at length so signally displayed? Here we approach the awful sacred fountain of love—we revolve that lofty name, "I am that I am." Our thoughts flow back as far as the wings of imagination and of faith can carry them into the abyss of the past eternity. We think of the self-existing essence of the Person first in Deity, in the earliest stirrings of divine counsel and affection, opening its ample stores of condescending love and compassion towards unworthy human transgressors. "Behold what manner of love the Father hath bestowed on us." See Him looking forth from the height of paternal Deity towards those countless multitudes of sinners, involved in the same condemnation and depravity which bring eternal ruin on their equals in transgression; but taking hold of each individual soul in all that multitude, with a love unspeakably more tender than that with which any human heart ever embraced the most select object of its dearest regards. Sacred awful fountain of love! In thee I discern the sublime cause of the great effect. How sovereign, yet how tender! How unobliged, yet how strong and determinate are thy movements! How personal, yet widely expanded! Let me, with revering ecstasy, approach this fountain of love of the first in Deity, while I hear its determinate voice in the word of promise, "All these gather themselves together, and come to thee. As I live, saith Jehovah, thou shalt surely clothe thee with them all."

III. A third subject of inquiry invites our thoughts in the words before us. They transfer to the Church of the living God *the honours of his surprising works of love.* These converted multitudes become his ornament, "Thou shalt surely clothe thee with them all, as with an ornament, and bind them on thee, as a bride doeth." What an image is here! I know not whether most to admire its august magnificence, or its condescending delicacy and sweetness. It reminds me of similar emblems in other parts of the sacred oracles, such as that (Rev. xii.), "A woman clothed with the sun, having the moon under her feet, and on her head a crown of twelve stars." I think of an ancient distinguished member of the Church, the patriarch Abraham, led forth by the divine hand under the star-bespangled glowing vault of heaven, and turning thither his heavenly-directed eyes, to see the emblem of the brighter multitude of believers who should call him father. In my text, honours like his are extended to the whole Church existing previously to those surprising and joyful enlargements.

Let this now be the subject of our inquiry, in what wonderful ways the vast extension of the powers of converting grace through the world shall be enjoyed, with the most delicious sense of ornament and honour, by the genuine Church.

1. By those converted multitudes the Church is honoured while they acknowledge the inexpressible value of the formerly existing spiritual Church of Jehovah. What are these peculiar treasures and excellencies? I hope, my brethren, many of you know them well. They are the treasures of divine truth, unfolded by a wisdom coming from above; they are the influences of the Spirit of truth conveying into the inmost soul, with certainty at once sweet and demonstrative, the most interesting and extensive discoveries of divine eternal truth. The treasures and prerogatives of the Church are the stores of salvation; they are the unsearchable riches of merit, righteousness, and redemption, the ransom price, powerful to rescue from the flames of eternity, and to open the paradise of immeasurable joys, and to do this for worlds upon worlds of the guilty. These treasures are the true medicines of diseased souls, the healing, purifying fountains; they are the riches of inimitable universal sanctity; they are the rivers, the floods of divine condescension brought down from heaven to earth, and lifting earthly beings to the delights and dignities of heaven.

While the multitude of converts in the various climes of this otherwise poor earth discern those glorious treasures deposited with the once despised Church, they come into the posture in which prophecy exhibits them, "And the Gentiles shall come to thy light, and kings to the brightness of thy rising" (Isa. lx. 3).

"They shall fall down unto thee; they shall make supplication unto thee, saying, Surely God is in thee, and there is none else; there is no God" (Isa. xlv. 14). "They shall bow down to thee with their face toward the earth, and lick up the dust of thy feet, and thou shalt know that I am the Lord; for they shall not be ashamed that wait for me" (Isa. xlix. 23).

2. Benevolence, philanthropy, goodwill to men. Venerable names, but often abused and falsely assumed. But it is to the singular and genuine benevolence of the true Church of the living God that the converted world shall gather its flowers and wreathe its laurels. That heaven-breathed benevolence, those supplications, those self-denied, persevering exertions, which originate in the knowledge and communion of the crucified Saviour, these bear the palm of victory in this warfare. I commiserate those well-meaning people who deceive themselves with words, and reasonings, and human authority, while they disregard the loud testimony of Scripture and experience concerning the inutility of all the productions of unrenewed human nature when brought to the work of subduing the stubborn pride and rebellion of an apostate world.

It is in the period to which our thoughts are guided by the prediction in the text, when the face of the covering cast over all people and the vail spread over all nations shall be destroyed,—it is then that the sentiments of mankind shall be rectified on this subject, and that the world shall discern its real enemies and its true friends. When the fruits of that benevolence, which long sighed and mourned in secret places, or pursued its unostentatious exertions under the shade of obscurity and contempt, appear overspreading and beautifying the whole earth, then the delivered nations shall bless that pious love, that heavenly kindness which, from the days of Abel, the Redeemer of sinners hath infused into the breast of his spiritual spouse.

3. But in what *diversified forms*, and in what *overflowing abundance*, shall the honours of the Church, mingled with those of her high Redeemer, flow in upon her from every quarter of the world !

The unfolded secrets of error, superstition, and vice in every land shall spread new lustre on the fair lines of eternal truth and holiness. The multitude of human beings inspired with heavenly energy, combining all the variety and extent of human genius and industry, in investigating and adorning the truth, and in shewing forth the praises of the God of salvation, and through the attending influence and blessing of the Spirit from on high, shall enrich and adorn the cities of our God in an unexampled, unimaginable manner. Blessed shall be those eyes which shall see a new train of Christian heroes, philosophers, politicians, princes, patriots, orators, and poets walking forth in every clime, and gathering in the honour and glory of the nations, to be collected at the feet of the Lamb who was slain, and to decorate the bride, the object of his eternal conjugal regards. Instead of the iron bond of connection, formed by a selfish, sordid, and often blood-stained spirit of commerce or of conquest, the nations, drawn into union by the silken cords of heavenly love, and formed into fair, symmetrical, peaceful combination, shall be actually assumed by the Church of the Redeemer as her ornament and glory, and "she shall clothe her with them all, as with an ornament, and bind them on her, as a bride doeth."

This adorning, these honours, however, shall by no means be confined to the happy race of believers then found on the earth; when such august scenes open they shall reach backward through all ages,—they shall embrace the spirits of the righteous in glory, especially "the souls under the altar of them who have been slain for the Word of God, and for the testimony which they held." In the living esteem and honour of these truly enlightened and dignified ages, the sufferers of all periods shall virtually rise from the dust of death, and appear as having judgment given to them from on high, as clothed with white robes, as sitting on thrones, the objects of universal esteem, admiration, and praise throughout the new-born world.

IV. But have we entered the regions of airy fancy, the fairy land of fiction? Are those things a dream, or *is there certainty attached to them?* A distinguished heathen poet, addressing himself to one of the fictitious objects of his admiration, speaks in this manner: "Do you hear her, or am I deceived by a lively fancy? I see myself wandering with delight among the groves of the blessed, watered with sweet streams, and fanned with delightful breezes." Such elegant pathos of a poor idolater will be pardoned by the philosopher, and will command the admiration of the man of classical sensibility; but both the philosopher and the man of classical sensibility, if impious, will pronounce it an intolerable enthusiasm, a madness not to be forgiven, if our souls are set on fire by the burning rays of truth coming from the true and eternal God. Shall we stand in awe of such censures? No; we are bound to despise them; for we have examined the grounds of our confidence; we have heard in the sacred oracles that inimitable voice of the Holy One, which shall at length silence all their voices; we know with a certainty, firm as demonstration, and sweet as the joys of heaven, that the Spirit of inspiration speaking in the Scriptures is truth. That Spirit summons us to joy, while he spreads out the wonderful scenes of salvation to be transacted in this sinful world. And he exhibits the bright seal of Deity, assuring us that in the indulging such hope we do not follow cunningly-devised fables. "As I live, saith Jehovah, thou shalt surely clothe thee with them all, as with an ornament."

The oath of Deity! The life of Deity! What securities are these!

1. It is difficult for us, who know so little of God, to apprehend in a becoming manner the solemn grandeur and authority of the oath of God.

The habits of a devilish profaneness debauch the human mind, otherwise we would feel inexpressible awe under the idea of an oath when emitted by the meanest individual possessed of the power of reason. What, then, would be the solemnity attached to the oath of a seraph, one of the sons of the morning, in the celestial regions? The oath of an angel would rise in its solemnity and force above that of the wisest of human beings in proportion as he possesses deeper reverence of Deity, and is capable of looking farther than mortals can do into those infinite perfections to which the appeal is made. But, when the uncreated Majesty itself in the heavens rises from the throne, and before the appalled multitude of angels, assuming the posture of swearing, appeals to that life of immense glory, whereof he is conscious, to procure belief of his promissory engagements, who shall then hesitate? Shall not unbelief then shrink away with horror? Shall not faith then lift up its head, and, walking on its high places, tread lightly over the tops of obstructing mountains of opposition? "As I live, saith Jehovah, thou shalt surely clothe thee with them all, as with an ornament."

2. The infinite life of Jehovah is the source of all existence, strength, and excellency; while therefore it is appealed to for the purpose of giving assurance of the promises, it exhibits the rich fountain of all those multiplied energies which shall operate as the instrumental means of fulfilling these great promises; "I have girded thee," saith God to the yet non-existing hero, "I have girded thee, though thou hast not known me." Even the irrational animals are witnesses of the divine power to impart vigour, sagacity, and invincible fortitude. The horse prancing fearlessly in the valley, the behemoth advancing

among the shady trees with bones like bars of iron, the leviathan with a heart like the nether mill-stone, looking forth like the eyelids of the morning, making the deep to boil around him; these are some of the innumerable visible monuments of the efficacy of divine operation in inferior animal beings. But what shall be the effects when Immanuel, the lion of the tribe of Judah, shall pour from the heavens the spirit of wisdom and of might, and shall bring into the world armies of such lions as the world never saw, excepting in some comparatively rare examples, in the days of bloody persecution? The man who shall bear the triumphant cross round the globe, shall exhibit strength and fortitude, not like the terrifying fierceness of partial selfish heroes, but holy, benevolent, irresistible, heaven-tempered, like the prowess of angels. Before such men in whom Jesus shall put forth his living powers, what obstructions, what terrors, can earth or even hell exhibit?

Jehovah lives; therefore the promise shall be accomplished.

3. After such securities it is hardly necessary to reason on the subject, otherwise a long train of arguments, in confirmation of the promise, might be brought forward. We might vindicate the superior preferableness of the Church's claims above those of any other of her haughty rivals; we might shew that so many millions of creatures made for eternity are too costly a sacrifice to be always offered up to the wild freak of bloody ambition, or to the equally careless, but more sordid monster, commercial avarice, or to the vain-glorious insolence of unfounded impotent philosophy. Such competitors as these must quickly retire when the Church of the living God rises in her brightness. Even the awful sovereign justice of Jehovah, which, in its mysterious range through the ages that are past, has devoured so many victims, will at length say, It is enough; and, smelling an odour of rest in the sacrifice of Jesus the Son of God, suffer the earth to become the joyful dominion of triumphant mercy.

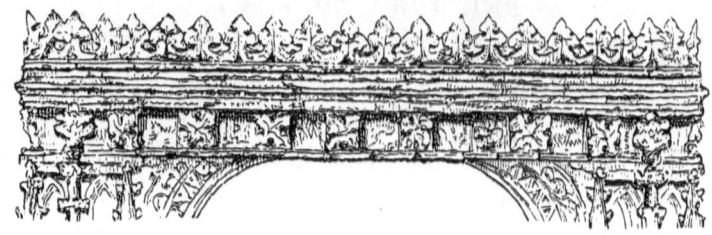

III.

Christ's Death and Resurrection.

BY THE REV. SIR H. MONCREIFF WELLWOOD, BART., D.D.

"For I delivered unto you first of all that which I also received, how that Christ died for our sins according to the Scriptures; and that he was buried, and that he rose again the third day according to the Scriptures," &c.—1 Cor. xv. 3-8.

I PROPOSE nothing more, in discoursing on this text, than to request your attention to the leading facts which the apostle here represents, as having formed the substance of the doctrines which he had originally received from the Lord, and had delivered to the Corinthians, at the time when the Church of Christ was planted among them.

I. "*Christ died for our sins.*" Assuming this fact, on the authority of the Revelation of God, I shall satisfy myself with general hints, rather than detailed illustrations of the place which it holds in the faith of a Christian; and shall endeavour to turn your thoughts to its general and practical influence on his state of mind through life, rather than to the solution of any real or supposed difficulties, which the perverted ingenuity of man may attach to it. How a sacrifice for sin was required to bring down the mercy of God to a fallen world, how Christ could die, or how the sufferings and death of the Holy One of God could be either appointed or received for the redemption of the creatures of his power, are questions suggested by querulous unbelief and presumption, not by the devout solicitude of humble and sincere believers.

The assertion of the text, "that Christ died for our sins," as far as it relates to the counsels of God, must of necessity contain a great deal, far beyond the reach of our understandings. But when it is regarded as a fact which involves the eternal interests of human beings, and is addressed to their consciences under the pressure of guilt, it sheds a glorious light on the path of human life, and awakens the most ardent affections of those who rely on it. As a fact addressed to a sincere and trembling penitent, who is humbled by his recollection of aggravated transgressions which he can never recal,—as a fact, on the certainty of which he can entirely depend, it comes home to his heart, as the tender mercy of God for the remission of sins which are past, through his forbearance; or is "like the day-spring from on high," visiting him who sits in darkness and in the shadow of death, to give him the knowledge of salvation, and to guide his feet into the way of peace.

"My heart is deeply wounded," will he say within himself, "by the consciousness of guilt which I cannot forget, and by the awful presence of that Holy and Omnipotent Being, who knows my sitting down and my rising up, and is acquainted with all my ways, whose wrath I know to be revealed from heaven against all unrighteousness and ungodliness of men. My repentance, were it ever so deep, will not fulfil the duties which I have not done; nor will it cancel deliberate guilt, where pure and perpetual fidelity is due. My recollections press heavily on my conscience, but I should have no reliance on the mercy of heaven, and no sound reason to rely on it, if I did not believe 'that Christ died for our sins,' because God set him forth to be a propitiation through faith in his blood, that whosoever believeth on him might receive the remission of sins. When I am assured of this fact, I am certain of another, that my sins, aggravated as they are, are not too heinous to be forgiven, and that they are not beyond the reach or the influence of the great atoning sacrifice which was offered for sins on the cross of Christ. I know that I have nothing personal to plead; but I also know in whom I have believed, and am persuaded that he is able to keep and secure whatsoever I commit to him. His blood cleanseth from all sin, and he is able also to save to the uttermost them that come unto God by him, seeing he ever liveth to make intercession for them."

It is in such language as this that the assertion of the text, "that Christ died for our sins," is recognised by well-informed and genuine believers as the foundation both of their principles of duty, and of all their hopes of salvation. There are those, no doubt, who with better and worse intentions, affect to represent the doctrine which rests the remission of sins on the fact "that Christ died for our sins" by the will of God, as if it were calculated to relax the obligations of morals and religion, and to separate the mercy held out to sinners by the death of the Lord, from the indispensable obligations of those to whom much is forgiven. But every attempt to misrepresent or pervert the grace of God to our fallen world must be completely defeated when we seriously examine and fairly estimate the views and feelings of a genuine penitent, who finds his consolations at the cross of Christ. There he receives the precious assurance of pardon from the throne of God, and of "good hope through grace." But he receives it there, inseparably conjoined with the passion and the agonies of the Holy One of God, suffering, the just for the unjust, to bring us to God, when God lays on him the iniquities of us all. And where then can he learn, with such irresistible conviction, that sin is at perpetual enmity with God and men—with God, as the avenger of his own law, and with men, whose guilt and impenitence are the cause of all their miseries? Where can he receive a more powerful admonition that there is no peace to the wicked, and no salvation for the human race but by his obedience unto death, "who died for our sins"? Or finally, where can he be taught, with the same authority, that the pardon which a sinner can only obtain by the blood of atonement is in no case to be separated from the promise of the Father, "to put his spirit within them" for whom Christ died; and that purity of life, and the fidelity of "a conscience purged from dead works to serve the living God," are both the result and the pledge of the faith by which he has peace with God, and of the grace wherein he stands?

Is it possible to imagine any other circumstances which have the same commanding power over those who feel their influence—which bring home to their consciences the indispensable obligations of a holy and circumspect and conscientious life with the same irresistible authority—which are as effectual as these to persuade them of the inseparable relation between purity of mind and the communion of God, between their abhorrence of the sins for which Christ died, and every hope or consolation which they can derive from him? There are no doubt hypocrites in every age who presumptuously assume a reliance on the sacrifice of Christ, while they secretly reject his authority; and there are also many individual sinners, who look with desire to the cross of Christ for the remission of sins, from uncertain and unsettled convictions, both of duty and of salvation, which often return, but are successively abandoned. But Christianity is not to be tried except by its genuine efficacy among those who believe to the saving of their souls. *They* embrace the salvation of the gospel for time and for eternity. They estimate the consolations derived from it by the sanctifying power of the cross of Christ, and "by Him the world is crucified unto them, and they unto the world." In proportion to the earnestness and affection with which they rely on the sacrifice of Christ for the remission of sins, their progress in purity of mind and in all Christian fidelity, becomes every hour more and more the object of their lives. By the sanctification of the spirit and the belief of the truth, they go from strength to strength, and they are kept by the power of God, through faith, unto salvation. The sacrifice of Christ, "who died for our sins," is not therefore to be regarded as a subject of mere speculative belief or inquiry. It is a great practical truth which affects the most essential interests of personal and vital religion. "If any man be in Christ, he is a new creature." His mind is purified by obeying the gospel, and "he walks not after the flesh, but after the spirit."

II. The text affirms, that after our Lord's crucifixion "*He was buried, and that he rose again from the dead on the third day.*" Though he was arraigned and insulted and condemned to death by the high and the low, and though he was followed to the cross by the execrations of the deluded multitude, he was, notwithstanding, honoured in his burial as no crucified man had ever before been honoured in Judea. Two men, of the highest distinction among their countrymen, with the consent of the governor, received his body from the cross, and with the most significant ceremonies and symbols known among the Jews, laid it in a sepulchre hewn in stone, wherein never man before was laid; a striking memorial of the affection and reverence with which they had regarded him, which neither the ignominy of the cross nor the hopeless aspect of his crucified body had been sufficient to destroy. But it is more important to remark, that when it is specially related that our Lord "was buried," this fact is presented to us on the record of the gospel, to certify the reality of his death, and to make all men know that he who bare our sins in his own body on the cross submitted to be charged with the penalty of sin in the grave itself, when he was laid in the tomb among the multitude of sinners for whom he had offered himself a ransom to God. "O death," he said, for that day, "I will be thy plague. O grave, I will be thy destruction;" and from that time "was death swallowed up in victory." And we have now to recollect that though our Lord Jesus Christ "died for our sins" according to the determinate counsel and foreknowledge of God, it was not possible that death could hold him, and that "he rose again from the dead on the third day," as he himself had distinctly foretold to his disciples. "He is not here," said the angel of the Lord to the women who came sorrowing to the sepulchre, "He is not here; for he is risen, as he said. Come, see the place where the Lord lay: and go and tell his disciples that he is risen from the dead."

Our Lord's resurrection, as a verified fact in the history of the gospel, is the corner-stone of our most holy faith. "If Christ has not risen, then there is no resurrection of the dead. Then is our preaching vain, and your faith is vain; ye are yet in your sins. Then they also which are fallen asleep in Christ are perished" without redemption. Glory to God, we know, on the most incontestable evidence, of which no inconsiderable part is detailed in the text before us, and will be afterwards adverted to, that "the Lord is risen indeed, and hath become the first-fruits of them that sleep." He was crucified in the weakness of his humanity, but "his resurrection from the dead declared him to be the Son of God with power." And the evidence of this fact is a demonstration to every age and generation of men, that Christ crucified is the power of God unto salvation to every one who believeth; and that "neither death, nor life, nor angels, nor principalities, nor powers, nor things present, nor things to come, nor height, nor depth, nor any other creature, shall be able to separate us from the love of God which is in Christ Jesus our Lord."

This is the precious testimony which God hath given of his Son, whom he sanctified and sent into the world "to seek and to save that which was lost." The Lord is risen indeed, and "them also who sleep in Jesus shall God bring with him," when he shall come at last, "to be glorified in his saints," and to receive them to himself. The dead in Christ shall rise together, to meet the Lord at his coming, at the sound of the archangel, and the trump of God. Every one of them shall stand in his place before him. They shall all be there. Not one of them shall then be wanting. Not one of them all shall be without his share in the triumphs of that great day. The hoary head which went down to the grave in peace, and rested from the labours of a long and eventful life, shall rise from the grave with the vigour of the sons of the morning to triumph and to share in the glories of the first resurrection. The men who died before their time, in the strength of their years, servants of the Most High God, and benefactors of the world—men who were followed to their graves by the regrets and the reverence of the multitudes who survived them—shall then rise to meet the welcome of the Prince of Life, and to join the glad hosannas of the highest heavens. Many shall be there who lived and died in the fear of God, unnoticed and unknown in their humble sphere, and who were scarcely remembered when they died, except perhaps by the unexhausted affection of the wife or of the child of their youth. Every one of them shall be there; but then many that are first shall be last, and the last shall be first.

The mourners in Zion shall be there. They who lived under the pressure of many sorrows—afflicted, but not forsaken; cast down, but not destroyed—they who always bore about in the body the dying of the Lord Jesus, and often suffered more than is common to men—the mourners of every age and of every tribe, shall rise from the grave to meet the multitudes "who have come out of great tribulation, and who have washed their robes and made them white in the blood of the Lamb." And the youth and the child shall rise together, among the sufferers who wept over their untimely graves, perfect as the first-born of the sons of light; welcomed by that gracious Lord who said of *them* in the days of his flesh, "Suffer little children to come unto me, and forbid them not, for of such is the kingdom of God." All shall be there together to meet the Lord at his coming—"redeemed unto God by his blood, out of every kindred, and nation, and people, and language"—all blessed and everlasting partakers of the glory hereafter to be revealed.

Oh! it is a precious and powerful recollection, that He who died for our sins, rose again from the dead for our justification; that our faith and hope are therefore secure, and do not stand in the wisdom of men, but in the power of God. We can therefore believe with confidence that "blessed are the dead who die in the Lord," and that the time is fast approaching when there shall be no more death, and when grace shall reign through the righteousness of God unto eternal life, by Jesus Christ our Lord. I now observe—

III. That the death, the burial, and the resurrection of Christ were events clearly foretold in the prophecies of the Old Testament, of which they were the unquestionable and visible accomplishment. He "died, and was buried, and rose again the third day, *according to the Scriptures.*" This is a point on which our Lord insists in his conversation with the two disciples on the way to Emmaus. The Apostle Paul also, in his address to King Agrippa, brings forward precisely the same facts on the same authority. "Having obtained help of God," he said, "I continue unto this day; witnessing both to small and great, saying none other things than those which the prophets and Moses did say should come, that Christ should suffer, and that he should be the first that should rise from the dead, and should shew light unto the people and to the Gentiles." It is unnecessary to specify particular prophecies. I shall sum up all in an abridged view of the distinct prophecy of Isaiah with regard to all these points. "Surely," said the prophet, "he hath borne our griefs and carried our sorrows; smitten of God, and afflicted; wounded for our transgressions, bruised for our iniquities, for the Lord laid on him the iniquity of us all; taken from prison and from judgment; cut off out of the land of the living. For the transgression of the people was he stricken, and he made his grave with the wicked, and with the rich in his death. It pleased the Lord to bruise him, and to put him to grief, though he had done no violence, neither was there deceit in his mouth; yet when thou shalt make his soul an offering for sin, he shall see his seed, he shall prolong his days, and the pleasure of the Lord shall prosper in his hand." This identity of the prophetic representations with the events for which they were intended to prepare the way, presents to us a glorious view of the wisdom and of the uniformity which predominate in the revelations, as well as in all the works, of God. There is one grand and uniform plan carried on, from the fall of man to the resurrection of Christ, in which there are many subordinate agents and events, removed from each other by ages and generations, and with no apparent influence or co-operation to connect them together; detached prophecies and revelations, far asunder, with no visible relation to unite them till, when the fulness of time arrives, all are seen to centre in one result. The subordinate parts of this plan have each a place and a form suited to the circumstances immediately connected with them, while all of them are subservient at last to its ultimate issue. The most remote events are employed to accomplish the designs of God, *according to the Scriptures;* and the Scriptures of the prophets bear witness, in the minutest points, to the spirit and the power of the gospel preached to us by Christ and his apostles. "O the height and the depth both of the wisdom and knowledge of God! how unsearchable are his judgments, his ways are past finding out! For who hath known the mind of the Lord? or who hath been his counsellor? For of him, and to him, and by him, are all things: and to him be glory for ever. Amen." On this point I have only to add, that when our Lord was buried, according to the Scriptures, this event (like every other fact in his history) was intended to hold a place in the faith and consolation of those who should believe on him to the end of the world.

It is one of the most humbling recollections of human life, that the bodies of those whom we have most loved and honoured from youth to age, and by whose hands the blessings of Providence have been longest and most affectionately dispensed to us, are consigned at last to the dust of the grave, as their common depository, shut out for ever from all that is visible in the living world. It is a painful and an aggravated recollection. But the gospel tells us that the grave itself is not beyond the reach of Christian consolation. It is "the place where the Lord lay," the place which he hath sanctified and blessed by his own presence, for them who are his; a place for them, where the wicked cease from troubling, and where the weary are at rest. But it is never to be forgotten, that though "the small and the great are there," the Lord himself "made his grave with the wicked, and with the rich in his death," to the end, that no variety of characters, mingled in the tomb, might lessen our reverence or disturb our faith in "the rest which remains for the people of God." The least and humblest of them all enters into peace, and rests in his grave till the resurrection of the just; and shall hear at length the sound of the archangel's voice, and the trump of God, when the dead in Christ shall rise together, redeemed from the dust of the grave, to give glory to him that sits upon the throne, and to the Lamb for ever and ever. Before I leave the subject, I have still to direct your thoughts—

IV. To the *several appearances* of our Lord, after his resurrection, which are detailed in the text by the apostle. "He was seen of Cephas, then of the twelve. After that he was seen of above five hundred brethren at once; of whom the greater part remain unto this present, but some are fallen asleep. After that he was seen of James; then of all the apostles. And last of all he was seen of me also, as of one born out of due time." All these different instances in which our Lord was seen by his disciples after his resurrection, excepting the three last, are detailed in the gospels; and in all of them, it is to be remarked, that he attended to every circumstance calculated to remove every doubt, which either their prejudice or their want of presence of mind could suggest to them of the reality of his resurrection. At one time when they were terrified, and supposed that they had seen not their Master but a spirit, "he said unto them, Why are ye troubled? and why do thoughts arise in your hearts? Behold my hands and my feet, that it is I myself: handle me, and see; for a spirit hath not flesh and bones as ye see me have. And he shewed them his hands and feet." On another occasion he said to Thomas, who had been more incredulous than the rest, and had declared, "Unless I shall see in his hands the print of the nails, and put my fingers into the print of the nails, and thrust my hand into his side, I will not believe;" that even this satisfaction might be given to him, he said to him, "Reach hither thy finger, and behold my hands, and reach hither thy hand and thrust it into my side, and be not faithless but believing;" and then, "Because thou hast seen me, thou hast believed: blessed are they who have not seen, and yet have believed." On other occasions he ate and drank in the presence of his disciples, and particularly at the sea of Tiberias conversed with them familiarly on different subjects, intimately connected with their mission into the world. Circumstances which demonstrate to the satisfaction of every reasonable man, that while he remained on earth nothing was neglected which was necessary to furnish them with the most incontrovertible proofs which they were afterwards to give to the world of the reality of his resurrection from the dead, which declared him to be the Son of God with power. His appearance to five hundred brethren at once, of whom the greater part were alive when Paul first wrote to the Corinthians, though it is not recorded, is evidently referred to by both the evangelists Matthew and Mark, who mention that after his resurrection the disciples went away into Galilee, into a mountain, where Jesus had appointed them. There can scarcely be a doubt that this is to be referred to the appearance specified in the text, when he was seen of above five hundred individuals at one time; a striking proof that most interesting assembly of disciples was of the reverence and affection with which he was regarded by the multitudes of Judea and Galilee, which neither the reproach of the cross nor the malignity of his murderers had been able to extinguish. The fact, as given by the Apostle Paul, guided by the Spirit of God, is most important in the evidence of the gospel. It is a public appeal to a great multitude of men, who being still alive when this epistle was written, were competent and accessible witnesses still, and who had the evidence of their own senses that the Lord was risen indeed. No such appeal could ever have been made, in the face of so many living witnesses, except on the supposition that the facts were incontrovertible, and could not be denied. We have no particulars of our Lord's appearance to the Apostle James, though it must have been well known at the time among the believers, and given to the writer of this epistle in the most authentic form.

To all this is added his supernatural appearance after his ascension to the writer of this epistle, when on his way to Damascus he was called to be an apostle by a voice from heaven, by a voice uttered by the Son of God himself, arresting his progress in his infatuated persecution of the Christians, by those awful words, "Saul, Saul, why persecutest thou me? I am Jesus whom thou persecutest." We have there the testimony of the persecutor himself, to whom this most miraculous revelation was given. "Last of all," he says, "he was seen of me also, as of one born out of due time."

And after all these authentic testimonies to facts on which so much of the authority of the gospel of our salvation rests, what more could we imagine to have been done to complete the demonstration for every age of the world, that the Lord Jesus "died for our sins, and rose again according to the Scriptures"? "If it became him, of whom are all things, and by whom are all things, in bringing many sons unto glory, to make the Captain of their salvation perfect through sufferings," we are not less assured, on evidence of most incontrovertible certainty, that God hath made him, who bare their sins in his own body on the cross, both Lord and Christ; and that he is the Lord both of the dead and of the living. Him hath God raised up, and given him glory, that our faith and hope might be in God. A glorious completion of all that the prophets have spoken, or the Scriptures have told us! Christ proclaimed from the highest heaven, the wisdom of God, and the power of God unto salvation, to every one who believeth. This is "He that liveth and was dead, and behold he is alive for evermore, Amen, and hath the keys of hell and of death!"

O how blessed to be able to bring home to ourselves this glorious consummation of the dispensation of grace! Christ proclaimed from heaven the power of God for salvation to the ends of the earth! He has the keys of the kingdom of God; and to every individual whom he acknowledges as his, he says, by the Holy Ghost, "I go to prepare a place for thee, and thou shalt be mine in that day when I make up my jewels." We are yet, in our most advanced state in this world, in our frail and mouldering tabernacle of clay, most fallible and imperfect beings; and struggles, and temptations, and death, and the grave are still before us. But if we believe in the grace which shall be brought to us at the revelation of Jesus Christ, we are certain that we shall go from strength to strength, and that at last when, according to his promise, we shall reach the new heavens and the new earth, wherein righteousness and blessedness for ever dwell, we shall be like himself, for we shall there see him as he is.

Glorious day! when the Son of God shall come again—when the grave and the sea shall give up their dead—when the redeemed of the Lord shall come together to Zion, from the east, and from the west, and from the north, and from the south, and sit down together in the kingdom of God—when the great redemption shall be completely finished—when the children of God shall all be one—shall all be blessed in one great and undivided society—when the infirmities, the struggles, the bereavements, the sorrows of mortality—the varieties in their lot, in their attainments, in their tempers, and in their expectations—shall all be lost in the vigour and triumphs common to them all, and in the fulness of eternal joy.

Amen. Salvation to our God and to the Lamb! Blessing, and honour, and glory, and power to Him who sits upon the throne, who liveth and reigneth through eternal ages, and to the Lamb for ever and ever! Amen and Amen.

IV.

𝔗𝔥𝔢 𝔏𝔬𝔳𝔢 𝔬𝔣 𝔱𝔥𝔢 𝔖𝔭𝔦𝔯𝔦𝔱.

BY THE REV. THOMAS M'CRIE, D.D.

"Now I beseech you, brethren, for the love of the Spirit."—Rom. xv. 30.

THE volume of nature has the name of its author inscribed upon it, and everywhere bears the most distinct and legible marks of his Godhead and perfections; but it conveys no information to us of his subsistence in three persons. In the unity of design apparent in the works of nature, and in the nice and admirable adaptation of all parts of the universe to accomplish the same grand ends, which we perceive the more clearly in proportion to the increase of our knowledge, we have a proof of the unity of God which yields satisfaction to a plain and unsophisticated understanding; but there is nothing either in the work of creation, or in the works of common providence, which indicates any personal distinctions in the Godhead, or, in other words, makes known the doctrine of the Trinity. The knowledge of this mystery we owe to the volume of inspiration, which not only teaches it doctrinally, but reveals and describes a work calculated to illustrate it, and to give us clear, though necessarily, from its nature, inadequate conceptions of the subject. Redemption is the work of one

God, but of that one Being existing according to distinct relations of an intrinsic kind, which we, for want of a fitter word, and to guard against the opinions of those who would explain away the whole mystery, are forced to call personal.

The doctrine of the Trinity, as revealed in the Bible, is far from being a mere speculative truth. It lies at the foundation of our hope; our blessedness is wrapt up "in the love of God, the grace of the Lord Jesus Christ, and the communion of the Holy Ghost." It is supposed in all acceptable worship, for "we have access to the Father through the Son, by one Spirit;" "our fellowship is with the Father, and his Son Jesus Christ," and this is the fellowship of the Spirit. And as our worship is animated by the distinct consideration of what each person has done for our salvation, so the duties of obedience are enforced upon our minds by the same consideration. Hence the apostle, in entreating the prayers of the Christians at Rome in his behalf, employs the plea in our text, "for the Lord Jesus Christ's sake, and for the love of the Spirit."

By the "love of the Spirit" I understand that love which the third person of the Godhead has displayed in the economy of redemption. Some indeed are of opinion that it refers to that brotherly love which is the production of the Holy Spirit in the hearts of believers, and binds them together as members of the same mystical body, so as to feel a deep interest in one another's welfare. Even though it should be allowed that this was the more immediate meaning of the word in this passage, we might still take occasion from it to speak of that love which is the spring of all the Spirit's operations. We judge of the qualities of a fountain from the waters which it sends forth, and of a tree from its fruits. "The fruit of the Spirit is love;" and what must be the love resident in and flowing from that divine Person, who is the author of every affectionate feeling toward God or toward man! But I apprehend the connection in which the words stand fully justifies the other interpretation: "I beseech you from regard to what the Lord has done for you, and the love which the Holy Spirit has shewn to you, that ye strive together with me in your prayers to God for me."

We often speak of the love of the Father in not sparing his Son, and the love of the Son in giving himself for us; and we do well, for we cannot speak of them too often, nor with too much fervour of gratitude and admiration. But the love of the Spirit is more rarely the topic of public discourse or private converse, and there is reason to fear that it is too little in our thoughts, for "out of the abundance of the heart the mouth speaketh." May not this deficiency have a hurtful effect upon Christian experience? God draws his children to himself "by the cords of love," meaning his own love; but if one of the threads in "this threefold cord" be relaxed, must not the influence of divine love upon our hearts be weakened and impaired? If we are deficient in this part of Christian exercise, it assuredly does not arise from any defect in the proofs and illustration of love on the part of this divine Agent. The subject seems entitled to our particular attention. Let us then, trusting to the aid of the Spirit, without whom we can neither speak nor hear aright, in the *first* place, contemplate the manifestations of the love of the Holy Ghost; and *secondly*, exhibit the influence which a due sense of this love would have on our minds and conduct.

I. Contemplate the manifestations of the love of the Spirit. The work of redemption, or of recovering man from the ruin into which he had fallen by his transgression, is to be traced to the spontaneous and boundless love of God. This wonderful love is held forth as exerted in distinct acts by the Father, Son, and Holy Spirit. To the Father we ascribe, agreeably to the analogy of the word, the purpose and superintendence of the plan of redemption, to the Son its purchase, and to the Spirit its application. The love from which the Spirit acts is equally divine with that from which the Father and Son act; indeed it is the same, for the love of God, like his will, is one. "There is none good but one, that is God;" and this epithet is repeatedly applied to the third Person in an absolute sense: "Thou gavest them thy good Spirit"—"Thy Spirit is good." The love of the Spirit is eternal, unchangeable, sovereign, independent; and in its breadth, and length, and depth, and height, it passeth knowledge.

1. *The Holy Spirit displayed his love in the readiness with which he undertook his mission and work.* We speak of the covenant of grace as made between the Father and Son, because, in contemplation of the Son's assuming human nature, there was an engagement and a promise, a work and reward. But we must not overlook the concurrence of the blessed Spirit, and the delight which he took in the prospect of his work of grace and power. As the Son was sent by the Father, so the Spirit is sent by the Father and the Son, and on this account is called economically their Spirit; but he was as free and cheerful in undertaking and engaging in his work as He who said, "Lo I come, to do thy will, O my God." When Jesus was about to leave his disciples he said, "I will pray the Father, and he will give you another Comforter; if I go not away the Comforter will not come, but if I depart, I will send him unto you." Observe, he is not only said to be "sent," to intimate the established order of the economy of grace, and the certainty of the gift, but he is said to "come," in order to point out his willingness to engage in the work. "When he is come, he shall convince the world." Hence the prayer of the Old Testament Church: "Awake, O north wind; and come, thou south; blow upon my garden, that the spices

thereof may flow out" (Cant. iv. 16). And hence on the day of Pentecost, "Suddenly there came a sound from heaven, as of a mighty rushing wind, and there appeared unto them cloven tongues as of fire, and it sat upon each of them." These were the emblems of the "love of the Spirit," in its ardour, impetuosity, and irresistible power. And as he was voluntary in undertaking, so he is sovereign in carrying on his work, "dividing severally to every man as he will." When we pray the Father to give us the Holy Spirit, we should remember that he whom we ask to dwell in us is a free and independent agent. "Uphold me with thy free Spirit" (Psa. li. 12).

2. *The love of the Spirit appeared in dictating the Scriptures.* Saints in every age have loved the Word of God, and from the time that it was first committed to writing, they have not ceased to take the highest delight in reading and meditating on its contents. In the Bible they find their meat and their drink, the life and the health of their souls. They could not live without it, and having it they can be contented with a slender portion. "Thy testimonies have I taken as an heritage for ever; for they are the rejoicing of my heart" (Psa. cxix. iii). The longest psalm that ever David composed is entirely occupied in expressing his esteem for the written law; there are few of his spiritual songs in which he does not commend it; and remember, brethren, his Bible was a small one compared with ours.

All Scripture was given by inspiration, or dictated to the sacred penmen by the Spirit. "Prophecy came not in old time by the will of man, but holy men of God spake as they were moved by the Holy Ghost;" and as they spake they wrote. This is true, not only of prophecy strictly so called, or the prediction of future events, but of all the contents of His inspired volume, whether given in the form of doctrine, reproof, exhortation, promise, or even history. Hence the formula used in quoting from any of the books of the Old Testament, "The Holy Ghost saith," whatever prophet was the penman (Mark xii. 36; Acts xxviii. 25; Heb. iii. 7, and ix. 8). Even those parts of Scripture which proceeded immediately from the mouth of the Redeemer himself, come to us through the inspiration of the Holy Ghost, who brought them to the remembrance of the evangelists; and to each of the letters which Christ ordered his servant John to send to the seven Churches of Asia is subjoined the same admonition: "He that hath an ear to hear, let him hear what the Spirit saith unto the churches."

Would you have a sensible sign and proof of the love of the Spirit? Here it is. Could there be a greater proof of love than the giving of this Book, so stored with everything that is necessary, and able to make wise to salvation the most simple? There are three distinguishing gifts of God—the gift of his Son, the gift of his Spirit, and the gift of his Word—and as to each of them we may say, "herein is love." Without the Scriptures, you would have been sitting in the region and shadow of death. Without the Scriptures, you would have known nothing of the plan of mercy and way of salvation; you would never have heard of the love of God, of the person, the undertaking, the incarnation, the sacrifice, the sufferings and glory of Christ; you would never have heard of remission of sins, of peace with God, of the adoption of children, of the inheritance laid up in heaven. If then at any time you have felt your consciences pacified, your difficulties cleared up, your fears dissipated, your minds fortified against temptation, strengthened for duty, or comforted in tribulation, your faith increased, your hope quickened, your love inflamed, your patience promoted, by anything contained in this precious volume—think, oh! think, of the "love of the Spirit." Christian children, who have been taught the first principles of the oracles of God, think on the love of the Spirit. Christian young men, who from your earliest years have known the Scriptures, think on the love of the Spirit. Christian fathers, who are strong because the Word of God abideth in you, think on the love of the Spirit.

3. *The love of the Spirit was manifested in preparing and endowing the human nature of the Saviour.* All the operations of the divine Spirit in forming those holy men who were raised up for carrying on the work of God under the Old Testament, such as Moses and David and Solomon, Isaiah, Zerubbabel, and Joshua, who were eminently furnished with gifts and graces for the faithful and wise discharge of their important functions, were nothing compared with this. In the miraculous conception, the Spirit "created a new thing in the earth," bringing "a clean thing out of an unclean," and from a corrupt mass forming a body which was without the least taint of, or tendency to, sin, and thus fitted for becoming the immaculate and blessed body of the Son of God. "The Holy Ghost shall come upon thee, and the power of the Highest shall overshadow thee; therefore also that holy thing, which shall be born of thee, shall be called the Son of God." This was the beginning of those miracles of love which were wrought with such heavenly profusion and prodigality during our Saviour's abode on earth. According to ancient predictions, the Spirit descended upon and dwelt in that holy nature which he had formed: "The Spirit of the Lord shall rest upon him, the spirit of wisdom and understanding, the spirit of counsel and might, the spirit of knowledge and of the fear of the Lord." And the miracle which accompanied our Lord's baptism held forth emblematically the source, and nature, and design of this unction. "The heavens were opened unto him, and he saw the Spirit of God descending, like a dove" (the emblem of love), "and lighting upon him." In the glorious person of

the Redeemer next to the grace of union, which is the effect of the assumption of human nature by the Son of God, the grace of unction is the most wonderful object of contemplation. "Behold my servant, whom I uphold; mine elect, in whom my soul delighteth: I have put my Spirit upon him." If the oil poured on the head of Aaron, which descended to the skirts of his garment, was precious, how much more precious was this heavenly oil which was poured on the Head, and was to descend to the meanest and least member of the mystical body; for God gave not the Spirit by measure to him, and he was given to be imparted to all that believe on him. "Thou lovest righteousness, and hatest wickedness: therefore God, thy God, hath anointed thee with the oil of gladness above thy fellows." This was the holy anointing oil which was poured on his sacrifice; and as it was through the Eternal Spirit that he offered himself without spot to God, so was he "justified in the Spirit" by his resurrection from the dead.

4. *The love of the Spirit is shewn in the first visit which he pays to the soul of a sinner, when he comes to take possession of it.* When he first enters the place of his future residence, he finds it in a very wretched and repulsive condition. The sinner himself, habituated to his own impurity, can form no conception of the disgust which this heavenly visitant must feel on approaching it, and is apt to wonder at the strong terms in which he has described it. No dungeon, at once dark and cold and filthy—no lazar who from the sole of the foot to the crown of the head is covered with wounds and bruises and putrifying sores—no corpse which has lain for days in the earth is half so loathsome to the senses as such a soul is to the Holy Spirit, who is "of purer eyes than to behold evil, and cannot look on iniquity." He finds the heart dead to all that is good, yet alive to all that is evil; the mind filled with ignorance of God, and enmity to him; the

whole man as proud as poor, as obstinate as foolish, as impenitent as guilty. His first approaches are shunned, his overtures rejected, his convictions stifled, his entreaties despised. Yet he perseveres in his gracious design, until he has conquered all opposition, won the soul to Jesus Christ, and formed the heart for a habitation to himself—" the temple of the living God!"

5. *The love of this blessed agent is further seen in keeping possession of the soul.* There is more love displayed in this, than in taking possession of the soul at first. We expect nothing but resistance and hostility from an enemy, but "he that hath friends, should shew himself friendly." Is this then what the saint evinces to his merciful deliverer? Alas! no. How often has the Holy Spirit reason to say, "Is this thy kindness to thy friend?" Who but the blessed Guest himself can tell what indignities and provocations he meets with from the time that he takes up his habitation in the heart of a believer? We can scarcely read the history of the unbelieving, ungrateful, and rebellious conduct of the Israelites in the wilderness without being provoked; yet it is a true picture of our own conduct: "He gave them his good Spirit to instruct them, but they rebelled, and vexed his Holy Spirit." And now often do professing Christians and genuine saints themselves rebel, and vex and grieve the Spirit by their slowness of heart to understand and believe the word which he hath spoken, and brought to their remembrance, by despising the hidden manna with which he has fed their souls, by indulging the wish to return to spiritual Sodom and Egypt, by calling in question those promises which he has sealed on their hearts, by quenching his motions, and acting contrary to those principles which he has implanted within them! On these accounts he is provoked to withhold his sensible and comforting influence, and threatens to withdraw from them. And yet he abides with

them. "How shall I give thee up, Ephraim? how shall I deliver thee, Israel? How shall I make thee as Admah? how shall I set thee as Zeboim? Mine heart is turned within me, my repentings are kindled together." "Many waters cannot quench his love, neither can the floods drown it."

6. *We have an additional proof of the love of the Spirit in the peculiar work which he carries on in the hearts of believers.* "The sanctification of the Spirit" is the comprehensive phrase under which his gracious work is held forth in Scripture. "We are bound always to give thanks for you, brethren beloved of the Lord, because God has chosen you to salvation through sanctification of the Spirit" (2 Thess. ii. 13). The blood of Jesus is the meritorious and procuring cause of our title to eternal life, but there is a meetness for, as well as a title to, eternal life, and the one as well as the other is necessary to our enjoyment of this beatitude. It is the work of the Spirit to renew us after the image of God—to conform us to the image of his Son, to make us partakers of a divine nature, and thus fit us for divine fellowship. And he it is who renders all the means of producing this effectual, whether the word, or sacraments, or prayer. "We all, with open face beholding as in a glass the glory of the Lord, are changed into the same image, from glory to glory, even as by the Spirit of the Lord" (2 Cor. iii. 18). Those who preach the gospel, or dispense the sacraments, have only a ministerial instrumentality in advancing this work of God. The Spirit is the efficient agent and author of it. "Ye are manifestly declared to be the epistle of Christ ministered by us, written not with ink, but with the Spirit of the living God" (2 Cor. iii. 3).

There are many things comprehended in this work by which the Spirit manifests his love. He takes of the things of Christ —his atonement and righteousness, and shews them unto believers, giving them fellowship with the Redeemer in his death and resurrection; he sheds abroad the love of God in their hearts; he gives them access to God with boldness and confidence, enabling them to cry Abba Father, and helping them in their prayers; he seals them as the chosen of the Father, and the redeemed of the Son, and preserves them from the allurements of the world, the temptations of Satan, and everything which would entangle or draw them aside in their Christian course. His residence in their hearts is an earnest of the heavenly inheritance to which they have been predestinated, and his operations are the first-fruits of that glory which awaits them.

Here we are particularly to call to mind his character as the Comforter, in which he was promised by Christ, and the manner in which he discharges it in all the distresses, afflictions, and tribulations, outward and inward, to which believers are exposed in the present state. In none of these is the Comforter, who only can relieve their souls, far off. All the peace and solace and joy which they feel under their trials, and by which they are sometimes made to glory in them, are to be traced to this source. Hence we read of "the comfort of the Holy Ghost," and "joy in the Holy Ghost."

In fine, the Spirit manifests his love by the termination to which he brings his work in believers. "He that hath begun the good work will perfect it unto the day of Jesus Christ." He will make their souls perfect in holiness at death, and their bodies, in which he has resided here as a temple, he will raise up at the last day, fashioning them according to the glorious body of Christ. "If the Spirit of him that raised up Jesus from the dead dwell in you, he that raised up Christ from the dead shall also quicken your mortal bodies by his Spirit that dwelleth in you" (Rom. viii. 11).

II. I now proceed to exhibit the influence which the love of the Spirit ought to have upon us. It is calculated to have an influence upon the whole of our life and exercise. The person who feels it will "live in the Spirit," will "walk in the Spirit." There is no duty which it will not enforce, no sin from which it will not dissuade. I shall select a few instances by way of specimen.

1. *It should excite us to love the Spirit.* Love begets love; "we love him because he first loved us." Love and gratitude, as terminating on the Holy Spirit, and created by his gracious acts, is no less a Christian grace than love to the Father and Son. Indeed, love to the Spirit is included in love to the Father and the Son. It is the work of the Spirit to open up the fountain of redeeming love, and the wide and deep channel in which it flows, to sinners in all its refreshing and salutary streams. He cannot be dishonoured or his work be contemned, if the Father and the Son are loved and glorified. Yet there is an honour and a duty which we owe to him, and which ought not to be withheld. Perhaps the believer's experience in this matter may be illustrated by a familiar example. If a stranger should come to any of you with the intelligence of the safety of a son in a foreign land, whom you had given up as dead, you would be so overjoyed with the message, and so occupied in reading the letters, and looking on the pledges transmitted by your absent child, that you might forget the messenger, and allow him to stand at the door; but no sooner would the paroxysm of joy subside, than you would recollect yourself, receive the messenger with due respect, and load him with marks of gratitude for the kind service which he had performed. In like manner the believer may at first be so rapt in the contemplation of God, even the Father who hath loved us, and of the Son who gave himself for us, as for a time to overlook the divine Agent who opened his eyes upon such a discovery of grace; but when he recollects himself, he cries out,

"Is it thou, Lord? Come in, thou blessed of the Lord, why standest thou without?"

The self-evidencing light of the gospel, shining into the soul in the day of conversion, may be so strong and overpowering that the person may wonder that he should ever have resisted it for a moment; his conviction of its truth may be so clear, and his reception of it so cordial, that he may be apt to overlook the supernatural agency on his soul, and to think that he can never again call it in question. It is not till he has lost sight of it, and relapsed into partial unbelief and darkness, that he becomes thoroughly aware that he owed his discoveries to the illumination of the Spirit, and that this is necessary to preserve and revive them. Then he is ready to say, "O blessed Spirit, thou didst visit me when I was an outcast, and lying in my blood; I was dead in trespasses and sins, and thou didst quicken me; I was blind to the things which belonged to my peace, and thou didst unseal the eyes of my understanding; my heart was filled with enmity to God, and thou didst cleanse me in the laver of regeneration; I was diseased as well as loathsome, and thou didst heal all my diseases by the sprinkling of the blood of Jesus, and by thy precious ointments. By thy grace I am what I am. What shall I render unto thee for all thy benefits unto me?"

2. *It should beget love to the brethren.* All true saints are in common the offspring and workmanship of the Spirit; and "he who loveth him that begat, loveth him also that is begotten of him." There is a union among true Christians, and this is the unity of the Spirit. "There is one body, and one Spirit." "For as the body is one, and hath many members, and all the members of that one body being many, are one body, so also is Christ; for by one Spirit we are all baptised into one body, and have been all made to drink into one Spirit." True believers are all united to Christ by the same Spirit. They are

brought to the knowledge of the truth, and the love of the truth, and the comfort of the truth, by the same Spirit. By the same Spirit they live and move, and have their being in Christ. The love of the Spirit is, as it were, the common blood which flows in all their veins, binding them together as one family, and affectionately causing them to cleave to and sympathise with one another. "If there be any consolation in Christ, if any comfort of love, if any fellowship of the Spirit, be like-minded, having the same love, being of one accord, of one mind." In vain do we pretend to the Spirit, if we have bitter envying and strife dwelling in us, for the love of the Spirit cannot dwell with these malevolent passions; but "if we love one another, God dwelleth in us; and hereby we know that he abideth in us, by the Spirit which he hath given us."

3. *It should encourage us to depend upon and apply for the influences of the Spirit.* Without him we can do nothing; he works in us both "to will and to do of his good pleasure." Everything that is good about any person—faith, love, purity, patience—is of his production. When a Christian thinks of the duties incumbent upon him, their number and importance, and at the same time reflects on his own weakness, he is ready to exclaim, "Who is sufficient for these things?" In such circumstances let him think of the love of the Spirit, and that he is not only able but willing to "do for us exceeding abundantly above all that we ask or think."

The Spirit is promised, and we are encouraged to pray the Father for him. "If ye, being evil, know how to give good gifts unto your children, how much more shall your heavenly Father give the Holy Spirit to them that ask him." Oh! is not this encouraging, that so far from being reluctant to the work, he is as ready to go as the Father or the Son is to send?

Christians complain of their unfitness for duty, and they sometimes make this an excuse for neglecting it. There might have been some show of reason in this excuse had not God made such rich and suitable provision to relieve our necessities and help our infirmities. You are unfit for duty, even indisposed to it! Granted; but is not the Spirit able "to strengthen you with all might in the inner man"? And is he not willing, and waiting for employment? Have you applied to him particularly? If not, you have not received, and justly, because you have not asked. Or if you have asked, you have not asked in the faith of his love; you have had doubts of this, and these doubts have prevented you from relying on his influences.

4. *It should excite us to abound in prayer.* It is in reference to this duty that the apostle in our text avails himself of the argument from the love of the Spirit. "I beseech you, brethren, for the love of the Spirit, that ye strive together with me in your prayers to God for me." There is a twofold argument here—one bearing on the duty of praying for one another, founded on the Spirit's being the bond of union among all the members of the mystical body, which we have already adverted to; the other bearing on prayer in general, whether for ourselves or others. This implies that the consideration of the love of the Spirit is a great inducement to prayer. And how? Because one way in which he manifests his love is by assisting us in our addresses to the throne of grace. On this account he is called the "Spirit of supplication" (Zech. xii. 10), and is said to help our infirmities in this duty. "The Spirit also helpeth our infirmities: for we know not what we should pray for as we ought; but the Spirit itself maketh intercession for us with groanings which cannot be uttered" (Rom. viii. 26).

He sheds abroad the love of God in the heart, and thereby encourages us to come to him as our heavenly Father. Christ by his mediation has procured access for us to God; the Spirit gives us access by discovering to us the living way consecrated by the blood of Christ, and powerfully brings us near: "Through

Christ we have access by one Spirit unto the Father." The Holy Spirit is promised in the character of a Comforter, or, as the word also signifies, a patron or advocate. What rich and superabundant provision has a God of grace made for us in the new covenant! How inexcusable if we do not come to the throne of grace! We have an advocate without us, and within us, in heaven and in our own breasts. It is a great encouragement to prayer that we have in Christ an advocate with the Father, who is ready to present our petitions and to obtain a hearing for us. But is it not an additional incentive that in the Holy Spirit we have one who will draw up our petitions, and help us to put them into the hands of Christ? And this last is agreeable to the will of God, as well as the former: "And he that searcheth the hearts knoweth what is the mind of the Spirit, because he maketh intercession for the saints according to the will of God" (Rom. viii. 27).

How great an encouragement to prayer this is, those only know who have felt enlargement of heart and confidence in prayer, and who have also felt the want of these. Formerly they were dragged or driven to the throne of grace by conscience, or the urgency of external circumstances; now they come to it of their own accord and cheerfully. Formerly they thought it enough that they prayed publicly and at stated times; now they embrace every opportunity of engaging in the exercise, and "pray always." Formerly their prayers were formal and cold; now they pour out their hearts to God, order their cause before him, and fill their mouths with arguments. This is prayer—"praying in the Holy Ghost."

5. *It should make us careful to avoid everything that may grieve the Spirit.* We are uncommonly tender of offending a person who has done us a kindness, and will deny ourselves many things which are agreeable, from an apprehension that our indulging in them would grieve him. The very expression,

"grieving the Spirit," points to his love. An enemy is provoked if we injure him, and he is gratified if he see us injuring ourselves; it is a friend only—one who really loves us, and wishes our welfare—who can be *grieved* at our improper conduct. Unregenerated persons vex the Spirit; believers grieve him. "Grieve not the Holy Spirit of God, whereby ye are sealed unto the day of redemption" (Eph. iv. 30).

A persuasion and feeling of the love of the Spirit will dispose believers to act in such a way as is pleasing to him, and to avoid everything which grieves him. Nor is it difficult to know what pleases him on the one hand, or what offends him on the other. Saints know it by a divine instinct—the Spirit witnesses to it with their spirit. The fruit of the Spirit and the works of the flesh are as much opposed as light and darkness. All sin is displeasing to him, but there are some sins which are eminently offensive in his sight. He is the "good Spirit," and therefore all wrath, malice, and envy are opposed to him. He is "the Spirit of truth," and therefore all falsehood and lying are dishonouring to him. He is "the Holy Spirit," and therefore all impurity in heart, speech, and behaviour are offensive to him. You will see all these sins warned against, as grieving to the Spirit, in the fourth chapter of the Epistle to the Ephesians.

This subject affords matter of self-examination and exhortation. Let me ask you, what know ye of the love of the Spirit? There are persons present, I am afraid, who have no part or lot in this matter, who "have not so much as heard whether there be any Holy Ghost" (Acts xix. 2), who never saw any need for his gracious influences, who never were concerned to obtain them; who never read or prayed, or performed any other duty in the Spirit. "These be they who are sensual, having not the Spirit" (Jude 19). Let such consider the solemn declaration of an inspired writer: "If any man have not the Spirit of Christ, he is none of his" (Rom. viii. 9). Those who are strangers to the work of the Spirit are strangers to the work of the Saviour. All who are in Christ, and to whom there is no condemnation, "walk not after the flesh, but after the Spirit."

But though you know him not, you have to do with him, and he with you. He speaks to you in the Scriptures, he speaks to you by the preaching of the gospel, which is the "ministration of the Spirit." The apostle Peter tells us that "Christ was put to death in the flesh, but quickened by the Spirit, by which also he went and preached to the spirits in prison, which sometime were disobedient, when the long-suffering of God waited in the days of Noah." The inhabitants of the antediluvian world thought that they had to do only with Noah, and that it was easy for them to contend with him, and despise his warnings and exhortations. But it turned out at last that they had been resisting one infinitely greater: "The Lord said, MY SPIRIT shall not always strive with man;" and this added greatly to their sin and condemnation. This was the great sin of the Israelites in the wilderness, and it is still the sin of gospel despisers; "Ye stiff-necked and uncircumcised in heart and ears, ye do always resist the Holy Ghost." There are two things which aggravate the guilt of the finally unbelieving and impenitent under the gospel, and render their doom unspeakably more dreadful than that of the heathen. First, they have despised and repudiated the love of God manifested in the death of his Son; and secondly, they have resisted and quenched the motions of the Holy Spirit, and poured contempt upon his love in the application of redemption. "Of how much sorer punishment, suppose ye, shall he be thought worthy, who hath trodden under foot the Son of God, and hath counted the blood of the covenant, wherewith he was sanctified, an unholy thing, and hath done despite unto the Spirit of grace?" Contemptuous resistance of the motions of the Holy Spirit is the crowning part of their sin. And justly so; for (and this is the reason why the sin against the Holy Ghost is irremissible) it is an offence against the love of God in the last and most ample display of it. Oh, bring not down this fearful doom upon your head, gospel hearer!—and there is only one way in which you can avert it, by yielding to the call of the gospel, and believing on the name of the Son of God. Whither can you go from the Spirit of God, or flee from his presence? Though you should resolve never to hear another sermon, never again to open a bible, though you should resolve to leave a land of gospel privileges, and hide yourself in the darkest thicket of heathenism, you would carry in your bosom, like the stricken deer, the arrow of conviction and death. You have heard of a Saviour, and have rejected him; you have become the subject of the Spirit's calls, and have resisted them. But my text leads me to employ the allurements of the gospel, rather than the terrors of the law. "I beseech you by the love of the Spirit" to comply with the calls of grace—to come to the Saviour. "The Spirit and the bride say, Come; and let him that is athirst come; and whosoever will, let him come, and take of the waters of life freely."

Believers should not be contented with owning the nature and work of the Spirit; they should seek to know and believe his love, to taste that he is gracious. Have you ever had the love of God shed abroad in your heart, Christian? Has Christ been precious to you? Has the word been sweet to your taste? Have you had freedom at the throne of grace? Have you been made to eat at a communion-table of the things wherewith the atonement was made? Have you been comforted under affliction? These are just the fruits of the Spirit, and the evidences of his love. Lay open your hearts to his benign influences; cherish his motions, and honour the Spirit, even as you honour the Father and the Son. Let others scoff at the doctrine of divine influences, and the inhabitation of the Spirit, as the effect of enthusiasm; "but ye, beloved, building up yourselves on your most holy faith, praying in the Holy Ghost, keep yourselves in the love of God, looking for the mercy of our Lord Jesus Christ unto eternal life."

Finally, let us be instructed where to look for the cure and rectification of all the evils which afflict the Church in our day! —to the love of the Spirit. By our misimprovement and abuse of our privileges, by our unchristian temper and carriage, by our worldly spirit and untender conversation, we have provoked the Spirit to withdraw from us, and the consequence has been that the glory has departed from our Israel, and ordinances have become in a great measure inefficacious and unsuccessful. "Who hath believed our report, and to whom hath the arm of the Lord been revealed?" Who is convinced of sin? Who cries out, "What must I do to be saved?" Who receives the word gladly? Who brings forth fruit to perfection? Where are the fruits of the gospel, even where it is purely preached? "Woe is me! for I am as when they have gathered the summer fruits, as the grape-gleanings of the vintage: there is no cluster to eat; my soul desired the first ripe fruit. The good man is perished out of the earth; and there is none upright among men" (Micah vii. 1). Our carelessness, our conformity to the world, and our mournful divisions, have wasted and nearly consumed the vitals of true Christianity, and left us little more than a spiritless and unsightly skeleton. "Our leanness, our leanness, woe unto us! the treacherous dealers have dealt treacherously; yea, the treacherous dealers have dealt very treacherously" (Isa. xxiv. 16).

Yet there is hope in the love of the Spirit. It is divine, and therefore infinite, sovereign, and free. He is God, and not man; he will turn again, he will have compassion upon us; he will subdue our iniquities, and cast all our sins into the depths of the sea. Let us lament after the Lord, the Spirit, and implore his return. Come from the four winds, O breath of the Lord, and breathe upon the slain that they may live! Wilt thou not revive us again, that we may rejoice in thee? The love of the Spirit shed abroad in the heart would quicken, and restore, and soften, and sanctify. It would correct all the evils among us, private and public. It would remove all grounds of division, and, what is more difficult still, it would remove all that spirit of alienation and enmity and jealousy which our controversies have engendered, even in the hearts of those who have been contending for truth and purity. It would be like oil poured upon the waters of strife, stilling the noise of their waves, and the tumult which they have excited. It would induce the contending parties to confess their faults one to another, or rather bring both to their knees before God, in joint confession, and inspire them with a holy emulation to strive who should be first in repairing the desolations of Zion, and in bringing back the King of the Church to his own house.

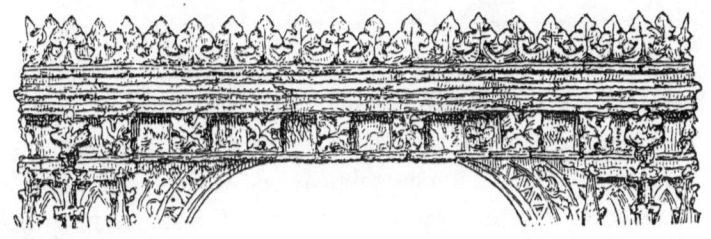

V.

Lovers of Pleasure more than Lovers of God.

BY THE REV. ANDREW THOMSON, D.D.

"LOVERS OF PLEASURES MORE THAN LOVERS OF GOD."—2 TIM. iii. 4.

WHETHER the times in which we live be the *"perilous times"* spoken of by the apostle in this chapter, it is not our present intention to inquire. This much at least is certain and indisputable, that every one part of the description which he here gives, to whatever period of the world or of the Church it refers, involves in peril every individual to whom it correctly applies. And it is too obvious that in our day there are not a few professing Christians of whose character the words of my text delineate a leading and predominant feature.

It is no doubt a serious charge against any who profess to be Christians to say that they are "lovers of pleasures more than they are lovers of God." And, if directed to them personally and individually, it would be apt, even though they were conscious of its truth, to excite no small portion of resentment and indignation.

The Scripture, however, declares that "all have sinned and come short of the glory of God" (Rom. iii. 23); and the history of the Church demonstrates that the profession of Christianity is frequently maintained by those who are leading worldly and wicked lives. Our sinfulness manifests itself in a variety of forms, arising from our peculiar dispositions, and temptations, and habits, and circumstances; but every varied form in which our sinfulness appears tends to establish the same melancholy statement respecting our spiritual condition. And as it is of vast consequence that we should be made sensible of our spiritual condition, and as the faithful ministry of the Word of God is one means of accomplishing that end, none can be reasonably offended when we illustrate and apply such parts of Scripture as seem calculated to unfold to them their real state, and demerit, and danger. Although the disclosure may be painful, it may also be salutary. And therefore those who are instrumental in making it should not be regarded as acting either an unkind or an officious part.

It should also be considered that "the heart is deceitful above all things" (Jer. xvii. 9); and that self-deception operates with peculiar force and effect in the case of those practices from which we are accustomed to derive our chief enjoyments. So that the sins of which we are least sensible may be the very sins to which we are most addicted, and against which we need to be most plainly warned.

Nor can the subject we are to consider be justly regarded as unseasonable. The preference mentioned in the text is one to which human nature constantly and powerfully leans. In past ages the love of pleasure has been a striking characteristic of fallen man, and the fertile source of misery to individuals, and families, and communities. And from all that we see and hear and read of the maxims and manners of the present times, it cannot surely be alleged that the tendency of human nature has become in this respect less decided or less alarming.

Suffer me, then, to point out to you, in a few particulars, the characters implied in the language of my text.

I. And here, it must be observed, in the *first* place, that these words are unquestionably descriptive of all who indulge in pleasures which are sinful in their own nature—in pleasures which are expressly prohibited by the divine law.

The great principle of moral obedience, as laid down to us in the divine law itself, is love to God (Deut. vi. 5, and Matt. xxii. 57). And "this is the love of God, that we keep his commandments." Every gratification, therefore, in which we violate any of these affords a decisive proof, either that this affection has no place at all, or that it holds but a very subordinate place in our hearts.

It will not do to say that the pleasures to which we are devoted are far from being the grossest and most debasing of those which prevail in the world—that they have the voice of fashion to commend and to sanction them—that we do not go so far in them as many others around us who have greater professions—that the temptations which they hold out to us are peculiarly strong—that, if their consequences be mischievous, they hurt nobody but ourselves—and that we have virtuous or benevolent qualities in our conduct, by which all that is wrong in them is more than counterbalanced.

These allegations are frequently offered by such as habitually "serve divers lusts and pleasures" (Tit. iii. 3), in order to extenuate or to justify their conduct. But they derive no countenance or support from the records or the statutes of Scripture morality. And they totally lose sight of the only feature of those practices they are adduced to vindicate, which, comparatively speaking, is worthy of being kept in view, namely, their contrariety to the revealed will of heaven. In all circumstances, and in every degree, they are forbidden by the authority of God. And not only has he denounced against them the threatenings of his wrath; he has also entreated us, by his mercies, to resist their influence, and keep ourselves from their pollutions. He has sent his own Son to "deliver us from that bondage of corruption" under which they have hitherto held us. He has appointed the Holy Spirit to purify our minds from those desires in which they originate, and to subdue those habits which they have already produced. And as it is the precept of his Word that we deny ourselves to every one of them, so it is the direct object of the whole of that system of grace under whose operation he has placed us, to encourage and assist us in the exercise of the self-denial which he prescribes. If after all this we still allow them to "have dominion over us," then surely it cannot be denied that we are "lovers of pleasures more than lovers of God." We permit the pleasures of sin to be competitors with God for our attachment. And, what is more, we permit them to succeed in the competition, and to occupy the throne on which he alone is entitled to sit and reign.

Examine yourselves, then, my friends, and see whether the pleasures in which you indulge be inherently criminal. If they be so, then you cannot hesitate a moment in admitting that the text applies to you. Do not cherish self-deception by fixing your regard on the grossly and openly licentious part of mankind, as if it could only be affirmed of *them*, or as if sin only deserved the name when it assumed its more hideous and disgusting forms. It is true, we observe too many sacrificing everything that is good and honourable at the shrine of vicious indulgence, and making it their sole business to gratify their unhallowed appetites without measure and without remorse. But then, while others cannot doubt, they themselves would not think of denying that they are "lovers of pleasures more than lovers of God." They are not ashamed of being lovers of pleasures; they make no secret of it, they glory in it. But they have no pretensions to be "lovers of God;" "God is not in all their thoughts" (Psa. x. 4), as he is not in all their ways.

Do not imagine, however, that because the text unequivocally embraces the character of such sensualists and profligates as these, its application to you, who have not gone quite so far, is either ambiguous or unfair. The simple fact that you are addicted to sinful pleasures is sufficient, upon the principles of the Bible, to include you in the guilt and condemnation of this scripture. Remember that there is no concord, and can be none, between God and sin. You cannot love, and you cannot serve both. You may be attempting to do so, but success is impossible. You may be hugging yourselves in the idea that you are moderate in the indulgence which you give to your passions. But if God prohibits it altogether, can you be said to love him with sincerity when you deliberately disregard his prohibition, and give to another object any portion of that affection which he requires exclusively to himself? You may not be open and shameless in your unlawful gratifications. But know you not that the eye of God penetrates the recesses of your heart, and follows you into your darkest and deepest retreats, and demands that you shall be pure there, as well as in the light of day, and in the face of the world? You may come regularly to his house of prayer—you may even lend your assistance to the propagation of his word and gospel throughout the world. But what avails it when you straightway go to contradict his will and dishonour his law, and to fulfil your own inordinate desires, at the expense of that unreserved submission which you owe to his authority? You may be able to boast of having done many good deeds to your fellowmen. But if these proceeded from love to God (and they were not good unless they did so), how comes it that the same principle does not constrain you to mortify your irregular propensities? or, how is your wilful indulgence of these in any case to be reconciled with devotedness of soul to Him who has commanded you to restrain and to subdue them?

No, my friends, such pleas as these are unsubstantial and vain. They are consistent neither with reason nor Scripture. They are the mere efforts of a conscience trying to relieve itself from compunctions occasioned by a sense of guilt. They are arguments forced into the service of sin by a mind that is perversely anxious to continue the enjoyments of which it knows it should never have partaken. And you must beware of yielding to the delusion with which they would soon overwhelm all your better feelings. Whatever you may be in other respects, yet, if in one point you are wilfully indulging yourselves in gratifications which the divine law forbids, you are among those whom the words of my text are intended to delineate; and whatever be the folly, whatever be the guilt, whatever be the danger implied in it, you are "lovers of pleasures more than lovers of God."

II. In the *second* place, the text describes those who indulge in innocent pleasures improperly or to excess.

Our heavenly Father has opened up to us many sources of sinless enjoyment in this the land of our pilgrimage. And a moderate and seasonable application to these is at once an expression of gratitude to him by whose kindness they are provided, and a means of fitting us for engaging with spirit and advantage in more serious occupations. Considered in this modified and regulated view, nothing would attempt to shut us out from them but ignorance of the nature and condition of man, and most unwarrantable views of the nature and obligations of true religion. They are furnished by God himself for our use and our satisfaction; and when we go to them under the government of good principle, and indulge in them, only so far as their purpose is duly served, we do nothing that is incompatible with the supreme regard which we owe to him.

But the case is quite altered when the pleasures of life, however unexceptionable in themselves, are abused or carried to excess. They are no longer innocent, or rather, *we* are no longer innocent, who in our pursuit of them overleap those bounds which the maxims of reason and of the gospel have prescribed. And the moment we enter upon forbidden ground, that moment we shew that the object for which we have done so is preferred by us to the favour and the honour of Him by whom the prohibition has been issued. We then, either directly or indirectly, fail in the duty which God imposes upon us, as the subjects of his moral government and the expectants of his heavenly kingdom. We are mindful, not of what pleases him, but only of what pleases ourselves. Instead of receiving with contentment and thankfulness the indulgences which he has seen proper to grant us, we go on to enjoy them in a way and to an extent which we cannot doubt will offend him deeply, because he has said, " Hitherto shalt thou come, and no farther." And thus abusing the bounties of his providence, and transgressing the limits which he has fixed, and listening to the voice of temptation rather than to the voice of his authority, we give evident proof that we are "lovers of pleasures more than lovers of God."

We are authorised to apply a still stricter rule. The divine injunction runs in these terms: "Thou shalt love the Lord thy God with all thy heart, and with all thy soul, and with all thy strength, and with all thy mind." Now, when we consider that our supreme, or rather our whole, affection is required in such absolute terms, it is not to be questioned that a much lower degree of attachment to the pleasures of the world than what is commonly felt will place us among those to whom the apostle refers. Not only must our esteem for these be infinitely less than the regard that we should study to cherish towards our heavenly Father, but our indulgence in them must be always in subserviency to his will and glory. So that if, in our eagerness to enjoy them, we neglect or lose sight of this paramount object, we are plainly chargeable with the delinquency mentioned in the text.

My friends, I would press upon you this view of the subject, for it is here that you are most likely to be deceived. When the gratification to which you are tempted is radically and obviously sinful, you can be on your guard against it from the very first. It carries the stamp of guilt upon its very front. At the moment it invites you to approach, it warns you of the precipice over which you are about to fall. And perceiving that it never was and never can be lawful, you are fixed in an attitude of firm resistance from which it will be difficult to displace you. But when the gratification is once clothed in the garb of innocence, and you have tasted of its sweets, you are unwilling to think that it can ever assume any other dress. What was allowable to-day, you will conclude to be just as allowable to-morrow. What was right and proper in others, you will presume must be right and proper in you. What was expedient in certain circumstances, and in a certain degree, you will be reluctant to admit, may not be expedient in all circumstances and in every degree. And in this manner you will be likely to flatter yourselves into the conviction, that what is at this moment innocent can never become criminal.

Such we believe to be a very common practical error; and to this cause we attribute in a great measure the prevalence of that character which our text describes.

The young in particular, to whose period of life it is natural to be gay and susceptible, who readily cherish the notion that it is not only allowable but becoming in them to be rather merry than serious, and who would scarcely think themselves prepared for the sedateness of advanced years but by a crowded course of amusements and pleasures in their earlier days—the young easily go into the delusion that they may indulge without limit and without control in those enjoyments against which there is no express prohibition.

The old, too, in the recollection of former times, and under the influence of former habits, though they may be forced to a different class, and confined to a narrower range of pleasures, seem to have similar conceptions of their lawfulness, and to think themselves entitled to persevere in the pursuit of them as long and to as great an extent as they have a mind, provided only they be not forbidden by name in any part of the decalogue.

Very little reflection indeed is necessary to discover that in all there is a grievous mistake. But, alas! the mistake is frequently committed, and the reflection is seldom made. And therefore it is that in these days of thoughtless and general dissipation, I would urge it upon you to remember that pleasures, however innocent in themselves, may be carried to a criminal excess; that it may be useful for you to consider how far you have been heretofore observant of this principle in morals, and that on every occasion on which you are hereafter asked or tempted to indulge in the gaieties and amusements of life, you should pause and inquire at your own hearts whether the word of divine truth does not justly describe you in these terms, "lovers of pleasures more than lovers of God."

If you ask me how this can be the case, when you keep to enjoyments that are lawful and harmless, I will tell you by offering to your consideration a few examples, requesting you to bear in mind that love to God is always to be proved and measured by obedience to his will, diligence in his service, and endeavours to promote his glory.

Now, is it not equally the language of nature and of revelation, that God requires you to provide for your own household? If then, instead of fulfilling this obligation, you squander upon your pleasures that property which should have ministered to your comfort, and secured the independence of your families, obtained for them the benefits of a useful or liberal education, and assisted them in the pursuits of honourable ambition, that is to be "lovers of pleasures more than lovers of God."

Does not God command you to be merciful to the poor, and kind to all your brethren? If then you shall spend on your pleasures what should have gone to relieve their wants, and to advance their welfare; if, instead of "giving them alms of such things as you have," and contributing to their temporal prosperity, you "waste your substance in riotous living," or in providing those luxuries and gratifications which "perish with the using," that is to be "lovers of pleasures more than lovers of God."

Is it not the precept of God's Word that you "redeem the time," and be diligent in "working out your salvation"? If then you devote to your pleasures the precious hours that should have been devoted to employments so urgent, so interesting, and so momentous, that is to be "lovers of pleasures more than lovers of God."

Is it not prescribed to you that you shall faithfully observe the ordinances of religion? If then you pursue your pleasures so far as to encroach on the sanctity of the Sabbath, to neglect the exercise of prayer, to forget the reading of the Scriptures, to "forsake the assembling of yourselves together," that is to be "lovers of pleasures more than lovers of God."

Are you not exhorted to guard against those temptations which might endanger your fidelity to God, and lead you to transgress his law? If then, in the pursuit of pleasure, you shall enter into scenes and mingle in entertainments which tend to corrupt the purity and cool the piety of your minds, that is to be "lovers of pleasures more than lovers of God."

Should not you be very jealous of the divine honour and authority, that the one may not be insulted, nor the other set at defiance? If then, for your pleasure, you countenance exhibitions and representations in which the name of the Lord is wantonly profaned, his Word exposed to ridicule, and the loose morality of the world boldly substituted for the dictates of his righteous will, that is to be "lovers of pleasures more than lovers of God."

Is it not a sacred duty, for the right discharge of which you must be responsible to the great Parent of all, to "walk in your house with a perfect heart," and faithfully attend to the improvement and virtue and comfort of those whom God and nature have committed to your care? If then, in the incessant chase of pleasure, you shall, day after day, and night after night, expose them to all the fascinations of folly, or leave them to their own wild misrule, or set them an example of idle dissipation, which they will take the first opportunity to imitate, that is to be "lovers of pleasures more than lovers of God."

Should not a regard to the divine authority, and to the interests of practical godliness, lead you to deny yourselves to personal indulgence whenever such a sacrifice is required for the advancement of these objects? If then you shall engage in exercises or amusements which, though not sinful of themselves, are yet calculated, from your situation, or character, or influence, to betray others into error, or afford them a handle for abusing what in your individual case was justifiable and proper; and if you thus sacrifice the prosperity of religion among your friends and neighbours to your own selfish gratification, that is to be "lovers of pleasures more than lovers of God."

Can you be sensible of the value and necessity of the gospel of the grace of God without being sensible at the same time how incumbent it is upon you to do what you can for propagating that which, in its doctrine, and in its plan, and in its effects, redounds so much to the divine glory, and to the happiness of man? If then, in the midst of your pleasures, you forget this transcendently important object, if upon these you consume the time, and the efforts, and the means by which you might have blessed thousands of your fellow-creatures with the knowledge of salvation; or if by degrading influence you have become a hindrance instead of a help to the progress of "pure and undefiled religion" in the world, that also is to be "lovers of pleasures more than lovers of God."

I mention these as specific illustrations of the general statement. Many more instances might have been adduced for that purpose. But these are sufficient to shew what is meant by the excessive or the improper use of pleasures that are innocent in themselves, fixing upon you the character described in the text. Let me exhort you to ascertain without delay how far any of them, or any modification of them, may be applicable to your conduct. Inquire not only whether the pleasures to which you are attached be lawful, but whether, being so, you have used them lawfully, whether you may not have carried them to excess, whether you may not have allowed some of them occasionally, or perhaps frequently, to interfere with the performance of religious and moral duties. And do not attempt to hide the truth from your own minds. But if you find in the words of my text the image of yourselves, let the conviction, however humbling and however painful, go deep into your hearts, that you are indeed "lovers of pleasures more than lovers of God."

III. In the *third* and *last* place, the text describes those who enter with greater eagerness and relish into the pleasures of the world, than into the exercises and pleasures of religion.

We do not suppose such persons to be altogether irreligious. They would be extremely indignant were we to apply such an epithet to them. And we would not willingly take from them a single portion of that of which, by the most liberal mode of judging, they can claim so very little. But though they are not altogether irreligious, still you may perceive from their manner, their conversation, and their conduct, that religion, even in the limited extent to which they profess it, holds but a very inferior place in their regard when it comes into competition with their darling pleasure.

Invite them to a participation of some favourite amusement, and observe with what delight they hear the invitation, and with what readiness they accept of it. But ask them to engage in a sacred exercise, the propriety and usefulness of which they are even forced to acknowledge, and see with what indifference they listen to your request, and with what sluggish reluctance they comply with it, if they comply with it at all.

Talk to them of any diversion in which they have been mingling, and they will speak about it for hours, and their eye will glisten with joy at the recollection of it, and they will expatiate upon all its adventures and charms, and they will never have done with it if you will only give them opportunity and encouragement. But try to introduce, with whatever prudence, the subject of religion—try to converse with them about the love of God to poor fallen creatures, such as they themselves are, about the grand work of their redemption by Jesus Christ, or about the heaven and the immortality to which even *they* would be thought to aspire—and you have all the conversation to yourselves. Such topics might be tolerable to them in church, or on a Sunday evening; but they are too serious for every day's discussion. They speak with no interest, no feeling, no rapture, if they speak at all, on themes which command the attention and awaken the hallelujahs of angels. They become not merely serious, but sad, and eagerly endeavour to escape from meditations to which neither their thoughts nor their tongues have ever been accustomed.

See them again actually engaged in the pleasures and amusements to which they are attached. They grudge no expense, no time, no inconvenience, no sacrifice of soul or of body, in order to secure, to diversify, and to perpetuate their indulgence. Everything they do demonstrates that their whole heart is alive with interest, and expanded with delight. But look to them when they are called to the discharge of Christian duties; how unwilling! how languid! how slothful! The Sabbath, which commemorates the resurrection of the Saviour, and is the jubilee of his disciples, is to them a weariness. A sermon that unfortunately exceeds the half-hour almost tires them to death. Exhort them to read the Bible—they sit down to it, and rise up from it as a distasteful task. When they pray, their prayer is anything but communion with God; it is short, and cold, and formal. Request them to give their personal labour to a work of charity—they have not leisure for it. Beg a little from them to assist in sending the Scriptures to the poor and the ignorant—they have no money to spare for such a purpose.

In short, to everything that is spiritual, everything that has an immediate relation to God, everything that forms a leading or essential part of the great work of faith and righteousness which he has given them to do—to everything of this kind they shew, because in truth they feel, a strong aversion; they engage in it with unconcern, not from inclination, but from a regard to form, or at best a dry sense of duty; they derive no satisfaction from it; they abandon it as soon as opportunity occurs, or decency will permit. And thus they exhibit a very marked and striking contrast with the activity and zeal and joy which characterise their attachment to the amusements and gratifications of the world.

Now, my friends, you will understand this delineation; you see the principles on which it proceeds; you see the manner in which it is to be applied. Apply it, then, to yourselves. And though you may not be able to trace the resemblance in every minute particular, yet if you find it faithful in its leading and substantial features, you cannot deny that, whatever be the shame or the consequences, you must be contented to rank with those whom the apostle condemns as "lovers of pleasures more than lovers of God."

Let the statements that have been made receive your serious attention. Plunge not again into the gaieties of life without reflecting deeply and impartially on what you have heard from the Word of God. If you have even a suspicion that hitherto you have been "lovers of pleasures more than lovers of God," stop your career till that suspicion has been disposed of by calm inquiry. And if conscience tells you that it is indeed the case with you, form the resolution at once, and keep it steadily, that you will no longer, no never even once again, yield to the solicitations of the world, or to the dominion of fashion, or to the corrupt tendency of your own heart, but that you will cast away from you all that interposes between you and your God, between your soul and its salvation, and that you will be devoted entirely and supremely to the fear and the service and the glory of Him by whom you are stationed upon earth, and whose favour alone will constitute your felicity in heaven.

VI.

The Terrors of the Lord.

BY THE REV. JAMES MARTIN, M.A.

"KNOWING THEREFORE THE TERRORS OF THE LORD, WE PERSUADE MEN."—
2 COR. v. 11.

THERE are not a few that object to the mode which the apostle here adopts to lead men to seek after, and to embrace the truth as it is in Jesus. It has been often said on this point, that such representations of divine truth are more likely to harden men in sin than to persuade them to relinquish it; that they are calculated to convey unfavourable views of religion, especially to young minds; that men are apt from this to regard it as an unwilling bondage instead of a service in which the affections are to be engaged; and not a few would resent it as savouring of an uncharitable spirit were you to speak to them of the terrors of the Lord, as if they required to be dwelt with as men who were void of any reverence for God or spiritual things. It would be idle to say that there has never been any room for these objections, or that the terrors of the Lord have never been so injudiciously set forth as to cause needless offence at the truth. Whenever they have been made the sole topic of address, or almost the single one—whenever they have been dwelt upon in such a way as that their subsidiary character as a means of persuading men to flee from the wrath to come has been forgotten—or whenever the minister of Jesus Christ has appeared rather a minister of the law than of the gospel, such objections as these may be well founded. It may be questioned, however, whether the evil that has ever resulted from this be at all equal to that which has resulted from an unworthy and sinful concealment of the terrors of the Lord, or whether the danger of offending, by setting forth the fearful misery which shall overtake sinners if they continue impenitent and unbelieving, can ever be so great as that of permitting them to remain undisturbed in their sin for want of faithful and solemn warning of the consequences in which sin must involve them. It is not natural for any of us certainly to entertain hard thoughts of our own condition; there is always enough of self-love in every man to make him think and hope well of himself; there are innumerable devices by which we are ever contriving to lull our conscience asleep, and under the influence of which we are led to apply to ourselves a very different rule of judgment from that which we apply to others; and the man perhaps lives not, however far he may be from God and his righteousness, who has not some palliative for his own fears and misgivings, and who cannot say to himself, "Peace, peace, though there be no peace." And I know no way in which this disposition, so ruinous to all true and lasting peace, can be broken in upon except by a faithful exhibition of the terrors of the Lord: by endeavouring to expose the delusions with which men are blinded, and make them alive to the danger and misery of continuing in them; and, by alarming their fears and wounding their self-interest, to drive them from those refuges to which they are so ready to betake themselves, and which will be found at last only refuges of lies. It is very true that all this will not make men religious, and that so long as they are moved to forsake their sins, or to obey the law of God, merely from terror, or from the dread of punishment, they want the spiritual principle of all true obedience. It is necessary before their hearts ever can be right toward God, that they should serve him from a principle of love and affection, and this principle no terrors can ever infuse into their minds—such a principle as this must come, not from the law, but from the gospel. But still, though it is not enough for the salvation of any man that you speak to him of the terrors of the Lord, it may be a means, and that a powerful one, of awakening his mind to the truth which can save him; by rousing his fears, it may lead him to look out for a place of security from the coming desolation; and the experience of thousands who may be at this moment rejoicing in the light and comfort of the gospel, and who may know the "love of God shed abroad in their hearts by the Holy Spirit," can testify that the thing which led to all their peace and joy and new obedience was some faithful discovery of the terrors of the Lord urging them "to flee from the wrath to come, and to lay hold of the hope set before them in the gospel." As for those who are ready to represent such a mode of address as unnecessary, as well as uncharitable, the question with them may be brought to a very short and speedy issue. If you are satisfied on good grounds that your condition is safe, and that you need not be alarmed for the misery that is to overtake the ungodly, what injury can it do you to hear that misery faithfully exposed? If you need not fear it, and if you feel that you have escaped it, then the more it is insisted on, the more will it awaken your gratitude to Him to whom you owe your deliverance, and awaken your compassion more freely for those who are yet exposed to it. If, on the other hand, you have a suspicion that things are not right with you—if you have fears at times, not indistinct, that were you weighed in the balance of the sanctuary you would be found wanting, and if the apprehension of having these fears awakened, and being thereby necessitated to look more narrowly into your spiritual condition, is the ground of your dislike to us when we preach the terrors of the Lord, does not this very circumstance shew the importance of inquiry on your part, and on ours the importance of employing every means which can urge you to it? And thus the very reason which many give for letting alone the subject altogether is the very reason for pressing it upon your attention—the very reason why, instead of but casually adverting to it, we should bring it at times fully before you; in other words, why, "knowing the terrors of the Lord, we seek to persuade men."

I am aware, however, that independently of those who object to the preaching of the terrors of the Lord altogether, there are others who would cast it aside on somewhat different grounds. They have, and can have, no objection to men being faithfully told their true condition, and the dangers of a state of sin and unbelief, nor would they, for any of the reasons now stated, have us to let this alone; but, as they apprehend it, the efficacy of this truth is a means of convincing and converting sinners far inferior to that of other truths equally revealed in the Word of God; and they would rather sink this truth in the view of those which, as they apprehend, are likely to be more prevailing. Aware that the exhibition of the terrors of the Lord will never of itself turn men from the love of sin, and having some foolish fears that men may contract false views of the divine character from hearing God's hatred of sin and the punishment with which iniquity shall be visited enlarged upon, the great and almost single topic on which they would have us dwell is the love of God. To give them such views of this attribute as would make them think and believe of God as though he were all love and compassion to them as sinners, constitutes, as they think, all that is necessary to the exhibition of the gospel; nor do they hesitate to say that such a view of the Godhead is the only means necessary or fit for turning men to the practice of all righteousness. We might reasonably ask those, however, who entertain such sentiments, how they can properly conceive of or estimate the love of God, if they be destitute of right views of his just indignation against iniquity, and whether it does not argue ignorance of human nature besides to suppose that such a view of the divine character is that which needs most to be inculcated upon men if they would turn unto God. As we have been accustomed to view the love of God to sinners by Jesus Christ, the only way in which we have any representation of the love of God to sinful men at all, we have always understood that the circumstance which gives that love its chief attraction, and ought to commend it most of all to our minds is, that such was the holiness and purity of the divine nature—such the hatred which God bears to sin, and such the unchangeableness of those threatenings which he hath denounced against it, that when he purposed to "seek and to save that which was lost," no less a sacrifice than that of his own Son was required in order that this salvation might be consistent with the truth of his declarations against sin, and his determination to punish it; that, in his sacrifice and death, "righteousness and peace met together," and that the chiefest glory of that grace which now comes accredited and sealed to us is, that it is in perfect harmony with every perfection of rectitude and purity and truth which the principles of our own hearts, as well as the testimony of the Bible, leads us to attribute to God.

If this be the view of the love of God as revealed to us in Christ Jesus—and that it is so we might appeal to every page of the New Testament—it might be asked, how, or in what way, you can rightly conceive of or estimate this love if you are ignorant or unbelieving of "the terrors of the Lord." If there was no holy necessity on the part of God to punish sin, then what becomes of the greatest manifestation of his love, in the gift of his own Son to suffer and to die for us? If the terrors of his wrath had no foundation, what foundation can there be for the greatest and most distinguishing characteristic of his love to rest upon? If the one is removed, the other falls with it; or if the one is not upheld in all its terror, you do, to the same degree, detract from the other; and in speaking to man of "the terrors of the Lord," therefore, there is no necessity that we should forget the tender mercies of the Lord; on the contrary, the more faithfully and fully we declare the one, the better fitted do we become for urging home upon you the other—the better fitted are we to warn your minds by the truth, that so great was his love, that even "when you were sinners, Christ died for you." When it is said that the love of God should form the great, if not the single topic of our preaching—that men have already, whether from the testimony of conscience or from the Word of God, sufficient conviction of the terrors of the Lord, and of the indignation which he bears, and will one day manifest, against iniquity—we may take this for granted as a topic which need not be insisted on, and may proceed at once to the manifestation of divine mercy in the gospel as a truth which, from their previous convictions, they are prepared rightly to appreciate.

Is this, however, agreeable to fact and experience? Do we, then, really find men impressed with the truth that God will, and must, punish sin, though he can never but wish that the sinner would turn from his way and live? Do we find the justice of God so uniformly admitted, that whatever else they may question in his character, this is never questioned, far less denied? Do men seem really alive to the fact, that his goodness is based on a rectitude unchangeable as himself, and which will be manifested in all his dealings with his creatures? Is it the case, that whatever excuses they make for their sins, they never reflect on the righteousness of God in punishing sin; or, whatever be the refuges to which they betake themselves, none of them can deny the purity of his character, and the indignation with which he will visit every worker of iniquity? What, then, were those palliations which they apply to their consciences, as though their sins were only infirmities for which God would not be hard to reckon with them? What mean those delusive schemes by which the mercy of God is rested in, as though there were neither truth nor justice in God at all? What mean those false and imperfect views of the gospel, by which the death of the Saviour is regarded as introducing a mitigated law, according to which the sinner's obedience is substituted for perfect obedience? Do these things tell that men are convinced of the terrors of the Lord, or that he is the righteous God who will and must deal righteously? or rather, do not these things shew that with multitudes the terrors of the Lord are reduced to an empty name, or, if they are regarded at all, are regarded only as a dead letter in the divine statute-book, which will never be produced in judgment against them? The truth is, I believe, that the whole of the controversy which men are at this moment maintaining with God, however various the forms which it may assume, is really a controversy with his righteousness, as the God who will carry out the righteous principles of his administration, in punishing sin and rewarding holiness. Let men assume the appearance of indifference to the discoveries of the New Testament altogether, or let them be found thinking of God as though he were a being of pure benevolence; let them wear the aspect of those who judge that only great sins or great sinners will meet his condemnation, or of those who, under pretence of magnifying the grace of the gospel, confound all moral distinctions as though the grace of

God permitted them to continue in sin: and still, in every case, the real ground of the controversy lies with the justice and holiness of God—the real subject of dispute is with the truth, that God will punish as he has threatened, every worker of iniquity; and they will ever continue to debate this till such time as, from right views of the purity of the divine nature, they see that it is impossible for God to accommodate his law to their sinfulness, and that it must be upheld in all its extent, even though they themselves should suffer everlastingly for it. Till this is done, the ungodliness of the human heart will ever be discovering some new refuge to which it may betake itself when you drive it from its old ones; and the only truth which can, under God, fairly dislodge it from them all, and lead the man to throw himself, as a lost and undone sinner, on the grace of God in Jesus Christ, is not the declaration of the mercy and love of God, of which we can very imperfectly conceive, but the declaration of "the terrors of the Lord," the full declaration of the truth, that not one "jot or one tittle of that law" which pronounceth a curse on him "shall in any wise pass till all be fulfilled." There is an expression of our apostle in another of his epistles which conveys the truth very strikingly and very exactly: "Before faith came," that is, before the way of salvation through faith in Christ was fully disclosed, were men "kept under the law, shut up unto the faith which should afterwards be revealed." These words, as is well known, represent the condition of men before the gospel came, as prisoners held bound by the law of God, while there is no way of escape opened from its threatenings, on every hand of them, except in the sacrifice and death of the Son of God. By the proclamation of its terrors it shut them up unto this as the only way in which there could be any deliverance, and left them no alternative but that of abiding its curse, or making their escape by the gospel; and the law, by the discovery of the same unbending and uncompromising justice, must do the same for us as it did for men before the gospel came; we must be thereby shut up unto the faith, and thus shall we be led to turn from all the devices by which our own hearts would deceive us. Never shall we give up attempting to make our escape from it in some other way than that which faith prescribes; never shall we be led aright to esteem and value and embrace the provided mercy until we see that every way by which we would pass from it is guarded by a faithfulness which never slumbers, and a justice and righteousness which no artifice of ours can ever elude; and that there can be no peace and no safety for us, but an immediate surrender of ourselves to the Saviour, to him in whom "God is just, although the justifier of him who believeth."

It is for these reasons then, that, instead of yielding to the objections of those, on the one hand, who would do away with "the terrors of the Lord" altogether, or those, on the other, who would dispute its efficacy compared with other topics embraced in the New Testament, we would comply with the exhortation of the apostle, and "knowing the terrors of the Lord, would persuade men." It is for these reasons that we know nothing more necessary than to follow a deceitful heart through all its labyrinths, and to expose the falsity of them all: and that, instead of "saying peace, peace, while there is no peace," we would expose the vanity of all pretences to its possession which are not derived from faith in the Saviour; it is for these reasons that, instead of encouraging you to believe that all is well with you because you may possess the ordinary virtues of the world, we would enjoin you to look narrowly into your goodness, whether it springs from the great source—from faith in the Saviour, and is really done in his name and to his service—and never to be satisfied that your calling and election are sure till you have been able to trace in your hearts and lives the marks of a regenerated nature. Such might be called a useless, as it may be in some respects a painful, jealousy, were not all of us to pass in review at the judgment-seat of Christ; but if we must all appear there to take our trial before a Judge upon whom it is impossible to impose by any appearance of goodness, however specious, or by any virtue, however fair it may seem, which has had no respect to their faith and to his grace, how necessary is it that we should judge ourselves now, lest we should then be judged and condemned with the world; and how necessary that we should look well to the foundation on which we build, lest in the desolation that shall then overwhelm the world, we and our works should be at once swept away! If this be painful, will it not be as painful to incur the sentence of everlasting "destruction from the presence of the Lord"? Would you wish that the face of the Judge should on that day be turned on you with a look of displeasure, bidding you away to the wailing and weeping of outer darkness? Would you wish to be then, even for a moment, in suspense, whether your place shall be among the "blessed of the Father"? Would you wish it to be with you, as the apostle says it shall be with some, that you shall be saved, "yet so as by fire," when the fire that shall then burn up the wicked shall have almost laid hold of you? Who would wish these things, and not rather "that an entrance should be ministered unto him abundantly into the everlasting kingdom of our Lord and Saviour"! And by those terrors, therefore, you are brought even now "to acquaint yourselves with God, and be at peace;" to betake yourselves to the Saviour, "as all your hope," and to "abound in the precious fruits of righteousness, which are through Jesus Christ to the praise and glory of God."

It was obviously to the judgment-day that the apostle adverted when he spoke of "the terrors of the Lord." "We must all appear before the judgment-seat of Christ, that every one may receive the things done in his body, according to that he hath done, whether it be good or bad. Knowing therefore the terrors of the Lord, we persuade men." The terrors of the Lord were in his view as certain as judgment was certain; if there were any doubt about the judgment, the terrors of the Lord would be exposed to the same dubiety; but because there was in his view no questioning of the judgment, there was as little room for questioning that the terrors of the Lord would be manifested. And the very nature of a judgment implied that there were certain attested principles of justice on which it was to be conducted; and not only a trial, but a sentence, and not merely rewards, but punishments; and not merely the blessedness of approval to those who should stand acquitted, but the misery of being outcast to those who should be condemned; and viewing these two things as thus intimately connected, has it never struck you how much there is in the condition of the world to lead you to respect the one and therefore to fear the other; and how the present system of things is so constituted, that you can draw out of it a stronger argument for a future and final reckoning than you could from any other, even from one that bore clear impress of a great Judge of all?

Amid all the apparent confusion around us, there are not wanting many testimonies that God is on the side of righteousness and against iniquity. There is that conscience which he hath planted in every breast, and which witnesses by its approvings, or its accusings, what he who planted it there approves or condemns; there is in the happiness which, more or less, attends right and virtuous conduct, and in the misery which, more or less, accompanies the indulgence of all sin, an evidence that virtue and happiness, sin and misery, are connected; and there are not wanting many proofs besides, in the case of individuals, and much more in the case of nations, of a righteous retribution, by which virtue is rewarded and sin punished and condemned; and from this we are justified in inferring—and every man whose conscience is not blinded by sin *does infer*—that there is a great moral Governor of all, a God who honours holiness and hates sin. Had the issue of things been more in agreement with the records of conscience; had virtue always and openly led to happiness, and sin been always followed by misery; had the retributive justice of God taken clearer effect upon guilty individuals or guilty nations; had this been the case, one might have inferred with some reason that this was all the judgment, and that there was to be no great and final settlement hereafter. Had there been no proof of justice and rectitude in the government of God at all, we could have had no ground to expect that judgment should follow us; had these been more perfect than we find them, one might have supposed that there was as little ground to expect anything beyond what we saw here; and it is because there is so much in the world to tell us that God judgeth, and because there is at the same time so little, that we derive our strongest argument for a great and final reckoning hereafter. Were there much less of it than we now see, the moral character of God might be doubted; were there much more than we see, there would be less call than there is for a great and final adjustment. There is enough to tell us that He who ruleth over all is righteous; but there is not enough to indicate his righteousness, and therefore we infer a time when that righteousness shall be fully displayed. And look at the world in this light, and see whether everything is not taking place as you might expect under such a system. Look at this world where God is so often seen, and at the same time so often hidden from us—where he interposes with sufficient clearness and frequency to prove what he loves and what he hates in his creatures, and yet where his love and hatred are not fully carried out. Look at this, and say whether it does not convey to your minds the impression that He who rules over all is only withdrawing himself for a season, that he may prepare a solemn assertion of his rectitude, and sending those messengers before as the proofs of a coming judgment, and whether it be not time for every one to "seek the Lord while he may be found, and to call upon him while he is near." I advert to this consideration, because the imperfect discovery which we have of the moral character of God in the world around us is often employed by men to set aside the truth of a future judgment, or to harden their hearts against it, whilst it confirms in fact the great foundation for it. It was on other and surer grounds than this, however, that the apostles knew the "terrors of the Lord;" they knew them not merely from the intimations of his nature and will scattered over the face of human things, or even from what he had himself declared to them by his Spirit; they know it from one great fact in the divine administration, and if that fact be admitted, there can be no question of a judgment in righteousness; that fact was the death of Christ. In the death of his own Son, God did manifest, even when his purpose was to save sinners, that he must save them righteously; in his person he carried out the principles of a righteous administration; he shewed that "not one jot or tittle" of his threatenings should fail, that "heaven and earth might pass away, but that his words should not pass away;" and having committed himself, if I may be allowed the expression, by this solemn act of justice in the person of his only-begotten and well-beloved Son, can you suppose that he will ever depart from it? If the cup did not pass from him till he drank it, can you think that it will ever pass from those who continue to disregard his grace, or that they can meet anything less bitter than that wrath which they shall not be able to abide? If this be not true, then Christ died in vain; then was the costly work of redemption fruitless; then was its victim prepared, and its sacrifice offered, to propitiate a justice which had no existence; and the manifestation which was then given of God's hatred to sin and his love of holiness, had no truth or reality in it. But because these things are not, and cannot be, therefore God cannot now pass from his purpose of judgment; and the death and the resurrection of the Saviour is as solemn an assurance that he shall judge the world in righteousness, as though the trump were already sounding, at which "the dead, small and great, shall stand before God." Let us seek to have our minds habitually impressed by these things—let us frame the whole tenor of our lives, so that we may be finally accepted of Christ at the judgment-seat; and this is the great and unspeakable consolation, that the very same truth which is in one light the most terrible to sinners, is in another the most supporting —the truth of the death and resurrection of the Saviour, which brings in a new and better hope, by the which we may draw near to God; and they who make it their trust and confidence now, shall have peace of mind in the midst of all their guilty fears, and shall receive the Holy Spirit to qualify and make them meet for the judgment hereafter. Amen.

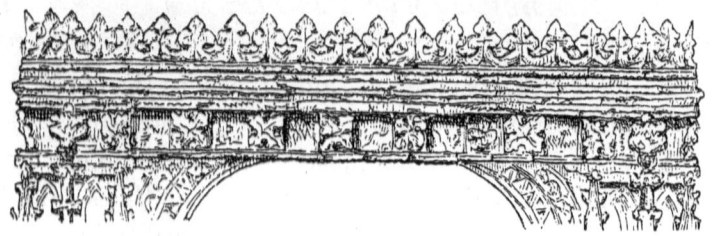

VII.

All Things are Yours.

BY THE REV. DAVID WELSH, D.D.

"ALL THINGS ARE YOURS; WHETHER PAUL, OR APOLLOS, OR CEPHAS, OR THE WORLD, OR LIFE, OR DEATH, OR THINGS PRESENT, OR THINGS TO COME; ALL ARE YOURS; AND YE ARE CHRIST'S; AND CHRIST IS GOD'S."—1 COR. iii. 21-23.

AT the time when the apostle wrote this epistle, there were divisions in the Corinthian Church, and it was forming itself into different sects and parties, each of which was attached to one or other of the apostles or teachers by whom the gospel was first preached. One said he was of Paul, another of Apollos, another of Cephas. In the commencement of the epistle, the apostle Paul points out the evil nature and dangerous consequences of such proceedings, and shews their inconsistency with the simplicity and purity of the gospel; and he sums up his various statements in the passage of which our text forms a part, the import of which passage is, that the Corinthians, in forming themselves into different bodies, and making their boast in different leaders, shewed that they had limited and erroneous views of their character and privileges—that the apostles were to be considered as their servants, and not their masters—nay, that under the gracious dispensation of the gospel all things—all the objects around them, and all the events which took place—were to be viewed as subservient to their spiritual interests: "All things are yours; whether Paul, or Apollos, or Cephas, or the world, or life, or death, or things present, or things to come." This spiritual possession with which they were invested, of all created things, arose from the relation in which they stood to Christ—as the members of his body, as the joint-heirs of his inheritance—"ye are Christ's." And this Saviour, who had purchased them with his own blood, was the Son of God, who acquired his mediatorial sovereignty over the creatures by becoming subject to the law of God, and fulfilling it, and all whose offices were assumed for promoting the glory of God—"Christ is God's."

The application of this statement to the particular case of the Corinthians is obvious. If such was their relation to Christ, and if in consequence of this relation they had such an interest in all created things, and if the end of all this was the glory of the Creator, the conclusion was irresistible, that in forming themselves into different parties, out of attachment to particular leaders, they were acting upon erroneous and pernicious views in regard both to the nature and extent of their privileges, and to the end of their profession. At present we do not intend to confine our remarks upon this passage to the special case which the apostle Paul had more particularly in view, but shall consider it in the general reference of which it admits, to the character and privileges of believers.

In our text, then, we have an account of the relation in which believers stand to created things and to the Creator, in consequence of their union with Christ, who in one person exhibited the mysterious union of a twofold nature—create and uncreate; the eternal Word having been *made* flesh. We have an account of the relation in which believers stand to all created things: they have a property in them; these things are theirs. This possession arises from their union with Christ, whose they are, and who himself is, they also in him being God's. All these particulars are strikingly represented in the holy ordinance which we have now so near a prospect of observing. In receiving the consecrated elements of this spiritual feast, we receive the seal of our right of "all things;" for if our Divine Master gives us his body and his blood—if he gives us himself—he must give us also all that he possesses, and he is "heir of all things." And in receiving these elements, we acknowledge our subjection to him as our Lord—that we are not our own, but his—that we are entirely dependent upon him—that we live upon him—and, living *upon him*, that we are bound to live *to* those great ends which he proposed in his mediatorial character. "Christ is God's," and we are bound to live to God in him. Let us make a few remarks upon the first of these particulars.

I. In the *first* place, generally, in regard to the possession of believers—"All things are yours." By this we must understand all *created* things; and that not as constituting an absolute, or undivided, or exclusive possession—that belongs to the Creator only—but all things exist for their use and benefit. This species of property which believers enjoy arises from the nature of the covenant of grace, and from that union which subsists between them and the Saviour. He made all things, and without him was not any thing made that was made, and he is the Lord of all that he created. Now, the believer being made one with Christ by faith, cannot look upon any thing that belongs to his gracious Master without feeling that he also has a property in it. Nor is this all. As Christ gave *himself* a ransom for his people, it is obvious that he will give them all that is *his*, so far as is necessary for their spiritual welfare, or for the ends he proposes in their salvation. The whole material universe was obviously at first formed in adaptation to the sentient beings which were afterwards to be called into existence. And the earth itself, and all the inferior tribes of living things, were placed in subjection to man, who was formed in the image of God, with dominion over his creatures. He was appointed lord of this lower world, and all things were his. This took place under the covenant of works; and when that covenant was broken, the system of things was altered, the ground was cursed for his sake—his authority was destroyed, and the world, like his own soul, presented a scene of insubordination and confusion. But under the covenant of grace, provision is made for this derangement which sin had introduced. Godliness has a promise of the life which now is, as well as of the life to come. The meek inherit the earth, and all things work together for good to them that love the Lord. And how this is accomplished must easily be perceived. Christ is the maker of all things, and as he makes nothing in vain, it must be for the good of his people. He has the control of all events, and he will direct them for the good of his chosen. Herein may be observed his perfect fitness for the office of our Redeemer—that he combines the character of God and man, and thus all the works of creation and of providence exist in harmonious subordination to the great work of redemption.

Oh, then, believers, consider well this most elevating and cheering doctrine. Your Elder Brother, who gave up his life for your sakes, is the sovereign of every creature, is the disposer of every event; and think you not that he will give you everything that you require, and direct everything in the way that he sees best for his purposes of mercy in regard to you? Can you look upon anything which you know to be his as if it were a stranger's? Can you see any event approaching which he will not be able to overrule for your good? When we look upon the followers of Christ merely in reference to the present world, we may see much to fill our hearts with sorrow for their sake. We may see them poor, neglected, afflicted—like their heavenly Master, despised of men, and carrying their cross in the midst of the scorn or hatred of a sinful generation; we may see them buffeted by the billows of adversity, the storm beating heavier on their unprotected head, and threatening to overwhelm them. Or we may see them struggling against temptations, going mourning all the day under the reproaches of their conscience, and fearing that God has cast off for ever, and will be favourable no more. Or more mournful still: we may see them for a time falling from their first love—the world with its pleasures, its business, its cares, regaining its ascendancy in their hearts—their eye dazzled with the returning sunshine of prosperity; and, amidst the friendships of this world, forgetting almost the friend that sticketh closer than a brother, and amidst the amusements of time overlooking the joys of eternity. When we thus look upon the followers of Christ, or when they reflect upon their own character only in reference to this earth, clouds of sorrow and sadness will overcast the soul. But when we consider them under their character of the ransomed of Christ, all these clouds again flee away. The Lord knoweth them that are his; he maketh all things work together for their good, and all things are theirs. It is good, my friends, on such a day as this, when we are to receive the pledge of every blessing, that we should cast our eye over the different parts of that blessed treasure with which the mercy of God has enriched us—that we should survey those wide and goodly possessions in which our lines have fallen, as calculated to increase our faith in the consideration of the amazing riches of the grace of God, who giveth liberally, and upbraideth not—to deepen our humility, and to stir us up to gratitude, as we joyfully exclaim, "What shall we render to the Lord for all his benefits?" While again, by dwelling on a theme like this, we may lead thoughtless and ungodly men to reflect on the incalculable loss they are sustaining, even when they gain the whole world at the expense of their own souls, and of this inheritance, in Christ, of all things.

II. In the *second* place, there is an enumeration of the most important of these possessions in the first part of the 22d verse, upon each of which I shall offer a very few remarks.

1. *The ministers of the gospel are yours.* "We preach not ourselves but Christ Jesus the Lord, and ourselves your servants for Jesus' sake." "We have not dominion over your faith, but are helpers of your joy." These are the words of the apostle in regard to the ministers of religion, and they are sufficient to shew the relation in which they stand to the people of Christ. Whatever talents or acquirements, whatever gifts or graces, they have received, they are all to be employed to the uttermost for the advancement of the best interests of those among whom they labour. They are appointed by the Almighty to serve in word and ordinances among *his* people, not their own. They are instruments in the hand of the Almighty, which he employs to instruct or admonish, or warn or comfort. If they are faithful in administering the mysteries of the gospel, no doubt they will save themselves, as well as those who hear them. But still they are chiefly to be viewed as labourers, whom God employs in the work of raising up his spiritual temple. And it is not till they are thus viewed by others, and till they thus view themselves, that there ever can be full comfort or benefit in their ministrations. Till there is a looking beyond the outward instrument—till there is a perception by faith of that great and gracious Being who employs it, and gives it all its success, the full benefit of the Christian ministry never can be experienced. "We have this treasure in earthen vessels, that the excellency of the power may be of God." And oh, the goodness of God to his people in this respect! The word is preached, ordinances are

administered, the sacraments are dispensed—and all these are yours. The reality of this possession may easily be proved to you. In the preaching of the gospel, where there might be little else to interest you, has a word ever come home to your secret conscience—has a text, as simply stated, appeared in a new application to your condition—has a description of character, or of some besetting sin, or committed evil, found you out—and all these in circumstances where you knew that he who spake could not know of your individual case, and did not himself speak in application to you? And does not this shew that in this respect, unwittingly even to himself, the preacher is employed by God for your warning and instruction, and that he is yours! Or does he come to your case in an expostulation that shews he has reflected upon your condition, that his heart's desire is for your salvation, that he inquired of God how he might make an impression upon you; that while speaking to all the rest he has, unconsciously to them, *you* especially in his eye—does not this shew that he is labouring for your benefit, that the Almighty is employing him in your service, that he is yours! The same remark is illustrated when, in dispensing the sacrament, he is made the means of shewing its application to your particular necessities; or when he comes to you apart from the world, and in dealing with you alone, finds an access to your conscience, which in the public services of the temple he never discovered; or when he waits till the hour of adversity or sickness, under the Divine blessing, prepares your heart for receiving the seed which never before had taken root or come to fruit. Many other illustrations might be added to these did time permit. But I trust that what has been said may be sufficient to shew how the ministers of Christ are yours.

I cannot dismiss this particular without remarking that the same view is indispensable for the comfort of those who minister in holy things. A sense of insufficiency for the least of the duties of our office would be altogether overwhelming, did we not consider that our sufficiency is of God, that neither he that planteth nor he that watereth is anything, but God that giveth the increase. We have this treasure in earthen vessels; and if we were to look only at them, our mind would sink within us. But it may comfort us to know that the power is not of us, but of God; that his strength is made perfect in our weakness; that the salvation of his people does not depend upon the way in which we set forth the truth, but upon the truth which is set forth; that we form but one out of many means which he employs for the edification and comfort of his chosen heritage; that he will make us sufficient for that end for which he employs us; and that what is weak or imperfect or even erring on our part, however much it is to be bewailed on our own account, will not frustrate his purposes of mercy towards those whom he has chosen unto himself.

2. *The world is yours.* The world is yours, because it is the workmanship and the property of him with whom you are united. It is yours, because he supports its whole frame, chiefly for his elect's sake. It is yours, because he will give you as much of it as is necessary for your real good. "Blessed are the meek, for they shall inherit the earth," not that they are to have it in that sense which constitutes in the language of this life possession, though even in this point of view they will in general ultimately succeed better than those who, hastening to be rich, fall into a snare; but they can view it all as manifesting the glorious perfections of their gracious Redeemer, they consider it as their own in him, and they have such a portion of it as is best for the welfare of their souls.

Even after this explanation, I am aware that there will appear to many a contradiction in the representing the followers of Christ as having the world. One may say, How can I have the world when I have been deprived of it? I have lost all that ever I possessed. I am poor, and destitute, and forlorn. But the Son of man had not where to lay his head, even in that world which he created, and of which he was Lord; and may you not in him, while you have nothing, possess all things? You have lost all that you had; but was it not attracting too much of your thoughts, was it not binding your affections to the earth, and now do not your spiritual desires arise to God with less to encumber them, have you not been led to much serious reflection, and has not your loss been a gain? Consider, then, your condition in comparison with those whom the world views as rich and increased in goods. Count your treasures, and balance them with theirs. You have only food and raiment, with a heart grateful to the Bestower of those blessings, and a contented mind. They have gained the world, but have lost their own soul. Which, think you, had the truest possession of the world—the young man who went away sorrowful from Christ because he had great possessions, or Levi who, when Jesus called him, rose up *and left all*, and followed him? Who was possessed of the truest treasure —Dives, who was clothed in fine linen, and fared sumptuously every day, or Lazarus, who lay a beggar at his gate? Let no sincere follower of Christ, then, complain that he is in want of this world's goods. Your Master sees what is necessary for your truest interests. In withholding, therefore, or in taking away what might retard your heavenly progress, or degrade your affections, he is giving you the world to use and not to abuse, and is making it truly yours. You may have been outstripped by a competitor in the career of life, though his exertions were less judicious and less persevering. Success has been his—disappointment yours. But if you have learned to submit to the will of God in this—if you acknowledge that you have received more than you deserved, if no envy stirs in your mind at the contemplation of greater prosperity, if you wish that he may enjoy and improve his blessings—in this submissive and tranquil state of mind you will acknowledge that godliness with contentment is great gain. Or perhaps you may have been defrauded by the injustice of man, deceived by him in whom you trusted. But if you can say that you forgive him who hath wronged you, that you wish him no evil, that no secret joy would fill your mind if adversity overtook him, then in this possession which God has given you over the workings of your sinful passions, you will perceive that, in the use which you are enabled to make of the world when taken away from you, it may be said especially to be yours.

3. *Life and death are yours.* Each one of the particulars mentioned by the apostle would afford matter for a separate discourse; but those which remain we must dismiss still more briefly than even those which have preceded, and we can offer merely one or two explanatory remarks.

Life is yours. It will be continued so long as suits the sovereign purposes of your heavenly Father in regard to you; its circumstances will all be directed for your spiritual improvement; the line of your life is drawn, its measure is determined in the Councils of Eternity, and it is yours.

Death is yours. Christ, my friends, has conquered this our last enemy. He has taken away the victory from the grave, the sting from death, and the king of terrors is yours. Yes, my friends, death is yours. You must indeed yield to it, for it is appointed unto all men once to die; but like your divine Lord, you yield to it only to triumph over it, and it is yours. The time when it is to take place, the circumstances with which it is to be attended, are all fixed for your good, and they are all adjusted with the tenderest regard for your happiness. The death of friends is yours, softening your heart, touching you with a feeling of human sufferings, and opening your sympathies in the ills of humanity, and loosing another tie that binds you to the earth. The death of enemies is yours—God thus delivering you from those who plot against you, or who tempt you to evil. The death which reigns in the world is yours—continually reminding you of the condition of our nature, teaching you to watch and to be sober, and crying to you aloud, "Prepare to meet thy God." The solemn harbingers of your own dissolution are yours—giving you due warning, and preparing the way for what is to come. And when death does come to you, it is yours—delivering you from all the ills of this mortal state, and ushering you into glory. To you to live is Christ, and to die is gain. Your last enemy is conquered. You have fought the good fight, and at length you gain the crown.

Doubtless death is an enemy, and in itself, and in many circumstances with which it is accompanied, it is calculated to fill the mind with alarm. But if we consider who has tasted of the bitterness of death for us, the glories to which it introduces the followers of Christ, and the good to our character which springs out of our very sufferings, we shall be taught that even in the dark valley of the shadow of death we have no evil to fear, for God is with us. "He that looks upon death (says Tillotson) only as a passage to glory, may look upon the messenger of it as bringing to him the best news that ever came to him in his whole life, and no man can stay behind in this world with the comfort with which a Christian man leaves it." "Death can do the saints no harm," says another (Boston). "It is one of the *all things* that work together for good. When the body dies, the soul is perfected. What harm did the jailor to Pharaoh's butler when he opened the prison-door and let him out? Is the bird in a worse case when at liberty than when confined in a cage? Thus, and no worse, are the souls of saints treated by death. It comes to the godly man as Haman to Mordecai, with the royal apparel and the horse, with commission to do him honour, though with a sullen mien and cloudy countenance. A dying day is in itself a joyful day to a Christian; it is the redemption day, when the captives are delivered and set free; it is the day of the pilgrim's coming home from his pilgrimage; the day in which the heirs of glory return to their own country and their Father's house."

4. *Things present are yours.* In whatever situation the believer may be placed he may reap advantage, and it is for his good to be there. It requires no ordinary measure of faith to believe this, for we are always prone to think we might have been better elsewhere; and yet there is no truth more clearly revealed than this, that things present are ours. If you are in prosperity, then you possess great means of usefulness; your gratitude will be quickened, you have more time to dedicate to the actual service of the Most High, and prosperity is yours. But can the same be said of adversity? Yes, my friends, it also is yours. In considering indeed the distresses of the afflicted, the sympathies of our nature are irresistibly called forth; sorrow fills the breast, and we cannot restrain the falling tear. Nor does religion forbid this; but then it teaches us to join mirth with our sadness. It makes known to us the uses of adversity. It reveals the sweetness that is to come forth out of the bitter—the glory that is to succeed the gloom. The tears of nature are thus brightened, if not in this world wholly dried; and faith rejoices while affection mourns. In this manner, even under the severest trials that come upon the believer, we see matter of heavenly joy. Though long-continued and increasing in their severity, we see the hand of a wise God who is making sorrow yours. Your "light affliction, which is but for a moment, worketh for you a far more exceeding and eternal weight of glory" (2. Cor. iv. 17). For the present, indeed, no affliction is joyous but grievous; yet

even in the severest affliction we see a real and substantial good. By many a repeated stroke the Divine Architect is hewing and fitting the stone for its appointed place in the heavenly temple. The sovereign Refiner is trying the gold in a fiery furnace; but it will come forth at last purified from all alloy. In short, my friends, if ye be following that which is good, your *present* situation, whatever it may be, is for your good, and is yours.

5. *Things to come are yours.* There is something portentous in the very sound, "the things to come." The things are so many and so great, so mysterious and yet so certain, that the boldest may well be appalled when he thinks on the "things to come." We can form no idea of what is to befall us. The events we are to witness, the feelings we are to experience, the scenes and changes through which we are to pass, even in the course of a few days or months, we cannot conjecture. How wonderful, how inconceivable, must be the number and the nature of years of ages of an eternity of things to come! The imagination of man cannot conceive them, language has no name to express them; and yet we know enough to excite every feeling of our nature to the uttermost, for death and judgment, and heaven and hell, are some of the things to come. Even without going beyond the present scene, there is enough to call forth many fears. Trials may, nay, they must befall you, temptations will assail you, troubles and misfortunes must needs come. But God maketh all things work together for good. He loves his people with a never changing affection. He loves them to the end. You know not indeed what may come upon you; but you know, at least, that nothing can come that is not according to the determination of your Father in heaven who careth for you.

You may be young, and going forth into the world, and you are not without cause of alarm in the snares and dangers of a world that lieth in wickedness. But if you put your trust in

God, he will guide you by his counsel and shield you by his might. You may be old, and perceive the decay of nature coming upon you, and you may be looking forward with apprehension to the greater decline to come. But the Lord knoweth your frame. He remembereth you are but dust. He will not forsake you when you are old. He can make your grey hair a crown of glory. Amidst the decay of nature he can revive strength in the inner man; and the trees that are planted in the house of the Lord shall still bring forth fruit in old age. Afflictions may be awaiting you, but they come from God, and he will bless them to you as a means of increasing your love to him, and of purifying you for his enjoyment. More arduous duties may be imposed upon you, but your strength is in God, and as your day is, he will make your strength to be. Your spiritual adversaries may set themselves in array against you, but greater is He that is for you than all they that are against you. Perhaps you may be tried with prosperity, the world may smile upon you, your table may be furnished, your cup may overflow, the praise of men, success in life, the riches of the world may be yours. But neither height nor depth—the height of prosperity, no more than the depth of adversity—shall separate you from the love of God. Look forward then, my Christian friends, to things to come; look forward, and rejoice. There may be darkness, there may be doubt, there may be danger; but with the word of truth to comfort you, of what need you be afraid? What real good can you ever want? Has not God given up his Son, and with him will he not freely give you all things?

But not only is the possession of this mortal life the property of Christians: the boundless felicity of the heavenly state is before you, and *eternity* is yours. "Blessed be the God and Father of our Lord Jesus Christ, which according to his abundant mercy hath begotten us again unto a lively hope by the resurrection of Jesus Christ from the dead, to an inheritance incorruptible, and undefiled, and that fadeth not away, reserved in heaven for you, who are kept by the power of God through faith unto salvation ready to be revealed in the last time" (1 Pet. i. 3–5). The prospect of this may well support us under all the trials of our earthly condition, or rather, it may teach us to rejoice in our tribulations, for, as has been beautifully observed, the greater troubles we come through, the kinder usage shall we receive when we come to our Father's house—that house where there are many mansions, and our Saviour is preparing a place for his people. There they are to enjoy an exceeding and eternal weight of glory—treasures, where neither moth nor rust doth corrupt—treasures inestimably precious and of endless variety—treasures abounding in all things—for he that overcometh shall inherit all things. However much may be enjoyed on earth, there is still something wanting; and the want of it takes away from the enjoyment of all the rest. But in heaven there is all that can contribute to complete happiness. They may go through that glorious land in the length of it and in the breadth of it, and all they see is their own. The Almighty shall rejoice in his works for ever, and they enter into the joy of their Lord!

Such, O believer, is your heritage! All things are yours, whether Paul, or Apollos, or Cephas, or the world, or life, or death, or things present, or things to come.

I cannot conclude without reminding all those who are strangers to the covenant, that while believers in having nothing possess all things, the wicked, though they possess all worldly comforts, have nothing. They may say, I am rich and increased in goods, but in reality they are poor; and surely this consideration should lead them to seek for those riches which endure, to come to Christ and buy wine and milk without money and without price.

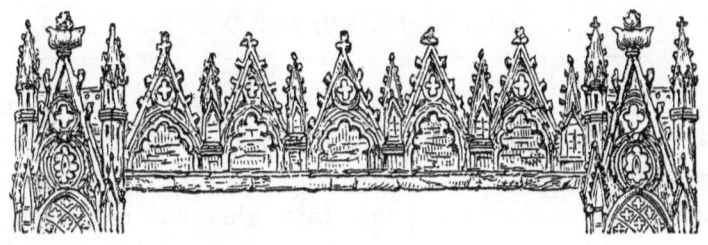

VIII.

Peace in Believing.

BY THE REV. THOMAS CHALMERS, D.D., LL.D.

"PEACE IN BELIEVING."—ROMANS XV. 13.

THE peace which is experienced in believing is relief from the terrors of wrath; it is not merely the removal, but the reversal of its anticipations; it is our altered view of God, when from an enemy we are taught to regard him as a friend; it is our assurance of his goodwill to us here, and a confident expectation of the promised bliss hereafter—these all spring in a disciple's spirit from the faith of the gospel, and these are the main elements of his peace and joy in believing.

Should a powerful and offended neighbour, under the threats of whose resentment I had been living for months in fearful insecurity; should he send to my door an offer of reconciliation, it is not difficult to understand how, at the moment of my reliance upon the truth and honesty of this offer, I would be at rest. Nor would it at all disturb the peacefulness of my heart, that I were given to know that the proposed friendship was only yet mine in offer, and not mine in possession, till I had performed certain conditions which I knew to be easily practicable. It would not, for example, abate the joy of the announcement, that I was told of an intended call on the part of my relenting adversary, and that I must give him a courteous reception, and stretch out my hand as the token of my having accepted his overture; and that then what was now mine in offer would become mine in possession also. If I consented to all this, and felt not merely the possibility, but the perfect ease of it, I would not postpone my gladness till the hour of the expected visit. On my faith in the reality and integrity of the offer, I would consider my before formidable enemy to be now my placid and my attached friend. An instantaneous peace would arise in my bosom, nor would I wait the coming formalities of reconciliation ere I threw aside the burden of my disquietude.

Now in the gospel of Jesus Christ, God addresses to me just such an offer; and I have only to believe in the truth of it, that I may cease from my apprehensions of God as an enemy, and God as an avenger. It is true that there is a difference between a thing being mine in offer, and a thing being mine in possession; and the difference still obtains, though that thing be forgiveness from God. But there is nothing in this difference which ought to serve as an alloy, or as an abatement, upon peace in believing. We have not, in the case of the gospel overtures, to look forward to any condition of future difficulty, ere the forgiveness that is now ours in offer becomes ours in possession. It is offered to us now, and it is competent for us actually to receive it now. The truth is, that it becomes ours simply upon our believing the truth of that message by which the offer is made known to us. No sooner do we believe than we possess; and let us cease, then, to wonder at the many recorded examples of the instantaneous peace which has dropped into the sinner's bosom from the word of the testimony.

And grievous, indeed, is their misunderstanding of the gospel, who think that peace must be postponed till we know that holiness is in progress within us, and that repentance is going onwards even unto perfection. It is true, that without holiness no man can see God; and it is as true, that unless we repent we shall perish. But just as the man who had the offer of reconciliation laid by an offended neighbour at his door, ought not to postpone his joy till the hour of certain easy and practicable formalities; so neither ought we to postpone it till the time when we know that repentance and holiness have been realized upon our characters. And that, not because these graces are easily attainable by us, but because these graces are actually included as so many offers in the communication of the gospel; because God holds them out for our acceptance, just as effectually as he holds out pardon for our acceptance; because He, in whom all sufficiency dwells, promises to make his grace sufficient for every one of our necessities; because He, who has given us his own Son, pledges himself to all who receive the gift, that he will also with him freely give them all things. The man who only hears the offer of pardon upon repentance, and looks to that repentance as a contingency which depends upon himself, may well hear such an announcement without being gladdened and tranquilised by it. But let a man hear the offer in the whole comprehensiveness of its terms; let him perceive that repentance, as well as the remission of sins, is included in it; let him understand that God holds out to him in the gospel a sanctifying Spirit as well as an atoning Sacrifice, and then let holiness be represented to be as indispensable to heaven as it may, no sense of impotency whatever will intercept the peace which ought to flow in upon his heart from such a communication. From the moment that he closes with these overtures, he may have peace; and the point at which belief enters into his mind, the point at which he recognizes in the gospel the view of Him who, when he commanded, made the winds and the waters to obey, marks the point at which the dark and fearful agitations of a sinner's bosom should cease into a calm.

And there is not a single reader of the Bible who might not thus appropriate to himself the offer of forgiveness, and have peace in believing it. Such terms as *all*, and *every*, and *whosoever*, bring this offer just as effectually to his door as if a special messenger had been sent to him from heaven, or as if he was the only person upon earth for whom the Bible was intended. That he may have the peace to which we refer, all that is necessary is to understand the message in the terms of it, and to believe in the trueness of it. If the word of salvation has reached him, the offer of salvation has been made unto him. In that word God holds himself out to every man as beseeching him to be reconciled; and proposes to all who will, the gift of that pardon and that preparation which are necessary for restoring them to an inheritance in the heavens.

Let me endeavour to urge a few distinct considerations, all grounded on the word of the testimony, and all fitted to confirm and to strengthen the peace of a believer, by being fitted to assure him of the reality of God's goodwill.

First, then, Christ undertakes to save all who believe in him, and his honour is at one with the success of his undertaking. As the economy of our redemption is constituted, had none believed, there would have been no trophy to exhibit of his redeeming power; Christ would have died in vain, or the whole fruits of his death would have been to aggravate the guilt of the world in rejecting him, and so to demonstrate more strikingly than ever the justice of God in its final condemnation. Had none believed, there would have been no actual salvation, no living triumphs of grace, no extension of the kingdom of righteousness, no inroad and no abridgement on territory of him who is at the head of that great moral rebellion into which he has seduced our unfortunate species. The prince of the power of darkness would still hold an entire ascendancy over the world,—would still boast an unviolated limit around his dominions,—would sit securely on his throne, and eye the enterprise and preparation of the Messiah as an impotent parade, and all this for the want of believing. It is said of Christ that he came to destroy the works of the devil, and yet, if there be no believers among men, he fails in his errand; and does not this prove, that the certainty of salvation unto all who do believe is in most inviting unison with the glory of him who is the captain of salvation? There is a consideration here that is fitted to draw sinners in trust and in expectation around him. It fully warrants them to venture their all upon Christ. It leads them to see that their security is in every way at one with his reputation. Every man who comes in the way of dependence to the Saviour, is just adding to the prosperity of that cause on which his heart is set, and rendering to him of the travail of his soul that He may be satisfied. And every man who has come may, by the thought which has been suggested, deepen and establish the foundations of his peace. Christ will never frustrate his own undertaking by casting off one who hangs upon his power, or looks with an expectant eye to the fulfilment of his promises. He will never so thwart the express and the special purpose of his own great achievement, as to withhold everlasting life from him who has been led by the terms of his own message, to regard it as the gift of God through Jesus Christ our Lord. He will never, in the face of his own declaration, that whosoever believeth shall not perish, leave any believer to perish; or give room to the great adversary to say, in a single instance, that here is one whom you have inveigled into confidence, but whom I still claim as my prisoner, and will torment as my victim through eternity.

The believer may gather an argument for security from such a contemplation. He may add to his peace and to his joy when he looks to this part of the testimony of God. He may view himself as the subject and the prize of a great competition between the Prince of light and the Prince of darkness. And as he places himself under the covert of the great and the appointed mediatorship, he may regard the honour of Christ and the glories both of his character and of his power as the guarantee of his own safety.

There is another consideration eminently fitted to stablish and to settle the mind of a believer. It is the same with that which strengthened the foundation of an apostle's hope. He expresses it in these words: "For if, when we were enemies, we were reconciled to God by the death of his Son, much more, being reconciled, we shall be saved by his life." It was when we were yet enemies that Christ died for us. It was when we were not so much as conceiving the wish of a return unto God, that God devised a way of return, and in the face of this world's determined wickedness did so much to reclaim to friendship with Himself its guilty generations. Had there been any movement on our part towards Him, which led him so to move towards us, the argument would have lost that peculiar emphasis which actually belongs to it. But, in fact, it was when we were prosecuting our rebellion with minds in the full bent of their enmity towards Him,—it was when, on the part of men, there was no relenting purpose toward God,—it was when, sunk in the deepest moral lethargy, we were altogether dead in trespasses and sins,—it was then, and in the midst of the most unalleviated depravity and provocation, that the whole plan of our redemption was laid; and the whole expense and labour of it was undertaken; and all the toil, and humiliation, and intense suffering of this great achievement were endured. Surely, if such be the goodwill of God to the world that no hostility of ours could quench it, and He would bring such a weight of agony on his beloved Son, rather than that the enterprise of mercy should be stayed, what shall we think now of his goodwill when the agony is borne, and all that is painful in the work of our redemption is finished, and Christ who was dead is now alive, and exalted at the right hand of God for the very purpose of carrying into accomplishment the design of his own undertaking. It is possible to conceive that ere Christ was humbled and crucified, he might have shrunk from the arduousness of the work that was before him. But it is not possible to conceive now, that he will not perfect into efficiency that which he hath already purchased with so much suffering; that he will not substantiate his own enterprise; that he will so nullify his own acts as that all the labour of them, and all the painfulness of them, shall be as good as thrown away. This, then, is a consideration that serves to deepen, and more firmly to establish, the foundation of a believer's peace. It is Christ's own cause, that he should obtain the inheritance. It is a cause which hath already been fought and conquered in the vale of humiliation, and which, now that he is exalted on high, he never will abandon. He will not throw away the spoils of his own victory. He will not, after having laid down his life for his enemies, now that he has taken it up again, fail to consecrate all its powers to the salvation and the service of those who are seeking to be his friends. "Who is he that condemneth? It is Christ that died, yea rather, that is risen again, who is even at the right hand of God, who also maketh intercession for us."

And every indication which God gives of his earnestness in the matter of salvation, is felt by every believer as a new argument for trust, and for the peace of assurance, or the peace of confirmation, which trust brings along with it. It is not merely when God declares acceptance through Jesus Christ, and so commits the glory of his truth to his actual acceptance of all who so come unto him. It is not merely the exhibition of an offer to all who will; but it is when, in the word of the testimony, we see God putting forth the expression of a desire after the creatures who had wandered away from him. It is when God makes use of a more active urgency, in order to prevail on us to comply with his overtures. It is when God invites, and entreats, and expostulates, and swears by himself that he has no pleasure in our death, and beseeches us to be reconciled, and bids us put him to the trial whether he will not, on our return unto him, himself return unto us, and pour out a blessing on the utterance of our prayers. It is when he represents himself, not merely as waiting to be gracious, but as longing after us, and rejoicing in common with all the angels of heaven, on the very first movement of our repentance towards him. It is when to reinforce, as it were, all these expedients for getting us to believe, he interposes his authority on the occasion, and positively commands us to do so. Nay, what is more, when, to shut us up to this measure as the only alternative of safety, he declares that they who believe not shall be damned. It is when such evidences multiply upon him, that by mere believing God is well pleased, and that faith is the very footing on which he wills us to stand. It is then that a disciple places himself more securely than ever on a foundation of reliance; and it just rivets him the more firmly to this basis when he reflects, that thus posted, and thus tenaciously adhering to his post, or, in other words, that, when cleaving unto Christ, and linking with his person and work all his tranquil convictions of present favour, and all his hopes of future glory, he ever says that I am doing what God wants me to do, and I am where God wants me to be.

The riches of Christ are said to be unsearchable. And as God reveals them by his Spirit to a believer, he is made to enter on such a region of manifestation, as to leave the general world exceedingly behind him. They cannot follow the movements of his exercised mind as he holds the communion of confidence with God, and tastes of that peace which passeth all understanding—a peace which bears no resemblance whatever to that momentary gleam of tasteful and tender emotion which is ministered by some faint imagination of the attribute of mercy, and leaves in utter darkness the place and the operation of the other attributes. A believer's peace is the peace of one who ever looks fully, and without dismay, on the whole character of God. His prayer for forgiveness is not that the righteousness of God may give way to his mercy, but that mercy may be extended towards him in such a way as to exalt and to vindicate righteousness. He comes in the name of the Lord his righteousness; and while this is the way in which he renders the most acceptable homage to the truth and the justice of God, he also finds it to be the way in which there is not a single intervening cloud between him and the friendship of a reconciled Father. Between him and Christ there is a welcome offer on the one side, and a confiding acceptance on the other. Between Christ and God there is an offering for the sins of men on the one side, and an entire satisfaction with the incense of that offering on the other. Goodwill to men on the part of heaven has, throughout the whole of this process, received its most abundant demonstration; and every one obstacle to the expression of this goodwill is now done away by him who travelled in the greatness of his strength for us. And the believer, to fortify the peace of his heart, is now warranted to look to the justice of God as already discharged on the head of the great Sacrifice; and to look to the truth of God, as vindicated in all its threatenings, and as now testifying its promises and its invitations; and to look to the tenderness of God, as now at liberty to call, and even to beseech, the return of the guilty; and to look to the glory of God, as much interested in the triumph of the method of redemption, as his mercy is gratified by our acquiescence in it; and to look to the way in which both the honour and the desire of the Saviour are linked with the object of salvation. In these contemplations, he sees nothing in the wish or character of the one party which does not stand in most inviting unison with the peace, and pardon, and deliverance of the other. Every restraint is taken away from the exercise of love with the former, and from that of an implicit confidence with the latter: and every view which he takes of the dignity of his Saviour's person, and of the reality of that work in which he toiled and suffered for the salvation of mankind, establishes the love of God more firmly in his heart, and strengthens within him that peace which the world knoweth not, and causes it to flow abundantly through his soul like a mighty river.

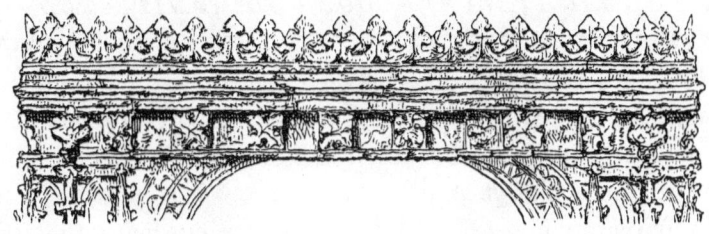

IX.

The Righteousness of God manifested for the Justification of Sinners.

BY THE REV. JOHN MACDONALD, D.D.

"BUT NOW THE RIGHTEOUSNESS OF GOD WITHOUT THE LAW IS MANIFESTED."—
ROM. iii. 21.

THE obvious design of this epistle is to illustrate and confirm the important doctrine of the sinner's justification before God—a doctrine which lies at the very foundation of Christianity —which includes in it, and connects with it, all the blessings of eternal life; and apart from which, no hope or comfort is left for man, either for time or for eternity. The Jews, though possessing all the advantages of a divine revelation, had fallen into sad mistakes regarding this doctrine. "For they being ignorant of the righteousness of God, and going about to establish their own righteousness, had not submitted themselves to the righteousness of God" (Rom. x. 3); and sought justification, "not by faith, but, as it were, by works of the law" (Rom. ix. 32).

The apostle, aware of the fatal consequences of such mistakes, not only to the Jews, but to the world at large, was led, under the guidance of inspiration, to write this epistle chiefly for the purpose of setting this doctrine in a just light.. Other points are noticed, it is true, and points of great importance, but these are evidently introduced in their subserviency to this doctrine, or as arising out of it.

In pursuing his design, the apostle sets out with the fact, which cannot well be denied, that the whole world, Jews and Gentiles, "are guilty before God," all having sinned and come short of his glory. And it follows by natural consequence, that "by the deeds of the law there shall no flesh be justified in his sight; for by the law," he adds, "is the knowledge of sin" (Rom. iii. 19, 20). Of course, if another method of justification, and a method altogether different from anything which man could devise, had not been revealed, man would have been utterly and eternally undone. Such a method, however, the apostle proceeds to unfold. "But now," says he, "the righteousness of God without the law is manifested, being witnessed by the law and the prophets; even the righteousness of God, which is by faith of Jesus Christ, unto all and upon all them that believe; for there is no difference: for all have sinned, and come short of the glory of God: being justified freely by his grace through the redemption which is in Christ Jesus; whom God hath set forth to be a propitiation through faith in his blood, to declare his righteousness for the remission of sins that are past, through the forbearance of God;—to declare, I say, at this time, his righteousness, that he might be just, and the justifier of him who believeth in Jesus" (Rom. iii. 21–26).

The whole of this interesting passage merits the careful perusal of every reader, as containing one of the clearest and most comprehensive views of the doctrine of justification that is to be met with in any part of the sacred volume. It exhibits to us at once a *righteousness* which constitutes the ground of the sinner's justification, and the *manner* in which a sinner obtains an interest in it, so as to enjoy the benefits resulting from it. This is by *faith*, and *by faith without the deeds of the law*. It points out to us also the ground upon which the sinner may warrantably receive it, and plead an interest in it; or that which may be called *the right of acceptance*, viz., the free offer of it in the gospel; for "*it is unto all*," as the light of the sun, for the benefit of the world. We learn from it, farther, that this righteousness is actually imputed to every believing sinner, or transferred, in law-reckoning, to his account, so as to avail him for the purposes of justification and eternal life. It is *upon* all who believe, as a garment (for to this the word alludes), in which they stand covered, clothed, and adorned before God. And finally, this method exhibits not only the *grace of God*, which it does in a marvellous manner —for believers are said to be "justified freely by his grace, through the redemption which is in Christ Jesus"—but also the *glory of his moral character*. For hereby "*his righteousness is declared;*" and it appears that he "*is just, and the justifier of him who believeth in Jesus*."

The limits to which I must confine myself will not permit me to enter on the consideration of each of these particulars. What I design at present chiefly is, in reliance on divine strength, to direct the attention of my hearers—

I. To that which may be called the foundation of the whole, in this procedure of grace—*the righteousness of God*. And II. To this righteousness, *as now manifested*.

The consideration of these points cannot be inapplicable on any occasion on which we have to address immortal souls; and it is hoped will be seen to be not unsuitable to that which has called us together this day. Our attention, then, is directed—

I. To that which is here called *the righteousness of God*, and which is represented as the foundation, or meritorious ground, upon which God bestows on man pardon, acceptance, and all the blessings of redemption. In Scripture the term "*righteousness*" is not unfrequently used in a different sense from that in which it is employed here; and it will not be foreign to our purpose for a little to advert to this. It sometimes signifies the righteousness of the divine nature, or that which has been commonly called the moral rectitude of God—a character which is inseparable from his nature, which is displayed in all his works, and by which he makes it manifest, that as he regards sin with infinite detestation, so he regards moral excellence or goodness with ineffable delight—a character, in short, which includes in it all the perfections of his moral nature, such as holiness, justice, and truth, and which is, therefore, essential to his very being. Hence he is said to be "a God of truth, and without iniquity" (Exod. xxxii. 4); to be "justified when he speaks, and clear when he judges" (Psa. li. 4); to be "righteous in all his ways, and holy in all his works" (Psa. cxlv. 17); the righteous Lord who loveth righteousness; and whose "countenance upholdeth the upright" (Psa. xi. 7).

It is evident, however, that this cannot be the import of the term in the passage before us. For the righteousness of the divine nature neither is, nor can be, a ground of justification to sinful man. It is rather that which reveals the divine indignation against sin, passes a sentence of condemnation on account of it, and renders it indispensable that sin be punished. Nevertheless, it is of the utmost importance to entertain just conceptions regarding this view of the divine character; for although this is not, and cannot be, the righteousness which justifies the sinner, and which is here referred to, it is not to be considered on that account as having no relation to that righteousness, much less (as many, alas! are too apt to think) as being at variance with it. On the very contrary, there exists the strongest affinity and harmony between the one and the other; for the righteousness of the divine nature is that which (on the supposition that sinners were to be saved) rendered it necessary that the other righteousness by which we might be justified, should be wrought out, and thus becomes the very reason of the existence of this other righteousness. This righteousness or character of God is, besides, the rule or standard to which the righteousness which justifies the sinner must be conformed, and with which, in all its essential characters of spirituality, equity, purity, and perfection, it must correspond. And, lastly, the righteousness which justifies the sinner must be such as to become a transcript of the other, and the mirror which exhibits its true character and glory to men.

Were these things but duly considered by many, they would not blindly or presumptuously trust in what they call the mercy of God, nor venture to approach him for pardon and acceptance on the footing of any deeds, or even sincerity and penitence of their own, while the righteousness of the divine nature stands in the way, precludes the exercise of mercy, except in consistency with justice, and fences around for ever the rights and prerogatives of divinity. They would, on the contrary, renounce every pretension of this nature, and most humbly and thankfully acquiesce in that wonderful plan, in which "mercy and truth are met together, and righteousness and peace have kissed each other" (Psa. lxxxv. 10).

But, as distinguished from this righteousness of the divine nature and character, that to which our text refers is evidently that which was wrought out by the Son of God in behalf of sinners of mankind. This, and this alone, is that righteousness, "which is by the faith of Jesus Christ unto all, and upon all them who believe;" the righteousness, on account of which God accepts the sinner, and which is manifested to the faith and acceptance of men for this purpose.

In regard to this righteousness, it is of importance to observe:

1. That it consists in the complete fulfilment of the law, in all its precepts and penal sanctions. The law, as a covenant of works, required of man perfect obedience, as the condition of life; and, at the same time, denounced death as the penalty of transgression. The Lord Jesus Christ, accordingly, met the law in both these respects, fulfilled its precepts, and endured its penalty; accomplishing the one by the holiness of his nature and the righteousness of his life, and the other, by the awful and unparalleled sufferings of his death. The whole course of his obedience, then, commonly distinguished into *active* and *passive* (with what propriety I do not at present inquire), is that which constitutes the right in question, and by which, in virtue of the divinity of the person who wrought it out, the law is "magnified and made honourable."

2. The righteousness thus wrought out in fulfilment of the law by the Son of God, was altogether of a *vicarious* nature—it was in behalf of others, and not for himself. He stood wholly in a *public*, never in a private capacity. He stood as the representative of sinners. In order to redeem them he assumed our nature, was made under the law, submitted to all its vast demands, and suffered its awful sanctions; for "He was made a curse for us," says the apostle. If he was wounded, it was for *our transgressions;* if he was bruised, it was for *our iniquities;* if he died the just, it was for *the unjust,* that he might bring us to God. Thus for men he lived, for men he died; and all that he hath done and suffered is to be considered as wholly on their account, and in their actual room and stead.

Some, indeed, talk as if his human nature owed obedience to the law for itself, and that only his sufferings were on our account, as procuring for us release from punishment, but that we are left to work for life as we can. This, to say the least of it, affords but poor comfort to the sinner, and in effect leaves him just where he was. But it should be remembered, that Scripture never represents the Son of God as having assumed the human nature *for himself*, but wholly for others—" Forasmuch as the children are partakers of flesh and blood, he also himself likewise took part of the same; that through death he might destroy him that had the power of death, that is, the devil: and deliver them who through fear of death were all their lifetime subject to bondage" (Heb. ii. 14–15). It should also be remembered, that the human nature in him never subsisted in a state of *distinct personality*, but always in inseparable union with the Godhead, in virtue of which, whatever conformity it might possess *to the law* as a *rule*, it could owe no obedience as a covenant; under which form it demanded obedience of man, and consequently of the surety. Let us hold, then, by the consoling truth, that our divine Redeemer fulfilled the precepts of the law, as well as that he endured its penalty for man; in consequence of which the righteousness which he wrought out has procured a title to life as well as a release from punishment, and bestows the twofold blessing of pardon and acceptance, on every one that believeth. Let us also rejoice, that if this righteousness was wrought out in behalf of others, it will also be readily conferred upon them, and eventually be applied to the myriads for whom it was thus accomplished. And let the guilty and condemned sinner avail himself of a righteousness which he is not only warranted, but invited, and even commanded to accept, for all the purposes of salvation.

3. It is a righteousness of infinite value, and therefore available to all the purposes for which it was designed. Wrought out by the Son of God in our nature, it was not only perfect as a complete fulfilment of the law, but a righteousness

of such value as to *merit* life and salvation for others. We can conceive of a perfectly holy human nature giving complete obedience to the law; but in all this, there is nothing that could avail for others. The obedience of the highest angel in glory could merit nothing for man; because a finite nature can never exceed that which it was its own duty to perform. But the Son of God, as was noticed already, having assumed the human nature into intimate union with the divine, all the actings and sufferings of that nature derived immediate and infinite value from the divinity, and, properly speaking, are to be considered (and in the estimation of law and justice actually are so), the actings and sufferings, not of a finite nature, but of him who is God in our nature. This is what stamps a value and glory on this righteousness, in consequence of which, the law is not only fulfilled, but magnified and made honourable, divine justice infinitely satisfied, redemption obtained for man; and "God is just, and the justifier of him who believeth in Jesus."

4. This righteousness has been actually sustained by Jehovah in behalf of sinners, and acted upon in all ages by him as the ground of their acceptance and complete salvation. This, indeed, might be inferred from what has already been stated; for, if wrought out in obedience to the law, in the room of the guilty, and by the Son of God, we must conceive it to be a righteousness worthy of God to accept and sustain. But, besides this, the resurrection of Christ from the dead, his ascension, and reception to glory—the outpouring of the Spirit on the day of Pentecost, and frequently since, the promulgation of the gospel in the world, the dispensation of means and ordinances in the church, the conversion of sinners, and the experience of saints in all ages—confirm the interesting truth that God the Father, as the righteous Judge, has actually sustained the righteousness of his Son in behalf of sinners, and has actually proceeded upon this as a foundation in receiving

sinners into his favour, and conferring on them all the blessings of eternal life. Oh, glorious rfghteousness, through which such blessings flow to man, and such rich revenues of glory accrue to God!

After what has been stated, it will be scarcely necessary to detain you by mentioning some of the reasons why it is here called the righteousness "*of God.*" It is so, as we have seen, because wrought out by him in our nature. It is so also, as exhibiting his glory and moral rectitude to man. It is a transcript of his moral character, and the mirror in which man may behold it. It is so likewise (and perhaps this is the principal reason of its being so called in the text), as being altogether of his provision and appointment. In this, as well as in many other respects, it is opposed to any righteousness of man, and the economy of grace connected with it, to the natural tendencies of his carnal, proud, and legal spirit; so much so, that it would never have entered into his heart to conceive of this astonishing method of salvation.

But further, it is called the righteousness of God "*without the law.*" Not that it has no reference to the law, for we have already seen that it was wrought out in fulfilment of it, and therefore that the interests of the law, in all its glory and dignity, were fully consulted in the working out of it. Nor are we to suppose that the sinner is to have no regard to the law in receiving this righteousness. On the contrary, he recognizes it in all the extent and spirituality of its demands; and it is under an impression of the equity of its demands, and of its awful sanctions, that he actually submits to the righteousness of God. But it is a righteousness conferred on the sinner without regard to *the deeds of the law*, or any works of his done in obedience to the law, as a covenant, and to which he looks, in whole or in part, as the ground of his acceptance with God.

There is a tendency in man to seek justification by works;

and he will, even when pressed hard by the law, endeavour to work up in himself convictions of sin, and certain penitential feelings, by which to recommend himself to God for an interest in the righteousness of his Son;—not recollecting that such convictions and inward feelings are designed to prompt us to accept of that righteousness, and not to entitle us in the least degree to an interest in it. The righteousness of God, however, neither proposes nor accepts of any compromise with the law in this respect; and it is the mercy of the sinner, did he but know it, that this is the case.

Lastly, This righteousness, it is said, is "*witnessed by the law and the prophets.*" The ceremonial law in almost all its types and sacrifices prefigured this substitutionary system, or justification by the righteousness of another. And though the moral law did not give any direct intimation of it, nevertheless, in the perfection of its demands, and the awful nature of its threatenings, it pointed out the necessity of such a righteousness. The prophets all witness concerning it. "Surely," says Isaiah, "shall one say, In the Lord have I righteousness and strength" (Isa. xlv. 24). "And this is the name," saith another prophet, "whereby he shall be called, THE LORD OUR RIGHTEOUSNESS" (Jer. xxiii. 6). And Daniel tells us that he —Messiah the Prince—should "bring in everlasting righteousness" (Dan. ix. 24). In short, "to him give all the prophets witness, that, through his name, whosoever believeth in him, shall receive remission of sins" (Acts x. 43). Of course, this was not a new and hitherto unheard of doctrine, as some of the Jews were apt to imagine. It was a doctrine known to their fathers, a doctrine recorded in their own writings, and which possessed a peculiar prominence in their system; which, therefore, nothing but wilful blindness and determined unbelief could prevent them from perceiving. And thus God in testifying concerning this righteousness by the law and the prophets, thereby declared not only his high approbation of it, but that it has ever since the fall of man been the exclusive foundation upon which he justifies the ungodly, and confers upon him that believes all the blessings of salvation.

This, then, is the righteousness to which our attention is directed in the text; a righteousness of infinite value and glory wrought out by the Son of God in behalf of sinful men, a righteousness without the law, and a righteousness witnessed by the law and the prophets, a righteousness which has procured for man deliverance from wrath and a title to life, and which actually confers on him who believeth these and all other spiritual blessings, in all the fulness of their extent and eternity of their duration.

II. Let us consider this righteousness, *as now manifested.* The apostle has evidently a reference here to the gospel dispensation, as having brought this subject, together with every other part of redemption, clearly to light. Under the law, these things were adumbrated by a variety of types, ceremonies, and sacrifices. But under the gospel, the vail is rent in twain, the shadows have given way to the substance, the Sun of Righteousness has arisen, and a day has dawned upon the world, in "the light of which men shall see light." We may observe—

1. That this righteousness is manifested in the gospel as *actually wrought out.* Here we see the Son of God no longer prefigured by types and sacrifices only, but actually appearing on the field of the world, tabernacling among us, suffering hunger, fatigue, poverty, and reproach, obeying the law in all its precepts, and during the whole course of his active life. We see him endure its penalty, enter the garden, his soul exceeding sorrowful there, ascend Calvary, suffer himself to be stretched on the accursed tree, and there, bearing the insults of

men, the malice of devils, and, what infinitely exceeded all these, those hidings of his Father's countenance, which led him to exclaim, "My God, my God, why hast thou forsaken me?" But we hear him at last cry, "It is finished!" And thus, having finished transgression, made an end of sin, and made reconciliation for iniquity, "he brought in everlasting righteousness." The gospel thus reveals to us a righteousness actually accomplished. The law pointed to it as a righteousness *to be* manifested, and ancient believers looked forward with longing expectation to its accomplishment; but the gospel points it out to us as *actually wrought out*, and manifested as such for the justification of sinners. What a confirmation is this to the faith of God's people, and how daring the presumption of the sinner, who, in the matter of justification, would propose to superadd any doings of his own to a righteousness thus manifested, as actually and perfectly wrought out!

2. It is manifested in the gospel, in the *universality of its benignant and beneficial designs* regarding sinners of mankind. Under the Mosaic economy, all the blessings connected with this righteousness were confined to one nation, and shut up within the pale of one church. This, with a few exceptions, was the state of things for ages; and the righteousness in question was, during that long period, unpublished and unknown to the world at large. But now, it is *unto all*, not only sufficient in itself for the salvation of all, but designed freely for the benefit of all, exhibited to the faith and acceptance of all indiscriminately, and commanded (for so the commission runs) to be preached *to every creature* for this purpose. For "there is neither Greek nor Jew, circumcision nor uncircumcision, barbarian, Scythian, bond nor free: but Christ is all, and in all" (Col. iii. 11). And this righteousness, which is *unto all*, starting from Calvary, whence it burst forth in its glory on a benighted world, shall continue its career until all nations shall

see its manifestation in the gospel, are brought within the sphere of its influence, and blessed with that salvation of which it is at once the medium, and the procuring cause to men. Oh glorious thought! what a warrant to sinners of every description, and of every nation to whom it is proclaimed, to accept of it. And what an encouragement! nay, what an imperious call to communicate the intelligence of it to all nations, far and near, that they may hear of, believe, and be found in this righteousness!

3. In the gospel it is manifested in the greater extent of its triumphs in the salvation of men. Under the ancient economy, confined as it was to one nation, there were but few among them who believed the report, and few to whom the arm of the Lord was revealed. But under the glorious gospel of the blessed God, thousands and tens of thousands have been led to believe the record concerning it; to rely on this righteousness as the ground of their justification, and to experience its justifying effects in the enjoyment of pardon of sin, peace with God, access to his presence, and the hope of eternal glory. They have also experienced its sanctifying effects; for it provides for the sanctification of all who receive it, and this remarkable change is inseparably connected with it, and is its never-failing result. For every believer finds that it is "grace reigning through this righteousness" that renews his heart, overcomes his prejudices, subdues his corruptions, detaches him from the world, elevates his affections to the things which are above, inspires him with zeal for God, and devotedness to his cause. In short, it directs, prompts, and strengthens him to abstain from all appearance of evil, to resist the devil, the world, and the flesh, and to follow that "holiness without which no man shall see the Lord." If these effects do not ensue, men but deceive, and sadly impose upon themselves, by imagining that they trust in this righteousness, while their

trust is but a mere pretension; for if any man be in Christ, and therefore clothed in his righteousness, he is a *new creature.* And Christ is made, to all who believe in him, not only wisdom and righteousness, but sanctification and redemption. And thus, instead of making *void the law,* they, on the contrary, *establish it.* And if such be the triumphs connected with the salvation of one sinner, what shall we conceive of those displayed in the salvation of the thousands and myriads who, in the days of the apostles, and in every succeeding age since, have been brought under its influence, and made to experience the blessed results of the imputation of this righteousness;— of thousands and myriads, too, of every description, rank, character, kindred, nation, and tongue; and thousands and myriads who have given evidence to the world, by their devotedness to God, their firmness and fidelity in his cause, their patience under affliction, and the holiness of their lives and conversation, that they owed all their ability thus to act, and all the hopes and prospects which animated them during their Christian journey, to the righteousness of God manifested in the gospel!

Thus the righteousness of God is manifested in the gospel more clearly than ever under the law. It is manifested in the gospel as wrought out; it is manifested unto all, in regard to its tendency and design; and it is manifested in its triumph or actual effects in the salvation of many. And does not the manifestation of it, in these respects, speak to us? Does it not proclaim to us the invaluable privilege which the Lord has bestowed on us, in giving us our lot under such a manifestation of his righteousness, whilst to many this is denied. How, then, should we remember, that "to whomsoever much is given, of him much shall be required." How inexcusable, besides, does it leave those who shut their eyes to its value, and refuse to submit to it, expecting by other means, and means of their own devising, to recommend themselves to the favour of God; or who, if they would not altogether reject this righteousness, for their own justification, yet would bring their own works, their sincerity, their repentance, and some even their faith, as a price in their hands, by which to acquire a title to this blessing; or who would conjoin these with the righteousness of Immanuel, in order to procure the desired acceptance in the sight of God; thus acting as foolishly as if one should, by lighting a taper, endeavour to assist and increase the light of the sun. Such conduct carries absurdity, as well as criminality, in its very face. And those who are guilty of it would do well to look to their state in time, and to betake themselves to the true foundation ere it be too late, and the door of mercy be for ever shut, otherwise they shall find that "the hail shall sweep away every refuge of lies, and that the waters shall cover the hiding-places."

A very extensive improvement might be made of this subject; but I shall confine myself to the three following observations which I deduce, by way of inference, from what has been said. And—

1. We may hence see of what importance it is, that every one of us, for himself, be satisfied that he has submitted to this righteousness, and so fallen in with the design of its manifestation, that we have received it as the righteousness of faith, that we rely upon it exclusively for pardon, acceptance, and eternal life; that we desire to be found in it, not having our own righteousness, which is of the law, and that we enjoy the benefits resulting from a personal interest in it, particularly peace with God, filial confidence in his presence, spiritual intercourse with him, the sanctification of our nature, and the hope of eternal glory. Everything depends on this. Oh, then, let us not rest satisfied without sure and scriptural evidence regarding this most important of all points. If we are right

regarding this, we cannot be materially wrong in regard to other matters relative to salvation; but if we are mistaken here, be it remembered that we are mistaken for eternity.

2. We may also from this subject see the necessity of divine influence to give effect to this important doctrine. The righteousness of God is manifested, but men do not naturally see it. The sun shines, but the blind cannot behold its light. A vail covers the face of man by nature, which hides the glory of this righteousness from his view. It is God alone that can remove this vail (Isa. xxv. 7). It is He "who commanded the light to shine out of darkness, that shines into the heart of benighted sinners, to give the light of the knowledge of the glory of God in the face of Jesus Christ" (2 Cor. iv. 6). It is the peculiar province of the Spirit to "convince men of sin, righteousness, and judgment;" "to guide them into all truth," and "to glorify Christ" (John xvi. 13, 14). It was He who led three thousand on the day of Pentecost to believe the report, and to submit to the righteousness of God. And it is he who, in all ages, discovers to sinners their need of this righteousness, reveals its glory, efficacy, and excellence, to their view, disposes them to acquiesce in it as the foundation upon which they would stand with acceptance before God, and enjoy all the blessings of eternal life and glory. And it is he alone that can give efficacy to the means appointed by God for the salvation of men, and to all the efforts of his creatures to communicate the knowledge of that salvation to their fellow-men, wherever it is preached. How necessary then is it that we should depend much on the Spirit in all our exertions, and pray that his power and presence may be felt by ourselves individually, and accompany our feeble endeavours to instruct others around us in the knowledge of those things which relate to their everlasting peace; that so the righteousness of God, which is manifested in the gospel, and whose light shines

around them, may thus be manifested in the hearts of many, bringing all the blessings of time and eternity in its train!

3. But, lastly. May we not from this see the obligations which lie on all who enjoy the benefit of the *righteousness* which is thus *manifested*, to communicate the knowledge of it to those who are still in darkness and ignorance regarding it? Many both at home and abroad are in this deplorable condition, and must be considered as "perishing for lack of knowledge." And are not we, upon whom the Lord has bestowed the privilege of this revelation, bound by every consideration to do all that we can to meliorate their condition? Are the means afforded us, and shall we withhold these means from them? By so doing should we not be accessory to, and even implicated in, their ruin? "If thou forbear to deliver them that are drawn unto death, and those that are ready to be slain; if thou sayest, Behold, we knew it not, doth not he that pondereth the heart consider it? and he that keepeth thy soul, doth he not know it? and shall not he render to every man according to his works?" (Prov. xxiv. 11, 12). But I trust that many among us are otherwise minded; and that from a regard to the glory of God, and love to the souls of men—from a view of the righteousness which is manifested in the gospel for the benefit of all—from considerations arising out of the love and grace of God manifested in this righteousness, and of the responsibility under which they are placed in reference to a final tribunal, they are willing to "know" the situation of "them that are drawn unto death," and to afford them the means of deliverance.

X.

Man's Redemption the Joy of Angels.

BY THE REV. ALEXANDER STEWART.

"Which things the angels desire to look into."—1 Pet. i. 12.

TO the man of the world the salvation of the gospel is one of the most insipid and uninteresting subjects imaginable. His apathy appears in his treatment of the holy Scriptures, the great record of salvation. The Bible is either read very carelessly, or it is altogether neglected. He sits with listlessness under the preaching of the gospel, indifferent often as to what is said, whether it be true, or whether he understand it or not. And this want of interest, or even a more positive feeling, is but too apparent in the manner in which he makes light of the invitation to the gospel feast, offering the most frivolous excuses for not complying with it. His understanding being "darkened through the ignorance that is in him, and blinded likewise by the god of this world, he is alienated from the life of God." The gospel is hid to him in respect to its glory; he has no apprehension of its transcendent excellence, and no desire to participate in its blessings. Even those of us into whose hearts the light of the glorious gospel has in some measure shined are likewise but too apt to be infected with the same spirit. Surrounded consciously by invisible objects, which are continually soliciting our attention, and yet living among men by whom the great salvation is habitually neglected, we are ever in danger of being overpowered by these unceasing influences, and so of relapsing into a state of spiritual slumber.

There are various ways in which this spirit might be opposed. We might address your fears in the language of the mariners to Jonah—" What meanest thou, O sleeper ? arise, call upon thy God, if so be that God will think upon thee, and that thou perish not." Or we might exhibit to your hopes the great things which God has promised to those who love him; and ask you, if a kingdom which cannot be moved, a crown which fadeth not away, be such trifles as not to be worth making some exertion to obtain them? Or the words of God might once more be re-echoed in your hearing, and the demand made, whether he has not a right to expect attention from his creatures. These might prove powerful considerations; but the one suggested by the words before us is different, and very peculiar. As Paul speaks (Rom. xi. 11) of provoking his brethren, the Jews, to jealousy by the Gentiles, *i. e.* of exciting by a holy emulation amongst the Jews that earnest attention and interest in the gospel which was felt by the Gentiles, so would we endeavour to provoke you to jealousy by the conduct of angels, beings of a totally different order from us. Learn, then, that the salvation of the gospel, the grace manifested to you, the incarnation of God's eternal Son, the life of holiness and beneficence which he led, the miracles which he performed, the grace and truth which, like the dew from heaven, dropped from his lips, the indignities which were offered him, the hardships to which he submitted, the complicated and unparalleled sufferings which he endured, the decease which he accomplished at Jerusalem, his resurrection from the dead, his ascension into heaven, the outpouring of the Holy Ghost, the conversion of sinners, the gospel dispensation, the restoration of the Jews, the calling in and fulness of the Gentiles, the millennial glory, the resurrection of the dead, the consummation of all things at the final judgment—all these, the sufferings of the Messiah, with the glories which were to follow, insipid and uninteresting as they may be to man for whom the mighty interposition was made, are, notwithstanding, things which angels desire to look into.

There seems to be an allusion in the words of the text to the situation and position of the cherubim in the Holy of Holies, a species of reference to the typical service of the law which is perpetually occurring in the New Testament (Exod. xxv. 17–20).

In further illustrating the interesting fact stated in the text, viz., that the sufferings of Messiah, and the glories which resulted from his sufferings, are a subject which strongly engages the attention of angels, it may be proper, in the *first place*, to advert shortly to some things respecting the nature, character, and employments of these celestial spirits; and then, in the *second place*, to inquire what in the mysteries of redemption, as a manifestation of divine glory, makes the subject so deeply interesting to angels.

I. Notice briefly some particulars relating *to the nature, character, and employments of angels.* — Who and what are those beings of whom the apostle speaks? This is evidently necessary in order to understand the passage, and properly to feel its force. If those who discover a deep interest in a subject be adduced as a recommendation of the study of such subject, and an inducement to imitate in this their example, it is obvious that very much indeed depends on the character of these persons. If it is a theme in which persons of exalted genius and of most excellent dispositions find peculiar delight, the inference is that the subject itself must be peculiarly excellent and interesting.

Angels are beings of very high mental and moral endowments. The Scriptures give us sufficient reason to believe that they are an order superior to us. The Psalmist, in the eighth psalm, although speaking of man as having dominion over this lower world, and crowned with glory and honour, still acknowledges, in the same passage, that he "is lower than the angels." The destruction of Sennacherib's army, the pestilence which wasted Israel, the death of the first-born in Egypt, and other similar events ascribed in Scripture to the ministry of angels, afford an appalling idea of that strength in which the Psalmist tells us in another psalm they "excel," so that there seems to be more than a mere poetical imagination in the idea of our great poet that they can arm themselves with the very elements by which we are surrounded. Satan, who is described in Scripture as possessed of peculiar subtlety and power, although an instance of a sadly perverted mind, affords a high idea of the intellectual superiority of angels. The apostle speaks not of fallen angels, but of those who kept their first estate, and *who are holy beings,* and are expressly called in the Scriptures *holy angels.*

Such being the high order of intelligences to which angels belong, attend next to the very peculiar means of improvement which they possess. They dwell in heaven, in God's immediate presence, the place of his glory, and the habitation of his throne. The angels see God's face. In this expression there is a reference to the practice of Eastern kings, who admitted none but their chief counsellors and favourites into their presence. This is an honour which is not granted to any sinful mortal man, for God said to Moses, "Thou canst not see my face, for no man can see me and live." But in the conclusion of the book of Revelation we are told that God's servants shall *in heaven* see his face. They shall enjoy a full manifestation of his glory, and be admitted, in a certain degree, into his counsels.

Now, this is a privilege which the angels have always enjoyed. They are represented as the immediate attendants of the King Eternal. When Isaiah saw in vision the Lord sitting upon a throne high and lifted up, the seraphim were in attendance, and worshipping, they cried one unto another, "Holy, holy, holy is the Lord of Hosts." "God's chariots," says the Psalmist (lxviii. 17), "are twenty thousand, even thousands of angels; the Lord is *among them*, as in the holy place." "Take heed," said Christ (Matt. xviii. 10), "that ye despise not one of these little ones: for I say unto you, That in heaven their angels do always behold the face of my Father which is in heaven." In the book of Revelation, where we have a glimpse of the heavenly world, we see that the holy angels surround the throne of God, they contemplate his glory, and they "do his commandments, hearkening to the voice of his word" (Psa. ciii. 20). They are angels of light, and they dwell in the world of light. No human being was in existence when God created the heavens and the earth. Man saw not then the wonders of creation. Hence God demands of Job (xxxviii. 4), "Where wast *thou* when I laid the foundations of the earth? Who hath laid the measures thereof, if thou knowest? or who hath stretched the line upon it? Whereupon are the foundations thereof fastened? or who laid the corner-stone thereof?" But when God prepared the heavens, and set a compass on the face of the deep, when thick darkness was the swaddling-band of the infant world, and when he commanded light to shine out of darkness, these sons of the morning were present, and sang together, these elder sons of God shouted for joy.

Not only did the angels witness the wisdom, power, and

goodness manifested in creation, they have likewise witnessed the events which have since then taken place in this world. They saw our first parents happy in Paradise, and afterwards expelled for their transgression. They saw Noah and his family enter the ark, and the avenging waters of the deluge sweep away an ungodly world. They saw Abraham leave his kindred and his father's house, and wander a stranger and a pilgrim in the land of promise. They saw Israel oppressed in Egypt, delivered by a strong hand and outstretched arm, led through the wilderness, and settled in Canaan. They have seen the rise and fall of empires, and interesting events of which we are in absolute ignorance. And we must take into account the advantage they had in understanding these events as a part of the dispensation of providence to them. Their knowledge of the facts must be correct, because they witnessed them, and likewise had access to know their causes. While not pretending to define the extent to which angels are acquainted with the purposes of divine providence, it is unquestionable that they have not only extensive knowledge of historical matters of fact, but likewise of the connection of such events with the general dispensation of providence as illustrative of the divine character. They are behind the curtain which conceals the invisible world from our view. What we call the light of revelation seems to be but some scanty rays of the noonday splendour in which they dwell penetrating this curtain.

Now apply these remarks to our present subject. The angels we have seen are superior beings of very high powers of mind. They are furnished likewise with most ample means of improvement and of increasing their knowledge. At what time they were created we are not told; but as Adam was tempted by a fallen angel, there can be no doubt they were created before man. For these six thousand years at least, then, with minds which were never darkened by sin, free from all the imbecility of infancy or of age, or the infirmity of mortality, with the wide field of creation and with a most extensive view of the dispensations of providence before them, God himself being their instructor, they have been contemplating His character, as illustrated by the wonders which He is continually performing. And what, think you, is the subject which rivets the attention of these exalted spirits? It is the sufferings of Christ, and the glorious consequences. The stable at Bethlehem, and the garden of Gethsemane, and the hill of Calvary, furnish illustrations of the divine character which they find nowhere else. And the angels, the inhabitants of heaven, leave its glories for a season to learn, from what is taking place in the earth, new songs of adoring praise.

Among us, if one discovers a star which no other observed before him, or writes a history of some nation, or accomplishes some literary or scientific achievement, he is straightway applauded as a man of genius and science, and among men he may he entitled to the distinction, nor do we by any means grudge him the honour; but when, like the philosophers of Greece, such an one begins to vaunt himself, and to despise Christ crucified as foolishness, it is high time to remind him that the angels who celebrated the creation of the very star which he has now discovered—the angels, any one of whom knows more of the destiny of the world than all the men on earth together—the angels who lived in heaven thousands of years before he was born—instead of considering the cross of Christ foolishness, turn to it with admiration as an object which eclipses every other manifestation of the divine glory! I apprehend their language would be similar to that of Paul, when speaking of the comparative excellence of the Jewish and Christian dispensations, "Creation is glorious indeed, but it has no glory in this respect, by reason of the glory (of the cross) that excelleth." But philosophers are not the only characters that see no excellence in the cross of Christ. We are surrounded by multitudes who can find in their daily worldly employments and amusements subjects of far keener interest. Oh! is it not wonderful, has it never struck you as surprising, that the angels who never sinned, happy although Christ had never come into the world, should yet feel more interested in the great salvation than the sinners for whom he died?

II. Consider now *what, in the mysteries of redemption, makes the subject so deeply interesting to angels,* i.e. why do angels desire to look into these things? Here, then—

Negatively, it is not vain or impertinent curiosity. One of the considerations which induced Eve to eat of the forbidden fruit was that the tree was desirable to make *one wise;* she and her husband expected "to be as gods, knowing *good* and *evil.*" They were discontented with the amount of information which God had been pleased to vouchsafe to them, and by unlawful means attempted to pry into what was forbidden. The same disposition continues to characterise their posterity; while, on the one hand, we continue in a state of ignorance of those things which are of the highest importance, and which God has been mercifully pleased to reveal to us, we are on the other very prone, curiously to search into what is not revealed, into what God purposely conceals from us. We are not diligent and anxious to be wise up to what is written, and yet we often attempt to be wise about what is not written. Hence it was that when God descended on Sinai, he gave solemn injunctions to Moses to set a fence around the mount to prevent the people breaking through to gaze.

But such is not the disposition of angels. These exalted and pure spirits have such views of the infinite majesty of God as humble them in the dust. The mystery of redemption is to a certain extent unfolded to them, and so far as God has been pleased to make the revelation, they shew their gratitude and admiration by studiously and earnestly contemplating it. But a step farther they presume not to go. Anything like an irreverent familiarity with God, anything like a scrutinising arraigning spirit, so common, alas! among foolhardy creatures on earth, is utterly unknown among them.

Since, then, to speak more *positively*, it cannot be from a principle of vain or impertinent curiosity the angels desire to look into the mysteries of redemption, the question recurs, What is it that thus so deeply engages their attention? Were you, my friends, to see the ark of the testimony, and the cherubim intently looking upon the mercy-seat, and were you at the same time made aware of the spiritual import of these emblems, might not the wish very naturally arise in your breasts, "Would that the cherubim spake, that we might know the subject of their thoughts, and the cause of their admiration, as they stand gazing on the wondrous mercy-seat!" Well, on one occasion they actually did speak, they did break silence—not the golden figures, but the angels themselves which these cherubim represented. One night (Luke ii. 8–15), as certain shepherds were watching their flocks on the plains of Bethlehem, "the angel of the Lord came upon them, and the glory of the Lord shone round about them, and they were sore afraid. And the angel said to them, Fear not: for, behold, I bring you good tidings of great joy, which shall be to all people. For unto you is born this day, in the city of David, a Saviour, which is Christ the Lord. And this shall be a sign unto you; Ye shall find the babe wrapped in swaddling clothes, lying in a manger. And suddenly there was with the angel a multitude of the heavenly host, praising God, and saying, Glory to God in the highest,"—in the highest heavens, among the highest order of intelligences, who are the inhabitants of the high and holy place—" on earth peace, goodwill toward men," *i. e.* salvation to men ! Such was the song of angels when they announced the incarnation of Him whom the mercy-seat typified ; such, as we learn from their own lips, are the sentiments which fill their hearts and minds as they steadily contemplate the humiliation of Messiah, and the consequences of his sufferings.

As holy creatures, they derive their chief happiness from beholding the glory of God. In the mystery of redemption the divine glory is manifested in a manner so singular, so remarkable, as to attract the notice and admiration of angels, and to afford them a delight so great that with incessant and unwearied earnestness they look into it. This indeed is one great end which was to be accomplished by the redemption of man. The apostle informs us that the unsearchable riches of Christ, and the manifestation of Him who was the brightness of the divine glory—the great mystery of godliness, God manifested in the flesh—that this mystery which, from the beginning of the world, had been hid in God, was so revealed—that Christ was now seen of angels—for this among other reasons, that unto the principalities and powers in heavenly places, might be known by the church the manifold wisdom of God (Eph. iii. 9, 10). And further, the angels' song discovers to us likewise that they not only desire to look into the singular manifestation of the divine glory, but also that, as beings of the highest and most disinterested benevolence, they delight in contemplating the blessed consequences of the Redeemer's sufferings in the salvation of myriads of the human race. "Peace on earth," they say, "and goodwill to men." Thus are we furnished with a twofold reply to the question, "Why do angels desire so earnestly to look into the sufferings and glory of Messiah?" They do so, *first*, because in these things they behold a peculiar manifestation of the divine glory; and *secondly*, because, as benevolent beings, they rejoice in the salvation of sinners.

Let us inquire, then, how the scheme of redemption affords a manifestation of the divine glory even to angels.

Here we must bear in mind the character and attainments of these exalted spirits. There are many things which to children are matters of the utmost astonishment, which excite no such surprise in persons of maturer years. Men, even prophets and apostles, are but children in comparison with these sons of the morning of creation. They are children *in capacity* compared with the elder sons of God. Were a person born and brought up in the retirement of the country to be introduced at court, made acquainted with the policy of the empire and the affairs of the State, and were he shewn the wonderful works of art with which the metropolis of a mighty empire abounds, he might very probably be overwhelmed with wonder, whilst persons born and bred in the metropolis would view them with comparative indifference. Now, the holy angels are the inhabitants of the metropolis of the universe, the city of the great King. They live and have always been in the court of the *King of kings*. If, then, the cross of Christ be an object which angels stoop from heaven to contemplate, if it be such as to rivet the attention even of these natives of heaven, who have for ages been favoured with various manifestations of the divine character, it can be no ordinary object. It must, if only in common with the other works of God, be glorious; but it must in some important respects excel in glory. What we have to inquire into, then, is the pre-eminence, the excellency, of the glory of redemption.

The mystery of redemption excels in glory, because in it each particular attribute is more illustriously manifested than in any of the works of God.

There are two circumstances which prevent us from experiencing the overwhelming astonishment on this subject which otherwise we certainly should. The *one* is the blindness of our minds, and our ignorance of the exceedingly rigid principles of the divine government. We are, as the Psalmist says, apt to think "God such an one as ourselves." The *other* is, that we are taught from our very infancy that *God's own Son* became *man* to save sinners; hence this great truth is to us very much deprived of its novelty, and also of its moral grandeur. But this is not the case with angels. They lived before a Saviour was known or needed, and while they experienced the riches of the divine goodness, a mysterious dispensation had deeply imprinted on their minds a most awful sense of the divine justice and the purity of God. They had seen their own companions, once holy and happy as they were, presuming to sin against their Maker. The punishment of the crime seems to have instantaneously followed the commission of it. The rebels were expelled from heaven, and cast into outer darkness. They had seen the earth when she opened her mouth and swallowed up Korah and his company, and had heard *their* cry as they descended alive into the pit. Had you seen the fiery destruction which overthrew Sodom and Gomorrah, had you seen the avenging waters of the deluge sweep away into perdition the myriads of an ungodly world, you might then have some faint conception of the feelings of awe and fear which filled the minds of the holy angels when they saw hell—that terrible and then unknown place—first open her jaws to receive the apostate spirits. Such a dispensation must have impressed their minds with a sense of the divine purity, justice, and majesty, which nothing short of annihilation could erase. Conceive then, if you can, with what sentiments of astonishment these celestial spirits must have witnessed this great and dreadful God, this consuming fire, assuming the character and the office of the SAVIOUR OF SINNERS. The *Creator* a *creature!*

The *Eternal* an *infant of days!* The *Omnipotent* a *man* compassed with infirmities! The Supreme *Lawgiver* made *of a woman*, made "under the *curse*" of a *violated law!* The Majesty *of heaven and earth* an object of insult and derision to those very devils whom so lately his own right hand had hurled into hell! He who is emphatically *the Living One*, the Author and the Prince of Life, stretched cold and lifeless in the tomb! And what I cannot but feel to be the greatest wonder of all, *the Holy One*—He whose absolute holiness angels adore with veiled face—submitting to have sin imputed to him, to have sin brought into immediate contact with him, to be charged with guilt—remaining speechless as if guilty, standing like a condemned criminal at the judgment-seat of God and man, to be numbered with transgressors, and suffering the vilest, the most ignominious of deaths, as if he were the very "chief of sinners"!

Every part of the work of creation displays skill and contrivance which manifest the Creator as the only wise God. But in the cross of Christ there is a *hidden and mysterious wisdom*, which excelleth all. There are two ways in which a law can be honoured—one by rewarding the obedient, the other by punishing the disobedient. But through the sufferings of Christ, the law of God is not only upheld simply in honour, it is actually *more glorified* by the salvation of the transgressor, who believes in Jesus, than it could possibly be by his condemnation (Rom. iii. 25). Sin is the greatest of all evils, the cause of all the suffering in the universe; but such is the wisdom of the cross that sin, the very essence of evil, is made the occasion of the greatest good. The apostle says, the foolishness of God is wiser, that is greater, than the wisdom of man. Through the cross, it turns even the deepest-laid devices of Satan into folly. How did the seed of the woman bruise the serpent's head? By *power?* No! but by *weakness!* By the aid of his friends? No! but by the machinations of enemies! He let them have their *will*. He permitted them to seize, crucify, kill, bury him; and it was in being thus defeated that he conquered. The ignominy of the accursed tree was his honour; his death was his victory. It was upon the very cross to which his enemies nailed him in malicious triumph that he triumphed over principalities and powers, and made a show of them openly. "In the day ye eat of the tree," said Satan to Eve, "ye shall be as gods, knowing good and evil," meaning, in his heart, that they should be such gods as he and his associates were, knowing *good lost*, by the bitter experience of *evil*. But such is the *wisdom of the cross*, that the *very lies* of Satan are converted *into truth*, to his utter confusion. Holy angels know *good* only. Satan knows evil, and *good* only by its loss. But redeemed sinners knew, as their deceiver meant, good lost by the experience of evil; but now, through the bitterness of evil and the sweetness of good, they are made like the Son of God. Oh, how truly incomprehensible is that wisdom which devised a scheme by which seeming impossibilities are performed, and things seemingly incompatible are reconciled! A holy God reconciled with sinful man; the law more honoured in the salvation of sinners than it is either in the happiness of angels or the misery of devils; the greatest good extracted from the very essence of evil; Satan's schemes frustrated by their very success; the cross of Christ the instrument of *his* triumph; and the world, where God had been most dishonoured, made such a theatre of his glory as attracts the very inhabitants of heaven! Well might the apostle exclaim, "Oh, the depth of the riches both of the wisdom and knowledge of God!"

How astonishing is *the power* of that simple word which created the heavens and the earth out of absolute nothing! But how more wondrous far is the greatness of that *strength* in which the Redeemer travelled when he made bare his arm, and came, "mighty to save." "Who knoweth the power of thine anger!"

said the Psalmist. Consider the manifestations of divine power which took place at the deluge, when the windows of heaven were opened and the fountains of the abyss were broken up, and the earth reeled and staggered like a drunken man. Contemplate the still more awful display of divine anger which shall take place on that day when the wrath of God shall be revealed from heaven, the elements melting with fervent heat, the heavens passing away like a scroll, the world in flames. Yet these are but the preludes of wrath. The flames of a burning world are but the glittering of the sword of divine justice when it is unsheathed. The devils are angels, and mighty angels, who excel in strength; but even they cannot endure the power of God's anger; it would annihilate them. They must endure it by degrees, and compensate by length of duration for an intensity of suffering which no created being could support. But the man Christ Jesus endured the wrath of God *alone*, and to the uttermost. Oh, what tremendous manifestation of power was there! The Prince of Life, sinking to the dust of death beneath his Almighty Father's wrath! In other cases, we contemplate God creating out of nothing, or doing his will with *mere* creatures which are supported by his hand. But here, we almost tremble as we speak it, we see a divine person inflicting a degree of suffering which nothing but the omnipotence of another divine person could support. Well might angels contemplate with wonder the sufferings of Him who is "the power of God." What an awful display of divine justice, of divine purity, and of divine hatred of sin was there! High in rank as angels are, they are still but creatures. Here however the Lord of angels suffers. In their case it was the personally guilty who suffered. In Christ's, the personally innocent. He suffered for others, not for himself. One might have imagined that his motive in suffering would disarm the hand of justice, that justice could not strike excellence so unparalleled. But such is the absolute inflexibility of this divine attribute, that when the Son of God himself stood in the room of the guilty, he was not spared.

Once more, how infinitely does the cross of Christ transcend every manifestation of the *divine love*. What are the riches of the universe, of heaven itself in all its glory, in comparison with the Creator himself—the unspeakable gift? They are but as the very dust of the balance—as dross, as nothing. " Herein is love" to make angels wonder; " God so loved the world, that he gave his only begotten Son, that whosoever believeth in him should not perish, but have everlasting life." The love of Christ in its length, and breadth, and depth, and height, is beyond the mighty grasp even of angels' comprehension.

Thus does redemption excel in glory, inasmuch as there is a *wisdom* in its contrivance, a *power* in its execution, a *goodness* in the deliverance wrought by it, and an infinite *rectitude* in the means by which the deliverance is accomplished, which immeasurably surpass all other manifestations of the divine perfections.

The pre-eminent glory of redemption appears further, in that excellencies which elsewhere are manifested separately are here combined. The works of creation afford abundant illustration of the wisdom and power of God; but the traces of his moral attributes are by no means so apparent therein. In heaven all exult in the goodness of God; but there is no practical display of His justice, and of the severer attributes of his nature. In hell God's justice and purity are awfully manifested. He appears as an offended King and Judge; but there is little evidence of his kindness as a Father who hath no pleasure in the death of him that dieth. Nor is there in this, you will observe, any discernible *inconsistency*. The miseries of a place of punishment may not directly illustrate the goodness of God, but they are not *inconsistent* with his goodness. The joys of heaven may not display God's anger, but neither are they *inconsistent* with his being angry. It is not an inconsistency, but rather a speciality in the occasion (as being a limited one from the very nature of things), in consequence of which there is but a partial illustration of the divine character. Now, the peculiar excellence in redemption, to which we at present call your attention, is, that it is entirely free from any such imperfection; that it illustrates the divine attributes, not separately, but in combination, not partially, but fully. It not only exceeds each, but it combines all. In the cross of Christ, not only is *divine justice* more awfully illustrated than in hell itself, *goodness* more gloriously than in heaven, *power* and *wisdom* more illustriously than in the works of creation; but the cross contains in itself all that is to be known of God in heaven, in earth, and in hell together. All the lovely tints of the rainbow that surrounds the throne blend here in purest, intensest, light. In the cross of Christ, the glory of God is manifested in all the colourless purity of meridian splendour.

The pre-eminence of redemption appears in its possessing a glory peculiar to itself, a glory found nowhere else. For anything we can learn from the Bible, an angel might traverse the vast extent of creation; he might, with the eyes of heaven, look into the depths of hell, and yet never discover that God was merciful, gracious, and long-suffering; that he both would and could pass over transgression and sin. Mercy seems to partake so much of human weakness that it might be deemed almost incompatible with the unsullied purity and unbending rectitude of the divine nature. But the cross of Christ demonstrates that God is merciful; that though he be infinitely holy, even a consuming fire, he can, nevertheless, without tarnishing his purity in the slightest degree, endure with much long-suffering the provocation of sinners; that although he be just and right, and without iniquity, he can, nevertheless, without deviating from the strictest rectitude, justify the ungodly. Nay, so far in this case is mercy from encroaching on purity, truth, justice, or any of those perfections towards which it seems most unfriendly, that these attributes are actually more glorified, more conspicuously illustrated, than if mercy never existed. Never did judgment appear more awfully sacred and glorious than at the very time that "mercy rejoiced over it."

But let us consider how such a manifestation could affect angels. For although they be sinless creatures, and therefore in no personal need of mercy, yet the fact that God is merciful, is a discovery of very high interest and importance to them as well as to us. We cannot say that angels in a state of innocence feel pain; yet when they considered the fate of their companions, and their own situation, they must at times have been filled with care approaching at least to painful apprehensions. They must have felt as if standing on the brink of a precipice—their footing not so secure, so firm, but a slight error might precipitate them irrecoverably—might infinitely remove them beyond the very possibility of restoration. God must have appeared to them utterly without mercy, incapable of anything like forbearance towards creatures—creatures certainly by no means incapable either of sinning or suffering—and this arising directly from the absolute perfection of his nature, as the polish and lustre of a diamond are due to its extreme hardness. In private life you may perhaps have met with a man of very high sense of honour—a man whom you would pronounce incapable of a mean or dishonourable action, but who, if you had inadvertently given him any cause of offence, would prove inexorable and unforgiving. In your intercourse with him, although his politeness and attention might be very agreeable while they lasted, you would yet be pursued by a disagreeable fear that they might be suddenly arrested. Something you may have thoughtlessly said has most unintentionally, but too certainly, given him great offence. The breach of friendship is irreparable, for he has no toleration for a failure of which he himself is incapable! Some such feeling as this—a feeling of the brittleness of the tenure by which they held their place, might sometimes have occurred to angels, an apprehension which the fate of their companions was by no means calculated to diminish. Now, the glory of redemption is that it removes all such painful apprehensions, so far as the character of the infinitely holy God is concerned. The Cross demonstrates the blessed truth that God is not only a Sovereign of infinite majesty, and a Judge of inexorable righteousness, but that the great God has the heart of a Father; that he punishes,—not because he has no feeling for the sufferings of his sinful creatures, for "his name is love," "he delighteth in mercy," "he has no pleasure in the death of a sinner," "and judgment is his strange work,"—but because the sovereign demands of righteousness in the All-supreme Governor require, when the occasion arises, that the irrevocable doom shall be pronounced.

Mercy, however, is His delight; what he does from choice—what it gives him pleasure to do. Oh! with what sacred, what intense interest must angels have pondered testimonies to the divine character in terms like these, "As I live, saith the Lord, I have no pleasure in the death of him that dieth" (Ezek. xxxiii. 11). "Like as a father pitieth his children, so the Lord pitieth them that fear him" (Psa. ciii. 13)—absolutely, unchangeably. Perfect as he is, he yet "knoweth and considereth the frame" of his creatures. "Can a mother forget her sucking child, that she should not have compassion on the son of her womb? yea, they may forget, yet will I not forget thee" (Isa. xlix. 15). "I could wish myself accursed for my brethren," said Paul; but God first took upon himself the nature of man, and then actually made himself accursed for his brethren.

When Christ came near and saw the city of Jerusalem, he wept over it. Angels might indeed adore with profoundest awe the Eternal Majesty seated on a throne, of which it is said that Justice and Judgment are its habitation. They might thank him with all their heart for his innumerable favours. But the Almighty God, in human nature, weeping over sinners —God in tears—is a sight which must have for ever enshrined him in their hearts! This is the all-surpassing glory of redemption, a circumstance in which it indeed excels in glory.

God created the worlds by Jesus Christ; and Christ by his Spirit made the heavens (Psa. xxxiii. 6). But from the work of creation itself we could never have learnt the distinction of persons in the ever-blessed Trinity. By the work of redemption, however, this glorious distinction is made apparent. We are thereby admitted into a view of the divine nature which we could never have imagined, nor comprehended otherwise. Not only God glorified generally, but each of the divine persons manifesting forth his own peculiar glory.

Finally, the cross excels in glory, because it illustrates, sheds a lustre on, everything else. The prophet says, "God created the earth not in vain, but he formed it to be inhabited" (Isa. xlv. 18)—words which evidently intimate that, were the earth not inhabited it would, in a certain sense, be a world in vain. What would the world and all its contents be were it not for man, were it not that it ministers to the support and education of spirits who shall live for ever? Many objects derive an interest and importance from circumstances to which nothing in themselves gives them any title. The admirers of ancient history know well the enthusiasm which classic names and classic objects inspire; and it were easy to make mention of places and objects in our own country, in themselves very insignificant, such as no traveller would think of observing, but they are hallowed in our remembrance—the spots where patriots have fought, or martyrs have fallen—or where our ancestors, driven by persecution from their homes, have met together to worship the God of their fathers. And that man is not to be envied who could walk unmoved throughout the highly-favoured land where patriarchs wandered as strangers and pilgrims, where prophets delivered their predictions, where apostles first proclaimed the gospel, where angels conversed with men, and where the Prince of prophets and apostles and angels lived and died.

What *Judea* is to us, the *earth* is to the angels. Insignificant the world may be in itself, poor and worthless we its sinful inhabitants may be—but this is our glory, that the Creator himself tabernacled for a time amongst us; that the earth we tread was trodden by him; that the sun that enlightens us shone on him; that the air we breathe was breathed by him. Once it was man's highest glory that he was beautified with the image of God; but his glory now is that God himself has become man.

The salvation of the cross sheds a lustre on the dispensations of providence. What are those mighty empires which, in our youthful days, we were taught to admire? In Scripture they are denoted by the emblem of "beasts of prey." The page of history is filled with pictures of human ambition, tinselled by what is only the semblance of virtue. To our apprehension, on a review of those dim ages past, their intrinsic insignificance and vanity are perceived. But this speedily disappears when we recognise the ever-ruling providence of the Eternal Sovereign, who guides all events, however insignificant, in preparation for that kingdom which cannot be moved.

The cross makes heaven itself more glorious. It is the place where God confers on his people the rewards of the Redeemer's sufferings; whilst hell is the place where are confined the enemies of the Redeemer, the place to save men from which the Son of God died.

Angels, as beings of pure and disinterested benevolence, we have said, delight in contemplating the happy consequences of Christ's sufferings in the salvation of myriads of the human race. Amongst us superior privileges invariably excite envy. Joseph was greatly beloved and favoured by his father Jacob; and this exposed him to the envy and hatred of his brethren. Were angels in the least disposed to envy, they could find far greater reason for it than they. That a race of beings inferior to themselves should be so peculiarly honoured as that God himself should take their nature into union with his own, would have been astonishing enough. But that this condescension should be exhibited towards sinful rebellious creatures, and that they should be exalted to an equality of rank and privileges with them, beings of undoubtedly higher order, would be peculiarly surprising, and that which, in fallen human nature, would have inevitably awakened feelings of jealousy and hatred. But angels have no pride of rank or of birth, for they greatly rejoice in the salvation of men and sinners. They rejoice in the addition of a new order of creatures to the heavenly society. They might have rejoiced at the prospect of this indeed at the creation of man; but the parables of the fifteenth of Luke inform us that the recovery of man, dead and lost, is, emphatically, their joy.

The general principles upon which a sinner of the human race is saved are precisely the same in respect to each individual. There is one common Saviour, one atonement, one faith, one hope; all are in this respect saved in the same way. But while there is thus but one Spirit, there is a great diversity of operation, according to the peculiar circumstances and dispositions of individuals. This must have occurred to every one who has read with interest the lives of Abraham, David, or any pious person, either recorded in Scripture or not. You

M

cannot say, after concluding the life of any distinguished saint, that you have found one who is saved in a manner different from other sinners; nevertheless there is a peculiarity always in each case which gives us new and interesting views of the manifold grace of God.

Such is a specimen of the society of heaven. Are we fit for that society? Are we preparing for it? Or are we still under the influence of the malignant fallen Angel? And are we content to be his wretched companions and captives for ever? What a reproof to the apathy of man is the deep interest which angels discover in the gospel! For us was the Saviour given—for us He suffered and died. To us has the word of salvation been sent and preached, yet what listless indifference do we manifest! What frivolous excuses do we make for that indifference! "How shall we escape, if we neglect so great salvation?" "Kiss ye the Son lest he be angry, and ye perish from the way!"

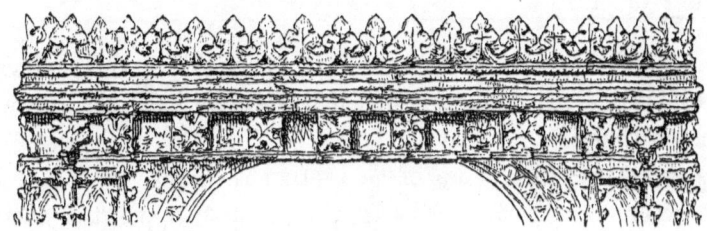

XI.

𝔗𝔥𝔢 𝔊𝔩𝔬𝔯𝔶 𝔬𝔣 𝔊𝔬𝔡 𝔱𝔥𝔢 𝔍𝔫𝔰𝔱𝔯𝔲𝔪𝔢𝔫𝔱 𝔬𝔣 𝔬𝔲𝔯 𝔖𝔞𝔫𝔠𝔱𝔦𝔣𝔦𝔠𝔞𝔱𝔦𝔬𝔫.

BY THE REV. PATRICK M'FARLAN, D.D.

"BUT WE ALL, WITH OPEN FACE BEHOLDING AS IN A GLASS THE GLORY OF THE LORD, ARE CHANGED INTO THE SAME IMAGE, FROM GLORY TO GLORY, EVEN AS BY THE SPIRIT OF THE LORD."—2 COR. iii. 18.

THERE is nothing more completely established by the history of the human race than that a man's moral character is moulded by his religious belief. The gods of the ancient Greeks and Romans were monsters of impurity and vice, and their character was reflected in those who worshipped them. "Even as they did not like to retain God in their knowledge, God gave them over to a reprobate mind, to do those things which are not convenient." Popery, with its masses and penances and indulgences and purgatory, bears fruit corresponding with the false conceptions which it conveys of God, and the way of acceptance with him and the path of obedience. Professing Christians, thoughtless and indifferent about religion, ignorant of the true God and eternal life, make a god of the world, and resemble the object of their idolatry. Their maxims and manners and habits of life are the maxims and manners and habits of life of those with whom they associate. Real

Christians, knowing the one living and true God, and believing in him, are "renewed in knowledge after the image of him who created them."

Accordingly the Word of God—that is, the revelation of his character and perfections—is the divinely-appointed instrument of the sinner's conversion, the instrument in the hand of the Spirit by which the soul is renewed, and the sinner becomes a new creature in Christ Jesus. It was when Saul of Tarsus beheld the glory of the Saviour on the way to Damascus—not his visible glory only, but the light of the knowledge of the glory of God in him—he lay prostrate before him, and exchanging the enmity of his unconverted state for humble submission to the Saviour, cried out, "Lord, what wilt thou have me to do!" It is the instrument of our sanctification also. It was when Job saw as it were with his eyes the glory of Jehovah, that he felt more deeply than he had ever done before, his own vileness, and in contrition and self-abasement exclaimed, "I heard of thee by the hearing of the ear, but now mine eye seeth thee: wherefore I abhor myself, and repent in dust and ashes."

The same important truth is declared in the words of the text. In the preceding part of the chapter the apostle, contending against the Judaising teachers, refers with joy and gratitude to the blessed influence of his preaching, and that of his fellow-labourers, on the life and conduct of the converted Corinthians, "Ye are our epistle," &c. (verses 2, 3). He then compares together the Old and New Testament dispensations, arguing, "if (ver. 7) the ministration of death, written and engraven in stones, was glorious, so that the children of Israel could not stedfastly behold the face of Moses for the glory of his countenance; which glory was to be done away; how shall not the ministration of the Spirit be rather glorious?" He alludes to the shining of the skin of Moses' face when he came down from his forty days' abode upon the mount, a splendour so bright that until he put a vail on his face, Aaron and the people of Israel were afraid to come nigh to him. That visible splendour was emblematical of the moral glory of the old dispensation; and the vail which was put on Moses' face represented the inability of the people of Israel to look stedfastly to the end of that which is abolished, namely, to Christ, the end of the Sinai covenant, "the end of the law for righteousness." Their minds were blinded; "for until this day," adds Paul, "remaineth the same vail untaken away in the reading of the Old Testament." It is otherwise with New Testament believers. "Where the Spirit of the Lord is, there is liberty;" liberty from the law as a covenant of works, liberty from the fear of the coming wrath, liberty to come boldly unto a throne of grace, the spirit of adoption, whereby we cry Abba Father; liberty to look with confidence on him as our reconciled God and Father in Christ, so that "beholding with open face as in a glass the glory of the Lord, we are changed into the same image, from glory to glory, even as by the Spirit of the Lord."

In discoursing from these words, I purpose, in the *first* place, to consider what we are to understand by "the glory of the Lord;" *secondly*, what is meant by beholding it as in a glass, with face unvailed; *thirdly*, the fruit or effect of thus beholding the glory of the Lord; and *fourthly*, the operation of the Spirit in this great work.

I. "The glory of the Lord," in the most extended sense of that expression, is *the glory of all his perfections* in all the relations in which he stands to his intelligent creatures; the glory of his power, and wisdom, and goodness, as these are manifested in the visible creation, in the preservation of his creatures, in his moral government, and, above all, in the scheme of redemption by Christ Jesus. The psalmist speaks of his glory in the first of these relations, when he says, in the nineteenth Psalm, "The heavens declare the glory of God; and the firmament sheweth his handy-work;" and in the 104th Psalm, "O Lord, how manifold are thy works! in wisdom hast thou made them all. . . . The glory of the Lord shall endure for ever." In the second of these relations, when he says, in the thirty-fourth Psalm, "The angel of the Lord encampeth round about them that fear him, and delivereth them." In the moral government of the world, when he says, "The Lord is in his holy temple; the Lord's throne is in heaven, his eyes behold, his eye-lids try the children of men;" and in the work of redemption, when he says, in the 102d Psalm, "When the Lord shall build up Zion, he shall appear in his glory. He will regard the prayer of the destitute, and not despise their prayer." And, in order to have just conceptions of Jehovah in any one of these relations, it is necessary to have just conceptions of him in all. We do not conceive rightly of the glory of his condescension, unless we apprehend him also in the glory of his power and majesty; or of his mercy, unless we see him in the spotless beauty of his holiness, and in his inflexible justice; or of his wisdom in the plan of our redemption, unless we have some understanding of the immutability of his character and government, and the eternal obligation of his law.

. It is of his moral glory, however, that the apostle speaks in the text; that glory which it is the privilege of his redeemed people, in their own measure and degree, to attain, when, through the Spirit of the Lord, they are metamorphosed into the image of their Father in heaven. They cannot resemble him in his infinity and immensity, in the unsearchableness of his wisdom, or the greatness of his power. But they may resemble him, and it is his will that they should resemble him, in the purity of his character, in his abhorrence of sin and his love of holiness, in his condescension and compassion; his forgiving mercy, his love, his abounding goodness, his unceasing beneficence. These constitute the moral glory of the God of our salvation—a glory which shines in creation and in providence, but above all in redemption. This is that glory which especially forms the subject of adoring wonder and gratitude in the hosts in heaven, and which ought from day to day to be the subject of humble inquiring contemplation by saints on earth.

If you ask me, Where is it to be seen? I answer, as I have already done, Everywhere; in all that you behold, in every work of his hand, in all that history—inspired and uninspired—records of his wonderful dealings to angels and men; in the creation of both, in the beauties of perfect holiness and the enjoyment of perfect bliss, in the punishment of the angels who kept not their first estate, and of man when he fell by his disobedience; in the promise of a Saviour to our guilty race, and in the long-suffering and forbearance of a God not willing that any should perish, but that all should turn unto him and live; in the flood which destroyed the world of the ungodly, in the mercy which saved a very small remnant, that they and their posterity might be witnesses to his faithfulness and love; in the mission of the only-begotten Son of God, that whosoever believeth in him should not perish, but have everlasting life; in the conversion and salvation of a countless multitude of the human race, and the final and everlasting punishment of the impenitent and ungodly. In all this we have the manifestation of the glory of the Lord. And there is this peculiar excellence in that manifestation, that no one divine perfection shines to the eclipsing or diminishing of another; but each adds to another's brightness. His majesty is not obscured by his condescension, his holiness is not tarnished by his mercy. Jehovah is perfect, his work is perfect, his character is perfect.

It is in the face or person of Jesus Christ that the light of the knowledge of the glory of God is most strikingly displayed; in the marvellous fact that the Son of God has become the Son of man, that God was manifested in flesh, that on this glorious divine Mediator the Lord laid the iniquity of us all; that he suffered the penalty due to our transgressions, and thus magnified the law and made it honourable, that through him, whosoever believeth in him should be justified from all things from which he could not be justified by his obedience to the law. It is here that God is revealed in all the immutability of his justice, and all the riches of his grace; here especially that there is everything to command the reverence, to melt the heart, and to win the affection and willing obedience of sinful and rebellious creatures. Christ crucified is the power of God, and the wisdom of God. Christ lifted up on the cross draws all men to him.

Add to this the manifestation of the divine glory in the life and character of the Son of man. Whoso hath seen him hath seen the Father. For he did no sin, he fulfilled all righteousness, he transgressed no commandment, he obeyed every ordinance; he was as pure in heart as he was without spot in external obedience. There was no defect, no imperfection in him. He was the Holy One of God, the Just, the Righteous One, the perfect image of the Father in holiness as well as in wisdom and in power; the brightness of his glory, the express image of his person.

II. Let us now proceed, as was proposed, in the *second* place, to consider what is meant by "*beholding as in a glass, with unvailed face,* the glory of the Lord." By "a glass," you are to understand a mirror or looking-glass. In ancient times these were made, as you learn from the book of Exodus, chap. xxxviii., not of glass, but of polished metal; and the reflection produced by them was more or less bright according to the perfection of the workmanship. We can look more easily on a brilliant light when thus reflected, than we can when we look upon it directly. For example, we can look upon the reflection of the midday sun on the smooth surface of a lake, while we cannot, without pain and even injury to our eyesight, look upon it directly.

In like manner, and for the reason to which we have now alluded, God has not communicated to us directly, and in its brightest radiance, the knowledge of his character and perfections. That is reserved for a higher and better state of being—that glorious state of being in which the saints shall see God face to face, and shall be like him, because they shall see him as he is. "Thou canst not see my face," said the Lord to Moses; "for there shall no man see me and live." There is something so awful, so overpowering in the full manifestation of the divine holiness, that sinful and imperfect creatures—and such are the holiest of God's people on earth—cannot behold it and live. They are permitted therefore to behold it as in a mirror. It is reflected from the works and the Word of the Lord; from his dealings with the children of men, and from the revelation which he hath given them; from the person and work of the Son of God, in whom dwelt all the fulness of the Godhead bodily, and in whom his faithful disciples recognised " the glory as of the only-begotten of the Father, full of grace and truth."

All men do not behold this glory. Some men refuse to look upon it. They would look on anything, they would think on anything, rather than on God. Others are not unwilling to contemplate God in his wisdom, and even in his power. They are philosophers. They cannot fail to be astonished at the stupendous nature of God's works, and to admire the wonderful mechanism in every part of creation. But they shrink from the contemplation of his moral perfections, except perhaps his goodness. They are afraid of his holiness; they tremble at his justice. These, even when reflected in the mild and benignant character of the Son of man, who came not to condemn but to save the world, they will not contemplate. They are wicked and profane, and these condemn them; or they are satisfied with themselves and their own goodness, and these find them wanting, and their pride is humbled. Another class do make God and divine things objects of study, their teachers and parents require it of them; but they contemplate them more as manner of form and Christian profession than with a view to their use and practical application. They want, and they do not pray for, the power of spiritual discernment, without which assurance they will read and contemplate in vain. For "the natural man receiveth not the things of the Spirit of God, they are foolishness unto him; neither can he know them, because they are spiritually discerned."

The "glory of the Lord" was revealed in Moses as well as in Christ. Even his glory as "the Lord, merciful and gracious," was then revealed; but the people of Israel did not behold it, for their minds were blinded, the vail was upon their hearts. "Even unto this day," says Paul, referring to the unbelief of the Jews in the days of the apostle—"even to this day," we may repeat, referring to their unbelief now, "when Moses is read, the vail is on their hearts." They have eyes, but do not see; they have an understanding, but do not perceive. And they are not alone in this. It is even so with all unconverted men who read the Word of God, blinded by prejudice, or sensuality, or worldly-mindedness, or self-righteous pride, or any other passion. They think they behold it; but they do not indeed behold in the gospel mirror, the glory of the Lord. They deceive themselves; for if indeed they beheld it, it would lead their minds captive to the love of God, and a cheerful and unreserved submission to his will.

This is what the apostle means by beholding the glory of God with "open" or unvailed face, or, as the original words mean, with the vail removed from our face. This is the true reading of the word—it is the beholding of the truth through the clearest possible medium, with no curtain or vail intervening. In the text there is a particular reference to the free and unimpeded contemplation of the truth as the means of our sanctification, when the Spirit of the Lord has set the soul free from the bondage of fear, and has introduced it into the liberty of the children of God. The people of Israel were afraid to look on the glory of the face of Moses. The blood of Jesus not yet having purged the conscience from dead works, the humble penitent has not received the spirit of adoption, and does not yet look with confidence on God. Let this vail be removed, let this slavish fear be taken away, and the glory of the Lord in the face of Jesus Christ is the object of his delighted believing contemplation. He can view it stedfastly; it awakens no alarm, it inspires no terror. On the contrary, it fills him with peace, it inspires with joy and confidence. It is the glory of a holiness which ensures to him the fulfilment of every promise; of a justice which, satisfied in the offering of Christ once for all, imparts to the believer a right to eat of the tree of life; of a love which has a height and a depth, a length and a breadth, which passeth knowledge; a glory in which the Christian finds a balm for every wound, treasures which all the wealth of this world cannot purchase, enjoyments which are pure, and satisfying, and eternal.

Let each one of us ask himself, Do I thus with unvailed face behold the glory of the Lord? The question is not, Have I knowledge? but, Have I a true faith? not, Have I an orthodox creed? but, Do I really and spiritually perceive and apprehend the truth as it is in Jesus?

III. Let us now proceed, as was proposed, in the *third* place, to consider the fruit or effect of our beholding the glory of the Lord—"We . . . are *changed* into the same image, from glory to glory."

It is no mere external character which is here spoken of. The character produced is a metamorphose—a transformation—so the word is rendered in the twelfth chapter of the epistle to the Romans. And it is not wonderful that it should be so called, for the character which is effected is a transformation into the image or likeness of the glory of the Lord. The beholder receives in a certain measure and degree a conformity to the glorious character of the infinitely holy, the all-perfect Jehovah. This is a transformation indeed, for assuredly between fallen man in his unconverted state and the God who created him there is no resemblance at all. The understanding is darkened, the will is enslaved, the moral perception is enfeebled and perverted, holiness is hated, sin is loved and pursued; in one word, "the carnal mind is enmity against God; for it is not subject to the law of God, neither indeed can be." If therefore any man be changed so as to resemble the holy God, that change must indeed be a transformation, a change from darkness to light, from sin to holiness, from a resemblance to the prince of darkness to a resemblance to the prince of life.

The transformation which is here spoken of is begun in regeneration. No sooner has God shined into the soul of the sinner to give the light of the knowledge of his glory in the face of Jesus Christ, than a pervading change is effected on the whole soul and character and life of the once impenitent and unconverted sinner. He arises from the dead, he awakes to righteousness, he becomes a new creature. The spirit of his mind, the affections of his heart, the habits of his life, become new. He puts off the old man, which is corrupt according to the deceitful lusts, and puts on the new man, which is renewed in knowledge after the image of Him who created him.

But regeneration is no more than the beginning of the character mentioned in the text, the blade which has sprung up from the seed of God's word in the heart, and is afterwards to ripen into the ear and the full corn in the ear. The transformation is "from glory to glory." It is gradual, it is progressive. The babe becomes a young man—a father in Christ. In regeneration there is the beginning, but not the perfection, of true holiness; the sinner has become a saint, but his sanctification is not complete; sinful dispositions are not wholly subdued; holy principles and affections have been implanted, but are not perfectly and completely matured. The work is gradual, and it is progressive. The transformation into the image of God is from one degree of holiness to another. Just as in the unconverted there is a downward progress from one degree of hardness and impenitence to another, so, in the sanctification of the people of God, there is a growing tenderness of conscience, a growing love of what is excellent, and a growing conformity to the image of God. True believers, though not without occasional backslidings, go from strength to strength, until they appear before God in Zion.

On these points, however, I do not intend to enlarge, it being my chief object under this head of discourse to shew how the beholding of the glory of God produces the effect described by the apostle in the text—how, and in what manner, it transforms the believer into the image of the Lord. The description in the text presupposes the frequent, the daily, beholding of the glory of the Lord. That act is not a single isolated act in the life of the believer. It is not the single act of a man when he receives for the first time the knowledge of the truth as it is in Jesus, and is convinced of it, and embraces it. It is the every-day work, the every-day privilege of a real Christian, a privilege which he finds it necessary to use habitually for the maintenance of the life of God in the soul, for his consolation under a sense of the guilt which daily cleaves to him, and for invigorating and animating him in the Christian warfare and the Christian race. He contemplates God habitually in his works and in his words, brings daily to his remembrance what he has already learned of him, and adds to the knowledge which, through grace and in the diligent use of the means of grace, he has acquired. With David, he says, "How love I thy law! it is my meditation all the day." "My flesh longeth for Thee in a dry and thirsty land, where no water is: to see thy power and thy glory, so as I have seen Thee in the sanctuary."

The natural effect of this daily contemplation of God is to assimilate the soul to him. It cannot be that he should be presented to our eyes from day to day in the glory of his character as the all-perfect Jehovah, a just God and a Saviour, without our feeling the desire and putting forth the earnest endeavour to be like him, if at least we be reconciled to him through faith in the blood of his Son, and would be renewed of the Spirit. For we must be at amity with God, our sins must be forgiven, and we must have learned to love Him ere we can take pleasure in meditating on him, and ere we should seek to imitate him. The conscience must be sprinkled from dead works ere we can serve him. Knowledge, and even meditation on God without this, may restrain from sin, but will not be productive of resemblance to him. But let sin, the cause of enmity between God and our souls, be removed, let the once alienated affections be again brought near to God, and fixed supremely on him, and the habitual beholding of his glory cannot but be producive of resemblance to him. In our intercourse with our fellow-men, who has not felt the influence of the character and condition of a beloved friend in producing a similarity of thoughts and feelings and habits of life? We may be in some measure unconscious of its operation, we may not always be able to trace the effects to their cause, but the effect is produced; the influence is in every such instance more or less powerful. It cannot be otherwise, in the experience of the true believer, while daily and habitually engaged in beholding the glory of the Lord. He cannot but feel its transforming power, its sanctifying influences. It is not more certain that the light reflected from the mirror will throw a radiance on the human countenance than that the glory of the Lord will be seen in the temper and condition of those who are in the habit of daily intercourse and fellowship with him.

We have said that reconciliation with God is essential to our being imitators of him, and that until sin be forgiven, and we be taught to love him who first loved us, we cannot be partakers of the glory of his moral perfections. Let it not be inferred from hence that the Christian reconciled to God, and adopted into his family, ceases to regard his heavenly Father as his Ruler and his Judge. No truly affectionate and dutiful child ever forgets that his father has authority over him, or supposes that his father's love has released him from the obligation to obey. It is quite otherwise. He reveres, he obeys his father, because his father loves him, and he has been taught to love his father in return. So it is with the child of God. He loves his Father in heaven, but he never forgets that he is his Ruler and his Judge, and that he and all men will one day be required to give account unto him. Holy fear is mingled with gratitude, loyal and dutiful submission with love. The truth is, that it is in God's actings as the moral Governor and Judge of men, that his people see in their brightest glory those perfections which it is their duty and their privilege to imitate. They behold God seated on his throne, denouncing indignation and wrath, tribulation and anguish, on every soul of man that doeth evil, and providing for the redemption of his chosen ones, not by any departure from the principles of eternal rectitude and truth, but in a way perfectly consistent with both magnifying his law and making it honourable, and making it more manifest than it would have been if man had never fallen, so that he has an infinite abhorrence of all sin, and that it is his will that men should be holy even as he is holy, and perfect even as he, their Father in heaven, is perfect.

Thus it is that the authority of a judge and the love of a friend are combined in God, and, on the other hand, that the affection of a child and the loyal submission of a subject are united in those who, believing in the record which God has given of himself, have just and enlightened and affectionate apprehensions of his character and glory. You may easily perceive whence it is that the transformation of believers into the image of God is gradual and progressive. If the knowledge of God's glory be the instrument by which that transformation is effected, it is obvious that the more perfect that knowledge is, the more powerful must be its influence. The more clearly the mirror reflects the glory of the Lord, the more deep and lasting will be the impression made upon our minds. The more completely the eyes of our understanding are unvailed—in other words, the more clear and enlarged our apprehensions of God and of divine things—the more nearly shall we resemble our Father in heaven. But knowledge is of gradual attainment, therefore believers grow in grace as they grow in knowledge. Every accession made to the one ensures, through the illuminating power of the Holy Ghost, an addition to the other. And they do grow, because they use the means of growing. Like Moses, they pray, "Shew us thy glory." Like the angels in heaven, they "desire to look;" they look intently and habitually on the mystery of redeeming wisdom and love, and beholding with face more and more unvailed, the glory of the Lord, they "are changed into the image from glory to glory."

IV. Let us now proceed, as was proposed, in the *fourth* and last place, to consider *the operation of the Holy Spirit in the work of our sanctification.*

There is no truth more clearly revealed, and none, perhaps, more frequently presented to us in Scripture, than that our sanctification is the result of the operation of the Holy Spirit in our souls. The word of God, the dispensations of providence, the influences of a holy life, and the ordinances of religion—prayer, preaching, and the dispensation of the sacraments—are no more than instruments in our hands, and are altogether unavailing, without the illuminating and quickening power of the Holy Ghost. And, in proportion to the measure in which the Holy Spirit is imparted along with the divinely appointed means, is the progress which the true Christian makes in conformity to the image of God. This, we apprehend, is the meaning of the words in the latter part of the text, "as by the Spirit of the Lord." There is probably a reference to the name given to the New Testament dispensation in the preceding part of the chapter, "the ministration of the Spirit," it being that dispensation in which pre-eminently the Spirit is given to those who ask him. When, therefore, under the New Testament believers are transformed from glory to glory in beholding the glory of the Lord, their transformation into the image of the Lord is more rapid and more perfect under the New Testament than under the Old, because the Spirit is poured out in larger measure, and the truth is carried home to the conscience with greater power and energy.

We have no conception of the mode of the Spirit's operations. It is as mysterious, not perhaps more mysterious, than the mode of the operation of our own minds on our bodies. The effects are visible, but the manner in which they are produced we are unable to comprehend. The first of these is the illumination of the understanding. How truly is it said of unbelieving men, that "the god of this world hath blinded their minds, lest the light of the glorious gospel of Christ, who is the image of God, should shine unto them!" It is not that they want the means of knowing the truth. The light shines around them. In a Christian country the light of the sun is not more clear or more freely enjoyed than is the light of truth, the opportunity, the liberty of knowing God, and the things which belong to their peace But if they have no eyes to see, what doth all this avail them? Seeing, they see, and do not perceive, and hearing, they hear, and do not understand. The Jews, of whom Paul speaks in the foregoing part of the chapter, were not favoured in respect of knowledge in the same measure as those under the New Testament dispensation, but their measure of knowledge was sufficient if they had possessed the power of perceiving it. But their minds were darkened; they wanted the power of apprehending the truth, which many of the saints who were before them understood, and believers rejoiced in. So it is with all, till the Spirit of the Lord illumines the darkened understanding, and so it is with real Christians when they seek not and do not enjoy, because they do not seek the illumining directing grace of the Holy Spirit. The word of God must be read and heard in humble dependence on him, if we really wish that it should give light and quickening to our souls. Our progress from glory to glory must be from the Spirit of the Lord.

Next to this is impression. Because the manifestation of the glory of the Lord is the chief instrument of sanctification, it were a most erroneous conclusion that the illumination of the understanding is all that is necessary to our conformity to the image of God. It is perfectly true that in every instance in which that illumination is given there is given along with it the deep feeling of the truth believed. But there may be the most brilliant light without heat, and it is quite conceivable that the understanding may be filled with the knowledge of God and divine things whilst the heart is unmoved. When the God of all grace gives to the darkened understanding the light of the knowledge of his glory, he changes the hard and stony heart into a heart of flesh, and when he carries forward the work of sanctification in the soul, he does it by the gradual softening of the heart along with the progressive light of divine truth. On this subject we may appeal to the experience of real believers. How varied their frames! how different the impression made on their minds by the same truths. Their transformation from glory to glory is just in proportion to the measure of grace vouchsafed—to the impression made on the heart by the Holy Ghost.

In the last place, the progress of a true Christian holiness is proportioned to the measure of the gift of the Spirit as a Spirit of adoption, a Spirit of liberty. To this we referred in the commencement of the discourse, and shall only add that it is abundantly obvious that so long as there is any remains of slavish fear, the necessary accomplishment of unpardoned guilt, the influence of the truth as a means of sanctification must be proportionably feeble. If we would be drawn to the imitation of another person or being, we must love him first. But we cannot love God till slavish fear be cast out. This is done by the Holy Spirit. Where he is, there is liberty. If we grieve him, our liberty is gone, and the Spirit withdraws. Let us then walk in the Spirit.

Application. 1. Aim at nothing short of conformity to the image of God. 2. Be diligent in reading the Scriptures, and let them be read in habitual dependence on the grace of the Holy Spirit. 3. See that ye be continually advancing in holiness.

XII.

Death Swallowed up in Victory.

BY THE REV. ANDREW SYMINGTON, D.D.

"He shall swallow up death in victory."—Isa. xxv. 8.

IT is the morning of the holy Sabbath. This hallowed day, as it commemorates the victory of Jesus over the grave, should be a season of joy and triumph to the Christian. Why do I observe so many worshippers clad in the apparel of mourners?* Why is every countenance so sad, and so deeply traced with the unequivocal indications of heart-felt sorrow? Alas! the countenance of him that so long and so lately gladdened you from this place is now changed and shrouded. The lips that instructed, and exhorted, and comforted you, are now silent in death. You shall see your lately beloved pastor no more till the morning of the resurrection. We have followed his mortal remains to the grave, and deposited them there to rest in hope. While proceeding through the streets of your city in the performance of the last sad offices, we were forcibly reminded that death prevails over all, and leaves behind it everywhere memorials of its universal reign. Your deserted palaces, your dismantled and untenanted castles, and your effort to give immortality to mortals, in the monuments you

* Preached on the occasion of the death of the Rev. William Goold.

have erected to the soldier and the senator, the philosopher and the bard, as well as your garnished cemeteries, are so many memorials of the victories of the universal conqueror. Death is indeed a great conqueror, but there is a greater; and to direct your view, to inspire your faith and hope, and to comfort your hearts on this mournful occasion, I am to tell you of a greater conqueror than death, one who encountered and vanquished this great destroyer. Refrain your voice from weeping and your eyes from tears. Jesus, your Saviour, has conquered death; and yet a little while, and shall be brought to pass the saying that is written, "Death is swallowed up in victory."

The Christian hearer knows at once to whom and to what the brief and memorable words of this prophetic oracle apply; but it may contribute to our satisfaction to mark the connection in which they stand. Isaiah has predicted in the preceding part of his prophecy the fall of the enemies of Sion. Moab, Syria, Ethiopia, Egypt, Babylon, Dumah, Arabia, and Tyre, sink in succession under the burden of divine judgment. From the uttermost part of the earth, songs are heard reiterating, Glory to the righteous—the Righteous One, the Blessed Saviour. The moon is confounded and the sun is ashamed in the splendour of Zion's triumphs, and the Lord of hosts reigns in mount Zion, and before his ancients gloriously. Then follows the song, in the chapter from which we have taken our text. From the first to the eighth verse the prophet celebrates blessings enjoyed and expected, and the concluding verses give a response of gratitude and exultation. From the first to the fifth verse, the prophet speaks to God in the name of the Church, and from the sixth to the eighth he speaks in the name of God to the Church. This not only presents a variety, at once relieving and agreeable, but seems instructively to express the reciprocation of joy which obtains between God and the Church. She celebrates his praise, and he rejoices over her with joy. Whatever immediate reference may be supposed to be made to Babylon, or other vanquished enemy of Zion, the text must refer to Him whom the ancient deliverances prefigured, whose day they prepared and pre-indicated, and must be applied to the victory and triumph of the Messiah on his cross, in his gospel kindgom, and in the ultimate resurrection of the just, when the last enemy shall be destroyed.

In the text we have Death, the grim king of terrors, the formidable foe of man, the great devourer of the human race. And conspicuous, and placed in opposition to Death, we have Jesus Christ, the Lord of hosts, the Seed of the woman, the Child born, the Lion of the tribe of Judah, the Mighty God. The two are supposed to meet in dire encounter. The issue is a victory on the side of Christ. "He will swallow up death in victory." Mark the language, which of course is figurative. Animals swallow their food. The lion swallows up his prey. In the prophetic dream, the lean and ill-favoured kine swallowed up the seven fat kine. The rod of Aaron, in ancient miracle, swallowed up the rod of the Egyptian sorcerers. Water swallows up the heavier substances cast into it. A numerous army swallows up a smaller. An earthquake swallows up men and their habitations, as it did Korah and his associates in rebellion. Death is the great devourer, swallowing up the successive generations of the human family, and may be fitly described by the prophet: "Hell hath enlarged herself, and opened her mouth without measure; and their glory, and their multitude, and their pomp, and he that rejoiceth, shall descend into it." This devourer came upon Jesus, gaping upon him with his mouth as a ravening and roaring lion, but it was swallowed up in victory; language expressing, if not the ease with which the foe was vanquished, his entire and final destruction.

Let us direct our attention to this glorious victory. It may be contemplated in three aspects,—as achieved by Christ in his immediate personal conflict with death,—as prosecuted in the deliverance of his redeemed people,—and as consummated in the resurrection, and in the ultimate triumphs of the celestial state.

I. *Jesus has swallowed up death in victory in his personal conflict with death.* Whence is it, we naturally inquire, that Jesus must encounter death? He is not a transgressor of the law, which declares that the wages of sin is death. He is not connected by natural descent, or federal representation, with the one man by whom sin entered into the world, and death by sin. His encounter with death is connected with the gracious design of God to save others from sin and death. Rebellion had been raised against the throne of God in the angelic and human families. Divine justice took effect in the expulsion of rebel spirits from heaven, and in the condemnation of man, who, through the instigation of Satan, had been seduced into disobedience. As in matter of fact, so by an unimpeachable constitution, the human race is implicated in the sentence of death pronounced upon Adam; and, in holy and retributive judgment, Satan has received a judicial power in carrying the sentence into execution. But it was the sovereign and gracious purpose of God to save sinners of the human family, and arrangements are made to carry this into effect in consistency with the divine perfections, the honour of the divine law, and the interests of the divine government. Accordingly we read that the designs of mercy were conditionated on the sufferings and death of Christ, and that by these he was to obtain the victory over Satan. "Therefore will I divide him a portion with the great, and he shall divide the spoil with the strong, because he hath poured out his soul unto death." In ancient prophecy, he is boldly represented as eagerly anticipating the contest, and exulting in its issues. "I will ransom them from the power of the grave ; I will redeem them from death : O death, I will be thy plagues ; O grave, I will be thy destruction!" And when the fulness of time came, he assumed human nature for this very end, "knowing, intending, and contemplating all the results of that act of assumption, through the period of the designed humiliation, and for ever." "He was made a little lower than the angels for the suffering of death ; and forasmuch as the children were partakers of flesh and blood, he also himself likewise took part of the same ; that through death he might destroy him that had the power of death, that is, the devil ; and deliver them who through fear of death were all their lifetime subject to bondage." Thus in the arrangements of mercy, and in the prospective and comprehensive view of the Saviour, death has an essential connection with his delivering others from death. Accordingly, no sooner was the Saviour born than death marks him for its prey. The dread monster stood at Bethlehem to devour Mary's child so soon as he was born. Thirsting for his blood, Satan found a ready instrument in the jealous Herod, but he was defeated. Though disappointed, he still pursued his object, and conducted the Redeemer to the pinnacle of the temple, seeking to engulph him, as he had done man, in self-destruction. Still defeated in his aim, he instigated the inhabitants of Nazareth to destroy him by violence ; he stirred up the priests and scribes against him ; he instigated the traitor ; he united the mocking Herod and temporising Pilate in enmity against him ; he prompted the false witnesses ; he animated the popular cry, Crucify him, crucify him ; and they hurried him to the cross. Death pursues Jesus from the manger to the tree, and seems to challenge him as the Philistine did David, "Come to me, and I will give thy flesh to the fowls of the air, and to the beasts of the field." But stay, proud Goliath! a stone from the sling of the despised Bethlehemite may yet penetrate thy forehead ; and thy sword, red with the blood of thousands, may yet sever thy head from thy body, and proclaim thy power destroyed. The combatants close in bloody, mortal grapple. Jesus dies, and death seems to have the victory; a victory, if won, the most signal and illustrious of his numerous victories. But is it so? Just views of the case will shew the contrary; Jesus is the conqueror, and death is swallowed up in victory.

This will appear if we reflect on the perfectly voluntary nature of the death of Christ, and the power he put forth in it. We observe about the Saviour a perfect willingness in all that he did and suffered; and in a sense peculiar to himself he died voluntarily. "There is no man that hath power over the spirit, to retain the spirit; neither hath he power in the day of death." Believers in the triumph of faith on their beds are ready to die, and holy martyrs have triumphed over all the pains and the fears of death on the scaffold; but they had no power over the spirit in the moment of death. Jesus had this power. His life was not taken from him by wicked men, nor by Satan; no, not by God himself. He laid down his life. His death was his own voluntary act, in a sense in which no saint or martyr ever did die, or could die. Having commended his spirit into the hands of his Father, he bowed his head and gave up the ghost; and, voluntarily dismissing his spirit, he expired. He died with the dignity and majesty of the Prince of life. He died a conqueror. The Serpent had succeeded in Eden, but was defeated here; for his head was crushed by the very heel which he bruised. The conflict was dreadful, and the Redeemer fell, but "death was undermost in the struggle."

But we must consider here, the intensity of his sufferings, and the infinite merit of his death. Jesus, in his death, had something more to contend with than the dread and murderous malignity of Satan. Death is the proper expression of the holiness and righteousness of God, as embodied in the sanction of the divine law; and when carried into execution, it is the law put into operation by the divine power. Death is the wrath of God revealed from heaven against the unrighteousness of man, and it takes effect upon the soul; and this appeared in the unutterable mortal sorrows of the Redeemer. Not the fear of natural death, not the fear of failing to support a proper deportment in the last scene, not the desertion of his disciples, not the miseries coming upon Jerusalem, could make him cry, " My soul is exceeding sorrowful, even unto death." It was not the crown of thorns, nor the pains of crucifixion, nor the taunt and contempt of man, nor the assault of devils, that called forth the shriek, " My God, my God, why hast thou forsaken me?" Sin appeared to him in all its atrocity and desert; and that countenance whose light is the life of saints and the joy of angels, was hid in penal frown, and a sense of wrath seems to have penetrated the soul. He stood in the room of the guilty, and suffered and died the just for the unjust. Upon no other principle can the providence of God, in the sufferings and death of the innocent and holy Saviour, be vindicated from indelible imputation. In his death Jesus made atonement for sin, and abolished death, and destroyed him that had the power of death, that is, the devil; and thus he obtained the victory. " Blotting out the hand-writing of ordinances that was against us, which was contrary to us, and took it out of the way, nailing it to his cross; and, having spoiled principalities and powers, he made a show of them openly, triumphing over them in it." The demerit of sin was swallowed up in the infinite satisfaction of his death. His sufferings were appointed of God, and they were endured voluntarily; and they derived an infinite value from his divine dignity. And thus was Satan's power destroyed. The secret of Satan's strength lay in the law. And the victory was won in the satisfaction of the law. Satan's main strength did not lie in his physical power, nor in his intellectual subtlety, nor in his moral malignity, which could easily have been over-matched by the infinite power and wisdom and love of the Saviour ; but the secret of his strength lay in the divine law, and the victory was achieved in the satisfaction of this law. " The sting of death is sin, and the strength of sin is the law. But thanks be unto God who giveth us the victory, through Jesus Christ our Lord." Through death, he destroyed (abolished the power of) him that had the power of death, and thus was death destroyed by itself, as Goliath's head was severed by his own sword. Satan was thus taken in his own snare, his power of death abolished, and he fell down at the foot of the cross, like the lords of the Philistines, when the pillars of the house were shaken by the right and left hand of him whom they had blindfolded.

This victory is further manifest in the resurrection of Christ. When they had fulfilled all that was written of him, they took him down from the tree, and laid him in a sepulchre. His burial was necessary, to fulfil ancient prophecy, to give full evidence of the fact of his death, to confound further his enemies, to prepare consolation for his friends, and to make his entrance into heaven and his glory more illustrious. His enemies crucified him, but his friends buried him. With all the mitigation of this circumstance, death seems for the time to prevail. The grave is death's territory, but in this case it was entered only to be spoiled, as the event of the morning of the third day declares. The house appointed for all living never had such a tenant ; but it was not to Christ a long home. There is not time to erect his monument. Let us go to his grave. He is not here, but he is risen, and in circumstances that indicate triumph. He arose from the dead by his own power. His resurrection was authorised by the Father, and it declared his entire satisfaction ; the quickening of the dead body was the work, in respect of efficiency, of the Holy Spirit ;

and the resumption of the body into union with the briefly disembodied spirit was the glorious victorious act of the Redeemer himself, the Lion of the tribe of Judah going up from the prey. We may say at the tomb which is opened by sin, SWALLOWED UP IN DEATH, but at the tomb of Christ, DEATH SWALLOWED UP IN VICTORY. There are many indications of victory. The trembling keepers, the composed state of the grave-clothes, the quaking earth, the attendant angels, all proclaim a victory. Let us lift the napkin which was left behind, wipe away our tears, and looking up to our exalted Saviour, ask in triumph, "O grave, where is thy victory?" O death, thy dark escutcheon is for once inscribed, ALIVE FOR EVERMORE. Death has been pursued to his last quarters and slain, like the king of Chaldee, in his own capital. The ever-hungry grave, the great devourer, when it caught the dead body of Christ, swallowed its own destruction.

And we must not overlook here the power with which the Saviour is invested in consequence of his death. The power of death has been taken out of the hand of Satan, and put into the hand of Christ. He conquered on the cross, and descended to the grave only to strip the slain, and to come forth with the spoil. He has now the keys of hell and death, emblems of his universal power. To him now belong the issues from death. He will henceforth take the prey from the mighty. At the very cross we see his power put forth, the opening graves at his feet and the dismission of a soul to paradise proclaiming his victory. It was promised, "He shall divide the spoil with the strong;" and he declared this as an object of his immediate anticipation in his death. "Now is the judgment of this world; now shall the prince of this world be cast out. And I, if I be lifted up, will draw all men unto me:" and again, "And when he, the Comforter, is come, he will convince the world of sin, because they believe not on me; of righteousness, because I go to the Father; and of judgment, because the prince of this world is judged." Little did Satan think of the results of that dread work which he was hurrying on in the condemnation and crucifixion of Jesus! The crown of thorns became a crown of gold, the reed a sceptre, and the very cross a throne of glory, and a triumphal chariot in which the Redeemer would ride prosperously, conquering and to conquer.

II. *Jesus swallows up death in victory in the deliverance of his redeemed people.* Death extends its power beyond the body of man. The body is not now in its state of primeval beauty and vigour; but in its deformity and infirmity and disease and subjection to the service of sin and to dissolution, it resembles the mangled carcase that has been in the mouth of a beast of prey, enfeebled, bleeding with wounds, and ready to be swallowed up at the pleasure of the devourer. But, oh! this is the least part of the evil of death. Death has extended to the soul, and appears in the privation of the moral image of God. The eye of the understanding is darkened, the spiritual senses are benumbed, and no pulsation indicates the operation or existence of any holy affection toward God. The soul is dead in trespasses and sins, and man is thus emphatically dead while he lives. The entire privation of life is predicated of those who are without faith. "He that hath not the Son hath not life. Except ye eat the flesh of the Son of man, and drink his blood, ye have no life in you. He that loveth not his brother, abideth in death." Alas! we are sometimes deeply affected when we think on the mortality of the body, while we are utterly unconscious of the dominion of spiritual death in the soul; and this unconsciousness is itself strong evidence of the mournful fact! No instruction, argument, reproof, allurement, or terror can take saving effect upon the soul of man, till the spirit of life in Christ Jesus set it free from the law of sin and death. But he shall see his seed,

"Therefore will I divide him a portion with the great, and he shall divide the spoil with the strong; because he hath poured out his soul unto death." Having achieved the victory, the Redeemer takes the spoil. His Father distributes to him many for his portion, and he shall take them as a spoil from the great adversary. In consequence of his death, the Redeemer has received power to take the prey from the mighty, and to deliver the lawful captive. He sends his gospel "to give light to them that sit in darkness and in the shadow of death, and makes it powerful to turn men from darkness to light, and from the power of Satan unto God. The hour cometh, and now is, when the dead shall hear the voice of the Son of man, and they that hear shall live."

The Redeemer swallows up death in victory, in the regeneration of the spiritually dead, and in the justified state of all believing in him. He quickens whom he wills, and every converted sinner is spoil taken from the enemy, is a lamb plucked from the mouth of the devourer, a soul saved from death. In imparting spiritual life to the soul, death is destroyed; for the soul is born again, not of corruptible seed, but of incorruptible, by the word of truth, which liveth and abideth for ever. Whosoever liveth and believeth in Christ, shall never die. This spiritual life is of a high order of excellence. It is not only more excellent than the animal and rational life possessed in common with others, but it is more excellent than that possessed by Adam in innocence, which was subject to mutability, and than that of angels in their first estate, which also was subject to change; it is life specially hid with Christ in God, and it is grafted into the life of Christ, in whom it shall live for ever and ever, beyond the reach of change, of decay, or of destruction. All this is secured in the justified state of the believer, and in the inhabitation of the Holy Spirit. He is pardoned all his iniquity, and accepted in the beloved.

He has everlasting life, and shall not come into condemnation, but is passed from death unto life. Is not death swallowed up of life in the glorious statement of evangelical doctrine by the apostle Paul? "If by one man's offence DEATH reigned by one; much more they which receive abundance of grace, and of the gift of righteousness, shall reign in LIFE by one, Christ Jesus." And fear of condemnation is swallowed up in the victory of Christian faith and hope inspired by the triumph of the arisen Saviour. "Who shall lay anything to the charge of God's elect? It is God that justifieth; who is he that condemneth? It is Christ that died, yea rather, that is risen again." And ample provision is made for sustaining the Christian life, in Christ himself, the living bread that came down from heaven. The bread that perisheth sustains by the divine providence the perishing body, and death gets the victory at last; but "if any man eat of the living bread, he shall live for ever." And in it death is swallowed up in victory. Paradise is regained, the flaming sword is quenched in the blood of Christ, and a way is opened to the tree of life, whose laden boughs, pendent with immortal fruit, invite to eat and live for ever.

Is not death also swallowed up in victory, in the warfare of believers on earth? Sin, and Satan, and the world, and every enemy have been overcome by Christ, meritoriously in the satisfaction of his sacrifice, exemplarily in his own life and death, and efficiently in the power and grace imparted to his people; so that in their warfare, however hot and obstinate, they have assurance of ultimate victory, and this is the victory that overcometh even their faith. A troop may overcome them for a time; but they shall overcome at the last. They may lose a battle, but not the war. And how is death swallowed up in the peace, the joy, the consolation, the assurance of the Christian, in all these things more than a conqueror through him that loved him? And in the believer's death itself there is victory. Mark the triumph of Christian faith over the last enemy. "Though I walk through the valley of the shadow of death, I will fear no evil. I am persuaded that death shall not be able to separate me from the love of God which is in Christ Jesus my Lord." Death and the grave and hell have no power over the redeemed in the hour of dissolution. Death has power indeed over the wicked, and it is said to feed upon them, and the first-born of death to devour their strength; but to the Christian death is a conquered foe, and so swallowed up in life that the day of death is better than the day of birth; the soul is in safety in stronger than in angels' hands; and when the body dies because of sin, the soul lives because of righteousness. And in the moment of dissolution it triumphs in immortality, not merely in that immortality which it holds of God by natural constitution, and by which it survives death in every case, but in that glory, honour, and immortality which it has in union to Him who was dead and is now alive for evermore. Death is to the believer not a curse but a blessing, and has been transferred from the penalty of the law to the promises of the covenant. It has still its repulsive form, but it is harmless as the serpent without its sting; and the believer finds in reality what he had anticipated in his triumphant faith, "O death, where is thy sting! Thanks be unto God who giveth us the victory!"

III. *Jesus shall swallow up death in victory in the resurrection, and in the ultimate triumphs of the celestial state.* The scenes of the Redeemer's victories already contemplated have been on earth, on his cross, in the soul of the believer, and on the death-bed of the Christian. We must now carry our view upward to the heavens, forward to the resurrection, and onward and upward to the final celestial state of eternal glory.

We have satisfactory evidence that the heavens have received Christ until the times of the restitution of all things. In the epistle to the Hebrews his entrance into heaven is described in reference to his priesthood, in that after offering a sacrifice for sin, he entered into the most holy places not made with hands. He made this entrance into human nature, as the representative of his people, with infinite acceptance on the part of the Father, with infinite joy to himself, with unspeakable gladness to the angels and saints in heaven, and with infinite advantage to his people on the earth. He now lives to make intercession, and has taken his seat at the right hand of God, prosecuting the ends of his sacrifice, and expecting till all his enemies be made his footstool. The entrance of Christ into heaven is also represented in the light of a triumph, bearing more immediately on his kingly character. To nothing short of this do the lofty descriptions in the book of Psalms ultimately refer. "Lift up your heads, O ye gates; and be ye lift up, ye everlasting doors; and the King of glory shall come in. Who is this King of glory? The Lord strong and mighty, the Lord mighty in battle. God is gone up with a shout, the Lord with the sound of a trumpet. Sing praises to God, sing praises unto our King, sing praises. Thou hast ascended on high, thou hast led captivity captive." This is the language of triumph, the victory follows the battle, and triumph follows the victory. Jesus after a most dreadful battle and a decisive victory received a glorious triumph when he ascended to heaven, laden with the spoil, greeted by angels and the redeemed hosts, and above them all welcomed by his Father to sit down with him on his throne. We can conceive of nothing so magnificent as the triumph of the Saviour ascending to heaven, death and the grave and hell, and Satan who had the power of them all, now conquered and dragged at the glowing wheels of his triumphal chariot, while thousands of thousands shout, "Sing unto the

Lord a new song, for his right hand and his holy arm have gotten him the victory." There he triumphs in life, having left the shades of death for the light of heaven. He feels not now, as in his humiliation, the infirmities and pains of the body, or sorrow of soul in penal separation from the face of his Father. "He asked life of thee, and thou gavest it him, even length of days for ever and ever. His glory is great in thy salvation; honour and majesty hast thou laid upon him. For thou hast made him most blessed for ever; thou hast made him exceeding glad in thy countenance." In that blessed place where there is no death, the words have been fulfilled to him, "Thou wilt shew me the path of life; in thy presence is fulness of joy; and at thy right hand are pleasures for evermore."

Death is also swallowed up in victory in the glorification of the spirits of the just. The soul of man has by the will of its Maker a natural immortality, and is not subject to dissolution with the body. But this is not the victory of which we speak, nor is this a consequence of the death of Christ. The natural immortality of the soul must prove a death that never dies to the impenitent. But the souls of the redeemed are at their death made perfect in holiness, and do immediately pass into glory. Witness the soul of Lazarus carried by angels into Abraham's bosom; that of the penitent malefactor dismissed to paradise; the spirit of Stephen received by Jesus standing at the right hand of God; and under the altar the souls of them that were slain for the Word of God and for the testimony which they held; and a great multitude which no man can number, standing before the throne, and before the Lamb, clothed with white robes, and having palms, the emblems of their victory, in their hands. They formerly triumphed in their faith and hope, but now in complete realisation; and, made more than conquerors over sin and Satan and the world, and affliction and persecution and death, through him that loved them, they triumph in life eternal. The spirits of just men made perfect sleep not with the body, nor are they sent to purgatorial fires, but they are with Christ, trophies of the victory which he won on Calvary.

Nor must we overlook here the progressive triumphs of the Redeemer's kingdom on earth. For though gone to heaven, he is still prosecuting his victory on the earth, conquering and to conquer. This world is covered with death's shade; but, through the tender mercy of our God, the day-spring from on high has visited us, to give light to them that sit in darkness and in the shadow of death. The cross on which the Saviour conquered is the grand instrument of converting sinners from the error of their ways, and saving souls from death. The preaching of it is the institution of the Saviour, and though a stumblingblock to the Jews, and to the Greeks foolishness, it is unto them that are called the power of God and the wisdom of God. The power of the gospel is forcibly represented by Paul, in allusion to the successful operation of military engines upon a strongly-fortified city. "For the weapons of our warfare are not carnal, but mighty through God to the pulling down of strongholds, casting down imaginations, and every high thing that exalteth itself against the knowledge of God, and bringing into captivity every thought to the obedience of Christ." "Gird thy sword on thy thigh, O most mighty! and in thy majesty ride prosperously, because of truth and righteousness. Thine arrows are sharp in the hearts of the king's enemies, whereby the people fall under thee." Heaven looks down with interest to earth, while this warfare of love and mercy proceeds. Every sinner that repenteth swells its song of triumph. The cross has triumphed already in the erection and preservation of the kingdom of Christ on the earth. In opposition to the malice of Jews, the idolatry of the heathen, the learning of Greece, and the power of Rome, it spread abroad. It has triumphed in surviving the most bloody persecutions at the hand of pagan and papal Rome; and its very martyrs overcame by the blood of the Lamb and the word of their testimony, loving not their lives unto the death. And we are assured greater victories are yet to be achieved, when shall come the kingdom of our God and the power of his Christ. And the cause of truth shall prosper over all opposition, and those that have gotten the victory over the beast, and over his image, and over his mark, and over the number of his name, shall stand on the sea of glass, having the harps of God, and singing the song of Moses the servant of God, and the song of the Lamb. Truth shall obtain a victory over error, and in the spread of the gospel and its power by the Spirit of God, death shall be swallowed up of life in the conversion of thousands of millions. It is cheering to think of the ultimate triumph of Christ in the spiritual conquest of the world, and to know that the crowns of many victories are to shine on the head of Him who conquered on Calvary, and who is now in heaven, where his glories are being celebrated with increasing triumphs.

But our text is to receive its fulfilment in the resurrection and glorification of the bodies of the redeemed. It is well to mark the connection between the Old Testament and the New, and to study both Testaments in the light which they reflect on one another. As in the burial of Christ death seemed to prevail, so it seems presently to have the victory over the bodies of the saints. Soon was the victory declared in the case of Christ; and his resurrection is the pledge of that of all his saints. "For this corruptible must put on incorruption, and this mortal must put on immortality, and then shall be brought to pass the saying that is written, Death is swallowed up in victory." It thus appears that the victory in our text has a special reference to the hour that cometh, in the which all that are in their graves shall hear the voice of the Son of God, and shall come forth, and they that have done good to the resurrection of life. The body which has borne the image of the earthly Adam, shall also bear the image of the heavenly. Freed from all disease and deformity and weakness, it shall become celestial, incorruptible, immortal, glorious, powerful, and spiritual; and a fit receptacle for the glorified spirit. The temples of the Holy Ghost which had lain for a time in ruins, shall be rebuilt, and of every one it may be justly said, the glory of this latter house shall be greater than of the former. "We that are in this tabernacle do groan, being burdened; not that we would be unclothed, but clothed upon, that mortality might be swallowed up of life." It is with us no incredible thing that God should raise the dead. We know the Scriptures, and the power of God, and the victory of the Saviour; and as soon shall the conquered grave recall Christ from the heavens and swallow him up, as retain the bodies of his redeemed children. Let the Christian triumphing at the grave of Christ adopt the challenge for himself, as well as for Christ, "O grave, where is thy victory!"

And here let us reflect on the completeness of this victory, in the perfect gathering together of the redeemed unto Christ. Mark the Saviour's words, as bearing upon a perfect comprehension of all the redeemed, "And this is the Father's will which hath sent me, that of all which he hath given me I should lose nothing, but should raise it up again at the last day." Not one shall be retained by death. All shall be raised or changed, and transferred to the enjoyment of eternal life, untouched by the second death. Over them the first death had some dominion, although no penal power. But over them the second death shall have no power. As expressive of the final triumph of the Saviour over death, we read, "And death and hell (that is, the bodies of the wicked and their souls that had existed in the separate state) shall be cast into the lake of fire: This is the second death." "Now he that overcometh shall not be hurt of the second death." While swallowing up its millions, it shall have no power over the redeemed.

And to crown the whole, Satan shall at this time be cast down into final degradation. He has had the power of death. As he had seduced man into sin, and brought death by sin, he received a judicial power to inflict death, and he is the executioner of the awful sentence in the case of the wicked, in the alarms of their consciences, in his full retention of them, and in the final inflictions of the place of woe. He shall be bound and cast into prison for a thousand years, and, after being loosed for a season, in the rampant wickedness which shall immediately precede the judgment, it is said, "the devil that deceived the nations was cast into the lake of fire, and shall be tormented for ever and ever." This is the judgment for which the angels that sinned and kept not their first estate have been reserved in everlasting chains under darkness. Now is come "the time" they dreaded, in the day of the Saviour's sojourn on earth. And now a long protracted and dreadful conflict closes in glorious victory. While mercy will triumph in the eternal salvation of the redeemed, justice will triumph for ever and ever in its victory over the unrighteousness of human and angelic criminals. Tell it now, seducer of Adam and tempter of Christ, whose is the victory? Death is swallowed up in eternal life, and he that had the power of death is cast into the lake of fire to be tormented for ever and ever.

Such, then, is the victory of the Redeemer over death and him that has the power of death. Glorious, final, everlasting victory! felt in the degradation and final punishment of the devil, his angels, and wicked men; and celebrated in the eternal jubilations of those who are around the throne.

Toward an improvement of this subject, one word in our text demands, in the first place, our attention. It is death. Dreadful thing! the object of universal fear. We see its effects upon the human frame, consuming its beauty, wasting its strength, and cutting it off with pining sickness or violent pain. We see its effects in the changed countenance, the pallid cheek and lip, the cold hand, the stiff limb, the shroud, the coffin, the grave, and the worm. We feel its effects in the rupture of tender ties, and in the irreparable blank and desolation which it leaves behind. Various are the instruments by which it works. It approaches us, not only in the diseases to which the body is subject, but it lurks and works in the air, in the fire, and in the water; in the food we eat, in the water we drink, in the path on which we walk, and in the vehicle in which we are conveyed; it is in the calm as well as in the tempest. It spares not rank nor sex. The very infant unborn, the suckling, the playful child, the blooming virgin, the ruddy youth, the man of strength in the midst of his days, and the man trembling on his staff, are alike liable to death; and the great and the mighty who keep the world alive, as well as the obscure and unknown. Gold cannot bribe it, wisdom cannot elude it, eloquence charm it, greatness awe it, power resist it, or tears melt it. It is everywhere; and has made the world a field of graves, and the inhabitants mourners.

To appreciate aright the nature of this great evil, we must view it in the light of the Scriptures; finding it first as the penalty annexed to the divine law when promulgated to man, and then as the sentence of the eternal Judge of all, when omniscient justice found man a transgressor. It is an evil of appalling magnitude, extending to the soul as well as to the body, and it is the just desert of sin. It is no debt of nature, or tribute of being, as some speak, no imperfection in the constitution of things, no arbitrary infliction, no paternal chastisement. It is the wages of sin ; and its universal prevalence confirms the divine word, and pleads God's holy cause against man's rebellion. But we see the least part of it, for when the dust returns to the dust whence it came, the spirit returns to give account to God. We feel the beginnings of this evil in the conscious fears of our own minds, but we would require to contemplate it in the alarms of a conscience awakened to a sense of sin, in the case of a sinner who feels that his diseased body cannot live and his guilty soul cannot die. It were well to look at Death as sitting on his pale horse, and Hell following with him, and making his advance to ourselves. We would require to look down into the place where the worm never dies, and the fire is not quenched, and to see hell from beneath moved to meet the sinner at his coming. Our busy occupations, our thoughtlessness, our procrastination, our doubtings and scepticism cannot change its certainty, mitigate its nature, or give us safety and hope. It has reigned from Adam to Moses, and from Moses to the present generation, and it is continuing to make havoc of the human race, and is menacing the generations to come, like the Dragon in the Apocalypse standing to devour the child so soon as it is born. Insatiate monster, gorging up the human race, who shall contend with thee?

Let us turn from the appalling scene, and direct our thoughts to Jesus' victory over this great foe. Warriors that have slain their thousands become at last the powerless victims of this destroyer; but here is one who has triumphed over death. He was not its victim when he died on the cross, nor its prisoner when he lay in the grave, for to both he voluntarily submitted, and in both he conquered. And now the Redeemer has not only dissipated the natural darkness which broods over human destiny, by certifying the immortality of the soul, and the resurrection of the body; but he has chased away the deep penal gloom which sin has brought over the future state, having abolished death and brought life and immortality to light. These beam with a clear and steady light from the cross. The victory achieved there was won for others. Christ died for our sins according to the Scripture, he tasted death for us, and in the great truths of his atonement, and righteousness, and grace, the prey of a great spoil is divided. The death of Christ was the death of death to all that believe in him. "IT IS FINISHED!" was not the groan of dissolving nature, but the shout of victory. In his death and in his resurrection he accomplished his own words, "O death, I will be thy plagues; O grave, I will be thy destruction!" and the believer, standing at the cross and at the grave of Christ, may begin to triumph, "O death, where is thy sting! O grave, where is thy victory!"

The Redeemer's victory is the only antidote against the evil and the fear of death. The gospel proclaims this victory, and the believer rejoices in it, "as one that findeth great spoil." Realise it for yourselves, my hearers, by that faith which is the substance of things hoped for and the evidence of things not seen. You know it is appointed unto men once to die, and it is well to be prepared for this greatest and most important of all certainties. Your utmost care will not prevent it, your vigilance will not escape it. It will baffle your physician, it will pursue you to the most salubrious clime to be found beneath the sun. Be ye therefore ready. Wait not for intimations of its approach, for it may surprise you in a moment. Boast not thyself of to-morrow, for to-night thy soul may be required at thy hand. And oh! think what death is, when all relations to this world shall be broken up, and the soul be separated from the body and placed before the tribunal of God. Man cannot live for ever here, and though he could, his life perpetuated without holiness, and without the divine favour, could not meet the necessities of his nature, nor give him felicity; nor would such a boon, could it be conferred, be worthy to be compared for a moment with the peace and joy of a life of Christian faith and hope. But it is vain to speculate here. You must die, and it is wisdom to be prepared for it. You are not abandoned to the darkness and apprehensions of your own minds. You are not left to the ambiguous oracles of reason or the philosophy of the world. Look to the cross of Christ and to his grave, and meditate on his victory over death. Reflect on the satisfaction and merit of his obedience unto death, on the righteousness and salvation which are now brought near, on the abounding of sin and the super-abounding of grace, on the reign of sin unto death, and the reign of grace through righteousness unto eternal life, and on the love, and power, and grace of the Holy Spirit, and receive Christ Jesus the Lord, and live for ever. In view of death, commit your spirits unto the Saviour, confiding in the love that burns in his bosom, in the merit and virtue of his blood, in the fulness that it has pleased the Father should dwell in him, in the promises by which that fulness is accessible to you, in his intercessions within the veil, in the sympathies of his heart, and in the power that is in his arm. Thus shall you have peace with God, and be delivered from the tormenting fear of death; thus shall you have successive victories over sin, and Satan, and the world; thus shall you have communion with God and with heaven; and contemplating the present life as preparatory to another, you shall rightly appreciate your present state. And when death shall come, at the time, and where, and how, as it shall please the sovereign Lord, it shall prove not the executioner of justice, but the messenger of grace and deliverance to dismiss the spirit unscathed into the presence of Christ, and to leave the flesh to rest in hope of resurrection unto life. Alas! for the folly and the criminality of those who live without faith in the Saviour. Live for ever here they cannot, and though they could, it would be beneath the end of their being and their capacity of happiness. Die they must. Have you made a covenant with death? are you at agreement with hell? Your covenant shall be disannulled, and your agreement shall not stand. Death, and Hell following with him, approach you, and you cannot escape but under the sceptre of Him that conquered both. Remember the words of the wisdom of God: "Whoso findeth me findeth life, and shall obtain favour of the Lord. But he that sinneth against me, wrongeth his own soul: all they that hate me love DEATH."

Let this subject be improved for consolation, on occasion of the death of the righteous.

We are prone at such times to dwell on our privation, to indulge in mournful recollections and dark forebodings, and we are apt to be much carried off with what is merely sensible. Our thoughts wander around the tomb, and our imagination takes afflicting looks of the mouldering clay. Instead of this, it were more befitting that our faith follow the disembodied spirit into the presence of Christ, and that we rejoiced in the victory which has been wrought for the believer, in the triumph which he now celebrates, when he has exchanged the helmet for the crown, and the sword for the palm. Would we with our tears, and our repinings, bring him back again to the battle-field? This, were it possible, would be unkind. Rather let us put on the whole armour of God, fight what remains of the good fight of faith, and, looking at the cross, anticipate the victory through him that loved us, expecting through grace to join the happy throng who stand before the throne, clothed with white robes, and palms in their hands, and who cry with a loud voice, Salvation to our God and unto the Lamb. And what time we descend from these celestial contemplations, and "go to the grave to weep there," let us go in faith, and, in despite of sense, believe that we shall see the glory of God, when in the resurrection, "Death shall be swallowed up in victory, and mortality swallowed up of LIFE."

My friends, what blessed hopes and strong consolations does the faith of the gospel inspire! Can infidelity do anything like this? What do we lose should these hopes be in doubt, which God forbid we should entertain for a moment? What boon do unbelievers offer us for renouncing the Christian hope of immortality and glory? What promise do they give? Gloomy consolation! the promise of an eternal sleep; a promise, too, which they cannot make good.

And to conclude, let us all realise by our faith the victory achieved on Calvary, let us fight the good fight of faith under the Captain of our Salvation, and let us rejoice in the hope of ultimate victory over death and the grave, these universal conquerors. You have heard of the oft-repeated and instructive action of a Saracen conqueror, who immediately before his death, ordered his herald to fasten on a lance the shroud in which he was to be buried, and to carry it about proclaiming, "This is all that remains to Saladin the Great." Of similar import was the answer made to the complimentary question proposed to one by a courtier, riding with him in the splendour and shoutings of a triumphal procession, "What is wanting here?" "CONTINUANCE," was the reply. Ah! my friends, is a winding-sheet all that remains, is the pageant of a day all that the world can give to those who have slain their thousands? We have something better in the spoils of the Redeemer's victory, a certified and illuminated immortality, and a glorious resurrection, and all this enhanced by everlasting duration. Yes, "white robes" of celestial light, not to array the dead body for the grave, but to clothe the glorified person, and "palms" to wave in a triumph whose joys and splendour shall continue and increase for ever and ever.

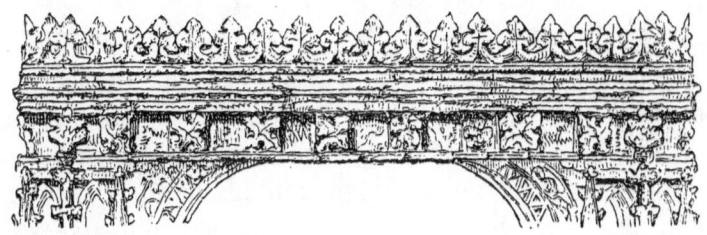

XIII.

Conviction of Sin.

BY THE REV. ROBERT MURRAY M'CHEYNE.

"AND WHEN HE [THE COMFORTER] IS COME, HE WILL REPROVE THE WORLD OF SIN, AND OF RIGHTEOUSNESS, AND OF JUDGMENT."—JOHN xvi. 8.

WHEN friends are about to part from one another, they are far kinder than ever they have been before. It was so with Jesus. He was going to part from his disciples, and never till now did his heart flow out toward them in so many streams of heavenly tenderness. Sorrow had filled their heart, and therefore divinest compassion filled his heart. "I tell you the truth, it is expedient for you that I go away."

Surely it was expedient for himself that he should go away. He had lived a life of weariness and painfulness, not having where to lay his head, and surely it was pleasant in his eyes that he was about to enter into his rest. He had lived in obscurity and poverty—he gave his back to the smiters, and his cheeks to them that plucked off the hair; and now, surely, he might well look forward with joy to his return to that glory which he had with the Father before ever the world was, when all the angels of God worshipped him; and yet he does not say, It is expedient for me that I go away. Surely that would have been comfort enough to his disciples. But no; he says,

"It is expedient for you." He forgets himself altogether, and thinks only of his little flock which he was leaving behind him: "It is expedient for you that I go away." O most generous of Saviours! He looked not on his own things, but on the things of others also. He knew that it is far more blessed to give than it is to receive.

The gift of the Spirit is the great argument by which he here persuades them that his going away would be expedient for them. Now, it is curious to remark that he had promised them the Spirit before, in the beginning of his discourse. In chap. xiv. 16-18, he says, "I will pray the Father, and he shall give you another Comforter, that he may abide with you for ever; even the Spirit of truth; whom the world cannot receive, because it seeth him not, neither knoweth him: but ye know him; for he dwelleth with you, and shall be in you. I will not leave you comfortless: I will come to you." And again: "But the Comforter, which is the Holy Ghost, whom the Father will send in my name, he shall teach you all things, and bring all things to your remembrance, whatsoever I have said unto you" (verse 26). In that passage he promises the Spirit for their own peculiar comfort and joy. He promises him as a treasure which they, and they only, could receive: "For the world cannot receive him, because it neither sees nor knows him;" and yet, saith he, "he dwelleth with you, and shall be in you." But in the passage before us the promise is quite different. He promises the Spirit here, not for themselves, but for the world—not as a peculiar treasure, to be locked up in their own bosoms, which they might brood over with a selfish joy, but as a blessed power to work, through their preaching, on the wicked world around them—not as a well springing up within their own bosoms unto everlasting life, but as rivers of living water flowing through them to water this dry and perishing world. He does not say, When he is come he will fill your hearts with peace and joy to overflowing; but, "When he is come, he will convince the world of sin, and of righteousness, and of judgment." But a little before he had told them that the world would hate and persecute them: "If ye were of the world, the world would love his own; but because ye are not of the world, but I have chosen you out of the world, therefore the world hateth you" (John xv. 19). This was but poor comfort, when that very world was to be the field of their labours; but now he shews them what a blessed gift the Spirit would be; for he would work, through their preaching, upon the very hearts that hated and persecuted them: "He shall convince the world of sin." This has always been the case. In Acts ii. we are told that when the Spirit came on the apostles the crowd mocked them, saying, "These men are full of new wine;" and yet, when Peter preached, the Spirit wrought through his preaching on the hearts of these very scoffers. They were pricked in their hearts, and cried, "Men and brethren, what must we do?" and the same day three thousand souls were converted. Again, the jailor at Philippi was evidently a hard, cruel man towards the apostles; for he thrust them into the inner prison, and made their feet fast in the stocks; and yet the Spirit opens his hard heart, and he is brought to Christ by the very apostles whom he hated. Just so is it, brethren, to this day. The world do not love the true ministers of Christ a whit better than they did. The world is the same world it was in Christ's day. That word has never yet been scored out of the Bible: "Whosoever will live godly in the world, must suffer persecution." We expect, as Paul did, to be hated by the most who listen to us. We are quite sure, as Paul was, that the more abundantly we love you, most of you will love us the less; and yet, brethren, none of these things move us. Though cast down, we are not in despair; for we know that the Spirit is sent to convince the world; and we do not fear but some of you who are counting us an enemy, because we tell you the truth, may even this day, in the midst of all your hatred and cold indifference, be convinced of sin by the Spirit, and made to cry out, "Sirs, what must I do to be saved?"

I. *The first work of the Spirit is to convince of sin.*

1. *Who it is that convinces of sin:* "He shall convince the world of sin, because they believe not in me." It is curious to remark, that wherever the Holy Ghost is spoken of in the Bible, he is spoken of in terms of gentleness and love. We often read of the wrath of God the Father, as in Rom. i.: "The wrath of God is revealed from heaven against all ungodliness and unrighteousness of men." And we often read of the wrath of God the Son: "Kiss the Son, lest he be angry, and ye perish from the way;" or, "Revealed from heaven taking vengeance." But we nowhere read of the wrath of God the Holy Ghost. He is compared to a dove, the gentlest of all creatures. He is warm and gentle as the breath: "Jesus breathed on them, and said, Receive ye the Holy Ghost." He is gentle as the falling dew: "I will be as the dew unto Israel." He is soft and gentle as oil; for he is called "The oil of gladness." The fine oil wherewith the high priest was anointed was a type of the Spirit. He is gentle and refreshing as the springing well: "The water that I shall give him shall be in him a well of water springing up unto everlasting life." He is called "The Spirit of grace and of supplications." He is nowhere called the Spirit of wrath. He is called the "Holy Ghost, which is the Comforter." Nowhere is he called the Avenger. We are told that he groans within the heart of a believer, "helping his infirmities;" so that he greatly helps the believer in prayer. We are told also of the love of the Spirit—nowhere of the wrath of the Spirit. We are told of his being grieved:

"Grieve not the Holy Spirit;" of his being resisted: "Ye do always resist the Holy Ghost;" of his being quenched: "Quench not the Spirit." But these are all marks of gentleness and love. Nowhere will you find one mark of anger or of vengeance attributed to him; and yet, brethren, when this blessed Spirit begins his work of love, mark how he begins—he convinces of sin. Even he, all-wise, almighty, all-gentle, and loving though he be, cannot persuade a poor sinful heart to embrace the Saviour, without first opening up his wounds, and convincing him that he is lost.

Now, brethren, I ask of you, Should not the faithful minister of Christ just do the very same? Ah! brethren, if the Spirit, whose very breath is all gentleness and love, whom Jesus hath sent into the world to bring men to eternal life—if he begins his work in every soul that is to be saved by convincing of sin, why should you blame the minister of Christ if he begins in the very same way? Why should you say that we are harsh, and cruel, and severe, when we begin to deal with your souls by convincing you of sin? "Am I become your enemy, because I tell you the truth?" When the surgeon comes to cure a corrupted wound—when he tears off the vile bandages which unskilful hands had wrapped around it, when he lays open the deepest recesses of your wound, and shews you all its venom and its virulence—do you call him cruel? May not his hands be all the time the hands of gentleness and love? Or, when a house is all on fire, when the flames are bursting out from every window, when some courageous man ventures to alarm the sleeping inmates, bursts through the barred door, tears aside the close-drawn curtains, and with eager hand shakes the sleeper, bids him awake and flee—a moment longer, and you may be lost—do you call him cruel? or do you say this messenger of mercy spoke too loud, too plain? Ah, no. "Skin for skin, all that a man hath will he give for his life." Why, then, brethren, will you blame the minister of Christ when he begins by convincing you of sin? Think you that the wound of sin is less venomous or deadly than a wound in the flesh? Think you the flames of hell are less hard to bear than the flames of earth? The very Spirit of love begins by convincing you of sin; and are we less the messengers of love because we begin by doing the same thing? Oh, then, do not say that we are become your enemy because we tell you the truth!

II. *What is this conviction of sin?* I would begin to shew this by shewing you what it is not.

1. *It is not the mere smiting of the natural conscience.* Although man be utterly fallen, yet God has left natural conscience behind in every heart to speak for him. Some men, by continual sinning, sear even the conscience as with a hot iron, so that it becomes dead and past feeling; but most men have so much natural conscience remaining, that they cannot commit open sin without their conscience smiting them. When a man commits murder or theft, no eye may have seen him, and yet conscience makes a coward of him. He trembles and is afraid; he feels that he has sinned, and he fears that God will take vengeance. Now, brethren, that is not the conviction of sin here spoken of, that is a natural work which takes place in every heart; but conviction of sin is a supernatural work of the Spirit of God. If you have had nothing more than the ordinary smiting of conscience, then you have never been convinced of sin.

2. *It is not any impression upon the imagination.* Sometimes when men have committed great sin, they have awful impressions of God's vengeance made upon their imaginations. In the night-time they almost fancy they see the flames of hell burning beneath them; or they seem to hear doleful cries in their ears telling of coming woe; or they fancy they see the face

of Jesus all clouded with anger; or they have terrible dreams, when they sleep, of coming vengeance. Now, this is not the conviction of sin which the Spirit gives. This is altogether a natural work upon the natural faculties, and not at all a supernatural work of the Spirit. If you have had nothing more than these imaginary terrors, you have had no work of the Spirit.

3. *It is not a mere head knowledge of what the Bible says against sin.* Many unconverted men read their Bibles, and have a clear knowledge that their case is laid down there. They are sensible men. They know very well that they are in sin, and they know just as well that the wages of sin is death. One man lives a swearer, and he reads the words, and understands them perfectly: "Swear not at all"—"The Lord will not hold him guiltless that taketh his name in vain." Another man lives in the lusts of the flesh, and he reads the Bible, and understands these words perfectly: "No unclean person hath any inheritance in the kingdom of Christ and of God." Another man lives in habitual forgetfulness of God—never thinks of God from sunrise to sunset, and yet he reads: "The wicked shall be turned into hell, and all the people that forget God." Now, in this way most unconverted men have a head knowledge of their sin, and of the wages of sin; yet, brethren, this is far from conviction of sin. This is a mere natural work in the head. Conviction of sin is a work of God upon the heart. If you have had nothing more than this head knowledge that you are sinners, then you have never been convinced of sin.

4. *Conviction of sin is not to feel the loathsomeness of sin.* This is what a child of God feels. A child of God has seen the beauty and excellency of God, and therefore sin is loathsome in his eyes. But no unconverted person has seen the beauty and excellency of God; therefore, even the Spirit cannot make him feel the loathsomeness of sin. Just as when you leave a room that is brilliantly lighted, and go out into the darkness of

the open air, the night looks very dark; so when a child of God has been within the vail—in the presence of his reconciled God—in full view of the Father of lights, dwelling in light inaccessible and full of glory—then, when he turns his eye inwards upon his own sinful bosom, sin appears very dark, very vile, and very loathsome. But an unconverted soul never has been in the presence of the reconciled God; and therefore sin cannot appear dark and loathsome in his eyes. Just as when you have tasted something very sweet and pleasant, when you come to taste other things, they appear very insipid and disagreeable; so when a child of God has tasted and seen that God is gracious, the taste of sin in his own heart becomes very nauseous and loathsome to him. But an unconverted soul never tasted the sweetness of God's love; he cannot, therefore, feel the vileness and loathsomeness of sin. This, then, is not the conviction of sin here spoken of.

What, then, is this conviction of sin? *Ans.* It is a just sense of the dreadfulness of sin. It is not a mere knowledge that we have many sins, and that God's anger is revealed against them all; but it is a heart-feeling that we are under sin. Again, it is not a feeling of the loathsomeness of sin—that is felt only by the children of God; but it is a feeling of the dreadfulness of sin, of the dishonour it does to God, and of the wrath to which it exposes the soul. Oh, brethren! conviction of sin is no slight natural work upon the heart. There is a great difference between knowing a thing and having a just sense of it. There is a great difference between knowing that vinegar is sour, and actually tasting and feeling that it is sour. There is a great difference between knowing that fire will burn us, and actually feeling the pain of being burned. Just in the same way, there is all the difference in the world between knowing the dreadfulness of your sins and feeling the dreadfulness of your sins. It is all in vain that you read your

Bibles and hear us preach, unless the Spirit use the words to give sense and feeling to your dead hearts. The plainest words will not awaken you as long as you are in a natural condition. If we could prove to you, with the plainness of arithmetic, that the wrath of God is abiding on you and your children, still you would sit unmoved—you would go away and forget it before you reached your own door. Ah, brethren! he that made your heart can alone impress your heart. It is the Spirit that convinceth of sin.

1. *Learn the true power of the read and preached Word.* It is but an instrument in the hand of God. It has no power of itself, except to produce natural impressions. It is a hammer, but God must break your hearts with it. It is a fire, but God must kindle up your bosoms with it. Without him we may give you a knowledge of the dreadfulness of your condition, but he only can give you a just sense and feeling of the dreadfulness of your condition. The most powerful sermon in the world can make nothing more than a natural impression; but when God works through it, the feeblest word makes a supernatural impression. Many a poor sermon has been the means by which God hath converted a soul. Children of God, oh that you would pray night and day for the lifting up of the arm of God!

2. *Learn that conversion is not in your own power.* It is the Spirit alone who convinces of sin, and he is a free agent. He is a sovereign Spirit, and has nowhere promised to work at the bidding of unconverted men. He hath many on whom he will have mercy; and whom he will he hardeneth. Perhaps you think you may take your fill of sin just now, and then come and repent, and be saved; but remember the Spirit is not at your bidding. He is not your servant. Many hope to be converted on their death-bed; and they come to their death-bed, and yet are not converted. If the Spirit be working with you now, do not grieve him—do not resist him—do not quench him; for he may never come back to you again.

III. *I come to the argument which the Spirit uses.* There are two arguments by which the Spirit usually gives men a sense of the dreadfulness of sin.

1. *The Law:* "The law is our schoolmaster to bring us to Christ"—"Now we know that what things soever the law saith, it saith to them that are under the law, that every mouth may be stopped, and all the world become guilty before God." The sinner reads the law of the great God who made heaven and earth. The Spirit of God arouses his conscience to see that the law condemns every part of his life. The law bids him love God. His heart tells him he never loved God—never had a thought of regard toward God. The Spirit convinces him that God is a jealous God—that his honour is concerned to uphold the law, and destroy the sinner. The Spirit convinces him that God is a just God—that he can by no means clear the guilty. The Spirit convinces him that he is a true God—that he must fulfil all his threatenings: "Have I said it, and shall I not do it?" The sinner's mouth is stopped, and he stands guilty before God.

2. *The second argument is the Gospel:* "Because they believe not on Jesus." This is the strongest of all arguments, and therefore is chosen by Christ here. The sinner reads in the Word that "he that believeth on the Son hath everlasting life;" and now the Spirit convinces him that he never believed on the Son of God—indeed, he does not know what it means. For the first time the conviction comes upon his heart: "He that believeth not the Son, shall not see life; but the wrath of God abideth on him." The more glorious and divine that Saviour is, the more is the Christless soul convinced that he is lost; for he feels that he is out of that Saviour. He sees plainly that Christ is an almighty ark riding over the deluge of God's wrath,—he sees how safe and happy the little company are that are gathered within; but this just makes him gnash his teeth in agony, for he is not within the ark, and the waves and

billows are coming over him. He hears that Christ hath been stretching out the hands all the day to the chief of sinners, not willing that they should perish; but then he never cast himself into these arms, and now he feels that Christ may be laughing at his calamity, and mocking when his fear cometh. O yes, my friends! how often on the death-bed, when the natural fears of conscience are aided by the Spirit of God—how often, when we speak of Christ, his love, his atoning blood, the refuge to be found in him, how safe and happy all are that are in him—how often does the dying sinner turn it all away with the awful question, *But am I in Christ?* The more we tell of the Saviour, the more is their agony increased; for they feel that that is the Saviour they have refused. Ah! what a meaning does that give to these words: "The Spirit convinceth of sin, because they believe not on me."

1. Now, my friends, there are many of you who know that you never believed on Jesus, and yet you are quite unmoved. You sit without any emotion, you eat your meals with appetite, and doubtless sleep sound at night. Do you wish to know the reason? You have never been convinced of sin. The Spirit hath never begun his work in your heart. Oh! if the Spirit of Jesus would come on your hearts like a mighty rushing wind, what a dreadful thought it would be to you this night, that you are lying out of Christ! You would lose your appetite for this world's food, you would not be able to rest in your bed, you would not dare to live on in your sins. All your past sins would rise behind you like apparitions of evil. Wherever you went you would meet the word, "Without Christ, without hope, and without God in the world;" and if your worldly friends should try to hush your fears, and tell you of your decencies, and that your were not so bad as your neighbours, and that many might fear if you feared, ah! how you would thrust them away, and stop your ears, and cry,

There is a city of refuge, to which I have never fled; therefore there must be a blood-avenger. There is an ark; therefore there must be a coming deluge. There is a Christ; therefore there must be a hell for the Christless.

2. Some of you may be under conviction of sin—you feel the dreadfulness of being out of Christ, and you are very miserable. Now, (1.) Be thankful for this work of the Spirit: "Flesh and blood hath not revealed it unto thee, but my Father." God hath brought you into the wilderness just that he might allure you, and speak to your heart about Christ. This is the way he begins the work in every soul he saves. Nobody ever came to Christ but they were first convinced of sin. All that are now in heaven began this way. Be thankful you are not dead like those around you. (2.) Do not lose these convictions. Remember they are easily lost. Involve yourself over head and ears in business, and work even on the Sabbath-day, and you will soon drive all away. Indulge a little in sensual pleasure, take a little diversion with companions, and you will soon be as happy and careless as they. If you love your soul, flee these things; do not stay, flee away from them. Read the books that keep up your anxiety, wait on the ministers that keep up that anxiety. Above all, cry to the Spirit, who alone was the author of it, that he would keep it up. Cry night and day that he may never let you rest out of Christ. Oh! would you sleep over hell? (3.) Do not rest in these convictions. You are not saved yet. Many have come thus far and perished after all; many have been convinced, not converted; many lose their convictions, and wallow in sin again. "Remember Lot's wife." You are never safe till you are within the fold. Christ is the door. "Strive to enter in at the strait gate; for many shall seek to enter in and shall not be able."

XIV.

𝔗𝔥𝔢 𝔍𝔫𝔳𝔦𝔱𝔞𝔱𝔦𝔬𝔫 𝔬𝔣 ℭ𝔥𝔯𝔦𝔰𝔱 𝔱𝔬 𝔖𝔦𝔫𝔫𝔢𝔯𝔰.

BY THE REV. ROBERT GORDON, D.D.

"COME UNTO ME, ALL YE THAT LABOUR AND ARE HEAVY LADEN, AND I WILL GIVE YOU REST."—MATT. xi. 28.

ON reading these words, the question naturally occurs, who are the persons to whom the invitation in the text is addressed, and of whom it is said that they "labour and are heavy laden"? and it will be found that the determination of this point is essential to the right practical application of the subject. It may, perhaps, appear to some at first sight that our Lord must necessarily refer to those who are under deep anxiety and concern about their spiritual interests—who, with a sense of guilt on their conscience, with the vivid anticipation of an approaching eternity, and, it may be, with the recollection of many an unsuccessful effort to dismiss their fears and soothe their disquietude, are ready to exclaim, "What shall I do to be saved?" Nor can it be denied, that such persons are included in the description given in the text; for, if it can be said of any that they labour and are heavy laden, it must surely be of those who are convinced of their sinfulness in the sight of God, and who cannot make their escape from the doubts and misgivings which the consciousness of sin awakens.

But applicable as the description is, and welcome as the invitation ought to be to such persons, it is not to them, I conceive, that either the one or the other is to be exclusively confined. From the manner and connection in which the invitation is introduced, we might infer that it was designed for all who had not already, through faith in Christ, found that rest which he promised to bestow on as many as should come to him. We find him saying, in the preceding context, "All things are delivered unto me of my Father: and no man knoweth the Son, but the Father; neither knoweth any man the Father, save the Son, and he to whomsoever the Son will reveal him." This, of course, is a general, an absolute statement, declaring of all men, without exception, that they know not the Father, and that they cannot know him, unless he is revealed to them by the Son. But it is elsewhere declared in Scripture, that ignorance of God constitutes the debasement and the misery of man, as a fallen creature; that, without the knowledge and the faith of a divine revelation, men are alienated from the life of God through the ignorance that is in them; that their natural feeling towards God, when he is brought vividly before them, is, "Depart from us, for we desire not the knowledge of thy ways; and that, "the Lord Jesus Christ shall be revealed from heaven with his mighty angels in flaming fire, taking vengeance on them that know not God, and that obey not the gospel of our Lord Jesus Christ:" and it is, moreover, expressly declared by our Lord himself, "This is life eternal, that they might know thee the only true God, and Jesus Christ whom thou hast sent." If such, then, be the natural condition of all men, it is true of all that "they labour and are heavy laden," whatever be the chief object of their pursuit, so long as there has not been made to them that revelation of God which Christ only can make; and every man, therefore, who has not already thus learned of Christ, is obviously included in the invitation, "Come unto me, all ye that are heavy laden."

Nor is this the only passage of Scripture in which the gracious invitations of Christ are addressed to all, without exception,—to those who are insensible to the guilt and misery of their condition as sinners, as well as to those who are earnestly seeking to be at rest on the great and momentous subject of their wellbeing as immortal creatures. It is the declaration of Christ himself, that "God so loved the world as to give his only-begotten and well-beloved Son, that whosoever believeth on him may not perish, but may have everlasting life." It was our Lord's commission to his disciples, "Go ye into all the world, and preach the gospel to every creature." And he had, long before, by the mouth of his holy prophet, thus addressed his ancient people, "Ho, every one that thirsteth, come ye to the waters, and he that hath no money; come ye, buy and eat; yea, come, buy wine and milk, without money, and without price." And, to shew that this proposal was not made to those alone who were really thirsting after the wine and milk—even the blessings of Christ's salvation—but to such also as were seeking and hoping to find, in some earthly object of interest and pursuit, all the happiness that they expected or wished for, he thus proceeds to remonstrate with them: "Wherefore do ye spend money for that which is not bread? and your labour for that which satisfieth not? hearken diligently unto me, and eat ye that which is good, and let your soul delight itself in fatness. Incline your ear, and come unto me: hear, and your soul shall live; and I will make an everlasting covenant with you, even the sure mercies of David." The persons described in these words, whatever was the object of their desire, and however ardent that desire might be, were assuredly not thirsting after the water of life; for it is the very subject of the prophet's complaint, that they were expending their strength and their substance in the pursuit of that which could not satisfy. Yet they are addressed as thirsting, and invited to come to the only water of which he that drinketh shall never thirst again; and therefore, on the same principle of interpretation, we are to consider our Lord as addressing, not only those who are earnestly desiring to be restored to the favour and fellowship of God, but all those also who have not yet attained to that blessed state, when he says, in the words of the text, "Come unto me, all ye that labour and are heavy laden, and I will give you rest."

It is assumed, then, in the text, as indeed it is everywhere in Scripture, that all men in their natural and unregenerate state labour and are heavy laden; and it is obvious, from the representation which the Bible gives of the condition and character of mankind, as sinners in the sight of God, that it cannot possibly be otherwise. We are there assured, that the true and permanent happiness of intelligent and immortal creatures is only to be found in God—in the enjoyment of near and friendly intercourse with him—in the sense of his favour which is life, and of his loving-kindness which is better than life—and in the exercise of all those feelings and affections towards him which are due from children to a father. And we are also assured, what indeed is necessarily implied in the enjoyment of such happiness, that they must be in all things conformed to his image—capable of perceiving and admiring his divine excellence—and ready to recognise and to obey his will as in all things holy, and just, and good. But the same record of unerring truth does everywhere bear witness, that the character and condition of mankind as sinners, and so long as they have not been transformed in the renewing of their mind, are the very opposite of all this—that "when God looked down from heaven upon the children of men, to see if there were any that did understand, that did seek God; every one of them is gone back; they are altogether become filthy: there is none that doeth good, no, not one,"—that "it is proved of both Jew and Gentile, that they are all under sin, being enemies to God in their heart by wicked works,"—and that "the carnal mind is enmity against God; it is not subject to the law of God, neither indeed can be." Being thus destitute, therefore, of all capacity for the enjoyment of what alone constitutes man's true happiness—having no relish for those things which must be the subject of the most delightful exercises of thought and feeling, if ever they are to be truly and permanently blessed—nay, having a positive aversion and dislike to any solemn and serious recognition of God at all, as a being who is really near them, and with whom they have immediately to do; it is obvious that, whatever objects they may pursue, or whatever means of gratification they may be able to command, all these gratifications must successively bring with them disappointment and vexation of spirit, and leave their votaries at last experimentally to know that they have all along been "labouring in the fire, and wearying themselves for very vanity." And, in point of fact, such is the actual experience of all men.

And surely I need not enter on any lengthened argument to shew that this remark is true of those who have unreservedly, and almost avowedly, surrendered themselves to the dominion of sinful propensities and passions—seeking their chief happiness in every ungodly indulgence which they can command, provided it can be attained without instantly bringing upon them some evil that would palpably outweigh the hoped-for enjoyment—and adding by every new gratification to the strength and the fierceness of those cravings of a depraved nature, the torture of mortifying which will be exceeded only by the misery of that death in which they must terminate. Of such unhappy persons, it is indeed perfectly true, that they "labour and are heavy laden." They are the subjects of a bitter bondage, the slaves of the most despotic of all taskmasters: nor are there wanting seasons in their history when they cannot conceal, either from themselves or others, that such is their state of degradation and misery; that all their past enjoyments have not only proved transient and unsatisfying, but have entailed upon them innumerable evils, from which they can find no other escape than a temporary forgetfulness of them by plunging deeper into sin and debasement; and that every new indulgence will assuredly be succeeded by its season of sorrow and shame. And if, at these times, there be occasionally awakened, as I suspect there frequently is, some gloomy foreboding of death and an hereafter, can there be conceived a heavier burden, a more intolerable load of wretchedness, than that with which, at such moments, they must be overwhelmed? And even where the pursuit of pleasure is not of so debasing a character as I have now referred to, where it is rather frivolous than flagrantly sinful; yet if worldly enjoyments, in some of the various forms which they assume, be the chief object that is sought after, the only kind of happiness that is either looked for or conceived of, not only will the pursuit terminate in disappointment, but it will prove throughout to be a laborious and thankless servitude. To say nothing of the actual disappointments to which the votaries of such pleasures are constantly exposed—the failure of some favourite scheme, on the success of which their whole happiness was for the time hazarded—or the jealousies and envyings which rivalship in the same pursuits is ever ready to generate, and by which the most valuable of their enjoyments are often embittered—what are these enjoyments, even when obtained in the greatest abundance and with the fewest disappointments, but toil and fatigue in another form?—every one of them falling short of what was expected, and the most permanent of them ending in weariness and satiety.

Nor is the case very different with those who are engaged even in the most laudable and important of worldly pursuits, so long as success in these pursuits is regarded by men as their chief good—as the only kind of happiness that they have ever looked or seriously longed for. Even when they have been successful to the full extent of their expectations, and have been permitted to make a fair experiment of what the world can do in ministering to their happiness, experience has proved, beyond all dispute, that the satisfaction of enjoying the accumulated comforts of this life never exceeds, and seldom equals, the pleasure of making the accumulation; that the object, when attained, has uniformly lost half the charms with which it was invested, while yet the attainment of it was distant and uncertain; and that, in retiring from the more active and laborious pursuits of life, with the view of enjoying the fruits of their long-continued efforts and successful enterprises, men leave behind them the main source of their gratification, and exchange what was wont to interest and excite them for what they find, in actual experience, to be dull and insipid. And if such be the result even of the most successful trials which men ever made to find a satisfying portion in the world—if they thus feel oppressed with the mere satiety and weariness of uninterrupted enjoyment—and if, in the consciousness of a growing incapacity for relishing such gratifications as they can command, they are compelled to anticipate the approach of that event which is to terminate these gratifications for ever, how true is it of all who place their happiness in present things, that they labour and are heavy laden, and that, through much toil of body and travail of soul, they seek rest, but find none!

It will be found, I believe, that there is nothing exaggerated in the view which we have now taken of human life, as a succession of laborious, but unsuccessful efforts for the attainment of permanent happiness, even when present enjoyments are the least interrupted by any misgivings as to the future. In most cases, however, such misgivings do make frequent and very serious inroads on the best and most substantial of these enjoyments; for though some may have succeeded either in shutting out all serious concern about eternity, or in lulling themselves into a state of false security and peace, yet with most men there are seasons when a feeling of insecurity will intrude, and with none in their unregenerate state has that feeling been so completely excluded as that it never can again perplex or disturb them. Though it should be nothing more, therefore, than a feeling of uncertainty as to what awaits them hereafter, it is enough to embitter every one of their earthly gratifications; and should it become with them the great and engrossing subject, it will not only lay upon their spirits a very heavy and depressing weight, but convert their very enjoyments, their most favourite pursuits, into a grievous and intolerable burden. Such, then, being the natural condition of all men, and such their actual experience as soon as they are awakened from that insensibility to future and eternal things, into which present pleasures and pursuits had lulled them, Christ here tenders to them permanent rest from their fruitless and unsatisfying labour: "Come unto me, all ye that labour and are heavy laden, and I will give you rest."

And what, then, is the nature of this rest? It is, in the first place, rest from the disquietude of a guilty mind,—the fear and the distrust which the consciousness of sin awakens, as often as they seriously contemplate the holiness of God, and anticipate the reckoning to which he may hereafter call them. And that this deliverance from a state of apprehension, or even uncertainty as to the manner in which God will deal with them, is necessary, in the first instance, to put sinful creatures in possession of anything like solid or permanent peace of mind, must be obvious to every one who reflects for a moment on the subject. Until they are assured that sin may be forgiven, and till they see clearly in what way, and upon what ground this forgiveness is extended to them, they must be every moment liable to have their comfort broken in upon, and their peace disturbed by anxiety and doubt; for though at times they may contrive to reason down their fears by some plausible conjecture as to what God may do, or though by an effort they may for a season dismiss their fears altogether, yet their real state is not hereby altered, and their security may at any one instant be overthrown by the simple reflection that peradventure their guilt is yet unforgiven. Nor is it merely in their worldly pursuits and enjoyments that this suspicion or uncertainty will depress and discourage them. It will affect also all the efforts which they make to yield obedience to the divine law; for even when they can no longer trifle with their eternal interests, when they are made to feel that salvation is the one thing needful, and are convinced that they never can be happy unless they are reconciled to God, and restored to his favour; and when, under this conviction, they give themselves earnestly and laboriously to the discharge of the duties, and the practice of the virtues enjoined in the law of God; still, so long as they are under any misapprehension or mistake respecting the way in which the guilty are forgiven, their obedience will be at best but a painful servitude, and a feeling of hopelessness will be ready to steal over them as often as they compare their heart and life with the requirements of the divine law, and seriously ask themselves whether they have yet made such attainments in holiness as will warrant them to conclude that God now regards them with favour and approbation.

It is from all this disquietude, then, this state of bondage and depression, that Christ promises rest; not by any vague and general representations of the mercy of God, which never can awaken anything better than a hope equally vague; but by revealing a definite principle on which God forgives the guilty, and accepts them as righteous in his sight. He came into the world "to seek and to save that which was lost;" he "suffered, the just for the unjust, that he might bring sinners unto God;" and having thus "put away sin by the sacrifice of himself, he has become the author of eternal salvation to as many as believe in his name." In consequence of His death, whereby he expiated sin, a free pardon is held out to all, and actually bestowed on as many as come to him; provision is thus made for removing the suspicion and pacifying the fears of a guilty conscience; there is presented to us a distinct and solid ground of hope towards God, whereon we are invited and commanded to rely; and being "justified by faith, we have peace with God through our Lord Jesus Christ."

But though the assurance that sin is freely forgiven through faith in Christ Jesus is the first and an essential step towards putting sinful creatures in possession of permanent peace, still it is but a step in that process whereby Christ fulfils the gracious promise in the text. Till the guilty know and understand how they are to be forgiven, in what way they are to be brought from under that condemnation which has passed upon them as transgressors of the divine law, nothing can ever afford them any sure or lasting peace; for so long as they have reason to fear that they are the objects of God's righteous displeasure, they must either be in a state of utter insensibility as to future and eternal things, or they must feel themselves perplexed and distracted with suspicions, from which it is impossible to make their escape. But even when they have discovered that provision has been made for their immediate deliverance from condemnation, that Christ has redeemed them from the curse of the law by being made a curse for them, and that, instead of being required to wait and to labour until they shall have wrought out a righteousness for themselves, they are justified freely through the redemption that is in Jesus; still this is but the commencement of their deliverance from that state of bitter bondage into which they had been brought by sin. Independently of all the fears and painful forebodings of coming judgment which did at times take possession of them, the dominion which sin has obtained over them is itself a most debasing servitude, unfitting them for the enjoyment of all that is pure and holy and heavenly, and making them dependent for their happiness on gratifications and pursuits which are as short-lived as they are unsatisfying, and which serve only to alienate them still farther from God and from righteousness.

Christ, then, gives rest to as many as come to him, not only by resolving their doubts on the most momentous of all questions—how they may be forgiven and received into the divine favour—but also by opening up to them a source of happiness which never can be exhausted, and the enjoyment of which will produce no satiety or weariness. In bringing them back to the favour, he restores them also to the fellowship of God, and imparts to them by his Spirit a capacity for the enjoyment of that fellowship; he removes from their minds that natural dislike of divine things, that enmity of the carnal mind against God, which characterises every individual of the apostate children of Adam; he quickens them to a lively apprehension of the glory and excellence of the divine character, especially of the riches of redeeming love; he takes captive the affections which were once given to vain and frivolous and sinful objects, by impressing them with an abiding sense of what they owe to him who bought them with His own blood; he brings them under the influence of his love, whereby they are constrained to live no more to themselves, but to him who died for them, and rose again; and having thus given them new powers, as well as new sources of enjoyment, he opens up to them the sure prospect of unending and uninterrupted blessedness in another and better state. With all this indeed there may be no change, either real or apparent, in their external circumstances. Their worldly comforts may be neither greater in their amount, nor more permanent in duration; their labour in providing for themselves and others may not be less, nor their disappointments fewer than before; nay, from the new motives by which they are influenced, and the new principles on which they act, they may be constrained to forego many an advantage, and to submit to many a temporal loss, which the less scrupulous morality of the world would not have required of them. But though their worldly condition, considered in itself, may have undergone no change, or if any, a change only for the worse; though they have no greater security than they had before, either for a larger or a more enduring portion of the good things of this life; and though they are as much exposed as ever to those vicissitudes which attach to every earthly enjoyment; yet a mighty change has taken place in their estimate of these enjoyments, and in the effect which the loss of them produces on their true happiness. Worldly things no longer constitute their portion; though not insensible to the pain of any sore bereavement with which God may see meet to visit them, they feel at the same time that no such bereavement can take away or impair their chief good; their treasure is safe, whatever may befall them as to the objects of their present interest and pursuit; and amidst all the disappointments which they may experience, and all the privations which they may be called to endure, they feel that Christ has given them rest, a rest which, so far from being disturbed by present afflictions, is only rendered thereby more valuable, inasmuch as they are persuaded that such afflictions form a necessary part of the discipline whereby they are trained to a meetness for the heavenly inheritance, and will "work out for them a far more exceeding, even an eternal weight of glory."

Such, then, being the rest which Christ has provided for the weary and the heavy laden, it ought to be a question of the deepest interest to every sinful man, how he may be brought into the actual enjoyment of this rest. And to this question the text furnishes a very simple answer. It is, by coming to Christ; "Come unto me all ye that labour and are heavy laden, and I will give you rest." In explanation of the expression, "coming to Christ," I might refer to other scriptures, where we find it represented as of the same import with believing on him. "I am the bread of life," said our Lord to the Jews on another occasion, "he that cometh to me shall never hunger, and he that believeth on me shall never thirst;" and everywhere in scripture we find the same effects ascribed to believing in Christ as are here said to follow on coming to him. "God so loved the world, that he gave his only begotten Son, that whosoever believeth on him may not perish, but have everlasting life." The apostle declares that the object of his mission to the Gentiles was "to turn them from darkness unto light, and from the power of Satan unto God, that they might receive the forgiveness of sins, and an inheritance among them that are sanctified by faith that is in Christ Jesus." When the jailor of Philippi, under a deep conviction of guilt, earnestly inquired of the same apostle what he should do to be saved, his prompt and simple answer was, "Believe on the Lord Jesus Christ, and thou shalt be saved." And he has elsewhere said, of himself and of all true believers, "Being justified by faith, we have peace with God, through our Lord Jesus Christ." But when we say that the expression, "coming to Christ," is the same as "believing on him," we do not perhaps make its true import much clearer than before. Indeed, I am inclined to think that it is itself the plainest and simplest form of expression, and may be employed to illustrate the other, and to remove some of the misapprehensions respecting the nature of saving faith which have given rise to so much unprofitable disputation. None at all events would be in any danger of misunderstanding the meaning of the expression were it applied to a person seeking deliverance and relief from any temporal calamity, for, supposing such a person to be in the same state of destitution and helplessness with regard to his worldly circumstances, as the Bible represents sinners to be in with respect to their spiritual concerns, and that he is urged and persuaded to betake himself to one who is alone able and willing to help him, would we not understand his coming to such an one to mean that he was ready cordially to acquiesce in the counsel, and thankfully to embrace the proposals which might be tendered to him? However little, then, men may know experimentally of what it is to come to Christ, they cannot fail to perceive that, from the very nature of the thing, it necessarily implies a willingness to accept and a desire to possess that rest which he tenders to the weary and the heavy laden; and they who are thus willing to receive and desirous of experiencing this rest are required to confide in the faithfulness of the promise, that it will be given them. And such I apprehend is the nature of saving faith. It consists not in a mere assent of the understanding to the general truth of the Bible, in the same way as men give their assent to a matter of fact—merely on the ground of competent evidence; the thing to be believed is of such a nature that the belief of it necessarily involves a perception of the reality, the value, and the desirableness, of what is tendered for acceptance; and implies, therefore, on the part of those who do believe, a change of heart—such a change as leads them to choose the rest which Christ has provided for all who come to him in preference to those pursuits and enjoyments in which they were naturally inclined to seek their chief happiness. And here we are to look for the explanation of the melancholy fact, that so many either reject the gospel, or only give to it a cold and formal assent. Their unbelief arises not from any lack of mere evidence, nor from anything intricate or perplexing in the nature of saving faith. It is because they are not willing to accept of the proposals which the gospel makes to them. Disappointed as they have frequently been, and weary and heavy laden as they still are, they have no desire for the rest which Christ promises, and will give to all who come to him. In their estimation such rest, so far from being desirable, would only be to relinquish everything that can yield them any real enjoyment; and though at times, therefore, they may have their misgivings as to the termination of all their pursuits, yet they cannot believe their condition to be so desperate as to require their immediate and unreserved compliance with the invitations in the text. They will not come to Christ "that they may have life, and that they may have it more abundantly."

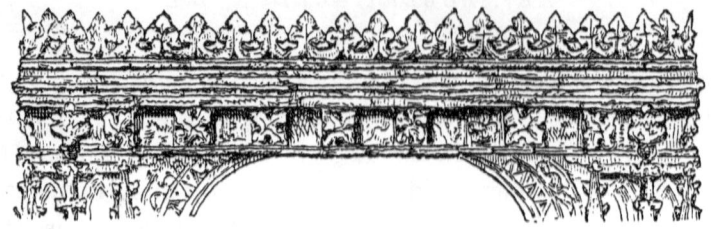

XV.

Godliness.

BY THE REV. WILLIAM CUNNINGHAM, D.D.

"HE THAT COMETH TO GOD MUST BELIEVE THAT HE IS, AND THAT HE IS A REWARDER OF THEM THAT DILIGENTLY SEEK HIM."—HEB. xi. 6.

THE existence and character and government of God are the foundation of all religion. The whole of religion, in the widest sense of the word, consists in, and is deduced from the knowledge and contemplation of God. Religion indeed may be, as it often has been, defined to be a right mode of thinking and feeling and acting in regard to God. When we think aright of God—that is, when we entertain correct views of his nature and character, and the relation in which we stand to him—when we are rightly affected by these views both in our feelings and in our conduct—we may properly be said to be religious, or to act under the influence of true religion. "He that cometh to God," says the apostle, "must believe that he is, and that he is the rewarder of them that diligently seek him"; or, in order that we may discharge aright the duties arising out of the relation in which we stand to him, we must know, first, that there is a God; and second, how or in what way he is disposed or affected towards us. From the knowledge of the existence and character of God results all the feelings or emotions with which we ought to contemplate him, and all the duties which we ought to perform towards him.

The great principle, then, on which all religion is founded—from which all religious feelings and duty are to be deduced—is the existence of God—a truth completely established by every sort of evidence, derived from every department of creation. There are indeed very few speculative atheists—I mean, very few who in words deny the existence of God and argue against it. But we are afraid there are not a few of those who admit and profess to believe in the existence of God who are practical atheists, or persons whose practice is scarcely, if at all, influenced by their professed or pretended belief in the existence of God—whose feelings and conduct are very much the same as they would be if they neither believed in God's existence, nor professed to do so. When we see men, as we may every day see them around us, professing to believe that God is, and that he is the rewarder of them that diligently seek him, and yet not coming to him—professing to believe in God's existence, and yet altogether uninfluenced in regard to it—the only conclusion to which we can come is, either that they do not understand what is implied in the proposition that there is a God, or else that they do not believe it.

Let us consider, then, what is really implied in the doctrine of the Existence of God, that we may see what effect it should necessarily produce upon the heart and character when understood and believed. What is God? What is it we mean when we use this word? God, we are told in the Catechism, in accordance with Scripture, is "a Spirit—infinite, eternal, unchangeable; in his being, wisdom, power, holiness, justice, goodness, and truth;" and there is no great difference of positive opinion with regard to what God is. For although men differ widely in the practical conceptions which they form of God and the divine character, there is little speculative difference of opinion with regard to what is implied in the general idea of God, at least in countries where the light of divine revelation is diffused. Endeavour then closely and carefully to fix your thoughts and attention upon what is implied in the idea of God, and in the existence of such a being as that word describes.

God is a Spirit. When we fix our thoughts and attention upon God, such is the weakness of our faculties, and such their subjection to things of sense, that we often find it very difficult, if not impossible, to form a distinct conception of God as a pure Spirit, and to abstract from our conception of him everything which has a connection, direct or indirect, with matter—to contemplate him simply by the eyes of the mind, without attaching to him any of those qualities which are perceived only by the external senses. In endeavouring, however, to fix our minds upon the contemplation of God— to come, as it were, into the divine presence—we must endeavour to withdraw from our idea of him everything corporeal, everything material, everything with regard to shape and form, everything which bears resemblance to the objects that come under the cognisance of our organs of perception.

But God is not only a spiritual being, free from the defects and limitations which necessarily attach to material beings; he is also infinite, eternal, unchangeable, in every perfection. He is a being of whose mode of existence, and of whose character and government we can form but a very inadequate conception. This knowledge is too great for us, we cannot attain to it. But we know at least that his power and goodness and wisdom and justice and truth infinitely transcend the degrees of these various excellencies which we have ever seen manifested in the character and conduct of any other being, and which we have ever been able to conceive, even in imagination. We may give full scope to our imaginations in forming a conception of the glorious excellencies of the Deity, provided our imaginations be under the influence of sanctified principle, and move in the track pointed out to us in Scripture; and yet our highest conceptions must fall infinitely short of the reality. God is infinite and unchangeable in his wisdom, possessed of a wisdom which is unsearchable, and which nothing can deceive or elude. He is infinite and unchangeable in his power, and possessed of a power which nothing can resist or withstand. He is infinite and unchangeable in his holiness, and possessed of a holiness which is at irreconcilable variance with all sin, and which cannot look upon iniquity but with abhorrence. And he is infinite and unchangeable in his justice and goodness, his whole conduct being regulated at all times by the dictates of exact and unerring justice, and at the same time guided by unbounded benevolence. We cannot form a clear and positive conception of these qualities, and still less of a being possessed of them all in an infinite degree, just because our finite understandings cannot comprehend fully an infinite object; but we are capable of forming some conception of a Being who is possessed of every excellence which we have ever seen exemplified in any degree in those beings with whom we may have had personal intercourse, and possessed of them in a degree altogether free from those defects and limitations which we have ever beheld attaching to them in all other beings, whether arising from their own nature, or from their relation to each other and external objects; and this Being, possessed of every perfection, and free from every defect, we call by the name of God. Now, if you really form to yourselves a clear and distinct conception—so far as it is possible for the human faculties to do so—of the qualities and character of God, as those which are commonly understood to be expressive of that name, and if you believe all these qualities to have an actual existence in a being who really exists, surely the idea of such a being must take a strong hold of your minds, and the contemplation of him must excite emotions of a very powerful and persuading character.

Conceive of a human being come to the full use of his faculties and actively engaged in worldly occupations, but who had never heard of the existence of God, and imagine that he was to be told at once, upon authority or evidence which completely commanded the assent of his understanding, of the existence of such a great and glorious Being as is meant to be described by the Word of God, would you not think it right and proper that this information should be received with the greatest eagerness, should make a powerful impression on his mind, and should ever after regulate his thoughts and feelings and actions as infinitely the most interesting and important object that had ever been presented to his understanding? How comes it, then, that men who profess to know God, and to believe in his existence, and who assent to the correctness of that account of him we have shortly stated, seldom think of him, are but little affected by the contemplation of his character, and feel very imperfectly, if at all, those emotions of profound humility and adoration which the contemplation of his character obviously and in right reason is fitted to produce? That this is the case is incontrovertible; and there is no way of explaining it satisfactorily, viewed merely as an exhibition of human character, except upon the ground that human nature is indeed in a diseased and disordered condition, that its functions are viciously and irregularly performed, and without admitting the truth of the scriptural doctrine that man's understanding is naturally darkened through the ignorance that is in him, that he desires not the knowledge of his ways.

Surely if men had anything like distinct conceptions of the

character of a Being infinite, eternal, and unchangeable, in wisdom, power, holiness, justice, goodness, and truth, and really believed in his existence, it might be expected that the idea of such a being would be often and habitually present to their thought, would keep alive in their minds feelings of profound reverence and respect, and of humble adoration, and would make them regard with the deepest reverence and submission everything connected with Him—everything with which the idea of him was in any way associated. But how many men do we see whose character and conduct scarcely afford any evidence of the contemplation of the character of this infinitely great and glorious Being producing the least effect upon them; in whom the conception of God, or the mention of his name, excites no feelings corresponding to what might be expected to rise from the contemplation of a Being glorious in holiness, fearful in praises, and continually doing wonders; who completely verify the scriptural description of being without God, and who, although they in a certain sense know God, yet glorify him not as God! There are even not a few, respected in society, who not only feel no emotion of awe and veneration in thinking or speaking of God, but who employ God's name for the most base and contemptible purposes, as if it had no meaning whatever, as if there was no Being in existence corresponding to the name which they use so freely, or as if he were altogether such an one as themselves, and not even entitled to the same respect and consideration which they would shew to one of their fellow-men.

This presents a most melancholy picture of the ungodliness of the human heart, and an ungodliness which is in the highest degree sinful and dangerous. Men are under a positive moral obligation to view God as he is, in all his glorious excellencies, and to be adequately affected by all those feelings which the perception and contemplation of his character are fitted to produce. Such however is the ungodliness of men's nature, and the hold which it has of them, that their nature must be thoroughly changed, and their hearts renewed, before they are enabled to pierce through the thick veil which it throws around the divine excellencies. It is only when the Holy Spirit takes of the things of Christ, and shews them to us, that we are ever enabled to behold his glory, and see him as he really is, to contemplate him in all his excellencies, and to feel in due measure the emotions which the contemplation of that excellency is fitted to excite. It is thus only that men are penetrated with a true spirit of devotion and enlightened piety, that they are led to see their own insignificance and meanness, compared with the holiness and majesty of the Godhead, and to fall down on the footstool of his throne with humble adoration; in short, that the contemplation of the divine attributes produces in any measure upon their heart and character the effects which it is both fitted and intended to produce. It is thus only that men are brought in any degree to a right way of thinking or feeling and acting in regard to God, as a Being of glorious and transcendent excellence, infinite in power, and wisdom, and goodness, and holiness.

God however is not only a Being possessed of every perfection, and of every perfection in an infinite degree, and therefore a right and proper object of holy and pervading adoration and self-abasement to all who possess capacities and opportunities of knowing him, simply on account of his own intrinsic excellence and glory, independently of any peculiar relation in which he might stand to us. He is also our Creator and Proprietor, our continual Preserver and Governor, and our bountiful Benefactor; and in all these characters he ought to be recognised and worshipped, and should exert a permanent influence upon our feelings and actions. When we view God as the Creator of everything that exists, as having originally called everything into existence by his creating word—then, if we understand what is meant by this statement, and are at all suitably affected by it, surely we cannot but be deeply impressed with the conviction that we ourselves, and all that we have, and everything that the world contains, are his property, and subject entirely to his disposal. If, however, we fully and rightly realised to our own mind God's original creation and continual preservation of the universe, and all things in it, animate and inanimate, we would see God in everything; we would view everything as his work, as an effect of his power, and proof of his wisdom and goodness. The habitual frame and tendency of our minds would be to see God, and to recognise him in all the works of nature, and in all other objects; to rise from the contemplation of what is great and glorious, beautiful and sublime, noble and exalted, in the objects of natural scenery, or in the exhibitions of human character and conduct, to him who is the great Author of every excellence, and the centre of all perfection. But, alas! how many are there who, in a world full of God, and teeming with traces of his power and wisdom and goodness, never recognise him—are never led by any of the striking and obvious marks of him which he has imprinted upon his works, to think of their great Author—whose hearts are seldom or never raised, with feelings of humble adoration and reverence, from second causes up to the great First Cause of all—who are never prompted from the bottom of their hearts to say, Lord, these are a part of thy works, and it is but a small part of them that we can behold!

But this great and glorious Being whom we call God is not only the Creator and Preserver of everything that exists, he is also the supreme and sovereign Ruler of the world, exercising a special providence over all the actions and concerns of men; and the contemplation of him in this character is well fitted to exert an important influence over the habitual tenor of our thoughts and actions, although, as in everything else connected with God, we are too much disposed to neglect and to overlook it. Would you only endeavour fully to realise to your minds for a single day, even for a single hour, the great truth which you all profess to believe, that God is everywhere, that he knows all you think, and hears all you say, and sees all you do; were this truth really brought to bear upon your thoughts and feelings, and to become a practical principle of conduct, surely you would think and feel and act very differently from what you do. How often in the privacy of our bosoms, and in solitude and secrecy, do we think and act what we could not endure that one of our fellow-men should know and behold! how often do we indulge in thoughts and imaginations, the indulgence of which would be checked and prevented if we knew that one of our fellow-sinners could perceive and trace them! and yet how little, comparatively, are we affected by the far higher and more important consideration that God sees us at all times, that he understandeth our very thoughts afar off, that there is not a a word of our mouths, but lo! It is altogether known to him.

God, as we all admit, is the great Framer of the world, to whose sovereign control and disposal our interests and prospects are at all times subject, on whom our happiness is continually dependent, who directs every event in our life, and arranges every circumstance in our situation; yet such is our natural aversion to think of God, and to recognise his authority, that men, unrenewed by the Spirit of divine grace, seldom or never see God's hand in anything that befalls them; they receive and look upon the various events in their life merely as the ordinary natural consequence of general laws, of the great principles by which the affairs of the world are regulated, and in this way they practically exclude God from the world which he has created, and which he at all times governs and superintends. Surely, if God does indeed govern the world, his authority ought to be felt, and his agency ought to be recognised. If he does indeed control all the actions and concerns of men, it is both our duty and our interest to feel this, and to act upon it—to set the Lord continually before us—to acknowledge him in all our ways that he may direct our steps. And yet how little of this is there practically in the conduct of the great body of mankind, and how strongly does the natural earthliness and grossness of our character shew itself, in thus blinding us to such an extent, to the plain and obvious traces of the working of an unseen but active and powerful Intelligence, which the heaven-enlightened eye can discover, and indeed habitually perceives, in the various events of life, and in the various changes of condition.

But while we acknowledge God's hand in controlling and superintending every event that befalls us, we should in an especial manner recognise him as our continual benefactor, the source of all our happiness, and the author of all our enjoyment. That He is so, we all acknowledge and admit, but how few of us, comparatively, feel and act upon it! Is it not, however, in the highest degree unreasonable that we should live continually in the enjoyment of the bounties of God's providence, and even admit that they are all his gifts, while yet we seldom feel our hearts filled with any emotion of gratitude to him, and seldom even feel that to Him we really owe them? It is lamentable to see so many engrossed with the gifts, so as to forget the Giver; and so occupied with the various pleasures addressed to their different senses, as to overlook him by whom they are all bestowed. How very imperfectly are even the best of us influenced by right views of our obligations to God for the bounties of his providence, for the benefits with which he is daily loading us! How far short do we come of the duty of giving thanks in all things, and of leading a life of gratitude to God! "Oh that men would praise the Lord for his goodness, and for his wonderful works to the children of men!"

We have thus attempted to explain shortly the leading ideas implied in the existence of God, both with reference to what he is in himself, and the relations in which he stands to us. We have pointed out to you the various feelings which the contemplation of God's character and government ought to produce in our hearts, and the various effects they ought to have upon the course of our conduct, if we were really affected by it as we ought to be; and we have endeavoured to contrast this, for it is a contrast and not a correspondence, with what we actually see exemplified in the generality of mankind. We have seen in many men an absolute want of those feelings with reference to God, which the contemplation of his character and his conduct towards us ought to have produced, and in all men a great deficiency, both in the depth and constancy of these feelings, and their habitual influence upon the character. We thus see how inconsistent the conduct of the generality of men towards God is with the dictates of sound reason and the principles of common sense, and how strikingly a rational survey of the moral aspect of society confirms the scriptural account of the fallen and depraved state of man's nature. Men do not feel and act towards God as even their own reason shews to be right and imperative, and therefore must stand self-condemned.

It is scriptural and requisite thus to point out, and to urge upon all, as we have been doing, their obligations with reference to God in their fullest extent, were it only in order to convince them of their guilt and sinfulness. But while we point out to you the great and radical deficiencies which too generally exist in our feelings towards God, and consequently in the conduct which flows from them, and while we refer these grievous deficiencies to their true source, in the ungodliness and depravity of our natures, and insist upon the guilt and danger of remaining even for a day in this state of alienation from our Maker, we must at the same time state that there is but one way in which fallen men can be restored to a right mode of thinking, and feeling, and acting in regard to God, and that is, by being born again, of the word of God, and through the belief of the gospel. We can never be led to right views, and adequate impressions of the glory and excellencies of the divine character, until we see it in the face of Christ Jesus. We can never be brought to feel aright towards God, as our Creator, and Preserver, and Governor, until we are led to look upon him as our Redeemer, as the God of our salvation through Christ. When, however, through the Holy Spirit, we are enabled to believe the truth as in Jesus, we are then impressed with a sense of God's glory, we are led to see that he is indeed infinitely amiable and excellent; we are constrained to adore Him, and constrained to love him. When, too, we are taught to view God as our Redeemer, this sheds a reflected lustre upon all the other relations in which he stands to us, and brings the contemplation of them to bear with power and effect upon our heart and character.

The true Christian, then, alone is impressed with anything like adequate conceptions of God's creation and preservation of the universe; of his upholding all things by the word of his power; of his providence or superintendence over all the actions of his creatures. It is only when men are brought to believe the truth as it is in Jesus that they are led habitually to recognise God's hand, to discover manifestations of his character and government in all the various objects around them, and in all the various events of their life. It is not until men have been enabled to understand and to feel that most wonderful illustration of the principles of God's moral government, shewn in the sufferings and death of Christ, that they ever fully realise to their own minds his constant government of the world, and his unceasing control over all the actions and concerns of men. It is only when they have been led in some measure to appreciate God's very best gift, Jesus Christ, the Son of his love, that they ever feel, in anything like a right measure and degree, their obligations to him for all the blessings of providence, and for the supply of all their temporal wants.

Religion, as we formerly stated, just consists in a right mode of feeling, thinking, and acting with regard to God,—in being duly affected by the contemplation of his character, and conducting ourselves suitably to the relations in which we stand to him. We are imperatively called upon to know and to feel these relations, and to live under their influence; for without this there can be no religion. Now, not only is the knowledge of Jesus Christ, and of him crucified, in consequence of the ungodliness of our nature, the only means of leading us to right views and suitable impressions of the relation in which we stand to God, and of our consequent obligations to him as the creatures of his hand, and the subjects of his government, but it is directly of itself the only source of our knowledge of another relation which we hold to God, and one of paramount importance, viz. that resulting from our character as sinners. It is only through the revelation of God's character in the gospel that we know with certainty anything of the way in which it would lead him to treat those who have violated his law, and incurred his displeasure. Our condition as sinners, as subject to the curse of a broken law, is the most important feature in our situation, it is that which bears most materially both on our duties to God, and upon our everlasting destinies; we can therefore have no saving knowledge of God, and of

Christ Jesus,—no such knowledge as will lead us to feel and to act towards him in a manner becoming our character and condition, and as he who sent to deliver us from that everlasting misery which we deserve, and to raise us to the possession of that eternal life which is the gift of God's free grace. Eternal life results from the knowledge of God, and of Jesus Christ whom he has sent. If we do not know Christ, then we cannot know God, as we ought to know him, and as it is indispensable for our salvation that we should know him. In short, it is in the gospel only that we can see God, see him as he really is, view him in his true character, and behold him in such a way, and in such aspects, as to transform us into the same image, and to lead us to glorify him.

If, therefore, you would cultivate true religion, if you would discharge the duties which you owe to God, and prepare yourselves for the everlasting enjoyment of his presence, you must habituate yourselves to view God's character in the light of the gospel, as revealed in the face of Christ Jesus; for it is in the gospel alone that we have correct views of God's character, in all its extent, that we find the grounds of all the feelings which we ought to entertain, and of all the duties which we ought to perform in regard to him; and it is through the gospel, and the powers and principles which it brings into operation, that these views will ever be effectual in producing their appropriate impression upon our depraved and ungodly hearts.

The great defect under which men's views of God are apt to labour, even when they do give some attention to the contemplation of his character, is a want of clearness and distinctness. When we attempt to form a clear and distinct conception of God, as an actually existing Being, we are very apt to invest him with material properties, inconsistent with his character as a Spirit; and in attempting to guard against this extreme, we are apt to fall into the opposite one and to lose sight of his distinct character as a personal agent. We are very apt to rest satisfied with a vague and indefinite notion of God, of which we have no very distinct perception, viewing him rather as a sort of power or principle, than as a person living and acting. It is of great importance, however, in order to our having right views of God, and being properly affected by them, that we get rid of this misty and vague conception of him, a conception which is too impalpable for our minds to grasp, and too uninteresting for the heart to be affected by it, and that we realise him to our minds, with all the clearness and vividness with which we contemplate a particular individual in his personal character. We should be careful of ascribing to God anything that partakes of human imperfections in his character or in his actings, and at the same time we must labour to have a clear and impressive view of him as he is; and this can be done only by removing from our idea of him everything of a vague and indefinite kind, and ascribing to Him, in all his actings and dispensations, the distinctness of personal agency.

This is certainly not easily effected by our feeble and darkened understanding; but God, in condescension to our weakness, has been pleased to give us a personal manifestation of the divine character in a human shape, in the person of his only begotten Son. "In him dwelleth all the fulness of the Godhead bodily." "He that hath seen Him hath seen the Father." "He dwelt among men, and they beheld his glory, the glory of the only-begotten of the Father, full of grace and truth." And God has been pleased, by the inspiration of his Spirit, and the superintendence of his providence, to transmit to us, in the gospel history, a full view of the life, and character, and conduct, and conversation of our blessed Saviour while he lived on earth, a view of which brings before us a faithful and accurate representation of the divine character in all its aspects and relations, and in a manner the best fitted to impress our understandings, and to affect our hearts. If, then, we would know what God is, and be suitably affected by the contemplation of his character, and the relation in which we stand to Him, let us view him at all times, and in all circumstances, as manifested in the person of his Son, even of Him who is the brightness of his Father's glory, and the express image of his person, and who is himself God over all, blessed for evermore.

XVI.

𝔗𝔥𝔢 𝔏𝔞𝔪𝔟 𝔬𝔣 𝔊𝔬𝔡.

BY THE REV. JAMES HAMILTON, D.D.

"THE NEXT DAY JOHN SEETH JESUS COMING UNTO HIM, AND SAITH, BEHOLD THE LAMB OF GOD, WHICH TAKETH AWAY THE SIN OF THE WORLD!"—JOHN i. 29.

THE sin of the world! Sin? Sin? What is sin? You see that holy law? Radiant with God's own purity, and bright with a divine benignity, it stands on earth a pillar of light and glory, a specimen of God, to tell us that he himself is holy, just, and good. And sin defaces that monument, dilapidates it, and casts filth on what it cannot destroy.

You see that God of love? Bending over an earth fresh fashioned, and beaming on it those looks of complacency which hallow while they bless; and behold him in his own image, man, concentring those regards of love and joy, which made him what they hailed him, "Very good"—and presently see man shaking the fist of defiance, and darting the glance of estrangement and hostility at the God of Love, and you see another aspect of sin.

Look to this man, made up of divers lusts and passions! Pride, ambition, envy; vanity, resentment, anger; covetousness, license, cruelty—these, and many evil appetites and emotions besides, flow through all his nature in fierce and malignant currents, and are his very being's poisoned blood and fevered pulse. And out they break in oaths and curses, in execrations and blows of violence, in debauchery and riot; in spoken falsehood and acted lies, in words of lewdness and deeds of shame; in the sanctuary forsaken, the Bible tossed aside, and prayer neglected or shammed over. And when, goaded by conscience, he makes an effort to amend, when to clear the cloud from affection's brow or reconcile him to himself, he makes a desperate struggle, and seeks to rend off some besetting sin, he finds he cannot. This evil habit he cannot tear away; for, like the poisoned mantle, it has grown into himself, and to tear it off is to tear fibres and nerves asunder, is to lacerate the quick and quivering flesh. This guilty affection, he cannot pluck it out, for his heart is at its roots, and nature could not stand the self-divulsion; and in this pervasive canker, this virulent and festering plague, you see sin it its malignity.

And look to this pure region, this holy paradise or radiant heaven. And what is this blot on the brightness, this shadow on the splendour? What is it which attracts so many eyes in wonder, and repels them again in horror? What is it they are expelling in amazement and disgust? Nay, rather, what is it which, abashed and self-conscious, expels itself? What is that object which from under Jehovah's burning eye, dark and dastardly, slinks away to its own place, and Eden again is bright, and heaven again is holy? What is it which, when confronted with Infinite Sanctity, would fain seek refuge in the deepest cavern of the pit, and from a region of light and elevation would gladly flee to hide its hideousness and pollution in the dungeon of despair?

Words cannot paint it. It is only in the light of the great white throne, or by the flames of hell, or in the revealing light of the Holy Spirit, that any one can see the real character of sin. It is the enemy of God. It is the transgressor of his law. It is the great soul-poison and heart-plague. It is the only thing which really defiles or deforms the man. It is pollution, misery, guilt, incipient hell. It is the only thing to which we can give, in its fullest sense, the emphatic name of evil.

But just as sin is our earth's great burden, and humanity's deforming blot, the design of the Incarnation was to do away this mighty evil in the case of a goodly number. For this end the Son of God was manifest, that he might destroy the works of the devil; and in the case of a multitude whom no man can number, the Saviour finished transgression and made an end of sin. And though here he be called the Lamb of God, there is one aspect in which the Lamb was wrathful, and his strength was leonine. There was one vindictive feeling which, like an oven, burned in his holy bosom, and one object toward which he was filled with exterminating fury. On sin he could not look without abhorrence, and the sight of that cursed thing which had insulted his heavenly Father, and filled a happy world with woe and horror, kindled his zeal and revenge; and whilst the Lamb's gentleness encouraged the sinner, the Lion's fury still flashed upon the sin. "Who is this that cometh from Edom, with dyed garments from Bozrah? this that is glorious in his apparel, travelling in the greatness of his strength? I that speak in righteousness, mighty to save. But wherefore art thou red in thine apparel, and thy garments like him that treadeth in the wine-fat? I have trodden the wine-press alone; and of the people there was none with me: for I will tread them in mine anger, and trample them in my fury. For the day of vengeance is in mine heart, and the year of my redeemed is come. I looked, and there was none to help; and I wondered that there was none to uphold: therefore mine own arm brought salvation unto me, and my fury, it upheld me."

But whilst it is important to remember that in Immanuel's bosom throbbed and swelled a purpose, not heroic only, because it was divine—whilst sworn to vindicate the perfections of the Godhead, and magnify the law—whilst darting an eye of annihilating hatred at sin, and through all the storm of intervening anguish borne sublimely by foreseeing the travail of his soul, and that new earth in which righteousness dwelleth, whilst the soul of the Redeemer was inwardly sustained by these big emotions and glorious prospects, his most obvious aspect was the one in which the Baptist hailed him—meek, gentle, and innocent, and doomed to suffer. Nay, for the sake of the one it was needful that he should become that other; and it was only in lamb-like guise that Ariel, the Lion of God, could fulfil his lofty purposes.

Consistently with God's wisdom and justice it would appear that there is only one way in which sin can be disposed of. It can only be ended by an exhaustive expiation, by the sinner or his substitute making full atonement for it. And as man could not atone, the Son of God undertook the atonement himself. He assumed the nature which had sinned, assumed it all except the sinfulness. He was formed in fashion as a man; and though he renounced no inherent perfection, for every attribute of wisdom, power, and knowledge would be needed in the work given to Him to do, he veiled them, he held them in abeyance, and as he moved about in Joseph's dwelling, and by and by in the streets of Jerusalem and on the hills of Galilee, seldom did anything meet the view except a very holy and benignant being. Though engaged about his father's business, hitherto that business was mainly a fulfilling of all righteousness; and few suspected that he was bearing our griefs and carrying our sorrows. And it was not till very near the close that the Saviour's character revealed itself as his people's sin-bearing substitute. In the greatness of his love he had volunteered to make reconciliation for the transgressors, and the time was now come for testing the powers of that ancient love. And just as when wrath began to sparkle in the old world's atmosphere, it was the signal for every creature which Jehovah had selected to seek the ark of refuge, so now, and in a very different way, when the hour of darkness came, it was the signal for the sins of all God's chosen to seek the victim of God's ordaining. One by one, and myriad by myriad, they came, and, dark and dismal, settled down on Immanuel's holy soul. A fearful hour to him! for, harmless and undefiled, he had never known sin except afar off, and now the sins of an elect world were counted to him, and accumulated on him. Abraham's lie and Moses' anger, Manasseh's sin who made Jerusalem run with blood, and David's who made God's enemies blaspheme, the sins of all the saved from Abel to the end of time, came in murky flight, and swarmed and clustered round the Saviour's pure and spotless soul. And as they well-nigh shut out the Father's love and the sight of accustomed heaven, that soul began to be exceeding sorrowful, even unto death. But unutterably dear to heaven as the beloved of the Father was, he was bearing the sins of many, and now or never must be made an end of sin. And as punishment alone can expiate sin, the vials of indignation burst, and on the Lamb of God they poured a momentary hell. "Father, if it be possible!" "My God, my God, why hast thou forsaken me?" But the work was done, the wrath was borne, the penalty was paid, and emerging from the flood of fiery wrath the Surety rose exulting, and flew back to the Father's bosom; but the sin was never found again. It was finished, drowned, dissolved; it was atoned for, and annihilated. Transgression was finished. An end was made of sin.

It was to this truth that by many types or pictorial lessons God turned the eye of his ancient people. For instance, every morning and evening in the temple the nation sacrificed a lamb, and at the great yearly festival, the Passover, every family selected from the flock a lamb without blemish, and having performed various rites, they slew it, and sprinkled on the door-posts and lintels its blood. And doubtless with that acuteness which personal solicitude produces, or rather with that sagacity which the Holy Spirit imparts, many a wistful eye saw deep significance in the familiar symbol, and when he viewed the fairest and most spotless selected from the fold, and saw it sundered from its companions, and conducted away from bright pastures where it had been alway rejoicing, and shut up in captive loneliness in the priest's or poor man's chamber, and then in silent innocence and uncomplaining meekness led forth to the altar, and then on its harmless head his own or his country's sin confessed, and the gleaming knife next moment soaking in its blood; in this process of obvious substitution and vicarious suffering intelligent piety must have glimpsed some better thing to come. But what enlightened devotion might have surmised, the sure word of prophecy revealed; and in words which scarcely needed a gospel to countersign, or a Philip to interpret, Isaiah expounded the whole:—"All we, like sheep, have gone astray; we have turned every one to his own way; and the Lord hath laid on him the iniquity of us all. He was oppressed, and he was afflicted; yet he opened not his mouth: he is brought as a lamb to the slaughter, and as a sheep before her shearers is dumb, so he openeth not his mouth. He was taken from prison and from judgment: and who shall declare his generation? for he was cut off out of the land of the living: for the trangression of my people was he stricken. Yet it pleased the Lord to bruise him; he hath put him to grief; when thou shalt make his soul an offering for sin, he shall see his seed, he shall prolong his days, and the pleasure of the Lord shall prosper in his hands. Therefore will I divide him a portion with the great, and he shall divide the spoil with the strong; because he hath poured out his soul unto death:

and he was numbered with the transgressors; and he bare the sin of many, and made intercession for the transgressors." And now when the Baptist, after fifteen centuries of passovers, and on the very eve of the last of them, when he who in his person was the isthmus of two economies, the final link between the law and the gospel—"Fibula Moris et Christi,"—exclaimed, "Behold the Lamb of God!" they were not only the two disciples who forsook John and followed Jesus, but all who heard were put on the tiptoe of expectation; and whether they acted as Andrew and his comrade did, whether they arose and went to see, they at least understood the allusion when the Baptist said, "Behold the Lamb of God, which taketh away the sin of the world!"

And having thus stated what sin is, and what Jesus has done to take it away, I would now conclude by repeating and enforcing the Baptist's exclamation, "Behold the Lamb of God!"

I. Behold Him, and *trust Him*. "Without shedding of blood is no remission;" and a soul taught of God is content that it should be so. Such a soul sees a grandeur in God's law, and a lustre in God's justice and truth, and much as it may covet pardon, thankful as it might be for a right to heaven, it would not wish to steal into heaven, nor receive a pardon which made God a liar. Ah no! let God be true though all mankind should perish; let the law be magnified, though the avenging bolt should fire the universe. And to such a soul it is relief unspeakable when it sees "mercy and truth meeting together, righteousness and peace embracing each other," when it learns that for the remission of sin blood has been already shed—a blood which cleanseth from all sin, even the precious blood of God's own Son, as of a lamb without blemish. And if any of you should this day be uneasy or anxious, if you wish to come to the Lord's table, but are hindered by the sense of guilt, if you are saying, "I would fain come to the Lord's table. I would like to join those who are keeping up the remembrance of redeeming love. How glad would I be to sit down with those to whom he says: 'Eat, O friends; drink abundantly, O beloved;' but I doubt if I dare. The iniquity of my heels encompasseth me about. I find something arresting me, and drawing me back, and whispering: 'How dare you?' I find my sin a weighty burden—too heavy for me. It crushes me down, so that I cannot arise. It is gone over my head, so that I cannot look up." But look out, look here, look to the Lamb of God. Look to Jesus and be lightened. Lay your sins on a sin-atoning and sin-exterminating Saviour. Behold the Lamb of God taking away the sins of the world, and see if He cannot bear yours away. And however heavy the burden of the past, and however depressing the body of sin, keep looking unto Jesus, and you will sooner or later find relief.

But if there be any among you to whom the Lamb of God has no recommendation, and the cross of Christ no attraction, how can you escape if you neglect so great salvation? It does not matter which way it be. Perhaps you deem your sin so trivial that you yourself can put it away; or perhaps you think it so terrible that it will need all your best efforts, all your watchfulness, and prayers, and repentance for years to come, to make you sure of salvation. Whichever way it be, you are not looking to the Lamb of God. In the one case you feel that you are not bad enough to need him; in the other, you think yourself too bad for him to save you. But in either case you deem yourself wiser or stronger than God—wiser, if you know another name by which men can be saved, except Jesus Christ—stronger, if you think that you can work out a better righteousness than the righteousness of God. "The justice of the Deity," as a great thinker has said it—"the justice of the Deity, not to be propitiated by any other means, pursues the transgressor over earth, and in hell; nothing in the universe can arrest it in its awful career until it stops in reverence at the cross of Christ." There, under the cross, is the sinner's sanctuary—there, my hearers, is the place for you and me. The first smiling look we shall get from God will be when looking unto Jesus; and the first time that we shall experience the alacrity of a lightened conscience, the relief and elasticity of the great life-burden lifted off, will be when we have laid our sins on the Lamb of God.

II. Behold Him, and *love Him*. In the estimate we form of others we are apt to be influenced by the opinion of the best judges—of those who have the largest opportunity of observation and the greatest powers of discernment. Here on earth we are subject to many disturbing influences, and are apt to admire or scorn, love or hate, very much as caprice may dictate or some casualty determine; but whilst our views are narrow, and our leanings partial, there is a world where all judge righteous judgment, and see as they are seen. What, then, with their loftier powers and larger observation, what do spirits made perfect think of Jesus Christ? Whilst he himself was still on earth, he saw that, with all their veneration, disciples had not discovered him. They admired him, but they scarcely adored him; they loved him, but they were not lost in him; and so it was one of his last prayers, "Father, I will that they whom thou hast given me be with me where I am, that they may behold my glory." Well, then, in the very place where Jesus is, what do they think of him, and what is thought by those who best can judge? "After this I beheld, and, lo, a great multitude which no man could number, of all nations, and kindreds, and people, and tongues, stood before the throne, and before THE

Lamb, clothed with white robes, and palms in their hands, and cried with a loud voice, saying, Salvation to our God which sitteth upon the throne, and unto the Lamb." And just as his service is rapture, so his society is the sunshine of the place, the meat and drink of its inhabitants. "They shall hunger no more, neither thirst any more; neither shall the sun light on them, nor any heat. For *the Lamb* which is in the midst of the throne shall feed them, and shall lead them to living fountains of waters: and God shall wipe away all tears from their eyes." But higher than spirits made perfect are the angels who excel in strength. If there be intellect more expanded, character more holy, affections more intense, and tastes more pure anywhere in the universe than what are found among the sons of men, they must be sought among these sons of God; and it is quite conceivable that objects which awaken our astonishment may be obscure or insignificant to capacities so transcendent as the principalities and powers in heavenly places. How then do these high natures deem of Jesus Christ? Why, all their superiority but gives the power of superior wonder. The marvels of Christ's person and work the angels desire to look into, and when God was manifest in flesh it was their privilege to see, their promotion to minister. When the Father introduced the only-begotten into the world, he said, "And let all the angels of God worship him;" "and I," says John, "heard the voice of many angels round about the throne, and the number of them was ten thousand times ten thousand, and thousands of thousands, saying with a loud voice, Worthy is the Lamb that was slain, to receive power, and riches, and wisdom, and strength, and honour, and glory, and blessing." And when the Son of man appears at last in his glory, he is to bring as his satellites all the host of heaven —all the holy angels with him. And if the Lamb of God thus receive the highest homage and deepest love of all the loyal minds and holy in wide immensity—if of all that is august and amiable, majestic and gracious, they concede to him the most glorious palm—if of all that is worthy their own verdict and eager voice be, Worthiest is the Lamb, there is only one Being in the universe more competent to judge, and his judgment is absolute. With full knowledge of all possible perfection, and with the wide universe inviting his complacency, and open to his choice, what does God himself think of Jesus Christ? Ere ever he quitted the bosom of the Father, he was alway his delight, rejoicing alway before him, and no less his delight when here. In the veil of flesh, and busied in this work of atonement, the voice from heaven again and again saluted him, "This is my beloved Son, in whom I am well pleased: hear ye him." Yes, brethren, among all the beholders of the Lamb of God, there was no eye which beheld him more complacently than Jehovah's own, and, whatever you may think of him, there is no object in the universe so glorious in the Father's view, nor so dear to the Father's heart, as the Lamb of God, which taketh away the sin of the world.

And oh, brethren, do you love him also? If you beheld him from that point of view from which the redeemed in glory see him, you would love him. If you saw the glories of his person as holy angels see them, you would love and adore him; and if you saw him as God himself beholds him, you would be filled with ineffable complacency towards him; he would be your delight. Yes. And if you do not love Him whom all the saved and all the sinless love, if your affection is not drawn towards him who has long since riveted to himself the heart of a holy universe, there must be something wrong with you. But brother, there is a reason why you should love him which angels and saints in glory have not. They are safe, but you are not; and if ever you get to glory, the Lamb of God must take you there. You are a sinner, and Jesus is the friend of sinners.

"All ye that pass by,
To Jesus draw nigh :
To you is it nothing that Jesus should die?
Your ransom and peace,
Your surety he is ;
Come, see if there ever was sorrow like his.

For what you have done
His blood must atone ;
The Father hath punished for you his dear Son.
The Lord in the day
Of his anger did lay
Your sins on the Lamb, and he bore them away.

He dies to atone
For sins not his own ;
Your debt he hath paid, and your work he hath done.
Ye all may receive
The peace he did leave,
Who made intercession. 'My Father, forgive.'"

3. Behold Him, and *follow Him*. "The next day John stood, and two of his disciples; and looking upon Jesus as he walked, he said, Behold the Lamb of God! And the two disciples heard him speak, and they followed Jesus." One of them was Andrew, the other is supposed to have been the Evangelist John himself. They first followed Jesus as inquirers. There were points on which they were perplexed. There were some questions which they longed to ask. They wanted more information, fresh data on which to make up their minds. But they had not courage to accost him. He was a stranger, and one whom their master reverenced. But Jesus soon shewed himself the Lamb of God. Instead of making himself shy to them or waiting till they

should hail him, he turned about and gave them the opportunity they wished. "What seek ye?" "Rabbi, where dwellest thou?" "Come and see." And should any among yourselves be in the mind of Andrew and John, wanting information, wanting light—confused and embarrassed, wishing to know Christ—be not afraid. Go to his servants; go to his ministers; go to his book; but above all, go to Himself. He will not quench the smoking flax; and if you desire to turn to him, to you, O inquirer, he says, "Come and see." They went and abode with him that night, and the next we hear of them is they are open disciples, following him in public and in full daylight, and bringing others to him. And if you really learn what Jesus is, if you go and see, you too will follow. Gratitude, love, and admiration, will make you open disciples; and whether it be in the sanctuary or in civil life, in a station high or low, where you meet with fellow-Christians or find yourself alone, in the workshop or the drawing-room, in the camp or the barrack, at college or at school, the language of your affectionate discipleship and frank consistency will be— "I'm not ashamed to own my Lord." And then from earnest inquirers and open disciples, you will become devout imitators; and just as the blood of the Lamb grows dearer as the ground of your hope and the price of your pardon, so will Christ's lamb-like spirit and demeanour grow more and more attractive to your emulous and admiring love. You will strive to copy his *gentleness*. He did not strive nor cry, nor cause his voice to be heard in the streets, and in moments of provocation you will pray, "O Lamb of God, calm the perturbation of my angry spirit." You will long to possess his *guilelessness* and *innocence*. He did no violence, neither was guile found in his mouth, and you will feel that till your character be "simplicity and godly sincerity," you are very different from the sincere and simple Lamb of God, and, as the most blessed distinction you covet here below, you will pray to be made holy, harmless, undefiled, and separate from sinners. And you will not forget his *meekness* towards men, and his *submissiveness* to God. He was oppressed and he was afflicted, yet he opened not his mouth; and after Christ's example, you will not always be apologetic and exculpatory, nor when they lay to your charge things that you knew not, will you feel as if a new thing had befallen you, and when some sore trial or stunning grief comes down, may the angel Jehovah strengthen you to say, "Father, glorify thy name. If this cup may not pass from me except I drink it, thy will be done."

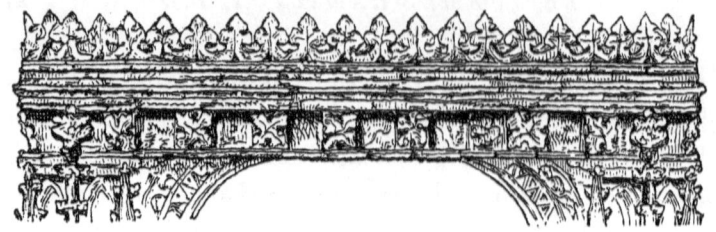

XVII.

The Pure in Heart.

BY THE REV. ALEXANDER DYCE DAVIDSON, D.D.

"Blessed are the pure in heart, for they shall see God."—Matt. v. 8.

WHEN these words were spoken, the ideas which were entertained respecting the nature of true religion, even by the greater part of those who had the holy Scriptures to guide them, were exceedingly erroneous. Extreme minuteness in the observance of outward forms, an ostentatious parade of sanctity in look and tone and deportment, and an affected reverence for the mere letter of the law, while the spirit of it was disregarded—these things were accounted the proper marks of those who could lay any good claim to the title of being pious and acceptable worshippers of God, and to be destitute of them was to forfeit all pretension to holiness of character. The religion of those times was, in the majority of cases, as different from that which is inculcated in the Word of God, as the statue of a man dressed out in some garments stolen from him is different from the living and moving man himself. Hence it is that we find our Lord so often exposing the sins of formality and hypocrisy, and urging upon his disciples the great truth that the service which God demands is pre-eminently a spiritual service, and that as he looketh upon the heart, he will be satisfied with nothing less than its undivided homage. And for the same reason the apostles are so earnest in enforcing the claims of spiritual religion in opposition to that which consists merely in externals, telling us in such brief but comprehensive sentences as these what true piety is : " Neither circumcision availeth anything nor uncircumcision, but a new creature ;" " the kingdom of God is not meat and drink, but righteousness and peace and joy in the Holy Ghost." These statements, as has been hinted, embodied no new truth, for the substance of them is contained in the Old Testament, in language as clear as could have been employed. " Circumcise your hearts and be no more stiff necked," was the injunction of Moses to the Israelites. " To obey is better than sacrifice, and to hearken than the fat of rams," was the address of Samuel to Saul. " Who shall ascend into the hill of the Lord? And who shall stand in his holy place? He that hath clean hands and a pure heart : who hath not lifted up his soul unto vanity nor sworn deceitfully," is the psalmist's description of God's acceptable worshippers. And that he took home to himself the lesson is manifest from his penitential prayer : " Thou desirest not sacrifice, else would I give it, thou delightest not in burnt-offering. The sacrifices of God are a broken spirit : a broken and a contrite heart, O God, thou wilt not despise." And to the same effect is the bearing of the prophetic writings, in so far as they relate to the nature of that worship which the Holy One of Israel required from his people. The externals of religion, while they are never stript of the value which truly belongs to them, are always represented as immeasurably subordinate to a right frame of heart and spirit on the part of those who observed them, as when Micah says, " Will the Lord be pleased with thousands of rams, or with ten thousands of rivers of oil? He hath shewed thee, O man, what is good; and what doth the

Lord require of thee, but to do justly, and to love mercy, and to walk humbly with thy God." Such then being the scope of the Old Testament Scriptures, there was nothing essentially new in those announcements which our Lord and his apostles made respecting the nature of spiritual and practical religion in such passages as have been quoted; and yet so completely had the perverse heart and the blinded understanding of man obscured the beauty of divine truth, and changed the living reality of divine worship into a cold and dead image, that the words of the text must have fallen upon the ears of the multitude to whom they were addressed with all the force of a discovery fresh from heaven itself: "Blessed are the pure in heart, for they shall see God."

The consideration of these words will, by the blessing of the Spirit, be profitable to us, for the doctrine which they contain can never be unsuitably enforced. The reign of formality has not been abolished among the followers of Christ, notwithstanding all the condemnation which is passed upon it in his word. The tendency is still strongly developed of overestimating externals to the neglect of the religion of the heart, and it must be met with such pointed weapons as that which is furnished in the text. There are many topics suggested for our consideration by this emphatic passage, of which the following may be selected. In the *first* place, we may consider generally what is to be understood by purity of heart; in the *second* place, how it is produced; in the *third* place, how it is maintained and promoted; and, in the *fourth* place, to what blessed issue it leads. The first and fourth points are those which chiefly claim our attention, as obviously arising from the words, "Blessed are the pure in heart, for they shall see God."

I. In the *first* place, then, let us consider generally *what is to be understood by "purity of heart."* Now, this is a weighty inquiry, as any misapprehension here would be most dangerous. Let it be observed, then, that it is not of any one particular quality, of any one single characteristic, that our Lord speaks when he refers to "purity of heart;" but that his words have reference to the whole state and frame of the inner man, to the fountains of affection and desire and thought and feeling, whence all activity flows. In this wide sense purity of heart is not the shunning and shrinking from certain sins which may more especially come under the designation of impurity, according to the ordinary forms of human speech; but it is a right condition of all the affections and desires and thoughts and feelings which prompt the outward movements of the man. The conformity of these outward movements themselves to the law of God is the most conclusive evidence. This principle requires to be particularly insisted on, because it does not correspond with the views which are usually held. The idea which is commonly suggested by the word impurity, when it is applied to the heart or to the conduct of a man, is that of his being under the dominion of the more gross and debasing appetites and passions of his corrupt nature. And certainly this is comprehended under the term. But it comprehends far more than this, as may be very easily shewn. For what, let me ask, is the great and unalterable standard of all moral purity? It is the divine law, which is founded upon the very nature of the Holy God. Every departure from this standard, therefore, however it may be glossed over by common language, is truly an instance of impurity, as really when it lies in the wrong state of the feeling within, as in the perceptible depravity of the conduct without. That is to say, in plainer speech, every act of sin, whatever that sin may be, let it be confined within a man's own bosom, or let it be exhibited in the outward violation of the law in his life, is an act of impurity. And that we do not overstrain the subject in speaking thus is obvious from the whole bearing of Scripture. When it is said, for example, "that the Lord is of *purer* eyes than to behold evil, and that he cannot look upon iniquity," is it not manifest that everything that may be called evil or iniquity, that is every sin, every departure from the law of God, is to be designated as *impure ?* Purity and holiness are used as synonymous terms in Scripture, embracing conformity to the divine law in all the movements of the heart and all the actions of the life; and therefore impurity and sin, their opposites, must also be synonymous, and must comprehend all transgressions of the law, whether in heart or life. You will perceive then what that is which our Lord pronounces blessed in the text, and to which he annexes such a glorious consummation. It is not merely abstinence from those evil thoughts which have their appropriate residence in the dark chambers of the heart of the sensualist, and which, in the strong language of Scripture, make it like a cage of unclean birds, but freedom from the bondage of all evil thoughts and desires. It is not merely the cultivation of right feelings and affections with reference to any one commandment of the law, but the having the whole heart and soul in such a frame that those things only are prized and counted excellent which are "true, and honest, and just, and pure, and lovely, and of good report." Let us try to elevate our minds for a moment above the narrow views of the pure and the impure, which the common forms of speech may have led us to entertain, and endeavour to realise such conceptions of these things as are cherished by the inhabitants of heaven. Would not any of the sinless spirits that are before the throne of God recoil, if we may so speak, with loathing at any violation of the law of truth, or from any manifestation of covetous desire, or, in a word, from any breach of the divine commandments, as indicating a nature depraved, perverted, and polluted? Must not the exhibition of any forbidden thought or affection be to any of these pure intelligences hideous and unsightly, just as any material object all defiled and filthy is disgusting to our eye. Then what is it that the Lord would have us aim at when he inculcates the cultivation of heart-purity, but just our having our tastes and likings and affections so refined, and so sensitive, as that *that* only will be pleasing to us which the law approves, and even a train of thought which is in opposition to the law will be loathsome? Yes, the purity of heart which he pronounces blessed is the love and the habitual pursuit of universal holiness; such an effective cleansing of the inner man, as that not even a desire will be tolerated which the law condemns.

Now, my friends, I need scarcely say that these remarks are well fitted to excite alarming misgivings and apprehensions in our minds. If only the pure in heart shall see God, then this seals the fate of all those who are contented to possess a blameless reputation in the world, without any endeavour to exercise a control over their desires and passions, and to bring them into subjection to the will of Jehovah. And if impurity of heart excludes from the vision of God, as the text obviously implies, then, we may ask, who will be admitted to this ineffable blessedness? When the torch of divine truth is carried into the secret recesses of the heart, what fearful disclosures are made! It is like darting a sunbeam into such a gloomy and polluted dungeon as was opened up to the prophet in vision when he beheld that chamber in the house of the Lord, wherein "every form of creeping things, and abominable beasts, and all the idols of the house of Israel were portrayed upon the wall round about." What unworthy thoughts of God are there not sometimes cherished, what rebellious desires, what unholy inclinations! What selfishness and worldliness are there not frequently to be detected in the motives from which even those actions proceed that seem to be most unexceptionable! What conflicts of unruly passion, what bitter enmity and malice and vindictiveness are there not to be found within, when the exterior is all bland and kindly! Verily, it needs but a glance at the condition and movements of the heart to corroborate the language of the Scripture, that "it is deceitful above all things, and desperately wicked;" and to extort the cry, "who can understand his errors;" and the prayer, "Set not our iniquities before thee, our secret sins in the light of thy countenance."

But, then, what shall we say concerning these things when we view them in connection with the words of the text? Are there none to whom that blessedness which is there promised belongs as being pure in heart? If we were obliged to answer this question *absolutely*, we would be constrained to say, "there is not one on earth;" for the holiest will be the most ready to acknowledge, from that tenderness and sensibility of heart and conscience which grace has wrought in them, that fearful corruption cleaves to them, that often when they would do good evil is present with them, and that if all the thoughts and desires which find lodgment in their breast were to be exposed to the scrutiny of men, they would be ashamed to hold up their heads. But still, speaking *comparatively*, the children of God are invested with purity of heart. If corruption cleaves to them, it has not dominion over them. Their delight is in the law of the Lord; their habitual aim is to bring thoughts and affections as well as actions under its holy authority. They will not be found taking refuge in the doctrine that perfect conformity of heart and soul and spirit to the law of God is unattainable, and converting it into an argument for remaining inactive, and suffering themselves to be dragged hither and thither by every sinful impulse. On the contrary, this doctrine combined with the other, that by the power of divine grace, God's people do make progressive advancement in the mortification of sin and in the cultivation of holy affections, stimulates them to watchfulness and prayer, and active effort for the suppression of every forbidden feeling and desire, so that there is in them the gradual development of that likeness to the Son of God in which is embodied perfect and absolute purity. Knowing that they have not attained, neither are already perfect, they are still pressing on; beat down often, and sadly troubled by that law in the members which wars against the law of the mind, they still breathe and pant after that freedom from sin which Christ hath promised them; tainted as they are with corruption, they still exhibit a heavenly spirit, which shines through that corruption, and demonstrates that they have been born from above; and so with all their shortcomings, their great characteristic is purity of heart.

These remarks might perhaps suffice upon this department of our subject; but as we would wish this discourse to be practical, we shall even at the risk of repetition advert very briefly to one or two of the marks by which those who may be truly designated "pure in heart" will always be distinguished, as this will serve to illustrate what is to be understood by purity. And this is one of these marks, that the pure in heart abhor *everything* that is sinful. You will often see among the professed followers of Christ a wonderful scrupulousness with respect to certain kinds of sin, while they are the very slaves of it in other forms. As for instance, a man may have such a reverence for truth and integrity and honesty, that he would not himself depart a hair-breadth from their strict requirements, nor tolerate such departure in others, and yet he may laugh to scorn the restraints and self-denial which the gospel of Christ enjoins. Some men are outwardly virtuous and of unblemished reputation, because a salutary fear keeps their evil propensities in check; others, because they have certain ends to advance, which can only be reached by the maintenance of a moral life;

others, because they have not the means of gratifying their desires. But all this is perfectly compatible with essential ungodliness of heart, and disregard of the sanctions of the divine law. But when the Spirit of God has taken away the hard and stony heart and given the heart of flesh, then whatever is denounced as sinful in the Word of God, whether it be the cherishing of a thought or the performance of an action, is in opposition to the tendencies and cravings of that renewed heart, and is abhorred and resisted. Hypocrites throw a cloak over their sin, and are contented when they can conceal it from the gaze of others; the pure in heart pass sentence of death against it, and are satisfied with nothing less than its complete extermination.

Again, this is another of the marks of the pure in heart, that they are exceedingly watchful against all *occasions* of sin. Many are foolhardy enough to thrust themselves into the very way of temptation, to play as it were on the edge of the precipice, to venture into a polluted atmosphere, as if they had sufficient power within themselves to stop at the precise point beyond which what is harmless becomes dangerous, or what is only somewhat questionable becomes positively sinful. Like the moth fluttering around the flame, they move for a short time within the circle of allurement, yet so far from the point of actual contamination, that they seem to be unscathed; but it is only for a short time. Imagined strength of principle gives way in some unguarded moment, and they become melancholy examples of the truth of the scriptural aphorism, "Can one go upon hot coals, and his feet not be burnt? Can a man take fire in his bosom, and his clothes not be burnt?" He that is pure in heart, on the other hand, knowing from sad experience how small a spark kindles up the flame of unholy passion, and how many a painful effort it costs to bring the heart back again into a right frame when it has once been drawn from it, shuns even the appearance of evil, and exercises a holy jealousy over himself, lest he be betrayed into sin, even through the instrumentality of that which seems in itself to be lawful. He may thus not unfrequently expose himself to the charge of being scrupulous over much; but it is safer to yield to the scruple than by disregarding it, to fall into sin, and pierce himself through with many sorrows.

Again, this is another mark of the pure in heart, that they are always panting after yet *greater purity*. Grace excites in the soul an incessant restlessness, an insatiable craving; not such restlessness and craving as ungodly men experience after higher worldly good, for this is accompanied with pain, sometimes with intense agony, but a craving after closer fellowship with God, and greater freedom from sin, and conformity to the likeness of Christ, which is so delightful in the measure that has already been attained. Thus, go into the secret chamber of the king of Israel, and mark the breathings of his soul: "Hide thy face from my sins, and blot out all mine iniquities. Create in me a clean heart, O God; and renew a right spirit within me." Observe the secret wrestlings of the holy apostle for complete emancipation from the bondage of corruption: "O wretched man that I am, who shall deliver me from the body of this death? I thank God through Jesus Christ our Lord." These are examples of the exercises in which the pure in heart are habitually engaged; and if we are satisfied with our present attainments, if we imagine that we are holy enough, it is a sad evidence that the work of purification has not even been begun, that we are still of the earth earthy, and therefore incapable of enjoying the vision of God.

Once more, this is another mark of the pure in heart, that they will uniformly be found cultivating *holiness of conversation* and of conduct. The two things indeed are inseparable. There may be, as has been already said, a virtuous and blameless life upon the whole while there is not purity of heart; but there cannot be the purity without the visible fruit of it in conformity to the law in speech and in action. Oh, it is a terrible infatuation in men to imagine that they are pursuing the path which terminates in heavenly glory because their life is irreproachable, while they carry within them the unsanctified desires, the carnal affections, and the grovelling appetites which mark only fitting companionship for the spirits of darkness! but the infatuation is not less ruinous of those who, while they seem to live in an atmosphere of sanctity, to delight in prayer, in devout reading, and in pious conversation, are as selfish, as grasping, as malignant, as passionate, as any of those who lay claim neither to the name nor to the hopes of God's children. Either make the tree good and its fruit good, or else make the tree corrupt and its fruit corrupt, for every tree is known by its fruit. As the accuracy with which the index of the watch points out the time is the only evidence of the correct movement of the complicated workmanship within; so the increasing conformity of the conversation and life to the law of God, or which is the same thing, to the example of Christ, is the only evidence of that growing purity of heart, without which none shall see the Lord.

We might very easily have singled out other marks of "the pure in heart," but those which have been given must suffice in the meantime. And now there is only one other observation which I would offer in connection with the present head of discourse. It is often a complaint with the real followers of Christ, and the more serious and earnest they are the more are they disposed to complain, that they are so troubled with vain imaginations, with unholy, yea, sometimes blasphemous thoughts, and with feelings and desires so worldly and sinful, as to make them afraid that their hearts have never even been touched by converting and sanctifying grace. Now, the time does not permit us at present to enter upon the full consideration of such trying and perplexing cases. But one remark may be made respecting them. The Scripture teaches us, that while there is a remanent corruption in the holiest on earth, the Tempter also is busy, injecting his poison into the heart, through every opening by which he can find access to it. The method by which he endeavoured, with his wicked suggestions, to move the spotless soul of Christ himself, is an example of the artifices he employs, with but too much success, against Christ's people. Then let this be noticed, that while the rising of a sinful thought or desire in the heart is in most cases too clear an evidence of the heart's natural corruption, it is only by your concurrence given to such thoughts and desires, by your giving them scope and room as it were to work, by your cherishing and fondling them, that they become actually sins in you, and that the way is prepared for your being drawn by them into outward transgression, by which the name of Christ is dishonoured. But if ye struggle against them, if ye strive to beat them down, if ye pray to be delivered from their contaminating influence, that the temple of the heart may be kept holy for God; then are ye really engaged in that sacred warfare which must be encountered in the path to glory, and with reference to which it is written, that where sin aboundeth, God maketh grace still more to abound. And if ye persevere in the struggle, giving no quarter to the sin by which you are beset, you will get the victory in the end; you will be raised to those blissful regions, the very air of which is holy, where there is nothing to hurt or to defile, where you will breathe freely after the fierce conflict, and wear the conqueror's palm and crown, and best of all, be pure as Christ is pure, and perfect as Christ is perfect.

II. Now we come to consider, in the *second* place, *how this purity of heart, of which we have been speaking, is produced.* And here we shall be very brief. The very term "purity," when denoting what does not naturally belong to an object, but what is imparted to it, suggests the idea of washing. And so as the heart is not naturally pure, but the reverse, when we read of its being purified, we think at once of its being washed. And accordingly the Scripture meets our conceptions here, and informs us of a twofold washing, sometimes also called a sprinkling, of which God's children enjoy the privilege. There is the washing in the blood of Christ, and there is the washing of regeneration. Let us advert to these two things. *First,* God's children are washed in the blood of Christ; or, more correctly, it is in virtue of this washing that any members of the human family are constituted the children of God. When the sinner is led through grace to feel himself guilty before God, and to realise the tremendous consequences of sin, and when to escape he lays hold of Christ, believing the divine testimony concerning him, that he is the only Saviour, and looking to the atonement which he offered for sin as the only ground of acceptance with God; then for Christ's sake his sin is freely pardoned, or blotted out, as the Scripture expresses it, or, according to the figure referred to above, he is washed from his guilt, and thus stands wholly free from the curse and condemnation of the law. He has no righteousness of his own, but the righteousness of Christ is imputed to him; he is clothed therewith as with a pure spotless robe, and thus all his natural deformity is concealed. The law recognises in that which covers him what answers all its claims, and its threatenings are hushed into silence. This is what is meant by being washed in the fountain of Christ's blood. Now, mark what changes are wrought upon the heart and feelings of the man who experiences this washing. While his conscience was all defiled and troubled with guilt, he regarded God with terror as his enemy. The law, with its inflexible requirements and its awful denunciations, was the minister of wrath, and was hated while it made him tremble. But now, pardoned and reconciled to God through Jesus Christ, his conscience is purged from dead works by the blood of Christ; he has peace with God, he can look up to him with humble confidence as the God of love, his own redeeming God; and the law, the reflection of the divine purity, becomes lovely too, for it is not with a voice of thunder, but with a Father's voice it speaks, pointing out the way in which he would have his children walk. And here then you see how there is provision made for the commencement of those breathings after purity, or conformity to the law in heart and life, by which the members of the heavenly family are known.

But, again, God's children are partakers of the washing of regeneration. Had strict arrangement of topics been regarded, this should have been placed first. For it is only when the sovereign Spirit has quickened the sinner, previously dead in sin, that the stubborn will is subdued to receive the divine testimony, and to embrace the offered Saviour. Faith is the first movement of the regenerated soul, the first real indication of spiritual life within. But the work of the Spirit does not terminate with the imparting of this life. He watches and fosters the heavenly germ he has implanted, until having reached the full maturity it can attain in the nursery here below, it is fit to be transplanted to the more genial clime above. We must not overlook or undervalue the operation of the Spirit. It is he who sheds abroad the love of God in the heart; it is he who excites holy desires and aspirations there; it is he who gives the transforming views of Christ through the word, of which the apostle speaks when he says, that we, "beholding as in a glass the glory of the Lord, are changed into the same image from glory to glory;" it is he who gives the thoughts their direction heavenwards; it is he who arms the soul with divine strength to resist the world and the wicked one ; it is he who assists the believer up every hill of difficulty ; it is he who refreshes him with the communications of his grace, when he is faint and weary; it is he who inspires him with that unquenchable thirst for holiness, which is to be crowned in the end with the full attainment of the likeness of God. And just because this glorious work of the Spirit is thus manifested in removing all the pollution of sin, in cleansing the heart from the leprosy which defiles it, it is called the washing of regeneration. Now, my friends, if there are any among us who think they are not altogether destitute of holiness, while yet they have never in earnest sought reconciliation with God through Jesus Christ, nor prayed in earnest for the Spirit's grace, they are still unwashed, and therefore unfit to dwell with him who is of purer eyes than to behold iniquity. Those only will be raised up in glory whose bodies are the temples of the Holy Ghost here, and who, by his indwelling and his mighty working, have the stamp impressed on them of holiness to the Lord.

III. Now, in the *third* place, we were to consider *how purity of heart is maintained and promoted.* Here there might be room for very lengthened remark, but we can only look for a moment at the subject. Let these three practical rules then be noted without any attempt to enlarge upon them. In the *first* place, if we would maintain purity of heart and make advancement in it, we must look often into the divine law, and make close and faithful application of it to ourselves. The law is likened to a mirror as revealing the character of those who look into it. Defects, shortcomings, sins of heart as well as of life, which would otherwise escape unnoticed, are there unmasked ; and the believer only learns what he really is, and what efforts he must put forth to become what he ought to be, by comparing himself habitually with that eternal standard of truth and rectitude. In the *second* place, if we would maintain purity of heart, and advance in it, we must often place ourselves in the company of Christ. And whether we are with him in thought, as he moved about on earth performing the work which the Father gave him to do, or as he suffered and died enduring the penalty due to his people's sin, or as he now reigns in the holy place into which no defilement can enter, we shall have before us at once the perfect pattern of purity, and the strongest and most constraining motives to the cultivation of it. In the *third* place, if we would maintain purity of heart, and advance in it, we must be often at the mercy-seat. And here let me take occasion to urge upon your attention the special advantage of ejaculatory prayer. We have already adverted to the fact, that Satan is ever ready to suggest unholy thoughts and desires to draw us under his power. Against these one of the most effectual weapons, and a weapon ever at our hand, is the short, pointed supplication, which like an arrow shot up pierces heaven, and is the signal that one of Christ's weak and helpless people needs his aid. The aid thus sought in time of need will never be withheld. My friends, when we think how the sinful thought suddenly suggested, when it is entertained, spreads its influence over the whole soul, first darkening it, and then destroying its peace and comfort; and when we think how easily deliverance could be obtained, if there was but a sentence uttered in faith for deliverance, we feel that we cannot too earnestly beseech you to avail yourselves of the help of such ejaculatory prayer. You cannot always find opportunity to betake yourselves in ordinary form to the footstool of the throne, when the flood of temptation sets strongly in; but you can never be without the opportunity, whether in private or in the company of others, whether engaged in your common occupations, or walking by the way, of turning your heart for a moment toward God. And that movement of the heart, although accompanied with no audible utterance, will be as the shield of faith wherewith the fiery darts of the wicked one are quenched.

IV. But now, in the *fourth* and last place, we come to consider *the blessed issue to which purity of heart leads :* "Blessed are the pure in heart, for they shall see God." The language employed in this precious promise is figurative. It seems to be used in allusion to the custom of eastern monarchs to exclude themselves from the gaze of the multitude, and only to shew themselves to their ministers of state, or their special favourites. Hence the expression to see the king's face, came to be equivalent to the enjoying of peculiar favour and distinction. Thus in the book of Esther i. 14, seven persons are mentioned as the seven princes of Persia and Media, which saw the king's face, and which sat the first in the kingdom. Thus also in Rev. xxii. 3, 4, the blessedness of the redeemed is described in these words, "His servants shall serve him, and they shall see his face, and his name shall be in their foreheads." And so in the text, "the pure in heart shall see God." The highest privilege and dignity then are implied in these words. But while the origin of the expression, and the general import of it, are thus brought out, it becomes interesting to inquire what is more particularly to be understood by the words, "they shall see God." Is it an actual or a spiritual vision that is here spoken of ? Obviously it cannot be an actual vision. For the Scripture says, "That God is the King of kings, and Lord of lords, who only hath immortality, dwelling in the light which no man can approach unto; whom no man hath seen, nor can see." But then, although the divine essence is infinitely beyond the reach even of man's highest conceptions, yet there is one sense in which, as the Scripture tells us, we can see

God. When Philip said unto Jesus, "Lord, shew us the Father, and it sufficeth us. Jesus answered and said unto him, Have I been so long time with you, and yet hast thou not known me, Philip? he that hath seen me hath seen the Father, and how sayest thou unto me, Shew us the Father?" The divine perfections are so manifested in Christ, that to see him is to see them; and we know that his people shall see him actually as he is. But this vision is reserved for the state of glory. We walk by faith here and not by sight. Here we see as through a glass darkly, but there face to face; here we know only in part, but then we shall know even as also we are known. At the same time, even in heaven the vision of Christ, as relating to the knowledge we shall obtain of the divine perfections manifested in him, will be spiritual; for though the eyes of the redeemed will behold his countenance, it is the soul that will perceive his glory.

But now, having made these explanatory remarks, I observe, *first*, that the pure in heart enjoy in a certain sense the vision of God, even while they are on earth. What is it that wraps the soul up in darkness, and renders it incapable of contemplating or appreciating the moral loveliness of the divine wisdom, holiness, justice, goodness, and truth? What but that corruption that is inherent in it. Do we not see that men blinded by passion and prejudice cannot perceive the beauty and excellence of truth; that men who are influenced by low and selfish cunning, cannot enter into the feelings of those who are of noble and disinterested and generous spirit; that the victims of sensuality, and of every grovelling and debasing vice, cannot comprehend either the motives or the enjoyments of the lovers of purity? And do we not mark, on the other hand, how men of kindred tastes and pursuits, engaged in the cultivation of those heavenly graces which are man's best and noblest ornament, can at once perceive each other's motives and feelings, can understand each other's experiences, and see as it were into each other's very hearts? Then just so, in the case more immediately before us, in proportion as the heart is freed from the pollution of sin, and brought under the power of holy principles, the character and dealings of God become more fully understood; in proportion as the believer is himself conformed to the divine image, he loves and rejoices in the divine perfections. As he grows in grace, the intimacy grows between him and the Holy One. He realises the presence of God, he lives and moves under a sense of it, his chief springs of delight are found in it, the more he becomes assimilated in affection to the Father of Spirits. His communion with God is more cheering and refreshing, the more he gets emancipated from the dominion of evil. His very life becomes a walk with God, and thus in sober earnestness he may be said in the language of Scripture, " to see him who is invisible." Such are the views we gather from the recorded experiences of holy men; and if we can but dimly enter into the meaning of these things, and but faintly realise it, it is because our souls cleave so tenaciously to the dust, and because our hearts are still so much under the bondage of corruption. But surely, my friends, we can perceive this much, that purity of heart, being from its very nature thus fitted to draw us close to God, to give us some power of comprehending the excellency of his glorious perfections, and to raise us to friendly converse and intimate communion with him, must be a source of highest and most exquisite enjoyment. And well may we ask, what can the poor slaves of sin have, under the name of pleasure or of profit, that can be compared with this living stream of purest felicity which flows into the sanctified heart, and which can never be dried up, because it is drawn from that " pure river of water of life, clear as crystal, which proceedeth out of the throne of God and of the Lamb."

But, *secondly*, I observe, that the vision of God which is promised to the pure in heart is more especially reserved for the life to come. There the redeemed, perfected and cleansed from every stain, will literally see Christ, whom to see is to see the Father. They will hear his voice, they will dwell in his presence, they will be for ever with the Lord. This will indeed be blessedness, this will be the accomplishment of the saying, that faith is swallowed up in vision. But still after all, as has been said above, it will not be the mere beholding of the Redeemer's face that will constitute the chief enjoyment of his saints, it will be the contemplation of his moral beauty, which is discerned not with the bodily eye, but with the eye of the soul. Resembling the Lord as they will then do, loving the very objects which he loves, having every feeling and every sympathy in unison with his, able now to relish whatever is truly beautiful and good, they will perceive in him the combination of all perfections, and that in infinite fulness and in glorious harmony. They will then truly know and feel what is meant by his mercy and his tenderness, although they will never be able to fathom their immeasurable depths; they will then feast with rapture upon his unspotted purity, they will bathe in the boundless ocean of his love. It is to this department of the blessedness of the redeemed, this power which in their thoroughly sanctified nature they will have to perceive and know Christ's perfections, that the apostle refers when he says, "we shall be like him, for we shall see him as he is." His meaning is, that as it is made sure by the divine promise that we shall see Christ as he is, this of necessity implies that we must be like him, as otherwise we would be destitute of the very capacity of enjoying this blessed and all-satisfying vision. As all the beauty of light and colouring is hid from the blind eye, so all the beauty of Christ is concealed from the impure, because the spiritual eye in them is darkened.

But the pure in heart have the eye of the understanding enlightened, in heaven it will be so perfectly; and therefore the light of the knowledge of the glory of God in the face of Jesus Christ shall shine with unclouded radiance upon their soul. Oh, then, let Christ's people be found ever striving to be cleansed from all filthiness of the flesh and of the spirit, that they may be fitted for that glorious vision which will burst upon them, when this mortal shall have put on immortality, and this corruptible shall have put on incorruption! And let the impure in heart bethink themselves what must be their eternal portion. As purity fits for heaven and for the society that is there, so impurity must have its place in hell, for there only is the society congenial to it. Oh, may the Lord himself quicken and purify us! and let our prayer ever be, and our actings and strivings in conformity to it, "Create in me a clean heart, O God, renew a right spirit within me." Amen.

XVIII.

The Equity and Benignity of the Divine Law.

BY THE REV. JOHN BROWN, D.D.

"Wherefore the law is holy, and the commandment holy, and just, and good."—Rom. vii. 12.

THE object of the following remarks is to prove and illustrate the general principle, that the law of God, which opposes man's natural inclinations in his fallen state, and which secures that he shall be punished for following these inclinations, is a most righteous and benignant appointment. "The law is not sin." There is nothing wrong with the law. It is a faultless institution. "It is holy," perfect, everything that it ought to be—"just and good."

A law that is inconsistent with truth and right, that infringes the rights of any being, is not a holy law—it is an unjust law. A law the native tendency of which is not to prevent or remove, but to create and increase misery, is not a holy law—it is a mischievous law; but a law which unites in it the characters of righteousness and benignity, which is at once "just and good"—*that* is a "holy" or faultless law.

That this is the character of the *divine* law is the proposition which I mean to demonstrate; and, in doing so, I do not at all feel as if I were undertaking an unnecessary work—wasting my labour, spending my strength for nought, in proving what no one denies; for though few will make the denial in so many words, the great body of mankind—all men, indeed, until they are taught of the Spirit—cherish doubts of the righteousness and benignity of the divine law; and, under the shelter of these doubts, try to shield themselves from the conviction that they are unprovoked and utterly inexcusable offenders in every instance in which they have violated that law; that every sin is equally foolish and wicked; and that it possesses both these qualities in a degree to which we can set no limits. Till these "refuges of lies" are entirely swept away—till the sinner's mouth is entirely stopped, and he is constrained to bring in himself guilty before God, till he is made to see that, in the quarrel between him and God, he has been uniformly and entirely in the wrong, and God uniformly and entirely in the right, he never will, he never can, be made to perceive the value and excellence of the Christian salvation, or gladly and gratefully to receive what is freely given him of God, but can never be obtained in any other way—pardon, peace, holiness, hope—"the salvation which is in Christ with eternal glory."

The law is a revelation of the will of God, for the regulation of man as an intelligent and active being, with this proviso, that if man refuse to regulate himself by this revelation, he exposes himself to such punishment as is adequate to the offence in the estimation of the Lawgiver. The law thus defined may be viewed in its *principles,* in its *precepts,* and in its *sanction;* and it is my object to shew that in all these, however rebel man may attempt to pursuade himself to the contrary, the law is "holy," faultless, excellent, being both *"just and good."*

I. First, then, the *principles* of the law are just and good. The principles of the divine law are three: *first,* That the will of God should be man's rule; *secondly*, That if man violate this rule, he should be punished; and *thirdly*, That the punishment should be such as appears to the Lawgiver adequate to the offence. Now, all these principles are just and good. Is it not just and right, that the will of the Being who is infinite in knowledge, in wisdom, and in moral excellence, should be the governing rule of all intelligent beings, especially as he is the Creator and they the creatures, entirely dependent on him for all they are and all they have? Is it not right, so far as *He* is concerned? Does he not deserve this honour? And is it not right in reference to *them?* What right of theirs does it invade? How can they have a right to govern themselves apart from, or in opposition to, his will? And is it not obviously as good as right? What can so directly tend to, what can so completely secure, the greatest possible happiness, as the execution of the will of Him whose nature as well as whose name is love? Just in the degree in which any will is concerned in the production of events, unregulated by, unsubjected to his will, must there be happiness prevented or misery induced.

Then, is it not right that the violation of the righteous, benignant will of God, should be punished? Would it not shock all our ideas of right, that he who regards and he who disregards the law and the Lawgiver, should stand on the same level? The justice of this principle is universally practically acknowledged; for all human laws are sanctioned by penalties. And is not this good as well as right? Is not the threatened punishment fitted to deter all from violating the law? and is not the inflicted punishment fitted to furnish those who have not offended with an additional motive to keep the law, the breaking of which, they see, leads to such painful consequences?

And then, as to the third principle. Is it not right that the punishment should be appointed by God? He is the supreme Sovereign, and properly, too, a disinterested person. His essential happiness and glory are not, cannot be, affected by the sin of man. He is infinite in wisdom, and knows exactly what is the degree and form of punishment which will best serve the great end in view—the exhibition of his own moral excellence in the order and happiness of intelligent beings; and his essential benignity secures that no unnecessary suffering shall be produced.

It is obviously good, too, as well as right, that this prerogative of sovereignty should belong to, and be exercised by, God. In what hands in the universe could such a power be safe but in his, whose infinite power is not only regulated by infinite wisdom, but by infinite righteousness; and in all its operations influenced by infinite benignity! That the fundamental principles of the divine law are just and good, is so evident, that it may seem to require an apology to have made even these few observations, for the purpose less of demonstrating the fact, than of shewing that it needs no demonstration.

II. I go on to remark, in the second place, that the *precepts* of the law are just and good. Now, what are the precepts of the divine law? They are very numerous, for the law is "very broad," and reaches to every part of man's nature—regulating his opinions, his dispositions, his actions, in all the variety of relation and circumstances in which he can be placed. But numerous as are its requisitions, we have a complete summary of them in the following very comprehensive words: "Thou shalt love the Lord thy God with all thy heart, and soul, and strength, and mind. This is the first and great commandment; and the second is like unto it, Thou shalt love thy neighbour as thyself."

Now, are not both these commandments *right?* Would there not be an obvious violation of right if they were otherwise than they are? Is it not right to love, to love supremely,

Him who is supremely lovely, who is infinitely kind; to fear supremely him who is supremely venerable, possessed, as he is, of infinite power, wisdom, and righteousness; to trust entirely Him who is supremely trustworthy? And could he, without injustice to himself, have demanded less of us? Would it not have been incongruous and monstrous for him to have enjoined less than the love of the whole heart, and soul, and strength, and mind? And as to the second great commandment, which is like the first, is it not right also? Does not its rectitude stand out in strong relief, when we contemplate it in the form in which our great Master exhibited it: "Whatsoever ye would that men should do to you, do ye even so to them"? Would the law have been right if it had required anything else, anything less, than this?

Their seems no gainsaying these statements. Yet there are two things in reference to the preceptive part of the divine law that many are disposed to think scarcely consistent with what is right, what is reasonable, in the whole circumstances of the case. The first is, the demand of absolute perfection in the performance of every duty; the other, the extending the preceptive part of the law to the inward principle, as well as to the external actions. But, with regard to the first, who does not see that for a law to permit imperfection, is to destroy itself? In the degree in which there is imperfection in obedience, there is a non-fulfilling of the law, that is, there is disobedience; and what kind of a law would that be which makes provision for being satisfied with disobedience? And as to the second, though it is not right for human laws to interfere with internal principles, for two reasons—that they cannot afford the means of obedience, and they cannot certainly discover disobedience, so as to punish it—yet, for the same reasons substantially, viz., that God can furnish the means of guiding the internal principles, and can discover when these means are honestly applied, it is right that the divine law should regulate conviction and dispositions, as well as actions. Indeed, it would not be right were not God, who is a Spirit, requiring worship in spirit and in truth. For *Him* to be satisfied with mere external services would be obvious incongruity.

But, it may be said, all this would be undoubtedly true, were man able to yield a spiritual and perfect obedience. But where is the rectitude of requiring spiritual and perfect obedience from so weak and frail a creature as man, who is not able to yield it, carnal as he is, and sold under sin? Now I have two answers to make to this objection—the *first* is, That in the only sense in which the objection could have any force, it is not true; and the *second* is, That in the only sense in which the objection is true, it has no force.

If God in his law were requiring anything that is physically impossible—anything which, from want of natural faculty, we are, in the strict sense of the word, *incapable* of performing—then, without doubt, such requisitions must appear to us not right, not reasonable. But this is not the truth; it is the very reverse of the truth. God requires of us nothing that is impossible, nothing but what, were our dispositions what they ought to be, would be found easy. God does not require of us the same measure of obedience as of angels. He requires and accepts of his creatures according to what they have, and not according to what they have not. Where "much is given, much is required; and where little, so much the less." He that has five talents is not expected to yield the same return as he who has ten. However weak our minds, however little our strength, were we to love the Lord with all our weak minds, with all our little strength, we should keep all his commandments, and none of them would be grievous to us. We surely *can* love God with the power of love we possess;

we surely *can* serve Him with all the strength we possess. To say anything else, is to involve ourselves in self-contradiction. It is to say, we *cannot* do what we admit we can do.

Bring the question to the test of experience. Go over all the demands of the divine law, as these are brought out in the Word of God, and ask yourselves, Is there any one of these which I could not comply with if I were so disposed? Is there any one of them which demands a faculty I do not possess—as in the case of a blind man required to read, or anything that absolutely and forcibly confines these faculties, as the fetters of the prisoner when he is required to walk? Am I in any case compelled to violate the divine law? Conscience very readily replies to all these questions with a strong negative. "No; there is nothing in the way of entire compliance with the divine law but strong disinclination. I do not obey the law, not because I cannot obey, but because I choose to disobey."

But this leads to the second remark: The only sense in which the objection is true, it has no force. It is true that man, depraved man, is so disinclined to obedience that, without a divine influence, he will not obey. "The carnal mind is enmity against God; it is not subject to the law of God, neither can be." But does this warrant the conclusion—Therefore man cannot be reasonably commanded, reasonably expected, to obey? What kind of reasoning is this? I have not a disposition to do my duty, therefore I cannot reasonably be required to do my duty. I have a great disposition to commit iniquity, therefore the law is unjust that forbids me to commit iniquity. Can it be unreasonable to require me to do that which I am disinclined to, which it would be quite right to require me to do if I had only an opposite inclination? The principle plainly lands us in this absurdity: No law can be just which requires any man to be better or to do more than he is disposed to be and to do. In this case, what would be the use of law at all?

The law would not be righteous if it altered with what has been termed man's measure of moral ability—in plainer words, man's measure of moral depravity. The law necessarily requires a creature like man to devote all his powers of action to the service of God. It cannot demand more. The nature of man makes it impossible he should yield more. It cannot demand less. The moral perfection of God makes it impossible that he should be pleased with less. No; however hard men may wink to hide the truth from themselves. The law of God is *right.* It requires nothing in the slightest degree unreasonable.

That the preceptive part of the law of God is *good,* calculated to produce happiness, may be very easily made plain to the mind of every reflecting person. Yes, we may truly say, with regard to all the ordinances and commandments of the divine law : "The Lord hath commanded us to do all these statutes for our good always." To love, fear, and trust God in the manner the law requires lays a deep foundation for true, permanent happiness. Without obeying these commands man cannot be happy. In the degree in which he obeys them he is happy, and he makes others happy. Is it not evident, that to pay a strict regard to the laws of truth, justice, and benevolence, is the shortest road to happiness ? Is not by far the greater part of the misery of man the direct effect of violating God's law? Are not all the commanded affections pleasurable ? Are not all the forbidden, malignant passions painful? Is not a benevolent man generally a happy man ? Is not a malignant man always a miserable one? Would the world have been happier had God permitted or enjoined gluttony and drunkenness, instead of temperance ; and if, instead of checking natural appetite, had given it loose reins? Fleshly lusts war against the soul, and the body too ; and the abstinence from them which the law of God requires is necessary for the comfort of the life that now is, as well as to the happiness of that which is to come. A man entirely conformed to the law of God would be as happy as it is possible to be out of heaven. And what a delightful scene would society present if the laws of piety, truth, justice, and benevolence were universally practised! "Violence would no more be heard in our land, wasting nor destruction within our borders." There would be universal, permanent peace among nations; and mankind would attain to a height of civilisation, a measure of happiness, which the most sanguine philosophical philanthropist has never dared to anticipate.

III. It only remains now that I endeavour shortly to shew, thirdly, that the *sanctions* of the law of God are just and good. The divine law is not a mere injunction of duty; it includes in it a provision that, if this injunction be neglected or disobeyed, the transgressor shall be visited with adequate punishment. This is ordinarily termed the penal sanction of the law. We have already seen, in our remarks on the first department of our subject, that it is just and right that the divine law should be thus sanctioned. My object at present is to shew that the sanction adopted is a just and good one.

The sanction of the law is stated in such passages of Scripture as these: "The soul that sinneth shall die," "The wages of sin is death," "Cursed is every one that continueth not in all things written in the book of the law, to do them." And they who are finally condemned for disobedience are doomed to the "everlasting fire prepared for the devil and his angels;" and are said "to go away into everlasting punishment." Every sinner exposes himself to the displeasure of God, to be manifested in the manner which seems fit to his wisdom and justice; and, unless pardon is obtained "through the redemption that is in Christ Jesus," this displeasure will continue to be manifested during the whole eternity of the transgressor's being.

Doubts have often been thrown out as to the justice and

goodness of this arrangement; and, on this ground, some have been rash enough to call in question, and even to deny, a doctrine very clearly stated in holy writ—the eternity of future punishment. With what justice such doubts are cherished will appear from the following remarks.

Few will deny that sin deserves punishment; and as to the degree in which sin is to be punished, assuredly the sinner is not the most qualified judge. Sin—any sin, every sin—includes in it an amount of moral evil; and therefore of criminal desert, which no human mind can fully estimate. There is in it unnatural conduct towards a father, ingratitude towards a benefacter, rebellious conduct towards a sovereign; and all these heightened inconceivably by the infinite excellence and the innumerable and inappreciable benefits of him who wears all these characters. He who reflects on this will be cautious how he asserts that sin cannot deserve unending punishment.

It is also worthy of his consideration, how far suffering can remove blameworthiness; and he would do well to ask himself if the statement does not seem agreeable to right and reason, that while just desert of punishment remains, there can be no injustice in inflicting the deserved punishment? When a sinner can stand up before the Eternal Judge and say, I have suffered so much and so long that I am become perfectly innocent, he may, on the ground of justice, plead that his sufferings should terminate; but not till then.* Besides, there is reason to believe that the finally condemned will continue for ever to sin; and on that ground it must be just that they should for ever continue to suffer.

The *goodness* of the penal sanction of the divine law may seem less susceptible of satisfactory proof than its *justice*. Yet we believe it to be capable of being shewn, beyond the possibility of rational contradiction, that this awful appointment is

* Smalley.

not only consistent with, but illustrative of, the divine benignity; not, certainly, of his permanent benignant regards to those who have abused so much goodness, and drawn from the reluctant hand of Jehovah the thunderbolts of his wrath—all proofs of love to them (and they were neither few nor small) are past—but of his benignant regards to the great body of intelligent moral beings in the universe. In punishing irreclaimable offenders, a wise and benevolent government discovers its benignant regards to its subjects generally; not to punish such offenders adequately would, in a variety of ways, be injustice and unkindness to their fellow-subjects. The manifestation of the true character of the supreme Legislator and Judge of all worlds, is the ultimate end of the universe; and it is the grand means, too, of securing the order and holiness and happiness of the intelligent part of it. This manifestation is made by appropriate works. By works indicative of design, he shews his wisdom; by deeds of power, he shews his omnipotence; by wonderful works of kindness, he shews his benignity; by awful judgments on the workers of iniquity, he manifests his holiness and righteousness. All these works are intended and fitted to produce in the minds of intelligent beings such impressions of the all-perfect character of Jehovah as go to form, in rational beings, that character which is necessary to their permanent happiness. That man gives clearer evidence of arrogance than of penetration, who, after reflecting on these statements, denies that the penal sanction of the law is not only consistent with, but illustrative of, benignity as well as righteousness. The effect which such a manifestation of the holiness and righteousness of God is calculated to produce on holy intelligences is strikingly illustrated in the Apocalypse, where the smoke from the ruins of the mystical Babylon, rising up for ever and ever, is represented as giving new energy to "that undisturbed song of pure concent aye sung before the sapphire-coloured throne, to Him who sits thereon, with saintly shout and solemn jubilee."* "And after these things I heard a great voice of much people in heaven, saying, Alleluia; Salvation, and glory, and honour, and power, unto the Lord our God; for true and righteous are his judgments: for he hath judged the great whore, which did corrupt the earth with her fornication, and hath avenged the blood of his servants at her hand. And again they said, Alleluia. And her smoke rose up for ever and ever. And the four-and-twenty elders and the four beasts fell down and worshipped God that sat on the throne, saying, Amen; Alleluia. And a voice came out of the throne, saying, Praise our God, all ye his servants, and ye that fear him, both small and great. And I heard as it were the voice of a great multitude, and as the voice of many waters, and as the voice of mighty thunderings, saying, Alleluia: for the Lord God omnipotent reigneth" (Rev. xix. 1–6).

Thus have I endeavoured to shew, as briefly and as clearly as I could, that, whether we consider its *principles*, its *precepts*, or its *sanctions*, the Divine law is "holy"—both "*just* and *good*."

It is a matter of very deep interest to every one of us to understand well the relation which we bear to this holy, just, and good law; for to it *we* do bear, to it every intelligent being in the universe bears, a relation; and our most important interests are dependent on that relation. There are multitudes who would fain have nothing to do with this law; they would fain have it abolished, annihilated. Many practically deny, some theoretically question, or even deny, its obligation on them. But the law is as stable and immutable as its author, God. Indeed, the law is God commanding, prohibiting, threatening. Men may forget it, but it never forgets them; they may put it away from them, but it keeps its hold; they may renounce

* Milton.

its authority, but they cannot escape from its grasp; they may deny its obligation, but they cannot destroy it. They may deny it now, but they will not always be able to deny it; they will be made to feel it in its painful effects. There are no sceptics in the invisible world.

It is of great importance that we should clearly understand the relation in which innocent man stood to this law, the relation in which fallen man stands to this law, the relation in which restored man stands to this law.

To innocent man, this law was the charter by which he held the fair inheritance of divine favour bestowed on him. The principle of the original economy was: "Do this, and live." Obedience to the law was the stipulated means of securing the divine favour, and of obtaining higher manifestations of this favour. It would have brought him into, and kept him in, a justified state; and, both as a statement of duty and incentive to duty, presented to a holy mind predisposed to holiness, it tended to make holy man more and more holy. The law was then strong to justify, to sanctify, to save.

With regard to fallen man, his relation to this holy, just, and good law has undergone a most melancholy change. He has broken the law; and he is, so far as all influence but divine is concerned, invincibly indisposed to keep it. The principle of the economy which sin brings man under is, "The wages of sin is death." The law says to the sinner: "Thou hast disobeyed, thou must, thou shalt, be punished;" and it says also: "Obey, obey perfectly every one of my requisitions. Every neglect, every violation, brings along with it a new sentence of condemnation, sinks thee deeper in guilt and in perdition." But not one word of promise, no ground of hope, does the holy, good law offer to the sinner. It would not be a holy, just, and good law if it did. To the sinner, then, the law cannot be the means of *justification*. No; "by the deeds of the law no flesh can be justified," for this plain reason: "By the law is the conviction of sin." Man is a sinner, and the law condemns him because he is a sinner; how, then, can it justify him? But this is not all. To the sinner the law cannot be the primary means of *sanctification*. For this purpose, too, "it is weak through the flesh." It cannot remove the enmity which conscious guilt generates and perpetuates. It merely authoritatively commands us to do what we are invincibly disinclined to do; and forbids us to do what we are strongly inclined to do, under the most fearful sanctions; and in this way, through our depravity, it either rouses our depraved propensities into a state of exasperated activity, or smites our powers of spiritual action with the torpor of despair.

With regard to restored man, he stands, too, in a peculiar and most important relation to the holy, just, and good law of God. He is delivered from its curse through union to him who "has redeemed us from the curse, having become a curse for us." "There is no condemnation to them who are in Christ Jesus;" and the law is not with him at all the means of justification, nor the primary means of sanctification. He is "justified freely by God's grace, through the redemption that is in Christ Jesus." To him "eternal life is the gift of God, through Jesus Christ the Lord;" and as to sanctification, "the love of God shed abroad in his heart by the Holy Ghost, given to him" by the faith of the truth, is the spring of holy obedience. Being "not without law to God, but under the law to Christ," he walks "at liberty, keeping the commandments;" not doing that he may live, but doing because he lives, and living because he believes; finding in the holy, good law of God "a light to his feet and a lamp to his path;" a stimulus when indolent, a guide when perplexed, a constant source of delightful contemplation and powerful motive, as an exhibition of the wisdom, holiness, and benignity of him "whose he is, and whom he serves." Such is a brief statement of the relation in which innocent, fallen, restored man stands to the divine law.

To the two classes into which my hearers, and into which indeed the whole human race, are divided as to their relation to the law, I conclude with offering a few affectionate exhortations.

All are by nature related to the law in the second of the ways I have been describing; "all have sinned"—all have incurred the curse—all are under the authority and obligation of the violated law; and all who have not been delivered from this state, by the atoning sacrifice and sanctifying Spirit of Christ, are so related to the law still. Not a few of those who are listening to me may belong to this class. Are there not some of them who know they are sinners, and who know, too, that they are unpardoned, unsanctified sinners? To such I say, Oh, think of your wretched, perilous condition, every hour becoming more perilous and wretched! Seek not to deny the fact that you are sinners. "If you should justify yourself, your own mouth would condemn you; if you say you are perfect, it also proves you perverse." Do not attempt to apologise, or excuse, or justify your conduct in violating the law. No excuse will bear examination at the bar of your own calm conscientious judgment now. How, then, will it bear to be urged at the bar of divine justice hereafter? "When he punishes you, you will have nothing to answer him." No, you will be speechless. Do not say the law was too strict in its requisitions, too severe in its sanction; we have seen that the law is every way worthy of its infinitely perfect author. Do not speak of the weakness of your nature; that is but another name for its depravity. Do not speak of the force of temptation; it was indeed too strong for your resistance, because you were not disposed to resist. You know you were never called to a duty which you could not have done if you would; that you *never* were *compelled* to commit a sin. The depraved inclination led the way to the criminal action. Do not harbour the thought that you can be saved without the law being satisfied, without your being both justified and sanctified. Do not attempt, for it is impious and vain, to obtain either the one or the other by works of righteousness which you may suppose you can do. Do not suppose that you can, in any degree, dissolve the connection between you and the law. No, you are bound to it by a chain indissoluble as the decrees of the Eternal. Do not suppose that you can have the law in any degree altered. When God changes, then, and not till then, can the law change; for what is the law but a declaration of God's mind and will as to what is right; and "He is of one mind, and who can change him?" Acknowledge the excellence and authority of the law. Acknowledge your own inconceivable folly and wickedness in violating it, and in being opposed to it in your carnal minds. Instead of seeking to have your connection with the law dissolved, or to convert it into an instrument of justification, seek to have your relation to the law changed. That can take place only by a change taking place either in the law or in you. The former is absolutely impossible. The created universe may be annihilated, but the law of God cannot change. Oh, dream not—it is a dangerous, if continued it will be a fatal, dream—of its demands, either preceptive or sanctionary, being lowered! The change must take place in you; you must "repent and believe the gospel;" you must change your mind respecting God; you must believe the truth with respect to Jesus Christ; you must, in good earnest, believe that God is the immaculately holy, the infinitely kind being he appears to be "in the face of Christ Jesus." Believing the truth as it is in Jesus—believing that "God is in Christ reconciling the world to himself, seeing he made him to be sin for us who knew no sin, that we might be made the righteousness of God in him"—believing that "he has redeemed us from the curse, having become a curse in our room"—believing that he hath "taken away sin by the sacrifice of himself"—you shall be "justified freely through the redemption that is in Christ Jesus;" and, "being justified by faith, ye shall have peace with God, through whom we have received the reconciliation." You will then be reconciled to God and to God's law; you will learn indeed to count it "holy, just, and good," and rejoice that it is "magnified and made honourable" in the finished work of your Lord; and loving God, you will be taught by his grace to "deny ungodliness and worldly lusts, and to live soberly, righteously, and godly in the present world," while you are "looking for the blessed hope, the glorious appearing of our Lord Jesus Christ, who gave himself for us that he might redeem us from all iniquity, and purify us unto himself a peculiar people, zealous of good works." And thus "what the law could not do, in that it was weak through the flesh," will be accomplished through "God sending his own Son in the likeness of sinful flesh and for sin." Through this wonderful manifestation of the united glories of divine holiness and love, set forth in the word of the truth of the gospel, understood and believed by you, "the righteousness of the law will be fulfilled in you, walking not after the flesh, but after the Spirit;" and, in the beauties of a consistent, holy life, you will shew forth the glories of the character and law of him who hath "called you out of darkness into his marvellous light." Such is the blessed result when a deep conviction of the righteousness of the law, and the impossibility of finding either justification or sanctification by it, leads the sinner to pardon, hope, holiness, and heaven, by leading him to Him who is "the end of the law for righteousness to every one that believeth." Yes—

> "So fares it with the sinner when he feels
> A growing dread of vengeance at his heels;
> His conscience, like a glassy lake before,
> Lashed into foamy waves begins to roar.
> The Law, grown clamorous, though silent long,
> Arraigns him, charges him with every wrong;
> Asserts the rights of his offended Lord—
> And "Death or restitution" is the word.
> The last impossible, he fears the first;
> And having well deserved, expects the worst.
> Then welcome refuge, and a peaceful home!—
> Oh, for a shelter from the wrath to come!
> "Crush me, ye rocks, ye falling mountains hide,
> Or bury me in ocean's angry tide.
> The scrutiny of these all-seeing eyes
> I dare not"—"And you need not," God replies;
> "The remedy you want I freely give;
> This Book shall teach you—read, believe, and live."
> 'Tis done! the raging storm is heard no more;
> Mercy receives him on her peaceful shore;
> And Justice, guardian of the dread command,
> Drops the red vengeance from his willing hand."

And what is the practical result?

> "A soul redeemed demands a life of praise;
> Hence the complexion of his future days—
> Hence a demeanour holy and unspeck'd.
> And the world's hatred as its sure effect." *

I have left myself room to say only a word or two to those whose relation and feelings to the law have been happily changed, "through sanctification of the Spirit and belief of the truth," to which, I trust, not a few of my hearers belong. Shew gratitude for deliverance from the curse of the law; by cheerful obedience to its precepts make it evident that you do indeed count the law holy, just, and good; that you delight to contemplate it, as exemplified in the all-perfect character of

* Cowper.

your Lord and Saviour, who fulfilled all righteousness; to study it in the writings of the holy prophets and apostles; and to reduce your studies to practice, in the cultivation of every holy disposition, in the performance of every prescribed duty. Oh, beware of giving the slightest ground to the world to suppose that the faith of these truths, the enjoyment of these privileges, has any tendency to make men say, "Let us continue in sin that grace may abound"! Make it evident that "the liberty wherewith Christ has made you free," is not a liberty to sin, but liberty in holiness. "Walk at liberty, keeping his commandments." "Serve him without fear, in righteousness and holiness all the days of your life." Having died and been buried, and raised again in your surety, who died by sin under the curse of the law once, but who now liveth for ever, by the power of God, made exceeding glad in the light of his Father's countenance, "reckon yourselves by this death and resurrection, dead indeed unto sin, but alive unto God through Jesus Christ our Lord;" and "let not sin reign in your mortal body, that ye should obey it in the lusts thereof; neither yield ye your members as instruments of unrighteousness unto sin: but yield yourselves unto God as those who are alive from the dead, and your members as instruments of righteousness to God; for sin shall not have dominion over you; for ye are not under the law, but under grace." Improve the high advantages of your new situation, act up to your principles and your privileges; and "whatsoever things are true, whatsoever things are honest, whatsoever things are just, whatsoever things are pure, whatsoever things are lovely, whatsoever things are of good report, whatsoever things are commanded in the holy, just, and good law, think on these things." Let your holy, happy lives proclaim, "His yoke is easy, his burden is light;" "his commandments are not grievous, his law is holy, just, and good."

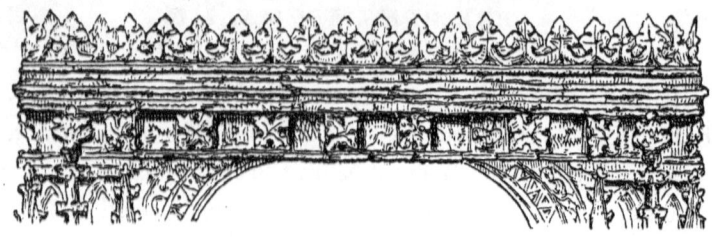

XIX.

God's Truth and Man's Freedom.*

BY THE REV. THOMAS GUTHRIE, D.D.

"THE TRUTH SHALL MAKE YOU FREE."—JOHN viii. 32.

IN great dry water-courses, with steep banks, and beds full of rounded stones, the traveller in Africa finds vestiges of a time when noble rivers rolled through these arid plains, clothing them with flowers and verdure. Here at home, beneath the surface of the black morass, in the skeleton roots of trees, that, laid bare by runlets or the spade, mat the ground, we see vestiges of a time when these unsightly bogs waved with stately forests. The coals we burn, the rocks we quarry, entomb in the remains of strange plants and animals the vestiges of a still older time, when the productions and climate of our country were those of a torrid, rather than a temperate zone. Everywhere we see vestiges of other and, in some instances, of better times; and nowhere more than in ourselves. Building his house, warming and lighting it with the ruins of a former world, man is himself a ruin; but one that, great in its decay, retains not a few traces of departed glory. Divines and philosophers find these in our conscience—the pleasure

* Preached at the opening of the Tricentenary of the Reformation, 14th August 1860.

which well-doing yields, and the pain which ill-doing inflicts ; in our intuitive belief in a God ; in man's eager craving for immortality, its bright and boundless hopes. To these traces of a divine image may I not add what is universal wherever cultivated, that regard for truth and truthfulness which, like the undergirding of Paul's ship, holds this shattered world together?

Is not lying considered one of the basest of vices, the worst promise of a boy, the meanest feature in a man? Is it not the deepest insult which one man can offer to another to say, You lie? What higher homage could the world pay to the majesty of truth than her rule, that one plain, palpable falsehood in a witness' evidence, like the dead fly in the apothecary's ointment, vitiates all his testimony. This regard for truth, this respect for truthfulness, blooms on the grave of every other virtue, and, like rose leaves, will retain its fragrance even when its life is fled. Have not I heard the lowest characters on these streets, those who seemed sunk beneath further disgrace, fiercely charge each other with lying, as with a thing of which even they might be ashamed? See how a bold, honest villain looks down on the sneaking cheat ; and how men of the loosest habits, having detected a religious hypocrite, turn him out to be worried, and think themselves at liberty to despise him, and reproach him, and tread him beneath their feet.

There is something inexpressibly hateful in lying. Our indignation against Judas turns into utter loathing when, as the tragedy goes on, the smooth-faced villain, with kindly looks and oily tongue, steps out from the crowd to betray his Master with a hail and kiss ; that looks the blackest spot of all his guilt ; more difficult to wash out than blood itself. Here his crimes culminate, and from this highest summit of sin, the traitor, detested of God and man, takes his fearful leap into the gulf below. I believe indeed that conscience will often less bitterly reproach a man for the crime he commits than for the falsehood by which he has attempted to conceal it; and thus the evil-doer has never felt so wretched, degraded, as when in solitude or dreary cell he thought of the falsehoods he had told to rob confiding man of his property, or, worse still, loving, trusting woman of her virtue. The last blush on the cheek has mantled for a lie. Now, in these things I trace the outlines of an old image; the features of Him who has a divine regard for truth. God cannot lie; no, not even to save his own, lost, loved children. He must keep his word; therefore his Son must fall, as much a costly sacrifice to his regard for truth as to his love for men.

"Buy the truth and sell it not," says the wise man; most precious of commodities, it is the only thing a man should buy and not sell. Secular or religious, all truth is, in a sense, divine; nor has the Fall left us any thing more godlike than that truth in its search is our keenest pursuit, truth in its discovery is our highest pleasure, and truth, in all its shapes and forms, is the object of our homage and admiration. The charm of the finest pictures or noblest poems lies not so much in their gorgeous colours or glowing language as in their truth. Charming because they are natural, and natural because they are true, they have the elements of universal and lasting fame; and thus the highest praise ever, perhaps, bestowed on the "Cottar's Saturday Night" was the disparaging remark of a peasant girl, who, not knowing what she said, declared that she thought nothing of it, for she had seen the self-same thing a thousand times at her father's house.

How precious is truth! Nothing, not gold, or the diamond, is so indestructible. Falsehoods, like meteors, after blazing for a while, go out. Truth never dies. It is immortal: the sword cannot kill it; the halter cannot hang it; water cannot drown it; fire cannot burn it; the grave cannot bury it; it shall have a day of resurrection. You can drown me, but not the truth I speak; you may burn its confessor, but it expires not with the martyr at his stake. To its immortality its discoverers owe their own. Bacon, Newton, Harvey, Watt, and others of the mighty dead, lie embalmed in the truths they have discovered, as I have seen a beautiful insect preserved in a mass of golden amber; on these truths their names stand inscribed on monuments that shall stand when the pyramids have crumbled into dust.

Precious, precious, above all things else, nothing lies so near man's present and future welfare as truth. All sin, wrongs, oppression, cruelties, crimes of every kind, stand on falsehood. The fall of man was wrought by a lie; our first mother, like thousands of her daughters, having been seduced from the paths of virtue. Tyranny rests on a lie!—that kings have a divine right to reign, and that subjects are under a divine obligation to obey. Slavery rests on a lie!—that man can hold property in man, and buy and sell his brother. Persecution rests on a lie!—that man has no right of private judgment, and is answerable for his faith to other than God. Intemperance rests on a lie!—that stimulants which intoxicate are a necessity to health and happiness. All vice rests on this lie, that it ministers more than virtue to our happiness; and by such lies as these—God is all mercy or has none—it is too late or too early to seek salvation—the greater number of lost souls are ruined. Too cunning to shew the naked iron, Satan baits the barb; and with gay, attractive falsehoods dresses all his lures. Called by our Master the father of lies, he catches his prey by these; and by these holds them. They are the foundation of the devil's power—the weapons he fights with, the tools he works with, the chains by which he binds his crowd of captives and drags them down to hell. And as the only thing that can destroy falsehood is truth, therefore our Lord says, in words which I proceed to illustrate, "The truth shall make you free!"

I. *To the truth we owe our spiritual freedom.* There is a system of medicine—on which I pronounce no opinion here—which professes to cure disease by the use of those substances that produce it. That was not the method of the great Physician. He did not cast out Beelzebub by calling in other devils. As cold snow is to a burning brain, warmth to the half-frozen traveller, oil to the stormy billows, water to a raging fire, so is the gospel to sinners. With truth, it encounters falsehood; that was man's ruin, and truth is his redemption. Conversion is not wrought by concussion, but by conviction; the triumph of light over darkness, of truth over error, it is not the result of blind force, but of persuasion. The Spirit of God reaches man's heart through his head; and therefore I may remark in passing, that all revivals which are not produced by the power of truth, like the swell of a passing storm, are agitations that must soon subside.

The truth shall make you free, and it does so. For example, a man thinks lightly of sin, and thinking as so many do that there is little ill in sin, he continues in it; by that the devil holds him. Now, truth comes in to shew that sin is exceeding sinful; that while one sin was enough to ruin, nothing less than the blood of God's Son was sufficient to redeem the world. Convinced of that, Satan's captive is free; and hasting to Jesus falls at his feet to cry, "Lord, save me, I perish!" Another, again, flatters himself that "God will not require," and therefore he continues in sin. But truth raises the curtain; and there, before the astonished man, stand an assembled world, a great white throne, the Judge of all, and at the bar—who? himself, giving an account of all the deeds done in the body, whether they were good or evil! Another, again, says, as many say—or rather perhaps believes, as many do—that God is too merciful not to overlook our offences. Did not he give us our appetites? Has he not placed us in the circumstances which expose us to temptation? Will he not, in consideration of the weaknesses of humanity, overlook what precise men too severely censure? Does not even the Bible itself say that he "knoweth our frame; he remembereth that we are dust"? and thus, lending a too ready ear to Satan's sophistry, the man continues in sin. But truth brushes away these cobwebs, telling him that "God cannot be tempted with evil, neither tempteth he any man;" that as he tempts none, he excuses none; and that the only answer his law gives to such pleas is, walking up to its debtor, to take him by the throat, and say, "Pay me that thou owest." The spell of these falsehoods broken, the man is free; and, alarmed for his soul, as a bird to the mountain, he flees to the refuge set before him in the gospel. The truth has made him free.

While thus seeking by lies to detain some from Christ, by these also Satan seeks to deter others; going off on the other tack, whom he cannot detain, he tries to deter. There is no hope for you, you are too old, or too bad to be saved; your application is too late, you have sinned against the Holy Ghost; others may be forgiven, but for you, hope is none, the door is shut; and thus, like Peter bound between two soldiers, barred and buried in the inmost dungeon, the sinner, poor soul! "sits in darkness and in the shadow of death, being bound in affliction and iron." But now, like the apostle's angel, truth steps in, and the prison is filled with light, it shines upon a cross—the Lamb of God dying for the chief of sinners, and proving in the thief he plucks from the very edge of hell, and carries in triumph to the skies, how he can save even to the very uttermost. The man believes, and is no longer bound; the fetters fall from his limbs, and truth his guide, he walks forth to breathe the air of heaven, to live like the just by faith, and enjoy the gladsome liberty of a son of God. Accompanied by the power and demonstration of the Spirit, the truth has made him free.

Now, this truth of God, which proclaims salvation by faith and not by works, salvation from bad and independent of good works, salvation by God and not by man, salvation through Christ and not through the Church, salvation by the Spirit and not by the sacraments, salvation by the Word and not by its interpreters—a salvation that deposes ministers as such from the priesthood, to make the humblest saint a king and priest to God, to crown a beggar, and put the priestly ephod on a little child—this truth is the only instrumentality to shake Satan's kingdom and emancipate the world. You never will persuade men to love God until you first convince them that God loves them. It is the cross, and nothing else, that is to conquer the world—a gospel that shews the Spirit brooding on the waters of a new creation in the gentle form of a dove, and Christ entering our hearts at their second birth, as he entered the world that night he was born, not amid the flashes of angry thunders, but under skies serenely calm, with a train of angels and songs of peace.

These saving, spirit-stirring, soul-emancipating and long-forgotten truths, it was the glory of the Reformation to bring out of prison, as she came forth, with the Bible in her hand, blazing like a torch of light; and it was the wisdom and glory of our fathers, clearing God's temple of many useless, and worse than useless ceremonies, to restore the pulpit with its open Bible, mother tongue, living preacher, and earnest looks. Thus the Reformation set free thousands and millions that lay in chains of darkness—God's spirit by God's truth giving them spiritual, eternal freedom. To its standard, unfurled often by burning stake and on bloody scaffold, the gathering nations came. Blown by the breath of Martin Luther, blown by the breath of John Calvin, blown loud and long by the brave breath of John Knox, the trumpet of salvation, as it echoed among Scotland's mountains, and rang from shore to shore, sounded like the trumpet of the last day—graves were opened; the dead came forth—not dead bodies, but spirits that had been long dead. The event which we are met to commemorate was life from the dead; light to the blind; liberty to slaves; a revolution that threw open the doors of dungeons; a resurrection to "the spirits in prison." Then religion, bathing herself in the celestial light, renewed her age like an eagle, and, with her eye on the sun, soared to the height of her earliest flights; in men whose memories cling to our city walls, whose heads, withering in the wind, were spiked upon our city gates, and whose honoured dust now sleeps in our churchyards—in these stout-hearted men God in heaven met the old powers of persecution with the old spirit of martyrdom. The truth made them free. They lived freemen, and though they died in dungeon chains, or bound to the stake, they died freemen; and now from their graves near by they seem to call us to follow them as they followed Christ.

II. *To the truth we owe secular freedom.* The pillar that rose from the desert sands, guiding the host of Israel to the land of promise, was at the same time a wilderness blessing—a cloud by day, it screened their heads from the glaring sun, and it lighted their tents by night. And, as a devout Israelite, lying on wakeful couch, looked out on that mysterious radiance, and listened to the voice of the stream, that, gushing from its rocky fountain, went murmuring through the camp, I can fancy how he recognised God's care for the present as well as future welfare of his people. Like that pillar, the gospel, guide of my pilgrim steps to a better world, sheds many precious blessings on this one. I believe it was intended to do so. This is no accident; 'tis the purpose of Him who, our pattern as well as propitiation, divided his time between the interests of this world and the next; taught us to care for men's bodies as well as for their souls, to carry a loaf of bread as well as a bible to the houses of the poor; and who, with the very hand that had been opening the gates of Paradise, dried the cheek of grief, bound up bleeding hearts, gave a brother to a sister's arms, and lighted with joy the dark abodes of sorrow. What Christ was in temporal things to a narrow circle, Christianity has been to a wide one. What country has she ever entered without a troop of earthly blessings in her train? Christianity is not all for the next world. We are too apt to forget this—ministers as well as people; and I am not the servant of Jesus I should be, unless I walk in the footsteps of him who spent his strength and passed his time as well in blessing men's bodies as in saving their souls. Let not the Church forget her duty to the world. Let not the world forget what she owes to the Church; nor, in persecuting religion, be the senseless infant that, ignorant of what it owes a mother, beats the kind breast it hangs on. Not only has the Church of Christ blessed the world in a thousand temporal ways, but for her the world itself is spared; the tares stand till the wheat is ripe; and vengeance, staying her hand till the last Lot is gone forth from Sodom, says with the angel, "I cannot do anything till thou be come thither."

In illustration of these remarks, so far as the blessings of freedom are concerned, I say,

First, To the truth we owe *mental freedom*. Until the advent of Christianity, and during the long dark ages that preceded the Reformation, the mind of man was in a profound slumber. I am not speaking of Plato and Solon and Socrates and Cicero, and such other rare and remarkable lights. I speak of the great mass of mankind; and so far as they were concerned, the range of human thought was limited to the circle of these wants, "What shall I eat, what shall I drink, and wherewithal shall I be clothed?" Read our ballad literature, and see how the great object of admiration in man was muscle, brute force, and brute bravery; and in a woman, personal beauty—what the worm feeds on; but as to mind, the higher faculties and nobler principles of man, its cultivation, like the green patches around the lonely house of some upland glen, that form such a contrast to the far-spreading and surrounding wilderness of brown moor and rugged hill, did not pass beyond the narrowest limits. I want to know where literature was. I want to know where free thought was. I want to know where science was. I want to know where politics were, where the arts were in this land before John Knox was with his compatriots, the great and noble men that fought at his side, or followed his steps. Let the world answer that! So far as the masses were concerned these had no existence. The human mind ran in the rut of a contracted circle. Men believed what their fathers did—no more, no less; and followed their leaders to whatever field they conducted them, with the stupidity, and more than the patience, of sheep.

The Word of God broke in upon this state of things. With its grand truths, its heart-stirring thoughts, it woke a sleeping world. It set all the wheels of man's mind in motion, and called him from low, sensual, animal pleasures, to employ his faculties on the loftiest subjects, and rise on the wings of thought even to the throne of God. The education of the masses, the diffusion of knowledge, the progress of science, the advances of art, the greater blessings of peace, and the diminished horrors of war, to what are these due but to the activity and liberty of thought which came into the world with the Word of God. Meet it was that the first book that issued from the press should have been a bible—the book that, preparing men's minds for the influence of the press, and purifying its thousand streams, has proved in every country the guardian of its freedom, and the best guide of its incalculable power. Calling us to think, to think freely and independently on matters of the highest moment, the truth of God emancipated the human mind, and sent man to expatiate on bold, free wing, into every other region of thought—the eye that had gazed upon the sun was not to be dazzled by lesser lights. Religion having set men a-thinking, the mind that was set in motion on the Sabbath, like a great wheel moved by some powerful cause, continued to revolve throughout the week, nor lost the old impulse till a new one was ready. Taught in matters of religion to think for himself, man took the liberty to think for himself in all things else. A free-thinker, in the right sense of the word, the devout and intelligent student of his Bible cannot be a bigot, or one who won't think—a slave, or one that dare not think—a fool, or one that cannot think. "The testimony of the Lord is sure, making wise the simple." "In thy light shall we see light." "The truth shall make you free."

Second. To the truth we owe *social freedom.* The Bible inculcates principles and precepts that appear to me as incompatible with slavery, as sin is with prayer. It has been well said that prayer will either put an end to sin, or sin will put an end to prayer; and is it not as true that the gospel will either put down slavery, or slavery will put down the gospel? What saith the Lord? that is the question; and "he that hath ears to hear, let him hear." *God hath made of one blood all nations. As ye would that men should do to you, do ye also to them likewise. Love thy neighbour as thyself. Love one another, as I have loved you.*

I will not sit in harsh judgment on others! Still, speaking

for myself, I hardly think that the devil himself has sophistry enough to make any man, not given over to believe a lie, believe that these most kind, tender, loving, gracious, glorious, celestial truths are compatible with slavery : a system that, as the inevitable and incurable source of oppression, cruelty, robbery, uncleanness, adultery, murder, is, to use John Wesley's immortal words, "the sum of all human villanies." With such crimes I do not charge all slaveholders; but where has this system not borne such fruits, and who can deny that these are its natural tendencies? And what doth God require of us? Is it to support or put down a system that bears such fruits? "What doth the Lord require of thee, but to do justly, and to love mercy, and to walk humbly with thy God?" and what but pride, or passion, or self-interest can blind men to this, that these duties are incompatible with slavery—that there is as plainly sin in slavery as there is slavery in sin? Take the last words I have quoted of our blessed Lord, "Love one another as I have loved you." By his most illustrious and divine example, by his glorious name, Redeemer, by the bloody cross of Calvary, he teaches me not to make the free a bondsman, but the bondsman free; not to steal another's liberty, but rather to give mine for his; not to betray or hunt a fugitive on his flight from chains and slavery, but to "bring the poor that are cast out to my house, and wash the feet that fetters have wounded. See him in yonder chamber, where he has stooped to wash the circle of wondering disciples, stand up to say, "I have given you an example that ye should do as I have done to you."

Tell me not that the system is old. Shame on its apologists! The age of the crime is no defence for it; it is only thereby rendered the more horrible, as a corpse long dead grows the more disgusting. Old! Murder is older still. Rocks and trees and ruins and man's grey head grow venerable by age—

sin, never. Tell me not that the poor black has lost his rights. The rights of the Crown, according to lawyers, never prescribe; still less those that are higher and older than rights of royalty, the birthrights of a man. Tell me not that the down-trodden negro belongs to an inferior race. On grounds of philosophy, of physiology, above all, as a believer in the Word of God—of that book which says that "God hath made of one blood all nations"—I deny it, indignantly deny it; looking on him who tortures Scripture to extenuate slavery, and thus tampers with sacred truth, as worse than an infidel—one who has denied the faith. But grant it; I have yet to learn that it is right to tread on weakness, that it is a magnanimous thing to insult a woman who cannot defend herself, rather than a brave stout man who can. The weakness of the oppressed may tempt, but can never justify the crimes of the oppressor. In the judgment of all generous men it rather aggravates them. Hence, Herod was the blacker murderer, that he sent his soldiers to fight with women, and stain their swords with infants' blood.

I cannot speak smooth things here for the sake of courtesy. Is this *not wise?* I reply that the "wisdom that is from above is first pure, then peaceable;" and I should be false to mine office were I not to speak the truth on such a subject when it meets me, as here, full in the face. In this matter, all to whom God's cause is dear, all who are jealous for the honour of Protestantism, all who tremble for the ark in the great battle between Christ and Antichrist, are called to listen not to those who talk with 'bated breath of caution and prudence, but to yonder old bearded prophet with his "Cry aloud, and spare not!" The trumpet must be blown in Zion, and God's great fast proclaimed from sea to sea, and from shore to shore, "Undo the heavy burdens, and let the oppressed go free!" Without fear or favour, crying aloud and sparing not, tell out what these words mean, "Love thy neighbour as thyself."

My neighbour! And who is he? I answer in noble words, read this morning in an American newspaper :—

> "Thy neighbour—'tis the fainting poor,
>   Whose eye with want is dim,
> Whom hunger sends from door to door ;
>   Go thou and succour him.
>
> Thy neighbour—'tis that weary man,
>   Whose years are at their brim ;
> Bent low with sickness, care, and pain,
>   Go thou and comfort him.
>
> Thy neighbour—'tis the heart bereaved
>   Of every earthly gem ;
> Widow and orphan helpless left,
>   Go thou and shelter them."

Shall I go on? Give out the full description? Thank God, I breathe free air; I live in a country where I am not tempted to suppress the truth.

> "Thy neighbour—'tis yon toiling slave,
>   Fettered in thought and limb ;
> Whose hopes are all beyond the grave,
>   Go thou and ransom him."

Third. To the truth we owe *political freedom.* Those who hold and wish to keep their servants in social—those who hold and wish to keep their subjects in political—those who hold and wish to keep their people in religious bondage, in other and plainer words, slave-holders, despots, and popish priests—a goodly company—in discouraging the spread of education, the free use of the Bible, and the full preaching of God's Word, are "wise in their generation." Observe their policy ! Self-interest sharpens men's wits ; and if others do not, they know that slavery and tyranny and priestcraft cannot stand with God's word.

Liberty was born that night that Christ was born—true liberty in all its shapes and forms. I challenge all men to shew me a nation that, till Christianity appeared to bless this world, enjoyed a constitution like our own. God be thanked for it, thanked for the sovereign that fills the throne, thanked for the loyalty of her people, and thanked for our calm but resolute determination, as this city lately saw, to stand by the liberties and protect the privileges which came down to us from battles which our fathers fought, and scaffolds where they fell.

What nation without its Bible had ever a country where citizenship is free to all men, whatever be their caste or colour; where the tribunals of justice recognise no difference between a king and a beggar, the prince and the peasant, the rich man and the poor; where, take it all in all, society is a ladder, up which the humblest at the foot, with a stout arm, a good head, and a bold heart, may climb to the topmost round? The like of it was never heard of till Christianity entered the world. The Bible is the mother of our liberties; and we will honour, and uphold, and defend her to the last! Tell me not about Greek and Roman republics. Republics! what's in a name? Does it make the fetters sit easy on the limbs of a slave, to assure him that he lives in a republic? Will that reconcile a father to see his boy set up to auction? or dry the tears of a mother that has the babe torn from her breast? The republics of Greece and Rome were cursed with slavery; and a republic with slavery is but the tyranny of many for the tyranny of one. It divides responsibility, and multiplies oppression; and is a hydra-headed monster which, having many necks to be smote (I speak figuratively), is but the harder to destroy.

Many years ago, I heard Gay Lussac, the great French philosopher, expatiating in the college of the Sorbonne, on the cause of Britain's greatness. He attributed it to our inexhaustible mines of coal and iron, lying not at great distances from each other, but in neighbouring strata within the same rock or field. Coal and iron! 'Twas all he knew about it. Coal and iron! what had they done to make Britain *Great* Britain—a mother of nations and the mistress of the seas—the home of freedom and an asylum for the oppressed, without the mind that has evoked their powers, without a peaceful, intelligent, religious people, inspired with the love of liberty, and animated by bravery to defend shores which the sea, not man, may invade? It is our freedom—our mental, social, political, religious freedom—which has made us great; and these, with God's blessing, we owe to his word. The Bible has been the source of our liberties. The Bible and the Shorter Catechism, read and studied by Scotchmen, these have toughened their intellects, and set all the wheels of their minds in motion.

Talk of Liberty! liberty without the Bible is either dead or delirious. Look at France, where they would have liberty divorced from religion! He who governs her, like a man in a morass, only keeps himself from sinking by ever shifting his position; beneath his feet the ice is bending, and he avoids his fate by constant motion. With a brave, a clever, a generous, a gallant people, still France, without a Bible, is just like a top—it keeps itself up by perpetual revolutions. Other nations envy Britain's fortune; if they would have her fortune, let them seek her faith. There are but two ways of it, rulers and people have no other choice—the bayonet or the Bible—the fear of man or the fear of God. Who suffers for his country wins admiration; yet the Christian is the truest patriot, the best subject of a good government, but the most formidable enemy of a bad one. Would to God that the patriots of Europe knew this! for we sympathise with their aspirations, and will cheer them on to plant the tree of liberty wherever they can. I have seen it as it stood in France, but it was withered, standing up against the blue sky, neither green leaf nor blessed fruit on its skeleton arms. Oh, that France would learn that if she would grow that tree, she must plant it in a soil nourished by the waters of the sanctuary! Then there is Italy, down-trodden, priest-cursed Italy; I feel the deepest sympathy with her patriots. The God of the oppressed crown their arms with success! But had I a voice to reach these brave Italians, it would tell them that their swords are drawn and their blood is shed in vain in Freedom's fight, unless the ground, thus roughly ploughed and richly manured, receive into its furrows the seeds of truth. No political regeneration has ever stood, or will ever stand, unless it is preceded, accompanied, or followed by a spiritual awakening.

In our case there was no failure. The Argyles and Guthries and Cargills of other days—Knox, with his indomitable spirit and bold endurance, the martyrs who sleep in the Greyfriars' churchyard, and those who lie on Scotland's hills, with nothing to mark their graves but a weathered stone, with its rude sketch of an open Bible and a naked sword, they neither prayed, nor laboured, nor bled, nor died in vain. And why? Why, but because they laid the foundations of our liberties deep in the Word of God. Therefore we have a sovereign, but no slaves in this land; we have authority, but no oppression; we have rulers, but no tyrants; we have liberty without licence, and religion without superstition: free trade, a free parliament, free justice, free thought; liberty, not the false, which is every man doing what he *will*, but the true, which is every man doing what he *ought*. The pious and noble ancestry who have transmitted to us this rich inheritance we have met here to honour; nor let this meeting depart without paying their memories a debt that has long been due. We have monuments to statesmen, to men distinguished in the walks of literature and in the fields of science, but no monument to the biggest man that ever trod the streets of Edinburgh — John Knox. It is not even known where his ashes lie; but we know where his memory is—it lives in the pages of imperishable history, it lies here, in a warmer place, in the heart of every Scotchman, be he Established or Free Churchman, Episcopalian or Independent, nay, in the heart of all men whose bosoms glow with the fires of freedom! And, in proportions somewhat corresponding to his greatness and our gratitude, let us raise a monument to the man who, more than any other, was in God's hands the instrument of making us illustrate these glorious words—

"He is the Freeman whom the Truth makes free."

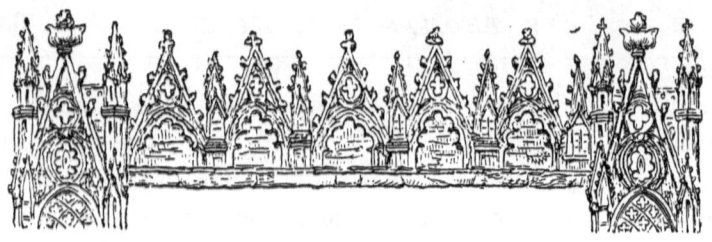

XX.

The Simplicity that is in Christ.

BY THE REV. ROBERT SMITH CANDLISH, D.D.

"But I fear, lest by any means, as the serpent beguiled Eve through his subtilty, so your minds should be corrupted from the simplicity that is in Christ."—2 Cor. xi. 3.

THE simplicity that is in Christ stands here contrasted with the subtilty of the serpent; and the instance given of the serpent's subtilty in his beguiling Eve illustrates what is meant by the simplicity which is opposed to it. In that first temptation, all on the part of God was abundantly simple; the command, not to eat of the tree, with the warning, "In the day that thou eatest thereof thou shalt surely die," was in fact simplicity itself. On the other hand, the subtilty of the tempter is apparent in the complex and manifold pleading which he holds with Eve. God has but one argument against eating, Satan has many for it; and there is no surer sign of subtilty than the giving of many reasons for what a single good one would better justify and explain. The apologist, conscious of a weak and indefensible case, usually has recourse to the multiplying of excuses, often enough irrelevant and inconsistent, as if the heaping of a number of weak explanations upon one another could make up for the impotency and insufficiency of each one of them apart. And the tempter also avails himself of the same artifice. He does not appeal to a single motive or depend on a single plea for success. He prevails by the variety rather than the strength of his weapons, as if he must first confound, before he can conquer his victim. First self-love and self-confidence are appealed to, suspicion is awakened, and discontent begins to rankle within. " Yea, hath God said, Ye shall not eat of every tree of the garden ?" Then, to lull asleep the just fear of God's wrath, as well as to mar the full love of his goodness, the specious insinuation comes in, " Ye shall not surely die." And to perplex the matter still more, obscure and ambiguous hints are thrown out as to the possible or probable issue of events, and the mind is cast loose on a vague calculation of chances and consequences : " Ye shall be as gods, knowing good and evil." Thus complicated is the subtilty of the serpent ; his lies, because they are lies, must be multiplied to prop up one another. But truth is one ; and as there is nothing but truth, so there is nothing, and there can be nothing, but simplicity in Christ—simplicity, as opposed to subtilty, is the characteristic feature of Christ himself, and of all that is his.

The simplicity that is in Christ ! It is a precious and blessed quality, and it may be discerned all throughout his great salvation, in every stage and department of that salvation.

I. In his own finished work of righteousness and atonement.
II. In the free offer of the gospel founded thereupon.
III. In the fulness of believers as divinely one with himself.
IV. In their following of him as their captain and example ; and,
V. In their expectation of him as their judge and reward.
In all these five instances of his grace, on the one hand, and of your experience and hope as his people on the other, this

distinguishing element may be noted; and in contrast with the subtilty of the serpent, we may trace the simplicity that is in Christ.

I. There is simplicity in Christ, as the Lord our righteousness, as the servant of the Father, and the substitute, surety, and saviour of the guilty. It was in this character that he came into the world; and with entire simplicity did he sustain it. It was the single object for which he lived and died. Indeed, without an apprehension of this leading aim, the Lord's ministry on earth is unintelligible, self-contradictory, and, as we might almost say, marked not by simplicity, but by manifold subtilty. Every theory that has been or can be proposed of the suffering life and cruel death of Jesus, the Holy One of God, apart from the recognition of his vicarious character and standing, fails, and must fail, to satisfy a simple mind. The whole story is a confused, inconsistent, inextricable, incomprehensible enigma; a dark riddle as regards the government of God; a strange anomaly that shocks the moral sentiments of men. It is the doctrine, or rather the fact, of his substitution for you, which alone harmonises and hallows all. On any other supposition the evangelical records are as void of clear meaning as any complicated tale of romantic fiction. At the very best, they are vague anecdotes and reminiscences of a remarkable person, of whose conduct and fate no intelligible solution can be imagined. It is the atonement that gives significancy and unity to the whole. Let him be owned as the righteousness of God in your stead, and the propitiation for your sins, what simplicity is there in Christ! Behold the Lamb of God, that taketh away the sin of the world!

That there is no mystery here—nothing that transcends man's finite understanding, and baffles his restless curiosity—we are far from saying. The substitution of that Holy One in the room of the guilty must ever be a wonder on earth, in heaven, and in hell. But, oh! is there not a simplicity in it that comes home to the heart of a poor despairing sinner? He lies bitten by the deadly fiery serpent, stung with remorse for sin, racked and tortured with the fear of eternal woe. Behold the serpent lifted up in the wilderness! Behold the Son of man, made sin, made a curse, for such precisely he is, for the lost world of which he is a most miserable portion, for sinners, of whom he is chief; behold this Jesus, living, dying, lifted up upon the cross, taking the place, doing the work, bearing the doom, of the condemned victims of everlasting justice—what simplicity as well as worthiness in the Lamb that was slain! How clear, how definite and precise, how plain and unequivocal is this marvellous transaction, this real atonement for sin! "Deliver from going down to the pit: I have found a ransom." "Awake, O sword, against my shepherd, against the man that is my fellow." Let the prisoner go free; let the guilty criminal be acquitted, justified, accepted; for an infinitely worthy substitute has been provided to undertake all his responsibilities, to meet all his obligations, to answer every charge in law against him, every demand in justice upon him, to plead for him in the trial, to stand for him in the judgment.

Alas! that this simplicity that is in Christ should ever fail to satisfy. Nay, that it should so often—this very simplicity—be the very offence of the cross itself! But it is the policy of Satan to mar it, and by his subtilty to corrupt your minds from its simplicity, from the simplicity that is in Christ, and him crucified. Hence the endless questions he has contrived to raise in connection with it, respecting the secret counsels of the divine mind, the abstract principles of the divine government, and other the like great matters and things too high for us; as if it were our part to care for God, rather than for ourselves, in this transaction—to be more anxious about his interests and concerns than about our own—to view the cross, in short, rather in its possible bearing on the unknown arrangements of heaven, than in its actual application to the wants and woes that press so sorely on the sinner here on earth. For it is a great thing for the enemy to have this whole affair transferred from the region of reality to the region of speculation; and hence taking advantage, not unfrequently, of the ingenuity even of wise and holy men, he tempts them to embarrass the simple fact on which the gospel rests, with sundry more than doubtful disputations on the philosophy or rationale of it.

It is indeed a noble exercise of mind to aim at seeing how God in his glorious majesty, as well as we in our miserable need, may stand related to the events of Bethlehem, Gethsemane, and Calvary; nor is the inquiry an unprofitable or unlawful one. The doctrine of the Atonement is a most reasonable doctrine; and to the understanding, spiritually enlightened, it opens up the largest views of God's character and ways, while it inspires the lowliest sense of the exceeding sinfulness of our sin. But it is still not to the wise and prudent, but to babes that these things are revealed; and as the Lord's new-born babes desire the sincere milk of the word, so do they delight in the simplicity that is in Christ. Ah! it is first as a fact, as an actual substitution of himself in their room, that they as sinners come to know the Saviour's cross, and it is through their acquaintance with redemption, as a real and literal transaction of awful import between the righteous Father and his eternal Son on their behalf, that they come, by means of that transaction, to have a blessed and rapturous insight into the very mind and heart of the Godhead, to perceive that God is light, to feel that God is love.

For subtle intellects, however, the snare of Satan's subtilty is often too seductive. Tempted to look on this great sight from a divine, rather than a human point of view, approaching it, as it were, from the side of God's high throne, rather than from the abyss of fallen man's misery and guilt, they seem to consult for God rather than for themselves, to settle beforehand how God ought to act, rather than believe what he tells as to how he has acted. And so they frame a theory of atonement and redemption accommodated to their own ideas of what the general government of God must be. They speak vaguely of his public justice as the ruler of the universe, rather than of his private justice in his controversy individually with themselves. They profess to determine what the ends of his universal administration demand, rather than what every sin deserves. They find manifold good and plausible reasons of state, so to speak, on the part of God, for the atonement, instead of one sad reason of necessity on the part of the sinner. And thus it ends in their representing the plan of redemption with a sort of undefined, abstract, and impersonal generality of statement, as an expedient for meeting an exigency, or getting over a difficulty in the divine government, harmonising certain opposite claims and considerations, and enabling God to shew himself good as well as holy, gracious as well as just; and all this with a studied avoiding of anything like the precise idea of a strictly real and literal substitution of Christ personally in the stead of the sinner personally; as if, after all, the cross of Calvary were a kind of stroke of policy in heaven's cabinet and heaven's councils, a pageant, a spectacle, an exhibition merely, and not that dread reality which made all hell tremble and all heaven rejoice, as, in the very act of pouring out his soul an offering for sin, the Lord addressed himself to one of those whose place he was then occupying, whose guilt he was then expiating, whose release he was then purchasing—"To-day shalt thou be with me in Paradise."

O my friends, let not your minds be corrupted from the simplicity that is in Christ. Others may be careful and troubled about the many reasons that may be found in the principles of God's high government to explain and account for the atonement; but for you, one reason is all that is needed—one good reason—alas! too good—that you have sinned, that without shedding of blood there is no remission, that the blood of bulls and goats could never take away sin, that the blood of Christ his Son cleanseth from all sin. Yes! "He has made him to be sin for us, who knew no sin; that we might be made the righteousness of God in him" (2 Cor. v. 21).

II. As in his own finished work of righteousness and atonement, so in the free offer of the gospel as connected with it, we may see, and seeing, we may bless God for the simplicity that is in Christ. How simple, in every view of it, is the gospel message! How simple in its freeness! "Ho, every one that thirsteth, come ye to the waters, and he that hath no money: come ye, buy and eat; yea, come, buy wine and milk without money, and without price" (Isa. lv. 1). "The Spirit and the bride say, Come. And let him that heareth say, Come. And let him that is athirst come. And whosoever will, let him take the water of life freely" (Rev. xxii. 17). How near does it bring Christ! "It is not in heaven, that thou shouldest say, Who shall go up for us to heaven, and bring it unto us, that we may hear it, and do it? Neither is it beyond the sea, that thou shouldest say, Who shall go over the sea for us, and bring it unto us, that we may hear it, and do it? But the word is very nigh unto thee, in thy mouth, and in thy heart, that thou mayest do it" (Deut. xxx. 12–14). "The righteousness which is of faith speaketh on this wise, Say not in thine heart, Who shall ascend into heaven? (that is, to bring Christ down from above;) or, Who shall descend into the deep? (that is, to bring up Christ again from the dead.) But what saith it?

The word is nigh thee, even in thy mouth, and in thy heart: that is, the word of faith which we preach; that if thou shalt confess with thy mouth the Lord Jesus, and shalt believe in thine heart that God hath raised him from the dead, thou shalt be saved" (Rom. x. 6–9). How very plain as well as pathetic is the Lord's pleading with sinners! "As though God did beseech you by us: we pray you in Christ's stead, be ye reconciled to God" (2 Cor. v. 20). "Come now, and let us reason together, saith the Lord: Though your sins be as scarlet, they shall be as white as snow; though they be red like crimson, they shall be as wool" (Isa. i. 18). How explicit, how unequivocal, are his assurances! "Turn ye, turn ye, why will ye die? I have no pleasure in the death of him that dieth, saith the Lord God: wherefore turn yourselves, and live ye" (Ezek. xviii. 32). "As I live, saith the Lord, I have no pleasure in the death of the wicked; but that the wicked turn from his way and live: turn ye, turn ye from your evil ways; for why will ye die, O house of Israel?" (Ezek. xxxiii. 11). "Him that cometh unto me, I will in no wise cast out" (John vi. 37). How clear, how undeniably palpable and peremptory, as it might seem beyond its being possible for any sophistry to torture it, is the declaration of the Lord's will that all men should be saved and should come to the knowledge of the truth, and his command that all men everywhere should repent.

Yet, need I say to you, my friends, that it is here very especially that Satan puts forth all his subtilty to beguile! You are not ignorant, I am persuaded, of his devices. You know how many reasons for doubt and unbelief he can contrive to set up against God's one reason for believing. Here am I, a lost sinner. There is Christ, a living Saviour. I am commanded to believe; and if I believe not, I perish. But here is a test. Is there ever any one of all his reasons that is not founded on a perhaps? It was upon a perhaps that he persuaded his poor beguiled victims at first to risk their paradise, their souls, their all; ye shall not *surely* die! And it is by a perhaps still, or by many a perhaps, that he would beguile poor sinners, to keep them away from Christ. Thus, as to the Father: it may be that you are not elected; that your name may not be in the book of life; or, as to the Son: Christ died only for his sheep, and you may not be one of them. Or again as to the Holy Ghost: as you may not be an object of the electing love of the Father, and the saving work of the Son, so you may not be a subject of the converting grace of the Spirit. You may have committed the unpardonable sin; you may have persevered in sin so long as to be beyond the reach of renewal and repentance; you may have offended God beyond the hope of his being ever appeased; or crucified the Son of God afresh, and put yourself out of the range of his sacrifice; or quenched the Spirit beyond hope of any revival: your sin may be so heinous, your backsliding so inexcusable, your hardness of heart so great, that though all other sinners might find mercy, there may be none for you. Or, yet once more, as to the supposed conditions of your being saved: perhaps you are not convinced enough of your sin, or sorry enough for it; or perhaps you are not repenting aright, or not believing aright, or not seeking and praying aright; or you may not be willing enough, or you may not be able enough, or you may not have knowledge enough, or faith enough, or love enough, and so on; with *may-bes* and *perhapses* heaped on one another, Satan, playing into your own natural fears and feelings, would keep you hesitating and halting, balancing scruples and weighing doubts for ever.

But it is upon no may-be, upon no perhaps, that the blessed Lord invites you to commit your soul to him. He does not multiply uncertain reasonings and pleadings. He has but one word to you. And that word is true. He has confirmed it by an oath. " As I live, saith the Lord, I have no pleasure in the death of him that dieth." He has sworn by himself, " I, even I, am he." " Look unto me and be ye saved, all the ends of the earth." He has but one voice, the voice of tender entreaty, Turn ye, turn ye. He has but one argument, the argument of the cross, a full atonement made for guilt of deepest dye, an everlasting righteousness brought in, a sufficient satisfaction made to the righteous law, and a welcome, without upbraiding and without reserve, awaiting the very chief of sinners.

O my friends, let no subtilty of Satan ever beguile you, or corrupt your minds from the simplicity that is in Christ, in his gospel offer of a free, a full, a present salvation. And be not careful to answer Satan's manifold subtilty; be content to set over against it the simplicity that is in Christ. Ah! there is nothing Satan likes better than to draw you into argument and debate; he would fain entangle you in his web of sophistry, by getting you to take up and discuss his specious reasonings in detail.

Thou poor soul, scarce escaped out of his net, thou knowest these wiles of the devil. It was in many meshes he tried to involve thee; it was by many ties he tried to bind thee; and while thou wast painfully seeking to unravel each miserable thread, to unloose each small and cunning knot, how did he keep thee fluttering and vainly panting to be free.

And, oh, the first glimpse thou didst get of the simplicity that is in Christ! the first apprehension, the first taste, of the free, the simple, the unencumbered gospel of the grace of God! What a relief! What a release! The scales fell from thine eyes! Like Samson awaking, thou didst tear off from thy limbs ten thousand chains of Satan's lying sophistry as, with a sovereign pardon in thy hand, thou didst walk forth out of thy prison, erect now and bold, in the broad light of God's reconciled countenance. It was then that by a single word of power and peace—" Come unto me," " It is I," " Thy sins be forgiven thee "—thy Lord dissipated the entire host of thy spiritual enemies ; and the new glad song of liberty he put into your lips was, " Blessed be the Lord, who hath not given us as a prey to their teeth ! Our soul is escaped as a bird out of the snare of the fowlers ; the snare is broken, and we are escaped."

III. As there is the simplicity of actual reality in the great Atonement, and the simplicity of earnest sincerity in the gospel offer, so in respect also of the completeness of believers as one with Jesus, we may note the simplicity that is in Christ. Here we speak to you in the language of the apostle, as espoused to Christ ; presented to him as a chaste virgin to a loving husband ; and we would be jealous over you with a godly jealousy ; for duplicity now on your part towards him is nothing short of spiritual adultery, and is sadly inconsistent with the simplicity that is in Christ towards you. And what, the apostle adds (ver. 4), would you have ? Would you have one to come to you with another Jesus to preach to you, another Spirit for you to receive, another gospel for you to accept ? Are ye so soon weary of the homely fare of the Lord's kingdom that ye would look out for new and foreign dainties ? Are your minds corrupted from the simplicity of Christ ? Alas ! it is to be feared that the serpent who beguiled Eve through his subtilty has been busy with your minds too. He contrived to make her dissatisfied even with the simplicity of Paradise. Is he making you, in like manner, dissatisfied with the simplicity that is in Christ ?

Call to mind here, my friends, the circumstances of our first parents, and the subtilty of Satan in that first temptation that beguiled them. In the garden of Eden they had all things richly to enjoy. Of every tree of the garden they might freely eat. It was a simple grant of all the happiness of which their pure nature was susceptible that was made to them by their bountiful Creator. But the very simplicity of the grant was a stumbling-block to them. The single test of their loyalty, in itself simple enough too, became irksome. Satan had a more excellent way. He would improve upon the divine method of Eden's holy joys, and make their position yet more perfect and more free. "Ye shall be as gods, knowing good and evil." It was a subtle snare. You are treated now as children ; your innocence is the innocence of ignorance, and ignorance, too, is all your bliss. Be knowing ; and be as gods.

So the serpent beguiled Eve through his subtilty, causing her to be discontented with the simple profusion of Eden's blessings and the simple tenure on which she held them. And the like spirit of discontent he would fain cherish in you in regard to the simplicity that is in Christ. Of that simplicity you that are in Christ have some experience. It is the simplicity of a rich and royal liberality, alike in his gifts and in his manner of giving. How simple in every view of it is his treatment of you, my brethren that are his—you that are in him. "Ye are complete in him." "All things are yours." All that he has is yours. The perfection of his righteousness, the fulness of his grace and truth, the holiness of his divine nature, the riches of his divine glory, his blessed relation of sonship to the Father, the unction of the Holy Ghost wherewith he was anointed, the love with which the Father hath loved him, the reward with which the Father hath crowned him, all his possessions, in short, and all the pure elements of his own inmost satisfaction, his rest, his peace, his joy, all, all he shares with you, simply, bountifully, unreservedly ; and all upon the simple footing of your only being in him, and abiding in him.

What simplicity is this! And yet, my friends, you may be tempted to weary of it. Even Paradise itself began to grow tame and insipid. The even tenor of its peaceful and placid way, the noiseless unbroken current of its smooth waters of delight, was felt to be dull and slow; and its inmates became impatient for a change. They disliked the level uniformity of mere creature innocency, and the humility of prolonged dependence on their most beneficent Creator. They would take a shorter and more summary road to perfection, they would be as gods themselves, knowing good and evil. Is there never anything like this, my friends, in your spiritual experience? Are there never seasons when the whole ordinary routine of your wonted spiritual exercises seems weary, stale, flat, and unprofitable? Is it a time of heaviness with you, of falling away from your first love, of collapse after excitement, of dulness after ecstasy, and listless languor following upon some agitating or exhilarating crisis in your history? Who shall prescribe for such a spiritual malady? What can we say to you that will not fall as a thrice-told tale upon your ear? To tell you again merely of Christ, to rehearse the old story of his sufferings and death, to assure you over and over of the sufficiency of his atonement, the freeness of his gospel, the promise of his Spirit—to speak to you still of nothing but the efficacy of faith, and the power of prayer, and the consolation of the word, and the lowly duty of simple waiting on the Lord, that he may renew your soul—all this is but to charm ache with air and agony with words, to patch grief with proverbs. It is all true, you say, incontrovertibly true; you know it all, and you believe it all; and yet you feel wretched and dull and dead. Is there no more sovereign specific for ministering to a mind diseased? Is there no fresh expedient for reawakening the dormant feelings of the heart? Is there no royal road to a holier and happier state?

Alas! my friends, yours is the very frame of mind for Satan's subtlest policy to work on. To you he comes as an angel of light, proposing some specious novelties in doctrine, refinements upon the commonplace threadbare preaching of the cross; or suggesting new modes of worship or of fellowship, expedients for improving upon the ordinary means of growth in grace and progress in holiness. It is the frame of mind with which heresiarchs of all sorts, whether cold and calculating, or warm and enthusiastic, know well how to deal. Let church history, modern as well as ancient, testify! At such seasons, brethren, be ye especially on your guard! Seek not relief impatiently by devices of your own or of others who may plausibly profess to pity you. Wait on the Lord. Stand on the old paths. Let his word still be your stay; continue in prayer, and faint not. Wait, I say, on the Lord. "It is good that a man should both hope and quietly wait for the salvation of the Lord." "Weeping may endure for a night, but joy cometh in the morning." Abide still in Christ. Look to him as at the first. Deal with him as a poor, empty soul, with a rich, full, loving Saviour. Go not elsewhere, but only to Christ. All things around you change. All within you changes. But keep on trusting in him. Though he slay me, he is the same. "Who is among you that feareth the Lord, that obeyeth the voice of his servant, that walketh in darkness, and hath no light? Let him trust in the name of the Lord, and stay upon his God." Let him not kindle a fire of his own, or walk in the sparks men may kindle. Let him still wait on the Lord, who will cause light to arise.

IV. Great and manifest as is the simplicity that is in Christ your Lord, in his work of righteousness and atonement for you, in the free offer of his gospel to you, and in his uniting you to himself, and associating you with himself in all that is his, it is not less apparent in his guidance of you, as your captain and example. I will guide thee, says the Lord to the happy man whose iniquity is forgiven, whose sin is not imputed, and in whose spirit there is no guile—I will guide thee with mine eye (Psa. xxxii. 9)—a manner of guiding peculiarly and pre-eminently simple. It is opposed to the use of mere brute force, or the mere compulsion of threatening and terror, the bit, the bridle, the uplifted rod, the inflicted stroke, the mere scourge or rein of absolute authority, softened perhaps by coaxing, flattery, and cajoling falsehood. To be guided by the Lord with his eye, what docility does this imply in you, what simplicity in Christ!

Observe the conditions of such a guidance as this. In all guidance of beings endowed with reason, conscience, and free will, four things are ordinarily indispensable : a rule, a motive, an inward power, an upward or onward pattern. In the case of men naturally, of you in your unconverted state, and out of Christ, what are these ? (1.) The rule—the law of course; but it is the law which you feel, if strictly applied, must condemn you, and therefore presume that it must admit of relaxation. (2.) The motive—a mere sense of necessity, a feeling that you must do some homage. (3.) The power in you—your own frail resolution. (4.) The pattern before you—some one of the better sort among yourselves.

But mark the change when, as pardoned sinners, ransomed criminals, adopted children, you are guided by the Lord with his eye. (1.) As to the rule, it is the law still; but it is not the dead letter, but the living spirit of the law. It is not the law in its condemning form of a covenant of works, bringing you under the sentence of death, and putting you to all subtle shifts to evade it. But it is the law as magnified and made honourable by our righteous and suffering substitute, the law as satisfied, and therefore justifying, the law of the spirit of

life in Christ Jesus, the law of liberty, the law of love. Then
(2.) As to the motive, it is not the desperate desire of some
sort of partial and precarious accommodation yet to be effected,
but the sweet sense of full and perfect reconciliation already
freely and graciously secured. Again (3.) As to the inward
moving power, it is the indwelling and inworking of the spirit
of Christ. You are strengthened with might by the Spirit in
the inner man; Christ dwells in your heart by faith. And
(4.) As to the ideal, or model, or example, it is Christ himself.
It is a guidance (1) according to the free spirit, and not the
mere servile letter of the law; (2) through the motive, not of
a servile dread of still impending wrath, but of love to him
who has first loved us; (3) by the power of that Spirit abiding
in us, who worketh in us, both to will and to do of God's good
pleasure; and (4) in the very steps of him who hath left us an
example, and to whom we are to look as the author and finisher
of our faith, who, for the joy set before him, endured the cross,
despising the shame, and is set down at the right hand of the
throne of God.

Surely there is great simplicity in such guidance as this. It
is throughout the guidance, not of arbitrary force, but of reason
and good feeling; not of fear, but of love; not of the flesh,
but of the Spirit; not of a miserably inadequate model, but of
a perfect pattern; not of the letter, but of the spirit of the
law. The simplicity of it lies in its appealing to our highest
sense of honour, our most generous and disinterested feelings
of gratitude and honour. There is unity, and therefore
simplicity, in the reference throughout to the one Lord, for the
rule, the motive, the inspiring power, and the animating
pattern.

But the subtilty of Satan, how manifold is it, how complicated are his insidious wiles, in this department especially, of a
holy walk, or of right and faithful discharge of practical duty!

What a subtle science is casuistry, the science in a special sense of Satan, in which he is peculiarly at home. How ingeniously does he multiply his pleas in reference to all the several parts of evangelical holiness, the rule, the reason, the power, the pattern.

(1.) For the rule—oh, it cannot always be the strict unbending morality of the ten commandments! That standard it may be right and necessary generally to maintain, to guard against flagrant antinomian and licentious abuses. But all men except recluses know that allowances must be made in social life, and regard must be had to circumstances, and within certain limits there must be an accommodation of what God requires to what the world will bear.

Then (2) the motive of all you do ought doubtless to be not servile fear, but filial love, not the mere dread of being visited with punishment, but the desire to please; and it is plain that this motive has a very large and wide sweep, and might prompt many a generous and even chivalrous service and sacrifice in God's cause, from which the other motive might hold you excused. Still, practically, as things now are, it is a great matter if a Christian mixing with society keep clear of what is positively forbidden, and if nothing palpably wrong can be established against him.

And so also (3) as to the power, it is admitted vaguely and generally, that you have a promise of divine aid to help your infirmities and strengthen you for the Lord's work and warfare. But this, alas! does not hinder a large measure of the very same apologetic pleading of human frailty by which worldly men are wont to palliate their shortcomings and excesses.

And finally (4), when we look to the pattern, how aptly does Satan teach us to evade the obligation of a full following of Christ, by suggesting sundry qualifications and limitations— as that there are many things in which Christ, being divine, must be admitted to be inimitable—until at last we come to feel practically, either that the imitation of him is a mere fiction, or that we are to fix for ourselves wherein, and to what extent it is to be realised.

O be not corrupted from the simplicity that is in Christ, as guiding his people with his eye according to the spirit of his own holy law, through the sweet constraining influence of love to himself, by the power of his Spirit abiding in them as in him, and after the high example he has left them that they should follow his steps. Ah, it is a blessed simplicity! It is the eye of Christian love. It is the charm of Christian life. To me to live is Christ: Christ the rule, Christ the motive, Christ the power, Christ the pattern. To live under Christ, for Christ, by Christ, after Christ; to live, yet not I but Christ living in me, and I living the life I now live in the flesh by the faith of the Son of God, who loved me and gave himself for me.

V. The simplicity that is in Christ may be noted in connection with his second coming and glorious appearing. Here Satan has been expending not a little of his subtilty, throughout all ages of the Church's history, sometimes hiding this great doctrine, or contriving to have it kept in abeyance, and at other times complicating and embarrassing it, mixing up with it a variety of questions scarcely, if at all, bearing on its real, vital, and practical import.

For, in truth, as to all that is essential and influential, it would seem to be simple enough. The Lord cometh as our Judge. He cometh as our exceeding great reward. We are to appear before his judgment-seat; we are to be with him where he is, to see and share his glory. And if we add that his coming for these high ends is to be apprehended by us as both sudden and near at hand, we seem to have the main substance of the believer's very simple, but very glorious and very awful hope.

Thus regarded, it is practically a most influential hope; influential for its very simplicity. It sets you upon working, watching, waiting for the Lord. You work for him as servants, not wicked and slothful, but diligent, as those who must give account to him. You watch for him with loins girt and lamp burning—not sleeping as do others, but watching and being sober, as children of the light and of the day, putting off sleep and drunkenness and all works of the night—putting on the whole armour of light, looking up, looking out, as not knowing at what hour the Master may come. You wait for him. You wait, with what ardent longing! I wait for the Lord. Yea, more than they that watch for the morning. When shall the day dawn and the shadows flee away? Oh, when shall I welcome my returning Saviour! You wait for him with increasing ardour, as your growing likeness to him makes his fellowship more congenial; and sorrows and separations set you more and more upon the anticipation of future reunion in him. You wait however still, how patiently! reconciled to every hard duty and every irksome trial by the promise of the Comforter now, and the sure hope of glory at the last. Now, to be thus working, watching, waiting for the Lord, how simple and how blessed an attitude! And thus to use for comfort and edification the great doctrine of his coming again, is surely to act according to the simplicity that is in Christ.

Other inquiries there may be, of interest in their place, respecting the times and seasons and events connected with the close of this world's dark history and the ushering in of a better day. But let not such detailed and complicated investigations, which surely after all are to the believer personally of subordinate importance, as well as of uncertain issue, be so blended with the one grand outline of Jesus coming again to receive his people to himself, as to mar the impression of its sublime and majestic unity and simplicity.

This was a warning needed in the early church, as the apostle himself testifies, when some used the doctrine to deceive and perplex; and he found it necessary, that he might prevent plain believers from being shaken in mind and troubled, to give an express and authoritative contradiction to some of the rumours that had been raised and circulated. And no intelligent observer, either of the past or of the present, will deny the necessity of a similar caution now.

I ask you to distinguish here again, and here especially, between the complex and the simple; and I remind you that what really is to produce the right moral and spiritual effect upon your souls is not the crowded canvas and complicated scenery of a picture embracing all the particulars of a world's catastrophe; no, not that, not that at all, but the one dread and holy image of Jesus, as he was taken up to heaven on Mount Olivet, so coming again, even as he was seen to go! Be that coming when it may, it is still, as the pole-star of the Church's hope, and the spur of her zeal, simple, solemn, in its very standing alone, insolated, solitary, separate and apart from all accessories of preceding and accompanying revolutions.

Yes! it is not earthquakes, or tempests, or deluges of fire; it is not falling empires, mighty wars and tumults, convulsions of all sorts over all the earth; it is not Babylon doomed nor Israel restored, nor all the vast upheaving of the social fabric that must attend such vicissitudes, though it well concerns the slumbering nations to give heed to these things, and watchmen in Zion must never cease to ring in the ears of a scoffing world the knell of its approaching dissolution; still, I say, it is not these, not these altogether, nor any of them, that I have before my eye, filling my whole soul and heart and mind when I turn weeping from the grave of buried friendship, or rise startled from the couch of despondency and sloth; no, but Jesus my Lord, himself alone, the centre of ineffable brightness and beauty. Angels and the redeemed are around him, but it is himself alone that fixes my regard; and I, poor miserable I, a sinner saved by his grace, a servant working for his hire, a watcher waiting for his coming, I rise, I rush forth, I run to meet—nay, I am caught up to meet—my Lord in the air. So shall I be ever with the Lord.

1. To *careless sinners* we have a word to say. The subtilty of Satan is very apt to beguile and corrupt; but we have to remind you that there is a simplicity in Satan that is more insidious and disastrous still. There are those whom Satan leads captive at pleasure, and on whom it is really not worth his while to waste or expend his subtilty at all. When the strong man armed keepeth his palace, his goods are in peace: he has no occasion for the use either of his arts or of his arms. It is when a stronger than he cometh upon him to overcome him that he needs to have recourse to the violence of threats, or the artifice of alluring wiles. It is for his victims that have escaped, or that are escaping from his grasp, that he reserves the practice of his stratagems; it is they who, alas! from personal experience, are not ignorant of his devices. With you, who are going on contentedly in the broad road, he uses no refinement: to you his lies are simple enough; nay, he scarcely needs more than one; his old lie with which he began, "ye shall not surely die." Ah, it may well be that all our discussions of nice and intricate points of conscience are unintelligible to you! You have little sympathy with the strange varieties of frame and feeling that attend a spiritual awakening, and you cannot comprehend the turns and windings of a poor soul,

hunted as the wounded hart in the desert, and panting for the water brooks. How it should be so very difficult to assuage the anguish of a guilty conscience, or to pacify the fears of a broken heart, or to get a sinner to believe in the forgiveness of sins, or to make him continue to rely on the mercy of heaven, you cannot understand at all; it seems all to you so simple, easy, natural; so much almost a matter of course, that you should be let alone now and let off somehow at the last. But I beseech you rather to look to the simplicity that is in Christ than to lean on the simplicity that is in Satan. The simplicity that is in Satan! Truly simple enough are they that believe his fond and simple lie! But hear another voice, simple enough too: "How long, ye simple ones, will ye love simplicity; and fools hate knowledge? Turn ye at my reproof. Behold, I will pour out my Spirit unto you, I will make known my words unto you." And hear another voice, yet the same, simple enough too, and awful!—awful for its simplicity: "Because I have called and ye refused, I have stretched forth my hand and no man regarded; but ye have set at nought my counsel and would none of my reproof; I also will laugh at your calamity; I will mock when your fear cometh." "Then shall they call upon me, but I will not answer; they shall seek me early, but they shall not find me!" "Seek ye the Lord while he may be found! Call ye upon him while he is near!"

2. To *anxious souls* I would say, Let not the subtilty of Satan distress you beyond measure. And above all, let it not surprise you. Count it not strange that you fall into divers temptations. When you are thus tempted, do not yield to the crowning temptation of imagining that your case is strange and your experience singular. This is a great snare. It ministers to a certain feeling of half-unconscious self-complacency, as you brood over difficulties and doubts and embarrassments; fancying that never was there soul-exercise, never soul-distress like

yours. Be sure that there hath no temptation befallen you but such as common to men. And remember your way of escape is not the way of combating in argument the subtilty of Satan; but the common, far safer and simpler way of simply acquiescing anew, and ever anew, in the simplicity of Christ. For you are no match in special pleading for the Master of that science. The question of your peace with God, and your comfortable walk with him, is one that never will be solved or settled beforehand by any processes of subtle reasoning. You must solve and settle it experimentally. Taste and see that the Lord is good. Venture your soul upon the simplicity that is in Christ, his simple faithfulness, the simplicity of his promise, "Him that cometh unto me I will in no wise cast out." Let Satan perplex the question as he may. Let him conjure up doubtful disputations by the score, by the hundred. Let him summon a very legion of dark surmises to disconcert you! Be you simple. Be you decided. Linger not. Hesitate not. Do to God—Father, Son, and Holy Ghost—the justice you would be ashamed to deny to an earthly friend. Simply believe that the Father means what he says when he beseeches you to be reconciled to him in his Son; that the Son means what he says when he cries, "Come unto me, ye weary;" that the Holy Ghost means what he says when, together with the Bride, he says, "Come, take of the water of life freely!"

3. To you who *believe* I would say, Let there be simplicity in you corresponding to the simplicity that is in Christ. In all simplicity, accept Christ as your substitute. In all simplicity, comply with his call to come to Him, and through him, to the Father. In all simplicity, abide in Him and be satisfied with his fulness. In all simplicity, yield yourselves to His gracious and loving guidance. In all simplicity, be ever looking out for his glorious coming. All on His part—in his treatment of you, in his offering himself for you, in his giving himself to

you, in his keeping you and making you complete in himself, in his guiding you with his eye ; in his coming again to receive you to himself, that where he is you may be also; all is simple, free, generous, unreserved ! There is no keeping back of anything, He opens his heart, his hand, to you. Let all on your part, in your treatment of Him, be simple too. Be upon honour with him. Be guileless, frank, cordial in your reliance with him ; your submission to him, your working and waiting for him. So will you taste the blessedness of fully realising the simplicity that is in Christ. Yours will be the enlargement of heart that, springing out of a simple faith in Christ, takes in all the fulness of his glorious gospel. Yours will be the alacrity, and cheerfulness, and joy of running with heart enlarged in the way of the divine commandments, and walking freely as well as humbly with your God. Your path will be as the shining light, shining more and more unto the perfect day. All embarrassment, all constraint, all reserve, being at an end, your fellowship in the Spirit is with the Father, and with his Son Jesus Christ our Lord.

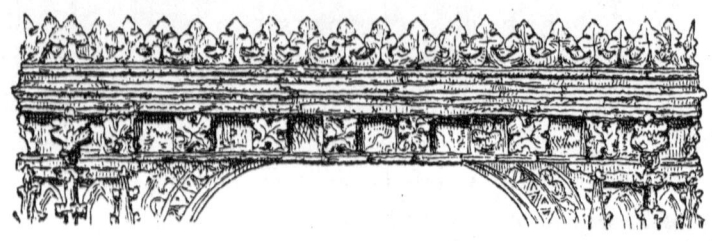

XXI.

Salvation by Water and Blood.

BY THE REV. PATRICK FAIRBAIRN, D.D.

"This is he that came by water and blood, even Jesus Christ; not by water only, but by water and blood. And it is the Spirit that beareth witness, because the Spirit is truth."—1 John v. 6.

IT is of importance to note the connection in which this remarkable statement is introduced by the apostle, and the more immediate purpose for which it was made. The special subject of discourse in the preceding context is the victory, which it was necessary for the cause of Christ, and for the well-being of their own souls, that Christians should gain over the world—that is, over the world in its present fallen and corrupt state, as the enemy and rival of God, the theatre of human pride and folly, the home of those fleshly lusts which war against the soul. As such the world must be overcome by the true followers of Christ; they must shew themselves to be animated by a spirit which resists and rises above the evil; and this spirit the apostle had just said is faith: "This is the victory that overcometh the world, our faith."

But faith in whom, or in what? This the apostle more exactly defines in the question, "Who is he that overcometh the world, but he that believeth (or hath faith) that Jesus is the Son of God?" It is, therefore, faith in the Christian sense with which the apostle connects the power that overcomes—faith in Jesus Christ as the Son of God. But even that he seemed to feel was not quite specific enough; for some might be ready to own as much about Christ, who yet desired concerning his mission and work that which alone could give life and energy to faith for spiritual and holy results. Therefore, to prevent misunderstanding or mistake, to distinguish in this respect between the true and the false, he further mentions what the really victorious faith in Christ must embrace respecting him: "This is he, who came by water and blood, Jesus Christ; not by water only, but by water and blood: and it is the Spirit that beareth witness, because the Spirit is truth."

Such is the explanation which the apostle gives of the faith that overcomes the world. But the explanation is so peculiar that some will perhaps feel as if it again required to be explained, for the language bears much of a symbolical form. "Came by water and blood!" does this not refer to what John elsewhere tells us he saw issuing from the side of our Lord, when pierced by the soldier's spear on the cross? It may do so; but then that water and blood themselves undoubtedly had, to the apostle's view, a hidden meaning; he looked beneath the surface and saw in them, not merely component elements of Christ's bodily frame, but expressive symbols of the nature and design of his mission. Let us then inquire, *first*, what is meant here by his having come by water; *second*, what further by his having come by blood; and *third*, how in respect to these the Spirit, as truth, can be said to bear witness.

I. What is to be understood by Christ having *come by water*. You may have noticed in the writings of St John, that the expression often occurs respecting Christ, of his *having come* in some particular way. Thus, near the beginning of his gospel, he says of Christ, that he "came into the world," and again, that "he came to his own," though they did not receive him; plainly implying that he existed elsewhere before he came—existed, namely, as the Eternal Word, or as the Only-begotten in the bosom of the Father; and thence "came down from heaven," as it is again said, "to give life to the world." Then, as to the precise manner in which he came or appeared among men, John in this and his second epistle lays special stress on his *having come in the flesh;* that is, having really assumed our nature, in its fleshly as well as its spiritual part, becoming indeed bone of our bone, flesh of our flesh; and not, as some began to speak in the latter days of the apostle, took these merely in appearance, or in some other manner than they are with us. To profess to believe in Christ, and yet not to confess that he had come in the flesh, the apostle declares, was to do the part of the Antichrist, in reality opposing, while in some sense acknowledging, the claims of Christ.

These things have respect to Christ's person; but they may help you to understand more distinctly the language of our text, which has respect to his mission and work. *He came by water*, or through water, as emblematic of his purpose in coming. When men were much used to symbolical rites in religion, water was ever taken as the symbol of purification. They washed their bodies or their garments in water when they had come into contact with defilement, in token of their dislike of it, and their desire to be rid of it. With reference, partly at least, to this religious usage, our Lord, you will remember, washed his disciples' feet, to impress them more deeply with a sense of the moral purity which they were called through his grace to maintain, as he himself explained at the close of the ceremony, when he said to them, "Now ye are clean." On the same account, and for the purpose of inculcating the same great lessons, the forerunner of Christ fulfilled his calling, not only by preaching the doctrine, but also by administering the baptism of repentance. It was the most impressive way of proclaiming, as things then stood, the necessity of a true spiritual renovation, in order to be prepared for the Messiah and his kingdom. Men must set about the cleansing of themselves by breaking off their sins, and applying in earnest to the work of righteousness. Thus, John might be said to come by water; but in a much higher and fuller sense Christ, to whom John merely pointed the way. For, what was the grand aim with which Christ came into the world? Was it not to bring a *clean* thing out of an *unclean;* to "purify unto himself a peculiar people"; or, as it is again more fully expressed, "to sanctify and cleanse them with the washing of water by the word, that he might present them to himself a glorious church, not having spot or wrinkle, or any such thing, but holy and without blemish"?

No one surely in the least acquainted with the simple records of gospel history can doubt that such *was* the object which lay nearest to the heart of Christ. Look to his manner of life, the surest witness of his thoughts and purposes, what a strength of moral earnestness shines in it! What a pure and heavenly elevation! He appeared indeed in the *likeness* of sinful flesh, but without the least taint of sin, or anything that bore on it the impress of human selfishness and corruption. He came to fulfil all righteousness, and he *did* fulfil it in spite of the contradiction of sinners which he had to endure, and the wiles of Satan which were plied against him to the uttermost. Amid all He never swerved from the integrity of his way; the sinew of *his* thigh never shrank; from first to last the law of his God was in his heart, and in a course of unwearied beneficence love did its perfect work. So that, not only could Satan find nothing of his own in him, but the Father, who knew him with the most intimate and perfect knowledge, proclaimed him to be the "Beloved Son, in whom he was well-pleased."

With the holy tenor of such a life the *character of our Lord's teaching* was in full accord. Its pure and sublime morality has been acknowledged even by many who have not otherwise believed on his name, and has made itself felt wherever his gospel has been preached. There is nothing in the past history of mankind to be compared with it. Its essential elements, indeed, are to be found in the earlier revelations of God; and occasionally even in heathen writings sentiments and precepts occur which are not unworthy of being mentioned along with some of Christ's. But, as a whole, his teaching stands altogether alone; none, *like it,* speaks to men's hearts and bosoms—so divine in its matter, yet in its manner and form so entirely human, so lofty in its views of truth and duty, yet so tender in its sympathies toward the erring and the fallen; so ready to encourage even the faintest efforts on the side of well-doing, and to acknowledge the smallest services performed for the glory of God and the good of men, going down even to the giving of a cup of cold water to the thirsty, yet calling men to such noble aspirations and firm resolves as shall dispose them, when the higher interests of the world require it, to scorn all earthly delights, and not count their very lives dear to them.

Could we picture to ourselves a state of things in which this teaching and example of Christ had reached their aim, or produced everywhere their proper effect, what a change should we witness! Not only would the greater crimes and the more violent outbursts of passion cease to be known, but also the more secret workings of ambition, avarice, and guile. Men would learn war no more; no more practise oppression and fraud; they would look with the feeling of a common brotherhood on those around them, and would do to others only what they would that others should do to them; they would be merciful and forgiving, not sullen and revengeful; and feeling habitually near to the All-seeing and Holy One, and anticipating the full disclosures and just awards of the great day, they would put away from them all hypocrisy and deceit, would think in their hearts according as they act in their lives, and would seek to have their lives even more and more replenished with the fruits of righteousness, the things which are at once pleasing in the sight of God, and profitable to man.

Were such a state of things in any measure realised, would it not seem as if the world had undergone a blessed process of cleansing, as if some mighty one had come by water to purge away its impurities? But it is nothing less that our gracious Redeemer aimed at in his divine mission; in so far as it is not realised, his aim still lies unaccomplished. And it is, let us remember, what he calls every one of his disciples to be and to do, what is in itself necessary to the perfecting of his work of grace in them, and to the true redemption of their natures. For so long as impurity remains, the disease of our souls is not cured. Corruption is the enemy of solid peace and blessing: it is the very root of hell. The pure in heart alone shall see God; they alone can drink from the river of his pleasures; and it is not possible for him, who seeks to turn again the tide of our misery, and raise us to the enjoyment of perpetual life and blessing, to do it otherwise than by delivering us from the dominion of sin, and creating in us the will and the power to do the deeds of our Father in heaven.

II. But this is still only one branch of Christ's work. There is another, and that even of primary importance. While the apostle tells us Christ came by water, he very expressly says, not by water only, *but by blood;* in other words, he came not as the Teacher merely, or the Reformer, or the Spiritual Guide and Pattern of humanity, but its High-Priest to atone for our guilt, and by his own obedience unto death for us to effect our reconciliation with God. For there can be no doubt that this is what is meant by *blood* here, and in other passages, as when it is said, "The blood of Jesus Christ cleanseth us from all sin." It is the language of sacrifice, in which the blood of the victim was given to make atonement for sin, because the life was in the blood, and so the blood came to be but another name for the death of the sacrifice. It signified life for life—a life free from the charge of guilt for one laden with guilt, and as such liable to death. To speak of Christ therefore as having come by blood is all one with saying, that he gave his life a ransom or propitiation for our sins; and this the apostle intimates he did, not as a mere accessory, but as a thing of vital moment, without which what he otherwise did would have been in vain.

It was not without reason that the apostle laid stress on this point, presenting it as an essential part of the faith which overcomes the world. For a tendency was then beginning to discover itself in certain minds, more imbued with the philosophy of the world than with the spirit of the gospel, which delighted to extol Christ's teaching and life, but could not brook the thought of his death as an expiation for human guilt. They would ascribe salvation to him only in so far as he brought the knowledge of God, and put men on the cultivation of virtue and self-discipline, and the higher attainments of a spiritual life. And have we not in our day indications enough of much the same way of thinking about Christ? Have we not views set forth of his character and mission which seem to make account of almost everything in his history on earth, save only this one thing—his death as the substitute of his people, that he might rescue them from the guilt and condemnation of sin?

But a Christ without this is not the Christ of Scripture. It wants that which most of all is needed to pacify the sinner's conscience, and render it possible for a righteous God to bestow life and blessing on those who have lifted up their hearts against him. Hence, whatever value is attached in Scripture to the matchless glory of Christ's life, and the singular excellence of his teaching, it is always with his death that the great good is associated—in *that* the grand foundation was laid. So Christ himself testified when he said that "He came to give his flesh for the life of the world"—or, that he *must* die in order that repentance and remission of sins might be preached in his name. And when He would set up an ordinance in his church for the express purpose of keeping him in perpetual remembrance among his people, in what light does he there present himself? Simply as the suffering and dying Saviour, giving his body to be broken and his blood to be shed for the remission of their sins. This is the image of him which, above all, he wishes to have embalmed in their heart and conscience; not Jesus Christ merely as the Son of God, but Jesus Christ as the atoning Redeemer. He will be remembered thus, or not remembered at all.

But does this aspect of Christ's work tend at all to supplant or disparage the other? When we hold the prime importance, the necessity of his coming by blood, and proclaim the virtue of his atoning death as the one refuge and hope of sinners, do we the less own and appreciate him as having come by water —the regenerator and purifier of humanity? No; not in the least. The two, indeed, hang inseparably together, and without the one the other cannot be accomplished. Sanctification through the Word and Spirit of Christ rests upon justification through faith in the blood of Christ. If we are to succeed in the great conflict with evil in our own soul and the world around us, we must stand on the firm ground of a crucified

Redeemer, like those of whom it is written, "They overcame by the blood of the Lamb;" or those again who, having passed triumphantly through the struggle, appear in the mansions above all perfect and complete. Why? Because they had "washed their robes and made them white in the blood of the Lamb."

This is the truth of Christ's gospel, not for one age merely, or for one section of mankind, but for all ages and all conditions of men who hold the truth in uncorruptness. A personal interest in the death of Christ carries everything of vital moment along with it. It secures first, indeed, our deliverance from the guilt of sin; but from that as a starting-point carries us forward in the love and practice of righteousness. *Doctrinally*, we must divide between the two results, in order to get a more clear and living apprehension of them in our minds; but *experimentally* they run into each other, and, like twin sisters, go hand in hand. Christ cannot be divided. If I have an interest in his atoning blood for the pardon of my sin, I have it also for fellowship with his pure and blessed life. If I can say, "It is God that justifieth, who is he that condemneth?" I can also say, "It is God that hath raised me in Christ to newness of life, who is he that can bring me again into the bondage of sin and death?" I have been accepted in the Beloved; the feelings of a child of God work in my bosom; Christ himself the Holy One of God lives in me by his Spirit; and so, the life which I now live in the flesh is not *after* the flesh, but by the faith of him who loved me, and gave himself for me.

Such it is to know Christ as having come by blood; it is to know him at once for righteousness and life, for peace and for purity. Oh, let us see that we do indeed know him thus!

III. Having thus seen what is meant by Christ having come by water, and not by water only, but by water and blood, let us look for a little to the third point presented here for our consideration, that which concerns the testifying of the Spirit; "*And it is the Spirit that beareth witness, because the Spirit is truth.*"

The work of the Spirit is here presented under the somewhat peculiar form of a witness-bearing; but this only because the work is viewed in connection with a *true* representation of the character and mission of Christ as opposed to a *false* or *imperfect* one. In itself, however, it is the same thing that is more commonly meant by the effectual application of the things of Christ's redemption, so as to give them a place in the experience and lives of men. For the great ends of Christ's mission this is just as much needed as the personal appearance of the Son in our nature, and his obedience unto death for us. Hence, before Christ's departure, very special prominence was given to the promise of the Spirit. It was emphatically *the* promise of the Father to the disciples; and was to be verified by the Spirit coming and resting upon them as a sacred unction, diffusing itself through their souls with quickening life and energy—awakening convictions of sin, righteousness, and judgment—taking of Christ's things and shewing these to their souls; as if till then they could only know *about* them, but then should come to know the *things themselves* in their real character and importance. And when, with reference to this work, the apostle says "the Spirit is truth," he means to tell us that the Spirit identifies himself with the truth as his material or instrument of working, he can make use of nothing but the truth; so that the views of Christ, which are rendered mainly instrumental by him in the conversion of souls and their growth in holiness, are thereby commended to us, not only as true, but as the more vital portions of the truth as it is in Jesus.

Now, the question is, what *are* the views of Christ which

the Spirit most peculiarly employs for this purpose? Nothing of course which really forms a part of God's revelation in Christ can be said to be either in itself unimportant, or excluded from the matter of the Spirit's testimony in the souls of men; for as the design of a preached gospel is to declare the *whole* counsel of God regarding the person and work of his Son, so there is no part of that counsel which may not, in one respect or another, be made to minister to the enlightenment, the strength, or the consolation of believers. But still there are differences; and there is especially a difference between the two great aspects of the work of Christ presented here under the water and the blood—that is, between Christ's work as the Reformer, calling men to repentance and righteousness, and his work as the Propitiation for their sins.

You see this difference clearly coming out in the records of gospel history. Look *there* at the practical result of all that Christ did and taught up to the period that he poured out his soul an offering for sin. The things were in themselves great and wonderful which filled up the history of his eventful life. He spake as never man spake, laying open the secrets of men's bosoms, and the purposes of divine mercy and lovingkindness as these had never been disclosed before, even by inspired lips. And the spiritual glory which shone forth in the whole of his earthly ministry was the glory of the Onlybegotten of the Father, full of grace and truth. Yet how little practically was accomplished by it! "Who hath believed our report?"—might he not have said at the close of it—"and to whom is the arm of the Lord revealed?" Even his immediate disciples but imperfectly understood his words, nor did they apprehend the proper design and import of his mission; while the great mass, among whom he had uttered his memorable sayings and done his mighty works, had only here and there caught some rays of gospel truth, and been impressed as with the vision of something great, mysterious, and wonderful. As yet it could not be said that any salvation had been wrought in Israel.

But turn to the death of Christ, and presently you see the commencement of a new era in the eventful history; you see what proved to be at once the climax of Christ's undertaking, and the spring whence life flows to a perishing world. And if it is asked, Why precisely this? No other answer can be given than that it was in his death he did the great thing that was needed for the world, since thereby he closed the gulf which our sin had made between us and God, and so unsealed in our behalf the treasures of divine grace and blessing—opened a channel by which the Spirit might freely descend and operate in the souls of men to their present and eternal good. So that, as Christ himself said, it is by his being lifted up on the cross that men are properly drawn to him; in other words, it is with the exhibition of Him as a crucified Redeemer that the Spirit's work of regeneration unto life and blessing most especially proceeds.

It was so at the first; and the beginning was here, as in other things, prophetic of the end. While the Spirit quickens through the truth, and testifies of all that pertains to it in men's hearts and consciences, it still is, and ever has been, pre-eminently the truth of a suffering and dying Saviour, in connection with which the power has gone forth. The triumphs of Christianity, in every age—I mean its real triumphs, its spiritual conquests over the corruption, the selfishness, and miseries of mankind—are all interwoven with that cross, on which as the Lamb of God he took away the sins of the world. The ministers of grace and mercy who have brought peace to men—the missionaries who have been honoured to turn foul and savage barbarians into peaceful and virtuous members of society—the martyrs who have nobly braved the persecutors' rage, and hazarded wealth, honour, comfort, life itself for the cause of God; or, in the quieter places of the field, the well-experienced and ripened believer, who has risen to the higher attainments of the divine life, and is approaching the condition of saints made perfect—all of them, if asked whence more especially they draw the inspiration that animates their hearts, and the power that has enabled them to overcome, will point with one accord to the Saviour on the Cross. It is the love, the unparalleled love, which shines forth there that constrains them, and the victory there once for all gained over the powers of evil, which supplies them with strength and courage for the conflict. But for their living and realising faith in a crucified Redeemer, they would have been weak and impotent as other men.

In conclusion, there arise out of this subject three important practical thoughts, which I would briefly press upon your consideration.

First, as regards the work of the Spirit, remember it is *the truth* with which he ever deals in carrying forward the work of our salvation—the truth of the gospel of Christ Jesus. Nothing is of avail, excepting in so far as it is a portion of this truth: Christ in his person and work is the truth, and it is the office of the Spirit to take this and apply it savingly to the souls of men. Therefore the grand lesson here is, to learn of Christ. Seek to have his word dwelling in you richly. And be jealous of everything in human refinement or speculation which would corrupt its simplicity, or come between you and it.

Remember, secondly, that there is a *central truth* in the gospel, which it is of unspeakable moment to have kept in its proper place—the truth, namely, of a suffering and crucified Redeemer. Without this we might have a revelation of God which would tell us much concerning his being and attributes and works; but we could have no gospel, in the proper sense, for sinners. Cling therefore to the doctrine of the cross as for your life; hold fast by it as the ground of your confidence, the source of peace and hope, and seek not merely to know it as a fact or doctrine, but to drink into its spirit, for thus only can it become life and power in your experience, and you shall be able to go thoroughly along with the apostle, when he says, "God forbid that I should glory, save in the cross of our Lord Jesus Christ, by whom the world is crucified unto me, and I unto the world."

Lastly, remember that in the truth, as revealed in the gospel and applied by the Spirit, there is a high practical aim, which must shew itself in your experience and life, as in the character and mission of Christ. This must still be the grand test, for the doctrine of Christ is pre-eminently a doctrine according to godliness. Is Christ as known and believed in by you a sanctifying power? Does it tend to make you Godlike in spirit and behaviour? Does it turn the blood which you trust in for pardon into a source of cleansing efficacy and faithful striving against whatever is corrupt and sinful? Search and see, for only when Christ is known thus, is he known as the wisdom of God and the power of God unto salvation.

XXII

Sin, Death, and Victory over them.

BY THE REV. ROBERT BUCHANAN, D.D.

"So when this corruptible shall have put on incorruption, and this mortal shall have put on immortality, then shall be brought to pass the saying that is written, Death is swallowed up in victory.—1 Cor. xv. 54."

THIS is the peroration of Paul's inspired and truly magnificent discourse on the resurrection of the dead. Beginning in that discourse with the great fundamental fact that "Christ *is* risen as he said," and having rapidly but clearly specified the leading proofs by which that fact had been conclusively established, he went on to shew how it involved and secured the resurrection to eternal life and glory of all those for whom Jesus died. Turning next to the unspeakable importance of this vital doctrine, he referred to his own career of self crucifying test and trial as a thing that would have been alike inexplicable and impossible but for the truth of that doctrine, and for its soul-sustaining power. Advancing from that point to the difficulties which ignorance and scepticism had been conjuring up against the doctrine of the resurrection, he assailed and overthrew them with arguments of equal force and beauty, derived from the phenomena of nature on the one hand, and from the whole analogy of things upon the other.

Having thus exposed the utter futility of all such objections, he goes on from the possible to the actual, and in terms the most explicit and emphatic describes the change which the human body is to undergo at the appearing and kingdom of Jesus Christ. And now it only remained that he should proclaim and celebrate the triumph which he had thus shewn to be in store for the people of God. This he accordingly does in the singularly striking and impressive language of the words before us, in which he brings the whole subject to a close.

In taking up such a text as this, it is impossible not to be affected with a painful sense of utter inadequacy to do it justice. There is in it a height and grandeur which it seems almost presumptuous even to approach. The thoughts and feelings which it awakens in the mind one has a painful consciousness of being utterly unable to embody in words. To many, at least, the very attempt to do so may seem only to enfeeble and degrade the apostle's theme. The human commentary may serve only to render tame and mean what his inspired language with so much majesty sets forth. To reconcile one, however, to the hazard of producing this disappointing result, there is this to be remembered, that in dealing with that language the preacher's business is not to make out of it a splendid picture such as may dazzle the eye and captivate the mind, but with simplicity and fidelity to present those views of the truth contained in it which, under the divine blessing, may be fitted to instruct and edify the soul.

In the immediately preceding context Paul had described the mighty and mysterious change that shall be effected on every member of the human family at the second coming of the Lord. In a moment, in the twinkling of an eye, that change shall be wrought, alike upon the living and upon the dead. Those who shall constitute the then existing generation of men shall have their natural bodies transformed into spiritual bodies; and in the same instant, and by the same Almighty power, the bodies of the many previous generations of men who had gone down to the dust shall be quickened with the breath of immortality. The long reign of death shall then be for ever at an end. That great destroyer shall be himself destroyed. And *then* "shall be brought to pass the saying that is written, Death is swallowed up in victory." The saying thus quoted occurs in the eighth verse of the twenty-fifth chapter of Isaiah, and forms part of a prophecy concerning the sufferings of Christ, and the glory that should follow. Beginning in that prophecy with a pointed allusion to the destruction of Jerusalem, and to the contemporaneous diffusion from that centre of the gospel of salvation, Isaiah briefly but beautifully sets forth the breaking up of that moral and spiritual darkness which had so long brooded over the nations of the earth, and their ultimate and universal conversion to Christ. It is when this blessed consummation has been reached that the event spoken of in our text is represented by the prophet as taking place. It is at this precise point the words come in, "He will swallow up death in victory." And to shew that this prophetic announcement had reference to that great and notable day of the Lord, to which Paul in our text applies it, it is immediately, in Isaiah's prophecy, followed up with these explicit words, "And the Lord God shall wipe away tears from off all faces"; while at the same time the redeemed, in thus meeting with their blessed Lord, are described by Isaiah as hailing his approach with this joyful tribute of gratitude and praise, "Lo, this is our God; we have waited for him, and he will save us: this is the Lord; we have waited for him, we will be glad and rejoice in his salvation." It is this sudden and marvellous transition from the dust and ashes of the tomb to incorruption and immortality that shall at once explain and accomplish what Isaiah foretold about death being swallowed up in victory.

The expression conveys the idea, not only of death ceasing, and ceasing for ever, of its utterly disappearing, and being, so to speak, annihilated, but it conveys the further idea of this taking place in circumstances that will cause death's dark and repulsive reign to be altogether forgotten by the people of God— forgotten amid the glory and felicity of that state of things by which, in their case, the reign of death shall be succeeded. As the woman that was in travail remembers no more the anguish for joy that a man-child is born into the world; as the dangers and terrors of a tempestuous voyage are lost sight of when the ship's anchor is dropped in the desired haven; or as the hazards and horrors of war are drowned in the swelling tide of public exultation which is raised by some decisive and crowning victory, even so the tears and the sorrows and the dark anxieties inseparable from the dominion of death will serve in the retrospect only as a foil to enhance the joy and the glory of life eternal. "Death shall be swallowed up in victory!"

The apostle, however, is not satisfied with simply announcing this truth. By one of these bold and striking figures which everyone instinctively feels to be in completest harmony with the grandeur of the subject, he powerfully strengthens and deepens the impression which the truth itself, even in its own naked simplicity, is fitted to produce.

In the fourteenth chapter of Isaiah there is something like a counterpart of the figure which is here employed. In that passage the object was to celebrate death's resistless power. He had gone forth in his might, and had struck down the proud and imperious monarch of Babylon. That haughty conqueror "who smote the people in wrath with a continual stroke, who ruled the nations in anger"—who, in the height of his strength and glory was like "Lucifer the son of the morning"—that gigantic oppressor, death, at a single blow, had cast to the ground. To signalise this triumph of the last enemy, as he is leading his captive into the dismal regions of the dead, their ghastly inhabitants are represented by the prophet as gathering together to look on the once mighty king, now stripped of all his greatness and reduced to a level with themselves. "Hades from beneath is moved for thee to meet thee at thy coming: it stirreth up the dead for thee, even all the chief men of the earth: it hath raised up from their graves all the kings of the nations. And they shall speak and say unto thee, Art thou also become weak as we? art thou become like unto us? Thy pomp is brought down to the grave, and the noise of thy viols: the worm is spread under thee, and the worms cover thee." It is that same all-conquering, all-subduing death, who is himself destined to fall and perish and disappear for ever. He triumphs over the first Adam, and over all his fallen race. But the second Adam shall triumph over him. Of this second Adam, the Lord from heaven, it had been written of old by the prophet Hosea, that to him it should belong to say concerning his people, "I will ransom them from the power of the grave; I will redeem them from death." And that to him it should also belong to say concerning the destroyer, by whose fatal dart they had been stricken down, "O death, I will be thy plagues; O grave, I will be thy destruction."

Now, it is obviously to the period of the fulfilment of that prophecy our text refers when it represents the saints of God, rescued at length from the corruption of the tomb and imbued with immortality, as now turning round upon their vanquished foe, and celebrating at once his destruction and their own deliverance in this triumphant song, "O death, where is thy sting? O grave, where is thy victory? The sting of death is sin, and the strength of sin is the law. But thanks be to God, which giveth us the victory, through our Lord Jesus Christ."

In these remarkable words there are three things set before

us—*First*, a figurative representation of death; *next*, an interpretation of that emblematic picture; and *last*, a grateful acknowledgment of the power and grace of Him who hath abolished death and brought life and immortality to light.

I. First, *there is here a figurative representation of Death*. The last enemy is personified as a hideous, serpent-like form, armed with a deadly sting, and incessantly and mortally wounding his victims, and consigning them to the grave. In the case of this graphic figure there is no doubt an intended reference to the great deceiver and destroyer of mankind. The subtilty of that tempter's arts, and their poisonous malignity, have too well merited for him the terribly significant designation, "that old serpent the Devil." Death is, so to speak, his hateful progeny, and the one ever follows fast upon the heels of the other. Since Satan prevailed with our first parents to eat the forbidden fruit, and thereby to break their covenant with God, death has passed upon all men, for that all have sinned. For now nearly six thousand years the last enemy has reigned upon this earth. There is no period of history and no quarter of the globe to which his destructive dominion has not extended. If we open the Bible and go back to the record of the long-lived antediluvian race, we still meet at every step with these significant words, "And he died." The history even of a Methuselah ends with these emphatic words, "And he died." Since the world began only two individuals—Enoch and Elijah—have escaped death's fatal stroke; and these escaped, not by any mastery of their own, but by the immediate supernatural interposition of Him of whom we shall have occasion hereafter to speak as having the keys of hell and of death. Neither the wit nor the wealth of man can provide an antidote to death's poisoned sting. It strikes the infant, and the smiling babe sickens and dies in its mother's arms. It strikes the youth, and his beauty fades like a flower that has been blighted in the hour of its fairest and freshest bloom. It strikes the man of mature age, and his strength departs, and the place that knew him knows him no more for ever. It strikes the grey-haired sire, and his venerable form bows down to the dust. The grave has been victorious over all the generations of men. And still, as in the days of Solomon, it "is not satisfied." It is as far as ever from saying, "It is enough." None of us can tell the day or the hour when we shall ourselves be called to go down into that silent and narrow house. This only we know that it is appointed unto all men once to die. From the warfare with this last enemy there is literally no discharge. At this very moment the insidious foe may be stealthily gliding toward us, like the venomous reptile, hidden among the long grass, and which strikes the unwary traveller before he is aware that any danger is near. Nay, who can tell whether, in his own case, the blow may not have been already struck; whether there may not have been already insinuated into his frame the *virus* of some hidden malady, destined to break out ere long with fatal force, and ere another Sabbath or another sun shall have risen upon the earth, to stretch him on the bed of death. Such is the enemy who is here apostrophised—an enemy before whom, sooner or later, we must every one of us fall. And, nevertheless, it is of that dreaded enemy our text teaches the believer to say— "O death, where is thy sting!"

II. But next, there follows in our text *an interpretation of this emblematic picture.* What is this sting with which death is armed? and whence does it derive its fatally destructive power! Anticipating such inquiries as these, the inspired apostle, in the language of that triumphant song which he has put into the mouth of the risen saints, tells us that "the sting of death is *sin,*" and that "the strength of sin is the *law.*" Yes, the sting of death is sin. It is *by sin* that death prevails. "By one man sin entered into the world, and death by sin." Had man never sinned, death would never have assailed him. Had there been no sin committed by Adam, he would still have survived as the honoured patriarch of his multitudinous race. Even after the long lapse of so many thousands of years his eye, bright as when it first beheld the glories of creation, would not have been dim, nor would the natural force with which his Maker then endowed him have been abated. His death was part of the great and awful penalty, inseparable from his transgression. And because in him all his posterity sinned, in him all his posterity die. Even the infant that has "not sinned after the similitude of Adam's transgression," that has not lived long enough—that is, to become, like Adam, an actual and conscious breaker of God's law—is nevertheless mortal from its birth. Involved by covenant in the guilty act of its primeval head and representative, it is involved in the curse by which that act was followed; and under that curse, accordingly, even infants die!

Sin is thus the envenomed sting with which death slays his victims. We can never approach a fellow-creature's death-bed without beholding an affecting memorial and evidence of our sinful state. Every funeral that passes along the streets proclaims the fact that we belong to a sinful race; and even the silence of the churchyard tells with more impressiveness than the most eloquent words that all men are sinners. But what is it that gives to sin this condemning and destructive force? It is "the law," the law of God—that law which some men would fain have us to believe was abolished and buried eighteen hundred years ago. "The strength of sin is *the law.*" If the law have this terrible strength, and be still putting it forth every day, what folly and madness is it to speak of that law as dead! The law denounced, in the beginning of human history, a curse against sin. The law said, "The soul that sinneth, it shall die."

It is *the law*, therefore, that gives to sin its potent strength, not only to kill the body, but to wound the conscience, and to torment it with the anticipated horrors of eternal condemnation. "By the law is the knowledge of sin," for the law defines sin and measures it, and makes known the light in which it appears to the Divine Lawgiver himself. The law proclaims sin to be "the abominable thing" which God hates; and tells us that he will by no means *clear*—that is, excuse or acquit—the wicked. In the case of offences against an earthly sovereign, what is it that drags the man who is charged with them to the bar of judgment, and which, when they are established against him, casts him into a dungeon, or consigns him to a scaffold? It is *the law* which does all this. The law is his accuser. He has broken it, and it therefore condemns him. It does so in vindication of the affronted power and authority of the holy, just, and good Lawgiver; and in the interests at the same time of eternal righteousness and truth. The strength which the law has to doom the sinner to death is thus twofold. The law has the strength of its own inherent righteousness, and it has the strength of that august and supreme authority which it is meant to express and enforce. In the case of mere human law, either one or both of these elements may be awanting. A human law may be unjust, while the authority which enforces it may be strong; or, on the other hand, it may be righteous, while the authority which sustains it may be weak. Or, still further, both may the law be an unjust law, and the authority which should sustain it be an authority destitute of power. But not any of these defects can possibly attach to the law of God. His law is holy, and the commandment holy and just and good. And for giving effect, whether to its promises or threatenings, it is backed by the resources of omniscience, omnipresence, and omnipotence. The very perfection therefore of both *moral* and *executive* strength resides eternally and universally in the law of God. And hence escape from it is impossible. Because the law is so righteous, even the sinner's own heart condemns him, and makes him miserable. Because its authority is so resistless, it can not only kill the body, but can cast both soul and body into hell fire!

III. And now, in the *third* and last place, we come to the grateful recognition which the text contains of *the saving power and grace of Him who hath robbed death of its sting, and who takes away its victory from the grave.* "Thanks be to God, which giveth us the victory, through our Lord Jesus Christ."

The victory here in question must needs be the victory over sin and death. How is this double victory secured? Our text tells us we are indebted for it exclusively to God. "Thanks be *to God,* who giveth us the victory." When we had destroyed ourselves by our apostasy and rebellion, help was found for us in Him—even in that very Being whom we had disowned, dishonoured, disobeyed. When there was no eye to pity and no hand to save, His eye pitied and his arm brought unto us salvation. "For God so loved the world that he gave his only-begotten Son, that whosoever believeth on him should not perish, but should have everlasting life."

God is therefore the true and only source and author of this victory. He found the Ransom. He gave and sent forth the Divine Deliverer, who came down from heaven to earth on this blessed mission; and he did so under no other constraint than that of his own free grace and sovereign mercy. But while the text sets before us the author, it also sets before us the instrument of our salvation—God giveth us the victory, through *our Lord Jesus Christ.* He it was that came up from Edom, with dyed garments from Bozrah, travelling in the greatness of his strength, mighty to save. *His* therefore is that only name under heaven given among men by which we must be saved, if we are to be saved at all. Let us see then what this

Mighty One had to do in order to rescue us from sin and death —in other words, to gain for us and to give to us the glorious victory of which our text speaks.

1. He had to *satisfy* the law. Before the law would or could relax its hold of the sinner, the debt due to the law must be fully paid. A perfect obedience must be rendered to all its requirements. Though as to his own divine nature as God's co-eternal Son, he was in the form of God, and thought it not robbery to be equal with God, and as such was above the law, it was necessary he should put himself under it, if he was really to redeem his people from its curse. For this purpose accordingly he took upon him the form of a servant, and was formed or fashioned as a man. Having been thus made under the law, he, as his people's Surety and substitute, fulfilled all the righteousness which the law revealed and required. From the cradle to the cross it was his meat to do the will of his Father, and to finish his work. He alone of all whoever appeared in human form and nature could hear the law's commands read out without exception before him, and say in perfect sincerity and truth, "All these have I kept from my youth up." The law, in all its purity and integrity, was not only exemplified in his whole outward life, it was within his inmost heart. He was holy, harmless, undefiled, and separate from sinners. The Prince of this world came to Christ, but in him there was nothing, absolutely nothing, to give even the faintest response to the tempter's seductive voice. Pilate came to him, fain to find if he could any pretext however slight on which to condemn him, in order that he might thus accomplish his own end, which was, if anyhow it were possible, to harmonise the dictates of his uneasy conscience with the base ends of a thoroughly selfish mind. But even he could find in Him no fault at all. Above all, God himself, the righteous Ruler of the

moral universe, came to Him—came to him again and again, and at the most trying moments of his earthly history—but it was only as often as he came to bear this conclusive testimony to his spotless innocence, "Thou art my beloved Son, in whom I am well pleased."

2. But while Christ thus rendered to the law the very uttermost of all it could demand from his people in the way of obedience, he also rendered to it the very uttermost of all it could demand from his people in the way of *penalty* for their sins. He hath redeemed us from the curse of the law by bearing that awful curse in our stead. Because the law said, "Cursed is every one that continueth not in all things that are written in the book of the law, to do them," He submitted to be numbered with transgressors, and to hang upon the accursed tree. He was thus wounded for our transgressions, and bruised for our iniquities; and suffered, the just for the unjust, that he might bring us unto God. And therefore it is that "there is now no condemnation to them that are in Christ Jesus!" Both actively and passively, he met and satisfied all the law's demands. And because this finished work of Christ was performed by one who was both God and man, it had of necessity an infinite value. It not only exhausted the law's claims, it magnified the law itself, and made it more honourable far than if its vengeance had been left to take full effect on our whole guilty race. And thus has it come to pass, that as by one man's disobedience many were made sinners, so by the obedience of one—that is, of the God-man, the Lord Jesus Christ —many are made righteous. Therefore it is that God is now in Christ reconciling the world unto himself, not imputing unto men their trespasses. He is just, and the justifier of the ungodly who believe in Jesus.

3. But, once more, in order to secure for us the victory spoken

of in our text, Christ becomes to all who truly believe in him *a quickening spirit*. He is made of God unto them, not only righteousness, but sanctification too. He creates in them a clean heart, and renews in them a right spirit. He sheds abroad in their hearts the love of God by the Holy Ghost which is given unto them. And this, too, is indispensable to the victory over sin and death; for except a man be thus born of the Spirit, he cannot see the kingdom of God. Without holiness, the very holiness which God's love reveals and requires, no man shall see the Lord. In the very nature of things there can be no communion between righteousness and unrighteousness, no fellowship between light and darkness, no concord between Christ and Belial. This great fundamental change accordingly is part of the great work wrought by Christ in every believer. He that is joined unto Christ is thus made "one spirit" with him. The believer is a branch of the true vine, partaking of its very life, and bearing its very fruits. He is a member of Christ's mystical body, animated and impelled by the living and life-giving Head. And being thus indissolubly united to Christ, he has been crucified with Christ, and nevertheless he lives, because Christ lives in him. Already, therefore, he has *part* in the first resurrection, *i.e.* in the quickening of his soul from its natural death in sin into a new life of loving service and holy devotedness to God. And though, indeed, his body must go down to the grave and see corruption, it too shall be made to live again. There shall be a redemption of the body too. Sown in weakness, it shall be raised in power; sown in dishonour, it shall be raised in glory; sown a natural body, it shall be raised a spiritual body. Then the victory shall be complete. The law satisfied, sin expelled, death destroyed; the once guilty and perishing sinner, washed and sanctified and justified in the name of the Lord Jesus, and by the Spirit of our God, shall then at length go away with his glorified

Redeemer into life eternal. And then, indeed, it will be his privilege exultingly to exclaim, "O death, where is thy sting? O grave, where is thy victory? The sting of death is sin, and the strength of sin is the law; but thanks be to God which giveth me the victory through my Lord Jesus Christ!"

It needs not however, brethren, let me say in conclusion, that we should wait till the resurrection day in order to be in a condition to take home to ourselves these joyful words. True, indeed, until that great and notable day has come, they cannot have their whole meaning fulfilled, and their full significance realised. But still all that is most essential in the testimony which they contain, it may be, yea it *is*, the privilege of every true disciple of Christ even in this present life to bear. Already for every true believer death has been robbed of its sting, for to him death is but the door-way to heaven. Confiding in the atoning efficacy of Immanuel's blood, he can take up, here and now, the language of Paul, and say, "Who is he that condemneth? It is Christ that died; yea, rather that is risen again, who is even at the right hand of God."

And though the grave must receive that tabernacle of clay, whose destiny it is to be dissolved, he knows and is assured that from that very grave it shall one day come forth in an unspeakably brighter and better form. "Flesh and blood cannot inherit the kingdom of God; neither doth corruption inherit incorruption." Therefore at his coming the second time, without sin unto salvation, the Lord shall give back to the believer his once frail and perishable body, give it back frail and perishable no more, but fashioned like unto the glorified body of Christ himself—no longer to know hunger or thirst, weakness or pain, sickness or death, but to be the fitting tabernacle for the inhabitation of a happy, holy, and immortal spirit, destined to be for ever with the Lord!

Let me ask my hearers, is this privilege yours? Has

God given you the earnest at least of this victory over sin and death? If there be any here who have to answer "No," be sure the fault is their own. You have not, let me say of such, really and truly sought it—sought it in the spirit of repentance towards God, and of faith towards our Lord Jesus Christ, and therefore you have not received it. You have never yet been aroused to an adequate sense of the preciousness of Christ, and of the infinite peril and misery of living and dying in your sins, without God and without hope. You have been setting your affections on things beneath, and not on those things which are above. You have been sowing to your flesh, of which nothing can be reaped but corruption. Oh, therefore, be admonished in time! No longer sleep, as do others. Awake thou that sleepest, and arise from the dead, and Christ shall give thee light. Ah, it will be too late to awake at the voice of the archangel and the trump of God! Then there will be no place of repentance. Then the compassionate Saviour will have been transformed into the righteous Judge. And for all those who would not that he should reign over them, and who therefore would not come unto Him that they might have life, there will be nothing in store but the wrath that cometh upon the children of disobedience.

It is to-day then, if ye will hear the Lord's gracious voice. To-day from that cross on which he was lifted up on very purpose that he might draw all men to him. He is calling to you and saying, "Look unto me and be ye saved. Come unto me and I will give you rest." Will you not look? Will you not come? By the terror of the Lord we persuade you! By the mercies of God we beseech you. Now is the accepted time, now is the day of salvation. Amen!

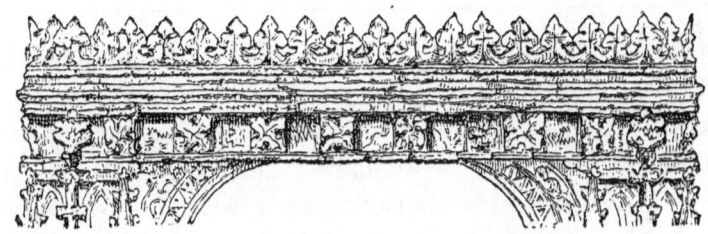

XXIII.

Apostasy and Recovery.

BY THE REV. CHARLES C. MACKINTOSH, D.D.

"ALL WE, LIKE SHEEP, HAVE GONE ASTRAY; WE HAVE TURNED EVERY ONE TO HIS OWN WAY; AND THE LORD HATH LAID ON HIM THE INIQUITY OF US ALL."— ISA. liii. 6.

MOST of us are familiar with this chapter, the subject of which is the humiliation of Messiah, and the glory that followed:—first, his humiliation, in its successive steps as he descended lower and lower till he was laid in the grave; and then, his exaltation and the fruits of his death. Our text, like the greater part of the chapter, is the language of the Church. Only the church of God makes this confession in truth, or beholds with unveiled face and a broken heart the suffering Saviour. Let us consider, *first*, The confession of the Church; and *secondly*, The Church's ascription of her deliverance to the Lord's having "laid on him the iniquity of us all."

I. *The confession.* The church of God, with one mind and one mouth, makes confession of common apostasy, and of particular individual transgression.

1. Confession of *common* transgression: and yet such confession as that every individual makes it for himself, while he

unites with others in making it. There are many expressions made use of in the Word to describe our natural state in its different aspects. Viewed in reference to man's original dignity and glory, it is a *fall*—we have "fallen by our iniquity." Viewed in reference to his having been seduced by the wicked one, and bearing now *his* moral image, Jesus says of it, "Ye are of your father the devil, and the lusts of your father ye will do." Viewed in reference to the change of heart towards God— from love to enmity—men by nature are a "generation of vipers." And viewed again in reference to the condemnation attached to sin, we are, "by nature, children of wrath." The simile of a lost sheep is frequently employed in God's Word to represent a sinful state; and there are three main ideas implied in it. (1.) *Apostasy* or *departure* from God: a ceasing to rest and delight in him as our chief good and portion; a slighting of his infinite claims on the love of the whole heart, and the service of the whole being; and a going away from him to seek our happiness in the world and in self. It is in this that the essence of sin consists, and therefore that its infinite evil is to be seen, according to those burning words of the Most High, "Hear, O heavens; and give ear, O earth: for the Lord hath spoken, I have nourished and brought up children, and they have rebelled against me" (Isa. i. 2). We have no sense by nature of the evil of sin in this its primary aspect. We have some sense of wrong in sins against our neighbour, such as deceit, fraud, or slander; or in open profanity and contempt of God; but no sense of the evil of sin as a practical renouncing of God as our Sovereign and our Portion, till the Holy Spirit convinces us of sin. *Then* this view of it fills and engrosses the mind, "Against thee, thee only have I sinned, and done evil in thy sight." (2.) *Folly.* Here is another very humbling view of the confession. "Be astonished, O ye heavens, at this, and be horribly afraid, be ye very desolate, saith the

Lord. For my people have committed two evils; they have forsaken me, the fountain of living waters, and hewed them out cisterns, broken cisterns, that can hold no water" (Jer. ii. 12, 13). Sin is a forsaking of our own mercy. It is a going away from the living God, the source of joy and happiness, to dumb idols; a choosing of the pleasures of sin for a season, rather than the "recompence of the reward." Men may be wise in regard to this world, and very fools in regard to their true interests and a world to come. Take but the one illustration of the worldling in Christ's parable (Luke xii. 16-21). If there *be* an eternal world, is any madness to compare with his who can say, "Soul, take thine ease; eat, drink, and be merry;" "forget thy latter end"? "O," says Jesus, "Thou fool! this night thy soul shall be required of thee." And yet "the heart of the sons of men is full of evil, and madness is in their heart while they live" (Eccl. ix. 3); and unless the grace of God interpose, this madness continues till "they go down to the dead." Is there any madness to compare with that of rejecting a Saviour? (3.) *Danger.* What more expressive image of utter helplessness than that of a poor stray sheep! And how does God's Word, in innumerable other places, set before us the danger to which we are exposed in our apostate condition. "Know, therefore, and see, that it is an evil thing and bitter that thou hast forsaken the Lord thy God, and that my fear is not in thee, saith the Lord God of hosts" (Jer. ii. 19). "The wages of sin is death." "The wrath of God abideth" on the impenitent and unpardoned sinner. "Broad is the way that leadeth to destruction." "It is a fearful thing to fall into the hands of the living God." "Where their worm dieth not, and the fire is not quenched." "*All* we," without one exception. We sinned in our first parents. We followed their steps. And I observe that this is such a confession as that every individual takes it home to himself in all its meaning. This is one great difference between the formal and the true worshipper. The one loses all sense of his own concern in the confession of sin, because it is true of all; and therefore with an unbroken heart he makes it. The other, feeling that he has to do with God and realising the presence of God, while he confesses the sin of our race confesses his own sin just as though he were alone with God, and smiting on his breast, says, "God be merciful to me a sinner." How many such worshippers are there now among us?

2. There is a confession of special *individual* transgression: "We have turned every one to his own way." (1.) Man, in departing from God, set up his *will* in opposition to God's *law;* and his own satisfaction as his chief end, rather than the glory of God. Look into your heart (if you are yet unconverted), and say whether it is not your own will that you follow, and not the will of God; and then consider, if there be a God who takes cognisance of the state of the heart, whether you can more directly insult and oppose him than by setting your will in opposition to his. (2.) Amidst men's general apostasy, there is wonderful variety of temperament and taste. There are innumerable diversities of character, and there is room in the broad way for them all. There is room in it for him who follows chiefly the lust of the eye;—he can have his own way: room for him who follows the lust of the flesh, or the pride of life: room for the open sinner; and for the decent moralist: for the young man whom Jesus loved, but who lacked the one thing; and for the scoffer: for the man with a false creed; and for the dead professor with a sound creed: for the despiser of divine ordinances; and for the almost Christian. (3.) Each has his *own* way, according to his tastes, and temperament, and outward circumstances. And one, in his own path, may have very little sympathy with another in *his* path. The Pharisee may look down with contempt on the open sinner, and the professed

believer in grace may pity the blinded Pharisee. But they are all alike in this, that every one has his own way of departure from God, and of unwillingness to return even when the voice of mercy follows them saying, "Turn ye, turn ye, why will ye die?" Oh! in what sad ways has the Lord found some who have obtained mercy! He met with Manasseh in his profanity, and obduracy, and horrid cruelty; with Mary Magdalene in her subjection to seven unclean spirits; with Zaccheus in his worldliness; with Saul of Tarsus in his persecuting rage; with Augustine and Newton in their impurity: and he turned them to himself. What was *your* way? Whether that of open sin or of dead profession, it was the way of false peace, of carnal security, of vain hope and vain chase after happiness in the world; the way of idolatry, of selfishness, of unbelief, of unthankfulness: and that way you would have pursued to the end, unless he who arrested Saul had arrested you.

Think then of your evil ways. Christ's people will desire to unite in the confession, "All we like sheep have gone astray, we have turned every one to his own way:" we were going further and further from God and from peace, deaf to the warnings of the Word and Providence, approaching nearer and nearer to eternal destruction: we deserved to have our iniquities laid upon us, and to lie under them for ever. There is a kind of religion of which we cannot be too jealous, for it is not from God; the religion which dispenses with the continued exercise of repentance on the part of the adopted child of God. The exercise of the spirit of adoption must, in this world, ever be combined with the exercise of godly sorrow. The believer, as he grows in grace, is not the less disposed to remember his sins, but the more. Every fresh sense of God's reconciling grace has, as its fruit, that "he remembers, and is confounded, and never opens his mouth any more because of his shame" (Ezek. xvi. 63). The Lord help his people to be thus exercised! They will be the better fitted to enter into the meaning of the wondrous words, "The Lord hath laid on him the iniquity of us all."

II. The Church's *ascription of deliverance* to "the Lord's having laid on him" ("made to meet on him") "the iniquity of us all."

Here there is an evident allusion to sacrificial rites. It is said (Lev. i. 4), "And he shall put his hand on the head of the burnt-offering," implying a transfer of guilt from the offerer to the victim, "and it shall be accepted for him, to make atonement for him." And in reference to the scape-goat, it is said (Lev. xvi. 21, 22), "And Aaron shall lay both his hands on the head of the live goat, and confess over him all the iniquities of the children of Israel, and all their transgressions in all their sins, and shall send him away by the hand of a fit man into the wilderness. And the goat shall bear upon him all their iniquities unto a land not inhabited, and he shall let go the goat in the wilderness." Aaron's laying both his hands on the head of the goat was a figure of the completeness of the expiation to be made by Christ, and of the forgiveness which is its fruit. It is said, " We have turned every one to our own way :" then, it is not added, "but through the wondrous mercy of God we are brought back," but (as accounting for this, and comprehending this) "The Lord hath laid on him the iniquity of us all."

1. The first truth to which our attention is directed here is, that *sin must be reckoned for*. God cannot pass it by. It must be laid somewhere, and, in the ordinary procedure of justice, laid on the sinner, and, *he* dealt with according to its desert God's holy law is the transcript of his own image; it is as unchangeable as God Himself; and it says, "the soul that sinneth, it shall die." One great end of the ceremonial law was to hold

up continually the truth, that "without shedding of blood is no remission." If God's justice is one of his essential perfections, if the principles of the divine government are fixed and stable, if the sacrifices were a figurative gospel, then no truth is more plainly held forth in the Scriptures, than that of the absolute necessity of satisfaction for sin ere sin could be put away from the sinner, a way of return be opened up to him, or God invite him to return. It is a trifling with the meaning of words, to deny this, and at the same time to profess to receive the Bible as a divine revelation. I have been referring to the *necessity* of repentance. I now notice that there are two kinds of repentance which are false : the repentance which can be exercised without a view of the atoning blood of Christ; and the repentance which is exercised, under the influence of a *supposed* view of God's graciousness in Christ, by those who have never felt their need of having light from heaven shed on the question, "How *can* a just God pardon sin?" But supposing this question put for the first time, or put afresh, I observe, as part answer to it—

2. The next blessed truth, *in order*, to which our attention is called is, that salvation has its source in the free sovereign love of God to sinners. "*The Lord* hath laid on him the iniquity of us all." His free love is revealed as prompting him to provide and open up a way of salvation The fountain-head of redemption is the love of the Father : " God *so* loved the world that he gave his only begotten Son, that whosoever believeth in him should not perish, but have everlasting life." "Blessed," says the apostle, "be the God and Father of our Lord Jesus Christ." This is the first dazzling truth which is presented before the sinner, and which comes first before the eyes of the saint in seeking to draw men to God. There is such graciousness in God's heart as moved him to purpose the restoration and salvation of guilty apostates. True, he did not purpose

the salvation of *all*. He chose whom he would to everlasting life. And "is there unrighteousness with God"? No: this grace in the purpose of salvation is not a grace which has respect of persons. And it is revealed and exhibited to us in his Word as the *free* grace which is needed by the sinner, and which continues to be needed by the child of God.

3. God's wonderful way of securing the righteous exercise of his grace was by providing a *Surety or Substitute for guilty men;* one willing by reason of boundless grace, and competent by reason of the dignity of his Person, to mediate between them and an offended God ; one willing and able to do and suffer all that law and justice demanded in order that all the perfections of Jehovah might be glorified in their being brought back to God. Such a Surety was found in God's own Son. I know not which of the heresies is most opposed to the honour of Christ ;—that which represents him as a mere man ; or that which represents him as existing before his appearance in the world, but only as a creature. Certain it is that when the holy law unveils itself to us in its sacredness, asserts its authority over us, shews us its judgment of sin, and apprehends us in our consciences as transgressors, no deliverer will be realised by us as able and suitable, but one who unites the glories of divinity and the tenderness of humanity in his own person. Blessed be God, such is the Deliverer revealed in the gospel ; one willing to have "the iniquity of us all laid on him," and able to bear the load, and to put sin away (Heb. i. 1–3). Jesus Christ is the proper Surety only of his own people ; but in the gospel he is exhibited to you and to me—to all alike—as willing to be our Surety, as engaging to be a Redeemer, as coming in the flesh, as suffering, dying, and rising again, in the exercise of a grace ready to embrace the chief of sinners. Consider then—

4. This most wondrous act of God towards the Surety—his "laying on *him* the iniquity of us all." If it was thus that

redemption was purchased, we ought to see how it is altogether a divine work. (1.) If the Son of God engaged to be the surety of guilty men, he needed to assume human nature that he might be regarded by the law of the Most High as a suitable Surety; and he needed to take the very place of guilty men under God's law, that in their room he might obey, fulfil, and magnify it (Heb. ii. 10, 14, 16; 2 Cor. v. 21; Gal. iii. 13; Rom. v. 19). (2.) The whole of his life upon earth, the appointed time of his sojourn with sinful men, was fruitful in glory to God and in blessings to his people. There was the example he has left us; the lustre of holy love which beamed forth in all his sayings and actions; in particular, his obedience to the holy law in our room and stead: but all pointed to his death, not merely as that event which was to consummate his obedience, but as that by which reconciliation was to be made for iniquity, sin taken away, the covenant ratified, the Church bought; and which was specially to display his purity, his love, and the glories of his obedience. And therefore it is that Jesus, in speaking of the design of his coming into the world, sums it all up in this—"to give his life a ransom for many" (Mat. xx. 28), "to give his life for the sheep" (John x. 11). There was, then, an "hour," the like of which never has been nor shall be; which had in it not only the importance of all time but the value of eternity, when everything as it were came to a height, to *full* manifestation; when Satan got power (a circumstance not to be overlooked in considering how low the faith of the Church then fell); when the wickedness of the heart was fully manifested; when the righteousness and the grace of God were displayed to the uttermost; when there was suffering without any parallel in kind, in depth, in purity, in preciousness. (1.) "The Lord laid upon him the iniquity of us all" in infinite grace towards us, and in righteousness as the Judge, because *he* represented sinners. It is this twofold consideration, that

Christ was the surety of his people, and that the Father dealt with him in righteousness, that not merely accounts for his sufferings, but shews a becomingness, so to speak, that he should *thus* suffer; that he should be apprehended and condemned, and spit upon, and crowned with thorns, and nailed to the tree, and be derided in his sufferings. The omniscient and infinitely holy and righteous One "*made* him to be sin for us, who knew no sin." Being made sin, he was made "a curse," *i.e.* he endured the proper punishment of sin; and was forsaken of God, because God hates and cannot look upon sin. The only view we can take of this is, that there was an entire suspension for the time of all comforting influences to his holy soul, while the wrath due to sin in all its unknown severity was endured by him. (2.) This is the most solemn of all subjects. We are reminded that we are on holy ground; and that there is a depth here which we cannot fathom, whether we consider the Person who suffered, the intensity of his sufferings, or their very nature as those of a voluntary surety and a holy sufferer. We are warned to avoid all rash speculation, and to look up for the Holy Spirit to guide us in the understanding of the record of his last sufferings. We know that the Lamb of God could not have suffered as sinful beings do; that he was a stranger to any such feeling as remorse, or despair, or the anguish arising from the conflict of evil passions. We know at the same time that he suffered the punishment of sin, and that his holiness gave an intensity to his sorrow of which we can have no adequate conception. But the *measure* of his sufferings, when "it pleased the Lord to bruise him," when "the waters came in unto his soul" (Psa. lxix. 1–3), when in Gethsemane he said, "O my Father, if it be possible, let this cup pass from me," when on the cross he cried out, "My God, my God, why hast thou forsaken me?" this is what none of his people can comprehend. And not only *what* he suffered, but *how* he suffered; in the exercise of what love and zeal and faith he offered himself up " a sacrifice of a sweet smelling savour."

"The Lord laid upon Him the iniquity of us all :"—but to lie on him only for a time. He " made reconciliation for iniquity ;" He put away sin by the sacrifice of Himself; dying to sin *once*, but conquering death in dying, he rose from the grave, and liveth for evermore. The God of peace brought from the dead the Lord Jesus, that great Shepherd of the sheep. And therefore did He charge his apostles to proclaim to sinners to the end of the earth, " Return unto the Lord, and he will have mercy upon you; and to our God, for he will abundantly pardon." Therefore did he, and does he, pour out his Spirit, to make the proclamation of grace effectual. Therefore have there been, and are there, those who, " once far off, but are made nigh by the blood of Christ;" and who, thus restored, seek as with one voice admiringly to say, "The Lord hath laid on Him the iniquity of us all."

XXIV.

The Drawing Power of the Cross.

BY THE REV. JOHN DUNCAN, LL.D.

"Now is the judgment of this world: now shall the prince of this world be cast out. And I, if I be lifted up from the earth, will draw all men unto me. This he said, signifying what death he should die."—JOHN xii. 31-33.

THE death by which he should die was now fast approaching. Jesus appears on the occason to have had a foretaste both of "the travail of his soul" and of its fruits, of which it was promised him he "should see and be satisfied." Certain Greeks had come up to worship at the feast; not Greek Jews, but native Greeks, who yet appear to have been worshippers of the Lord God of Israel, and to have come up to the feast. Having heard of Jesus, they applied to one of the disciples, expressing a wish to see him, and the disciple reported it to Jesus. Now, in this Jesus saw that though promises were budding forth to their fulfilment—that in the promised "root of Jesse the Gentiles should trust," and these, the first fruits of his death, were present—yet the death being itself first to be undergone, the very joys reminded him of its necessity. "The hour," said he, "is come that the Son of Man should be glorified." Already the hour had come, the nations, in their first fruits, look to "the root of Jesse, which should rise to be an ensign for the people, to whom the Gentiles should seek." But before this can be realised, his death was necessary. He must sow in tears, if he would reap in joy. He, the seed of corn, the root of the whole, must die. "Except a corn of wheat fall into the ground and die, it abideth alone: but if it die, it bringeth forth much fruit." "Much fruit"—here is the joy that was set before him. And he needed the joy set before him; for heavy, inconceivably heavy were the toils, the agonies, the sufferings that must precede. For the joy that was set before him he endured the cross, despising the shame. It to him was awful; only the joy was set before him. "He endured the cross," for he must die—must fall into the ground and die. And as this was the law for the Christ, so it is the law for the Christian. "He that loveth his life shall lose it; and he that hateth his life in this world shall keep it unto life eternal. If any man serve me, let him follow me"—follow me in hating his life—follow me in falling as a corn of wheat into the ground and dying. "If any man serve me, let him follow me," said Jesus, "and where I am, there shall also my servant be." Where I am—on the cross—there shall also my servant be. "If any man serve me, him will my Father honour."

Jesus, for the joy set before him, endured the cross. He endured the cross, but it was awful. Awful to us to think of. Awful to him. Even with the joy set before him, it was awful. Without the joy it would have been impossible to be endured: with the joy it could be sustained. "Now is my soul troubled: and what shall I say?" "Shall I say, Father, save me from this hour?" for so would I place the mark of interrogation. "Shall I say this, Father, save me from this hour?" Ah, no! he says, That I will not say. Father, glorify thy name. *That* will I say. Glorify thy name. I came for this cause. For the cause of this hour came I unto this hour. I undertook the work just for this. The whole of my mission, incarnation, all that I have done, all that I have endured up to this moment, was for this :—Christ not only being born and dying, but Christ being born that he might die. ' God sent forth his Son, made of a woman, made under the law, that he might redeem them that were under the law." " Forasmuch as the children are partakers of flesh and blood, he also himself likewise took part of the same." For it was necessary that this man should have somewhat to offer. " A body hast thou prepared me." " Lo, I come to do thy will, O God." " By the which will we are sanctified, through the offering of the body of Jesus Christ once for all." "For this cause came I unto this hour." And now, troubled in soul I must be ; I will not, I wish not to be otherwise. " Father, glorify thy name." " Then came there a voice from heaven, saying, I have both glorified it, and will glorify it again." I have glorified it in thee ; I will glorify it in thee still more. Of this voice some gave one interpretation—said it thundered : others said, an angel spake to him. Jesus explained it : " This voice came not because of me, but for your sakes." The voice came for their sakes, for the sake of those from whom we find afterwards Jesus departed and did hide himself. " For though he had done so many miracles before them, yet they believed not on him." For their sakes, of whom Esaias had prophesied that he had blinded their eyes and hardened their heart—for their sakes came this voice. Yes, for their sakes, and so for the sake of all unto whom this recorded voice comes. God speaketh to us from heaven, to the whole visible church—unto the visible church, in whose ear the testimony of the Father concerning his Son sounds—God speaks. He speaks in his Word to all to whom it comes. Not for Jesus' sake, but for the sake of these unbelieving people. And God does something for the sake of those whose eyes he has blinded, of those who cannot see with their eyes, nor hear with their ears, nor understand with their heart. He had not forsaken them utterly. It is to be feared multitudes of them forsook *him*. And now Jesus explains to them, to these unbelieving people, with the blinded eyes and hardened heart, Jesus explains to them the meaning of the voice, and the meaning of the death he was about to die. " Now," says he, " now is the judgment of this world, signifying, or giving to be understood to them, what death he should die."

I. We are here to contemplate the death of Christ as setting forth "the judgment of this world," the crisis. It was a mighty hour for this world. It was the hour of its judgment. The world is a lost world. But the lost world is a Divinity-visited world. In this world God had been dishonoured. In this world God had been already glorified; more glorified already had he been in this world, more glorified than ever he had been in the heaven of heavens. Jesus had glorified his name upon the earth. Truth had sprung from earth, while righteousness looked down from heaven. Here stood a guilty condemned world, with the Incarnate God tabernacling in it. Here stood humanity, the race which had been as smoke in God's nostrils, a fire that burneth all the day. There stood humanity in higher than Adamic glory. There stood man, the glorifier of God—man, the equal and fellow of the Lord of hosts. Human excellency in its perfection united to eternal Godhead, in the close union in which in Jesus the two natures was one person, Immanuel. So stood it. A sinful race—the righteous One. Man, God's dishonour—Man, God's glorifier. And now was coming the judgment of this world. Not the still future one, for Jesus said *Now*, signifying by what death he should die. Ah ! but that future one proceeds upon principles deducible from this one. In this one is the coming one in its seeds and principles already fixed and determined.

. . . Here the world is not taken unawares. The Son of God is not sent to an unprepared world. He came to his own. Prophets and holy men of God had for the previous thousand years been announcing his coming. People had been set apart and placed under a system of training for his reception. People had been taught to look forward to "the consolation of Israel." "In Judah's land God was well known; his name was great in Israel. In Salem also was his tabernacle, and his dwelling-place in Zion." He had not dealt so with any nation, and as for his judgments, these other nations had not known them. Now he comes, comes to his own, comes to the vineyard planted on the very fruitful hill, planted with the stones gathered out and the hedge planted round, planted with the noble vine, in that vineyard of which the Lord of hosts says, "What could have been done more to my vineyard that I have not done in it?" He had planted the vineyard long ago, and had sent seeking fruit, and they had taken one servant after another and killed and stoned them. But he had one Son, his well-beloved, and he said, "I will send him; when they see him, they will reverence my Son." And so he came—came to his own, and his own received him not. And that was in Judah's land: that was to men prepared with all appliances. And what was the reception? "Ye have both seen and hated both me and my Father." Here then is the judgment of this world: for there is no difference. "Are we," says the apostle, "better than they" Gentiles? I say what then are we better than they? "No, in no wise. We have before proved both Jews and Gentiles that they are all under sin." If there were a spark of good in fallen man it would have come out, it would all gather and cluster round him, and finding him, "increase with the increase of God."

If there were aught of good, it would find its way to the Christ of God when he came. He had indeed some that came to him. But how? "As many as receive him, to them gave he power to become the sons of God, even to them which believe on his name; which were born, not of blood, nor of the will of the flesh, nor of the will of man, but of God." "Ye have not chosen me, but I have chosen you, and ordained you, that ye should go and bring forth fruit, and that your fruit should remain." So it was, "he came to his own, and his own received him not." Those who received him were as little disposed as others; they received him, not in consequence of being born of the flesh, or of the will of man, but of God. Here then is the judgment of this world. This world received not the Christ. "Now is the judgment of this world." Ay, Adam fell, but Christ hath Come! "He hath finished transgression and made an end of sin, and brought in everlasting righteousness." Man hath gone away from God. God hath come to bring him back. But will fallen man go back? The two cherubim with flaming sword are not keeping the door to the way of life. The way into the Eden of God is open. God is standing in Christ reconciling the world unto himself, not imputing unto men their trespasses. Will they go back then? Oh, no, no! Speak not of Adam's fall. The second Adam reverses it. No return! Say not, "Adam fell." Who fell the second fall? When the second Adam came and ye said, Nay—who fell that second fall? To whom—to what gainsaying and disobedient people hath Messiah stretched out his hands all the day long? And who is worst—the man who went away from God, or the man to whom God said, "Come back by Jesus Christ," and he would stay away, and not go back? Now is the world judged. That's one point, shewing the equity of its condemnation. What was the condemnation, the punishment a guilty world deserved? Behold the Lamb of God;

and if these things were done in a green tree, what shall be done in the dry? If the pains of death encompassed him, and the sorrows of hell took hold on him, if Jehovah said, "Awake, O sword, against my Shepherd, and against the man that is my Fellow, smite the Shepherd," and he had done no iniquity, neither was any deceit found in his mouth, what is the estimate of sin now in what Jesus endured? Behold the judgment of this world! Behold what he endured! Behold that, by the endurance of which all saved are saved, because he endured it! What is the estimate of sin now, taking into view that they rejected all that when presented to them as the ground of a new hope and gracious acceptance?

And now, the world rises up against the Son of God. "Many bulls compass him, strong bulls of Bashan." "There be many that do fight against me, O Thou most High." "My strong foes and they that hate me are too many for me." "Verily, against thy holy child Jesus, whom thou hast anointed, both Herod and Pontius Pilate, with the Gentiles and the people of Israel, were gathered together." The world, the world, what hath it done? Ah, there are some crimes such that they would efface almost all minor criminality! Such, says God, were the trangressions of the apostate ten tribes compared with the sin of Jerusalem. Put now Adam's transgression and the whole mass of the transgressions committed since the world was, and what are they? They all meet, they all strike at the life of God inferentially, but this directly. God, as Divinity, cannot die. If man who is a Deicide in heart, is to get opportunity, God must have a mortal nature, and God takes the mortal nature, and in that nature is put to death. *That's* the world. The world that was, and the world that is. "Love not the world, neither the things that are in the world." "For all that is in the world, the lust of the flesh, and the lust of the eyes, and the pride of life, is not of the Father, but is of the world." "Now is the judgment of this world."

II. But next, Jesus says, "Now shall the prince of this world be cast out. This he said, signifying what death he should die." This world, this present world, is an evil world, and hath an evil prince, "the prince of the power of the air;" "the spirit that now worketh in the children of disobedince." This world is Satan's world—God's world, for he made it; but Satan's world, for he hath usurped it; and men made in the image of God have sold themselves for nought, to be his thralls, and he rules and lords it over them, "working in the children of disobedience." Men talk much of their own free-will and independence. Men scoff at spiritual influence, but every man is under it. Every man is under spiritual influence. Every man's body is either a temple of the Holy Spirit, or of Satan, the spirit that now worketh in the children of disobedience; and specially Satan exercises his power, if he possibly can, in keeping men from Christ. "If our gospel be hid, it is hid to them that are lost: in whom the god of this world hath blinded the minds of them which believe not, lest the light of the glorious gospel of Christ, who is the image of God, should shine upon them." "*Lest*,"—Satan is not satisfied with the corruption of man's nature; although he well might, yet he is not. He knows the gospel hath a mighty power; yea, though never but by the effectual operation of the Holy Spirit doth it convert a soul, yet it hath a mighty power. Even as a moral means, it has a mighty power of adaptation, which Satan trembles at, lest, notwithstanding all that he knows of the desperate wickedness of the heart, the light of the glorious gospel of Christ, who is the image of God, should shine unto them; therefore *lest* it should shine, he blindeth their minds. Every man then into whose heart God hath not shined, to give the light of the knowledge of his glory in the face of Jesus Christ, every man unto whom the gospel yet is hid, is devil-led and devil-bound. He hath a prince, the prince of this world, ruling and reigning; and under promise of liberty makes him the slave of corruption. "Now," says Christ, "shall the prince of this world be cast out. This he said, signifying what death he should die." . . .

He came that "by death he might destroy him that had the power of death, that is, the devil, and deliver them who through fear of death were all their lifetime subject to bondage." Satan had the power—the power of the jailer and executioner. Jesus died. The jailer's power was gone. Jesus died, but the foundation of Satan's kingdom was destroyed. Death snapped asunder the union which held together soul and body. It could not snap asunder the union which bound soul and body to Godhead. It was still Immanuel in the grave and Immanuel in paradise! The body of Christ was not separated from the Godhead. The soul of Christ was not separated from the Godhead. Death had put in his iron teeth as far as they could penetrate. And through the external they had penetrated to the separating of the soul and body of Jesus; his teeth, his iron teeth, found a hard adamantine union that could not be dissolved; and soon the body and soul of the Lord Jesus—never either of them separated from the Godhead—were speedily united to one another; God "loosing the bonds of death, because it was not possible that he should be holden of it." "He destroyed death, and him that had the power of death." And now, he appears living—a living Saviour, dead and alive again, and free and powerful to come as the strong man and snatch, come and legally take, his own redeemed, his own purchased—to come and condescend to open blind eyes, to turn from darkness to light and from the power of Satan unto God, that they might receive forgiveness of sins and inheritance among them which are sanctified through faith that is in him. And now the Spirit testifies of judgment, because the prince of this world is judged.

III. "And I, if I be lifted up from the earth, will draw all men unto me. This he spake, signifying what death he should die." "Draw all men to myself." The prince of this world held men in his thrall, but by his death Jesus judged the prince of this world. "Lifted up," he says, "I will draw all men to another prince. I will draw all men unto me." The crucified Saviour draws men from the prince of this world. Oh, Satan is sadly foiled! One crucified in weakness, hanging on a tree, the buffeted, derided, spit upon, despised of men, a Man of sorrows and acquainted with grief, despised and not esteemed; but he endured the cross, despising the shame, and draws all men to him.

Draws all men—away from the judged prince of this world. The proud run to the Meek and Lowly in his humility, crucified. Those who sought honour one of another, and seek not the honour that cometh from God only, run to the Taunted, the Condemned, Vilified, dying the malefactor's death on the accursed tree, and glory in the cross of the Lord Jesus. He draws. The worldling looks from all this world in which his heart was bound up, he looks to the One not of this world, lifted up above the world on a piece of wood, a poor despised dying man, and he leaves all, and runs to him. He draws him. The votary of pleasure, sinful pleasure, looks on this aspect of deepest pain, of holiest pain, and he quits his lusts, and runs to the holy Sufferer. He draws. He draws the miser from his hoards, draws the sensualist from his pleasures, draws the self-righteous from his efforts, draws the abandoned from his vices, draws the proud from his arrogancy, draws the stupid from his insensibility.

The dying One hath a drawing power. What kind of men will you find such that the Saviour draws none such? " I will draw all men unto me. This he spake, signifying what death he should die." *Christ is all attraction.* The world does not know that. The world thinks him and feels him all repulsion, but he is all attraction. He repelleth not, he draws. " Him that cometh unto me I will in no wise cast out." He is all attraction; but lifted up on the cross he is most of all attractive. All his drawing power is concentrated there. We might think there was more attractive power when he was lifted up on the Mount of Transfiguration—when he was lifted up and set on the right hand of the Majesty on high, far above all principalities and powers, and every name that is named; and there *is* attractive power, and these do draw when the cross has drawn; but till the cross draw these draw not. The heart may go out indeed selfishly after these things, but it goes not out after him. But in the Crucified, if you see not himself, you see nothing to attract. It's not a crown of glory that, it's a crown of thorns. These are not robes of heavenly splendour: it is but a mock robe. These are not all the angels of God worshipping him: they are knees bent in derision. That is not a mighty hand which is nailed to the cross: he is crucfied in weakness. There's no honour there, no splendour there. Nothing that all the world likes—everything that all the world hates in the circumstantials of it; and now unless there be attraction in himself, in his heart, and in his dealing as shewing his heart, there can be none extrinsic, there is none. If there be, and there is, it must be all intrinsic. And what say the drawn about it? What account do they give? Some of them possibly can give very little account of it at all, for the man may feel his heart affected when he can but ill tell what it is; a man may feel rightly and deeply, and not be very good at explaining, and those who can give some account may give an inadequate account. Woe is me for the man who can tell all he sees in Christ to draw him! Woe is me for the man who has not experience of more drawing than he is able to give account of in words; he sees but a measured degree of excellence in Christ. But surely the drawn can give some account. Grace, grace; and now, in connexion with grace, holiness. Till drawn, he was despised and we esteemed him not. When drawn, "surely he hath borne our griefs and carried our sorrows." What said one drawn man about it? " I am crucified with Christ, nevertheless I live; yet not I, but Christ liveth in me; and the life which I now live in the flesh, I live by the faith of the Son of God." "The Son of God loved me, and gave himself for me." " He is derided, to save me who deserved it from eternal ignominy and confusion of face. He endures the malice of devils and men, that I might be free from torment, everlasting torment. He bares his breast to receive the sword of God, which was about to pierce into my heart. He is taking and drinking that cup of sorrow, of the red wine of the wrath and indignation of Almighty God, which was my portion, and which, but for him, to eternal ages I should have been drinking, ever unexhausted—he hath emptied it. He hath put it empty of curse, full of blessing, into my hands. What have I to do any more with idols! God forbid that I should glory, save in the cross of our Lord Jesus Christ." " Ah! now," saith the voluptuary, " there is a bitter cup for Christ—a sweet cup for me of holy joy." "There," saith the ambitious man, " there is an awful degradation for that glorious one. It humbles me in the dust to think of it. Oh, there his crowned head is encircled with the mock crown of thorns, that I may wear the crown of life that fadeth not away!" " And there, then," saith the covetous man, " is he who was rich emptied. Though he was rich, yet for my sake he became poor—and what's the vile trash to me?—that I through his poverty might be rich with a treasure which fadeth not away, eternal in the heavens." He draws : " I will draw all men unto Me." And " who are these that fly as a cloud, and as the doves to their windows ?" He has drawn Jews, Romans, Greeks ; and distant lands and isles have heard, and hearing have submitted themselves unto him, and the strange gods have faded out of the strong places. He hath drawn men in Britain's isle ; he hath drawn men in Glasgow city ; and he is the same yesterday, to-day, and for ever. He hath drawing power. Lifted up once on the cross, his crucifixion in one sense is perpetual ; in the proclamation of it, and in the power of it, and in the remembrance of it, he draws still.

Hath he drawn me ? Hath he drawn thee ? From what, to what ? From what has he drawn ? Has he drawn from this world and from its prince ? All that he draws, he draws from that quarter—all fuel for the eternal burnings, and he draws to make pillars in the temple of his God. He draws, turning men " from darkness to light, and from the power of Satan unto God, that they may receive forgiveness of sins, and inheritance among them which are sanctified." Has he drawn you ? drawn you out of darkness into light, out of Satan's kingdom into his own kingdom—drawn you from the present evil world—drawn you from all its sentiments, likings and dislikings, wishes, efforts—drawn you, not grudgingly, out of its society ? A man may be drawn away out of the world into a convent, and carry the world with him in the shape of the love of it—his body drawn, his carcase drawn, his unwilling soul held back by the beloved world, to which he is not crucified, not crucified to all its godless sentiments, to all its selfish ways, to all its vain honours, by being drawn to the Crucified. Has he drawn you from yourself ? That requires the most drawing force of any, to draw man from himself. Has he drawn you from all your own sentiments, from all your own willings, from all your virtues and from all your sins, from your religions and irreligions, from your fancied good and real evil—drawn you away from all? Have you nothing now but him? "God forbid that I should glory, save in the cross of our Lord Jesus Christ." The apostle did not say, "God forbid that I should glory"—leaving out the cross of Christ from the causes of his glory—but "God forbid that I should glory, *save* in the cross of our Lord Jesus Christ." Mistake not that. You say, We put it in among the causes of our glorying. God forbid that I should glory if it has not a place. That's not it. "God forbid that I should glory, *save* in the cross of our Lord Jesus Christ." So it is. "By whom the world is crucified unto me, and I unto the world." I was not crucified. Christ, Christ crucified, that's the object drawing—drawn to *it*—drawn away from all that is not Christ, drawn to Christ—drawn to him in his person, covenant-engagements, work, gospel, law, grace, authority—drawn to him as your Prophet, and Priest, and King—as all your salvation and all your desire. Are you being drawn? drawn more and more? If Christ has begun drawing you, sure I am he has not finished drawing you. We are not so near Jesus as we should be, as we must be, as, if we are under his drawing, we shall be. All who have been drawn are being drawn still; and all who have been drawn and are being drawn are approximating, are coming to Christ. They have heard him who says "Come!" and they have set out to go to him, and they're going, going; and he is always saying "Come, come!" and they're coming and getting nearer.

What steps of progress are we making as the results of this drawing? Surely, surely if we are not coming, he is not drawing. He is drawing in one sense, in his sweet and powerful invitations, but so drawing as that we feel able to resist them all still. Surely there is another drawing than that, a drawing not to be resisted. Are we drawn by that drawing? There is a drawing with the cords of love and the bands of a man. Sweet affections, different from all constraints and contraries, but stronger than all constraints— more powerful than all necessity—the constraint of love. What stumbling-blocks in the way are you getting over? What other attractions are being loosed and letting you on? What bands untied? What swiftness given to the feet, making them like hinds' feet? What kindling up of the love strong as death, and the jealousy cruel as the grave? What sacrifices, what accounting of all things but loss for the excellency of Jesus Christ? What suffering for his sake of the loss of all things, and counting them but dung if so be we may win Christ and be found in him? Feel you ever his attractive power coming and drawing hard away from detentions? When you are slow and he goes away, putting in his hand at the hole of the door, and leaving the smell of the sweet myrrh, what meetings of heart—what openings even for the gone Beloved—and when he is not found, what rising and going about the city? What drawing to a crucified Saviour? Oh, the world likes a crowned Saviour tolerably well, if it were a crown without a cross, but a crucified Saviour—to draw men to be crucified! A crown without a cross for me, saith the natural heart. Jesus is drawing you to the cross. Do you love his cross, the cross he bore, the cross on which he was crucified, the cross he gives to you, that you may have some conformity in this too to the image of God's Son, being crucified with him? Has the cross grown sweet yet? Have any of the aloes, myrrh, and cassia dropped from his cross upon yours and perfumed it? Can you rejoice to be counted worthy to suffer shame and reproach for the name of Jesus—to do good and to suffer for it, like him who, when he was reviled, reviled not again, when he suffered, threatened not, but committed himself to him that judgeth righteously? Is death becoming more pleasant? Are you getting any nearer the mind of being willing to depart and to be with Christ? I give not this as a mark essential to the being of grace, but as a mark of its progress, of God's drawing—a point to which even the beginner is to be looking forward. Although the beginner may be more pleased that Christ come and be with him here, and think that better than to depart and to be with Christ, yet let him be drawn a little closer and he will alter his mind, and think that, though good—O how unspeakably good it is to have Christ here—it is better far to depart and be with Christ. What zeal, what revenge do you feel and exercise toward counter-drawing? What revenge? O take a good vengeance on the flesh, on the world, the lust of the flesh, the lust of the eye, and the pride of life. Take a good vengeance! What revenge do they stir up in the man who is drawn and counter-drawn? If he is led by the Spirit, if the drawing to Christ is the stronger and prevailing, oh, then, what a real distaste of the hindrances, and what shewing of that, not by bare complaining of them, but by setting-to in good earnest, in the strength of divine grace, to have all these bonds cut through, that the soul may escape as a bird out of the snare of the fowler, and rise singing, singing, "Our help is in the name of the Lord, who made the heavens and the earth." . . .

Undrawn sinners, you know nothing of this; you have not experienced this, and so the words remain to be fulfilled about you. He hath not ceased drawing. But, oh, how can we persuade you! We know we cannot, because we cannot do God's work, cannot open your eyes, cannot shine in your hearts, to give you the light of the knowledge of the glory of God in the face of Jesus Christ. But, oh, if but one ray would shine in there, you would not stay away, the devil could not keep you! If but one ray would shine, it would draw. Truly light is sweet to the eyes. O that ye but knew how sweet light is! O that ye knew what sweet blessings Jesus bestows! If ye but knew the treasures of loveliness and of love that are in him, if ye but knew the riches of that poor One, who, though rich, yet for your sakes became poor, that ye through his poverty might be rich, ye couldn't, couldn't hate him. Not but that you're bad enough to do it, but the attraction that is in him wouldn't let you. O be persuaded, if we cannot give you sight. O that the Lord would enable us his ministers to persuade you that you are blind, that the darkness is passed away and the true light now shineth, and it is only that the darkness hath blinded your eyes! O that we could persuade you of that! Then would be heard the cry to Jesus, "Lord, that I might receive my sight!" O that we could persuade you that there is an unknown attractiveness in Jesus Christ! Then you might come and say, "Lord, thou hast told me about it, and that is all. Thou hast told me the doctrine, that is all man can do. Lord, draw me. I shall never know what drawing is till thou draw, till thou put it forth."

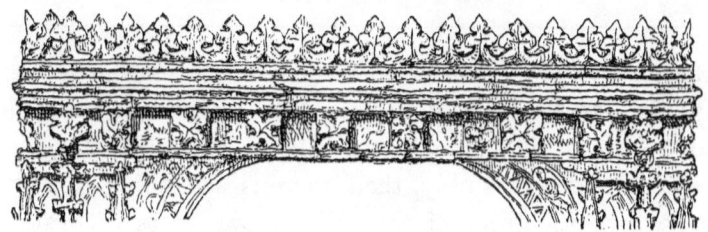

XXV.

𝔚𝔞𝔩𝔨𝔦𝔫𝔤 𝔴𝔦𝔱𝔥 𝔊𝔬𝔡.

BY THE REV. JOHN MACDONALD, A.M.

"ENOCH WALKED WITH GOD."—GENESIS V. 24.

THE attitude of a Christian should ever be that of observation. As the eyes of a servant are to his master, or of a child to his father, so ought the believer to have his faith directed to his God. He should especially seat himself under the vast heaven of providence, and with the glass of the Word sweep the whole canopy of events and providential movements; for these are fulfilments of God's will, and rich discoveries of his relative character, to the children of men.

Those of you, who are thus minded, we invite to turn aside with us for a little, to behold by faith one wonderful movement of the divine arm, which took place nearly five thousand years ago; when one bright luminary in the patriarchal firmament suddenly disappeared from man's vision, and re-appeared, as quickly, in the presence of the angels of glory. Behold your Lord, by an extraordinary and sovereign act snatching from this sinful, mortal world, Enoch his servant; divesting him, by an immediate process, of all corruption and mortality, transporting him to his kingdom of glory, and there setting him as his first crown-jewel, perfected from amongst men, in soul and body, for eternity. Such singular procedure was only once again repeated, in the case of Elijah, the great prophetic reformer of Israel; surely, then, there is something worthy of note in this, the prior of the solitary two cases of deathless translation.

Now, what was the *character* of this man, Enoch, whom God delighted so to honour, and in whose translation he gave so clear a manifestation of what that is which God most loves, and which he will have near to him in heaven? That character is simply described in these few words, "*Enoch walked with God.*" This was that which pleased God so—never was a biography written like this—"Enoch walked with God, and he was not; for God took him." If the Christian can have an object of envy, it must be such a character as that, and such an end, though in another form.

That which we know to be good and pleasing in the sight of God, it forthwith becomes our duty to seek after and practise with all our might; even as our Lord Jesus Christ says, "If ye know these things, happy are ye if ye do them;" and as also his blessed apostle says, "These things write we unto you, that your fellowship may be with us; and truly our fellowship is with the Father and with his Son Jesus Christ."

Let us then direct New Testament light to this Old Testament fact and statement; especially as we find that light concentrated on this very case in Hebrews xi. 5–6; and may the Lord the Spirit enlighten us?

I. The first idea that strikes us on this subject is, that if Enoch walked with God, then he must have been *reconciled* to God, and God to him. Reconciliation is essential to a godly life. God and man are at variance on account of sin; man hates the holy character of God; and God hates man's unholy character. God is angry with man's sin; and man is angry with God on this account. The sentence of eternal death is upon man for his rebellion, and hatred, and anger, towards his Lord; and the sinner contends against this sentence of justice unto death; and so sinks deeper and deeper under the curse. Such was the original condition of Enoch, and of every saint now in heaven, as well as of every believer now existing on earth.

How is this variance removed! How is reconciliation effected? How shall God's anger be removed, the sentence of death be executed, the curse cancelled, the enmity of the sinner be slain, and himself be justified? The world groans for an answer, but can find none from all her children, ; therefore the world, being unreconciled, cannot walk with God.

But the gospel tells us, " God was in Christ reconciling the world unto himself, not imputing unto them their trespasses." In the cross, or sacrificial death of Christ, the enmity is slain, and peace is made. In the sacrifice of Christ the evil of sin is seen, and its guilt punished; the character of God as a sovereign honoured, and the authority of his law magnified, in the sentence of death fulfilled, and in the curse fully executed: so that God may now righteously and graciously forgive whom he pleases, and reconcile to himself the guiltiest of Adam's race. In this cross of Christ, too, man sees displayed infinitely the love of God, and the loveliness of his character; and, being humbled in the dust on account of his own vileness and enmity, seeks reconciliation with his blessed and beloved Sovereign. Finding the way open, and hearing the invitation, " Be ye reconciled," he enters in and finds peace for his soul. " Being justified by faith, we have peace with God, through our Lord and Saviour Jesus Christ; and by him we have access also to this grace wherein we stand." The first promise, and the ordinance of sacrifice, were the avenues by which Enoch entered into a state of reconciliation with his God; and by the gospel of the grace of the Lord must we now become the "friends of God," so that we may walk with him in all godliness of life. "Blessed are the people that know the joyful sound! They shall walk, O Lord, in the light of thy countenance: In thy name shall they rejoice all the day; and in thy righteousness shall they be exalted."

II. *Renewal* of spirit in man must also be understood as necessary in order to walking with God, and as implied in such an exercise. As a fallen being, man is the very opposite of God, instead of being his image as at first. There is no congeniality of spirit, no oneness of mind between them. God is sovereign, but man is rebellious; God is spiritual, but man is carnal; God is holy and righteous, but man is unholy and unrighteous; God is light, but man is darkness; God is love, but man is hatred. How can parties, so different in character, ever walk together in real unity of mind, even if a reconciled relationship were established? It cannot be, without a change in one of the parties. But God cannot change—he is good and unchangeably perfect. Man, then, must be changed, in order to correspond with his Lord. But how shall he be changed in his inward nature? How shall he become a new creature? How shall he be born when he is old? Again the world groans for an answer; but in vain—her sons cannot solve the problem; therefore the world unrenewed cannot walk with her God. But in the gospel it is said, that a man shall be "born again of the spirit," and so shall he "enter into the kingdom of God." By the regenerating work of the Holy Ghost, a man becomes "partaker of a divine nature:" being "born of the flesh, he is flesh;" but, "being born of the Spirit, he is spirit," or becomes like the Holy Spirit. The life of God is in him, like a fountain of living water. His understanding is enlightened, so that he knows his Lord—his heart is renewed, so that he loves his Lord—his conscience is purified, so that he waits upon his Lord. He is thus in a capacity for walking with God in spirit and in truth: reconciled in state, and comformed in nature, the foundation of a blessed union is laid; and as regeneration grows up into full sanctification, and grace advances towards glory, so does the soul draw nearer to its God. Inward and sore conflicts there are with indwelling sin; and outward and painful trials there are, for the Lord's sake: but all these only send the believer more into the presence of his God, and make him more meet for dwelling with him for evermore. Thus was Enoch sanctified and ripened for heaven. That Spirit who ministered in the patriarchal world—who strove with sinners before the flood, until in anger he left them—worked effectually in him then, and has continued his gracious ministration in all saints to this day: and it is just in proportion as we walk in the Spirit that we shall walk with God. Let us remember and hold fast this precious promise, "I will put my Spirit within you, and cause you to walk in my statutes; and ye shall be my people, and I will be your God." (Ezek. xxxvi. 27, 28.)

II. In order to "walking with God," it is needful that we be possessed of *faith*. God is a Spirit invisible to the flesh; therefore, in order to commune with him, we must have some corresponding spiritual power, and some corresponding and spiritual medium of sight. That medium is divine truth, however it may be revealed; it is light to the soul, in which God is manifested. The power by which we see is faith; for it is the reception of light from the word, and the apprehension, in their nature, of the objects set forth. "Faith is the substance (or confidence) of things hoped for; the evidence (or conviction) of things not seen." This faith Enoch had; for it is written,

"By faith Enoch was translated, that he should not see death, and was not found, because God had translated him; for before his translation he had this testimony, that he pleased God. But without faith it is impossible to please him; for he that cometh to God must believe that he is, and that he is the rewarder of all them that diligently seek him" (Heb. xi. 5–6). Such faith must we have. Testimony being to faith what light is to the eye, we must see God revealed in his Word, as we see the sun revealed in his own rays; and so may we walk in the brightness of his face. Enoch saw God revealed in the promise, and in sacrifice; and on him so seen he firmly believed. No image made by hands, no imagination of the mind, can take the place of faith. When the gospel of Christ comes in word to us, and the Holy Spirit comes with power within us, then do we meet with "God in Christ reconciling us to himself." True faith never rests in the mere word, even as the eye rests not in the light; it passes on to the substantial object revealed in the truth, and terminates there its exercise. Such is the living faith of a true saint. It converses substantially with its objects according to their true nature, and walks with God according to his varied manifestations. When faith beholds him in his glory, *Humility* falls down at his feet and worships him. *Zeal* bows his head clad in armour, and says, "Lord, here am I, send me." *Hope* fixes her pure eye on his everlasting throne, and whispers, "He is the same, yesterday, to-day, and for ever!" *Joy* takes up his harp of grace, and sings, "Upon the harp will I praise thee, O God, my God!" *Sorrow* wipes her dewy cheek, and adds in a plaintive voice, "Why art thou cast down, O my soul, and why art thou disquieted within me? Hope thou in God, thy God!" *Patience* takes up his cross, girds up his loins, saying, "Thou doest all things well!" and *Love*, with fixed unwavering gaze, silently drinks in the divine glory, and unconsciously shines, reflecting, like Stephen's face, the lustre of the heavenly throne. O let us seek such faith as this! Let us seek the power of faith from the Spirit; the medium of it from the gospel; the object of it in our God and Father; and the end of it in the salvation of our souls by Jesus Christ. "Lord, increase our faith!"

IV. *Personal communion with God* is certainly involved in "walking with him." This naturally springs out of that living faith of which we have just spoken, and is in fact the "life of faith" in exercise. When the apostle John describes the chief privilege of believers, he says, "Truly our fellowship is with the Father and with his Son Jesus Christ." Who can read over the Book of Psalms without observing how it overflows with such communion? And who can study the Epistles without seeing that communion with the Father, and the Son, and the Holy Spirit, constitute the joy and glory of a saint's life in this world? There is a mutual acquaintance between the Lord and his people. "He knoweth them who are his," and "they know him in whom they believe." There is a mutual communication of mind between them; they make known their wants and requests unto him, and he reveals himself to them as their Father, Redeemer, and Comforter. There is reciprocity of action, in giving and receiving. The Lord gives himself to them as their covenant God, and they give themselves to him as his covenant people. The souls of the saints of God are affected by a sense of his presence or absence, his smile or his frown, his favour or displeasure. They "seek him," they "thirst for him," they "faint for him," they "cry out for him," and he is "found of them." "When thou saidst, Seek ye my face, then my heart said, Lord, thy face will I seek!" In prayer they speak to God; in his word, they hear him; in his Sabbaths, they rest with him; in his sacraments, they taste and handle the pledges of his love; in meditation, they walk in his secret chamber; in worship, they are openly with him in his courts. God's people go forth to meet him in the dispensations of his providence; sometimes lifting up their faces for joy in the bright sunshine; sometimes covering their heads for sorrow and shame; sometimes he taketh them up into his chariot for a little while in triumph; at other times they lie with their faces in the dust, whilst he passeth by. In the discharge of duty, saints seek communion with their Lord. They desire to have him ever, as their witness and their helper, yea, as the supreme end of their activity, present with them. They would make their own business the Lord's service, and so would they commune with him in all the common and constant details of life. This is the triumph, this is the crown of godliness, in this world. Blessed is the man who thus "walketh up and down" (for so the word is) "with his God!" Men may, and men do deny that there is any such divine fellowship; but the Christian, holding the Bible in his hand, can return the sigh of compassion for the smile of scorn. "Poor men," saith he "they are blind, and therefore they say there is no sun, and that we have no communion with his rays! Lord, grant them their sight, then shall they see the sun, and their fellowship shall be with us!" Let us seek such personal communion with God, and we shall then understand the benediction which saith, "The grace of the Lord Jesus Christ, and the love of God, and the communion of the Holy Ghost be with you all, for evermore!"

V. *Separation from an evil world* must evidently arise out of a life of communion with God. Enoch was distinguished and separated from the men of his day by his holy walk. He stood alone, as an oak in the midst of the tempest, as a rock amidst the raging of the sea. He was a witness for God against the world; and he constantly rebuked the rampant ungodliness by which he was surrounded. It is vain to think that we can walk with God and with the world too. We must separate ourselves from the world's principle, for it is pride; we must separate from its practice, for it is rebellion; we must separate from its profession, for it is hypocrisy; we must separate from its actuating end, for it is selfishness; we must shine as lights, making manifest the evil, that is around us—bearing testimony for God, and against sinners, even unto death—despising the world's censure as dross, and counting its reproach as the dust under our feet. "The friendship of the world is enmity with God," are the words of the divine Spirit; also is it written, "If any man love the world, the love of the Father is not in him." The world hates the character and the law of God, in proportion as these are made manifest, or brought into contact with its pleasures or pursuits. It hates, therefore, the people of Christ in proportion to their holiness or conformity to him. Oh, let us separate ourselves from such a world, save to do it good! and let us remember, that they who live with the world must also die with it, and share its doom for ever! The grand test of separation is in adherence to God's authority, and God's grace; these two things, sinful men cannot endure in practice; and if we abide in these stedfastly, we shall soon find that the world itself declares of us that we belong not to it. Let us never forget that description of true saints, embodied in Christ's intercessory prayer—"They are not of the world, even as I am not of the world." They of whom this cannot truly be said, have no place in Christ's intercession, and if so, who shall bless them?

VI. Lastly. *Patient continuance unto the end* is included in Enoch's walking with God; for it was only interrupted by his passage to glory. They who truly walk with God will not be deterred by obstacles ; for, "greater is he that is with them than all who can be against them." They will not be deterred by conscious weakness; for God's "strength is made perfect in weakness." They will not be afraid of the world, for Christ hath said, "Fear not, I have overcome the world." Indwelling sin shall not prevail to destroy them; for it is written, " Sin shall not have dominion over you, for ye are not under the law, but under grace." In tribulation they shall be found glorying; because it "worketh patience, and patience experience, and experience hope." The Spirit of God dwelling within them, and the Son of God interceding for them, and the fatherly love of God resting on them, according to the eternal covenant, they are thus kept " through faith unto salvation." Their duty is to walk in this their privilege even to the end. Enoch, whilst walking with God from day to day, was suddenly removed into glory. So shall it be with the saints of the Lord now. Some day, when groaning under the evils of life, it may be, ye shall receive a summons in your mortal bodies to depart and "be with the Lord for ever." Then shall ye see Enoch; and, above all, ye shall see Enoch's God. Blessed are the people whom the Lord when he comes shall find waiting for him : they shall enter into the joy tf their Lord.

Are there *saints* before me at this time ? To you I say, happy are ye, however few and despised by the world. Go on, and fear no evil. Walk ye in reconciliation with God, through the constant reception and sprinkling of the precious blood of Christ. Walk in conformity of mind, by a constant submission of yourselves to the blessed Spirit of grace. Walk in lively faith of the divine testimony. Walk in personal communion with the Father, Son, and Holy Spirit; carrying on spiritual and heavenly communion, "praying without ceasing." Walk in nonconformity to the world; whilst in it, be not of it; adhere to the Lord's word, grace, and cause always. Walk also in patience, "in all things giving thanks," and "casting all your cares upon the Lord, knowing that he careth for you." As you value your soul's salvation, the honour of your Lord and Saviour, and the good of your fellow-men—as you would value a holy and useful life, or a blessed and glorious eternity—as ye would be Christians indeed, and be found accepted at the coming of your Lord, let me beseech you to walk closely with your God, At last ye shall hear a voice say, " Come up hither !" and when ye are gone up, men will say of you too, in your measure, " These walked with God amongst us ; and now, they are not ; for he hath taken them. Arise, let *us* follow them !"

Men of the world ! God, for whom I speak, knoweth you ; and he knoweth all the secrets of your hearts towards himself. Ye do not walk with him, nor seek ye to do so. Self is your god, and according to your own course ye walk. Unreconciled through the blood of Christ, and unrenewed in the spirit of your minds, ye have no living faith in the living God. Ye make him to be an infinite shadow, and his Son to be an incarnate creed. No communion seek ye with the Father of your spirits ; but ye love his enemies, and ye rejoice in the company of hypocrites, apostates, Sabbath-breakers, fornicators, swearers, and infidels. The very idea of walking with God is a mystery to you, or else a nonentity. Now we beseech you to reflect—to repent—to turn from this most unnatural state of estrangement from God. In his name, and by his authority, we beseech you, "be ye reconciled to him !" Behold the cross, the symbol of peace, the meeting-place of souls for pardon, the starting-point of walking with God; behold that cross revealed to you ! for we preach to you " Jesus Christ, and him crucified." Come, be reconciled. Lay down your enmity, and take up divine friendship. Lay down your guilt, and take up a free pardon. Lay down the flesh, and take up the spirit. Lay down sight, and take up faith. Lay down the world, and take up heaven. Lay down your self-righteous works, and take up grace. Lay down sin, and take up salvation. Lay down time, and take up eternity. Lay down care, and take up peace. Lay down sorrow and despair, and take up joy and hope. Lay down all evil, and take up all good. All, all this is free to you at the cross of Christ! You are welcome, you are invited, you are besought, you are commanded to do all this freely, "without money and without price." Arise, then, O my fellow-sinners, arise! Seek ye the Lord whilst he may be found, and walk and commune with him; and be ye followers of them who through faith and patience do now inherit the promises, and are with Enoch in heavenly glory!

John Eadie Titles

Solid Ground is delighted to announce that we have republished several volumes by John Eadie, gifted Scottish minister. The following are in print:

Commentary on the Greek Text of Paul's Letter to the Galatians
Part of the classic five-volume set that brought world-wide renown to this humble man, Eadie expounds this letter with passion and precision. In the words of Spurgeon, "This is a most careful attempt to ascertain the meaning of the Apostle by painstaking analysis of his words."

Commentary on the Greek Text of Paul's Letter to the Ephesians
Spurgeon said, "This book is one of prodigious learning and research. The author seems to have read all, in every language, that has been written on the Epistle. It is also a work of independent criticism, and casts much new light upon many passages."

Commentary on the Greek Text of Paul's Letter to the Philippians
Robert Paul Martin wrote, "Everything that John Eadie wrote is pure gold. He was simply the best exegete of his generation. His commentaries on Paul's epistles are valued highly by careful expositors. Solid Ground Christian Books has done a great service by bringing Eadie's works back into print."

Commentary on the Greek Text of Paul's Letter to the Colossians
According to the New Schaff-Herzog Encyclopedia of Religious Knowledge, "These commentaries of John Eadie are marked by candor and clearness as well as by an evangelical unction not common in works of the kind." Spurgeon said, "Very full and reliable. A work of utmost value."

Commentary on the Greek Text of Paul's Letters to the Thessalonians
Published posthumously, this volume completes the series that has been highly acclaimed for more than a century. Invaluable.

Paul the Preacher: A Popular and Practical Exposition of His Discourses and Speeches as Recorded in the Acts of the Apostles
Very rare volume intended for a more popular audience, this volume begins with Saul's conversion and ends with Paul preaching the Gospel of the Kingdom in Rome. It perfectly fills in the gaps in the commentaries. Outstanding work!

DIVINE LOVE: A Series of Doctrinal, Practical and Experimental Discourses
Buried over a hundred years, this volume consists of a dozen complete sermons from Eadie's the pastoral ministry. "John Eadie, the respected nineteenth-century Scottish Secession minister-theologian, takes the reader on an edifying journey through this vital biblical theme." - Ligon Duncan

Lectures on the Bible to the Young for Their Instruction and Excitement
"Though written for the rising generation, these plain addresses are not meant for mere children. Simplicity has, indeed, been aimed at in their style and arrangement, in order to adapt them to a class of young readers whose minds have already enjoyed some previous training and discipline." – Author's Preface

Call us Toll Free at 1-877-666-9469
Send us an e-mail at sgcb@charter.net
Visit us on line at solid-ground-books.com

www.ingramcontent.com/pod-product-compliance
Lightning Source LLC
Chambersburg PA
CBHW021758220426
43662CB00006B/101